Intelligence Wars

American Secret History
from Hitler to al-Qaeda

Intelligence Wars

American Secret History
from Hitler to al-Qaeda

Thomas Powers

NEW YORK REVIEW BOOKS

New York

THIS IS A NEW YORK REVIEW BOOK

PUBLISHED BY THE NEW YORK REVIEW OF BOOKS

INTELLIGENCE WARS: AMERICAN SECRET HISTORY
FROM HITLER TO AL-QAEDA
by Thomas Powers

This edition published in 2002
in the United States of America by
The New York Review of Books
1755 Broadway
New York, NY 10019
www.nybooks.com

Library of Congress Cataloging-in-Publication Data
Powers, Thomas, 1940 Dec. 12-
    Intelligence wars : American secret history from Hitler to al-Qaeda /
Thomas Powers.
        p. cm.
Chiefly articles originally published in the New York review of books.
    ISBN 1-59017-023-7 (hardcover : alk. paper)

  1. Intelligence service—United States—History—20th century. 2.
United States. Central Intelligence Agency. 3. Espionage—United
States—History—20th century. 4. Intelligence service—History—20th century. I. Title.
    JK468.I6 P678 2002
    327.1273'009'045—dc21

                                                                        2002010877
ISBN 1-59017-023-7
Printed in the United States of America on acid-free paper.
November 2002
1 3 5 7 9 10 8 6 4 2

For Amanda, Susan, and Cassandra

Contents

Introduction

IT WAS THE Kennedys who introduced Americans to the world of secret intelligence. Before April 1961 the ordinary American citizen may have been half-aware that the United States had an intelligence service, but its size, its budget, its organization, its methods of operation, and the range of its missions—even its name—were a blank in the public mind. That national innocence ended in a hurry with the dramatic failure of an invasion of Cuba by a rebel army hoping to overthrow the Communist government of Fidel Castro. Every newspaper-reading American thereafter knew that CIA stood for Central Intelligence Agency. Covert operations are intended to be deniable but there was nothing hidden about the heavy American hand at the Bay of Pigs. American planes bombed Cuban airfields, an American fleet steamed offshore, Americans had trained the thousand rebels who went in over the beach, and American money paid for the whole endeavor. To pretend that the United States was merely an interested bystander was impossible, and President John F. Kennedy soon accepted responsibility for launching the invasion and for the failure that followed. By taking the blame the President doubtless hoped to quiet the public furor but whom to blame was not the big question—it was how we ever convinced ourselves this crack-brained scheme had a chance of success in the first place.

No answer to that question was possible without knowing a great deal about the history and leadership of the Central Intelligence Agency, which had turned a small plan into a grand one and then convinced the new president he had to let the invasion go forward or else turn loose a thousand angry Cuban rebels who knew a lot of American secrets. Inevitably some officials of the CIA thought others in the agency were to blame, and said so; naturally those attacked fought back. The architects of the invasion scheme let it be known that the chances of success had been really pretty good, until President Kennedy cancelled a critical round of pre-invasion air strikes on the timid ground that the American role would be too conspicuous. Defenders of the President countered that a few air strikes more or less were meaningless; the big mistake was to misread the overwhelming popular support for Castro. And so it went. Failure is a great tool for prying open locked doors, and succeeding generations of journalists, historians, and scholars, nailing down in ever greater detail the obsession with Cuba of President Kennedy and his brother Robert, have gradually dragged the world of secret intelligence into the light of day.

But the important word in the phrase "secret intelligence" is "secret," and no one should underestimate the tenacity with which an intelligence organization like the CIA will hold on to the secrets that can cause real trouble. These are not primarily the "sources and methods" which all directors of central intelligence are required by law to protect, but rather those things which government organizations, and the presidents who direct them, insist they would never stoop to do. Murder is at the top of this list, and especially that category of murder called assassination. In the history of the CIA there are no proven cases of assassinations committed under orders from the White House, but there are several almost-but-not-quite-proven cases, and some just-short-of-impossible-to-deny cases of attempted assassination. The most notorious of the latter were directed at Fidel Castro, and the architect-in-chief of the scheme to invade Cuba at the Bay of

Pigs, Richard Bissell, once told me that the plan would have worked a whole lot better if Castro had been killed on the eve of the invasion, as originally intended.

At the time Bissell had been the CIA's deputy director for plans, the second most powerful man in the agency after its director, Allen Dulles. Both men were fired after a decent interval by President Kennedy, who apologized for the necessity. Bissell didn't like being fired but had got over it before I met him in the late 1970s. He had a capacious memory and readily conceded astonishing things, once he had muffled their import with words like "probably," "perhaps," and "maybe." An hour of talk prepared him for a good lunch which he elected to precede with a martini on the rocks but it wasn't the martini that prompted his remark about the effect of Castro's assassination on the prospects for success at the Bay of Pigs. It was his intention that I should understand that the whole plan was not in fact crack-brained, but had several powerful factors going for it—killing Castro was number one, but another, just as vital, was the immense pressure that events exerted on President Kennedy to commit United States military forces to halt the tragedy unfolding on the beach. That would have ended the Communist foothold in the Western Hemisphere then and there. Bissell conceded that he and Dulles had not been candid with the President about this essential part of the plan, but he also made it as clear as he could that President Kennedy realized the role of factor one. How he withstood that pressure to act Bissell still couldn't understand; he violently swirled the ice at the bottom of his martini glass at the memory. But there it was. The President stood fast, the invasion collapsed, Castro survived, and Bissell retired to Farmington, Connecticut.

Bissell was being honest, not indiscreet. None of what he told me qualified as an official secret. By the time we talked the CIA's efforts to kill Castro were all part of the public record. Rumors of the assassination plots began to circulate in the mid-1960s and a twisted version

of the facts was published on March 3, 1967, by the political columnist Drew Pearson, who reported that Senator Robert Kennedy was
tormented by the possibility that plans to kill Castro, which he had
pushed, might have triggered the assassination of his brother. But the
truth behind the Pearson column did not emerge until a decade later
at the end of a cascading chain of events of the sort rightly described
as one damned thing after another. It happened like this: on December 22, 1974, the investigative reporter Seymour Hersh published in
The New York Times a major story about CIA intelligence-gathering
activities inside the United States, something prohibited by law. President Ford did what any president would do—he asked William
Colby, then director of the CIA, how big the problem was. Colby
responded as intelligence officers rarely do; instead of construing the
question narrowly, and revealing as little as possible, he gave Ford
"the family jewels"—a document compiled some months earlier of
just about every questionable undertaking by the CIA since its birth in
1947. Within a few days Ford knew the worst. Early in the New Year
Richard Helms, Colby's predecessor at the CIA but one, was called
back to Washington from his post as ambassador to Iran to warn the
White House what fresh horrors might lie ahead. After talking to him
National Security Adviser Henry Kissinger reported to Ford, "Helms
said all these stories are just the tip of the iceberg. If they come out,
blood will flow. For example, Robert Kennedy personally managed
the operation on the assassination of Castro." When Helms himself
talked to Ford a few minutes later he warned that "a lot of dead cats
will come out" if a commission probed too deeply. "I plan no witch
hunt," Ford responded, "but in this environment I don't know if I can
control it."

Hersh had spied the tip of the iceberg; Ford, knowing the behemoth
still out of sight, proceeded cautiously, according to his lights. At an
off-the-record luncheon with editors of *The New York Times* Ford
said he had asked former New York governor Nelson Rockefeller to

head a blue-ribbon panel of inquiry because he knew Rockefeller could be trusted to act with judgment and discretion, by which the President meant keeping under wraps the secrets too explosive to reveal. Like what? Like assassination, said President Ford.

Off the record means off the record only up to a point; Ford's use of the word "assassination" went way beyond that point. The editors of the *Times* printed nothing themselves but in short order the CBS television reporter Daniel Schorr had the story and went on the air. In a moment the CIA's reading of private mail and spying on anti–Vietnam War dissidents was old news and the House and Senate investigating committees, already up and running, were in effect handed a charter to rip the lid off the CIA's department of dirty tricks, as it came to be called. The result, in a year's time, was a five-foot shelf of green and gray paper–covered official reports on the clandestine operations of the CIA which put American citizens and government officials for the first time on the same page when it came to the question of what American intelligence organizations had either done or tried to do in the past. In this way it became possible for me to discuss CIA plots to kill Castro with Richard Bissell, who said he personally had never spoken to President Kennedy about them—he thought it was probably Allen Dulles who handled that. But the President's brother Robert told him repeatedly that the CIA's job was to get rid of Fidel Castro, and the attorney general made it unmistakably clear he meant *get rid of him.* [Bissell's italics.]

The role of the Kennedy brothers in stripping away the veil was not something that came to me all at once, but instead emerged gradually and incidentally after I agreed in 1976 to write an article for *Rolling Stone* magazine about Richard Helms. He was much in the headlines at the time: he had testified often during investigations into the crimes and misdemeanors collectively known as Watergate, and he was facing a charge of perjury for lying to a Senate committee about CIA operations in Chile. Helms was clearly a figure of interest but I had no idea where to begin. A friend suggested I seek the help of the writer Frances FitzGerald. She gave me the name of John Bross, who had joined the CIA in 1951 and held a succession of high-level jobs over the next three decades. It would be hard to think of a better place to begin.

Stony looks and sealed lips were what I expected to find when I got to Washington but I soon discovered that I had arrived at just the right moment with exactly the right question. The moment was at the end of three years of sensational newspaper headlines portraying the CIA as a nest of unprincipled thugs, killers, torturers, coup-plotters, and second-story men. The question was, what can you tell me about your old friend Richard Helms, facing the clink for trying to keep the secrets? Many of the people I talked to shared a history in the agency's World War Two predecessor, the Office of Strategic Services, and most had recently retired with the first generation of CIA officials. They were free to spend long mornings and afternoons talking in suburban Virginia and Maryland living rooms to a reporter who had never heard any of their stories. Most of these, inevitably, had to do with human personality, or long ago events no longer secret, or what the agency had been trying to do, which, when you had cleared away the underbrush, was mainly the effort to answer the questions and carry out the wishes of American presidents. What the old hands thought of Dick Helms wasn't classified; they felt he had been getting a raw deal from Congress and the press, and that went for the agency, too. Maybe Helms did lie to the Senate about Chile, but he had no choice. The senators jumped him with questions of the kind they had always saved for executive session; if he'd told the truth a lot of secrets would have come out.

One thing leads to another in an interview and a defense of Helms about Chile led naturally enough to the way presidents sometimes demand the impossible—a coup to overthrow the government of Salvador Allende in Santiago on short notice, for example, which was about as feasible, really, as the instant revolution the Kennedy brothers wanted the CIA to mount in Cuba after their humiliation at the Bay of Pigs—an unrealistic project, by the way, with which Dick Helms had nothing whatever to do, leaving that up to Richard Bissell and General Edward Lansdale, whose enthusiasm for covert operations matched Wild Bill Donovan's in the OSS. Helms wasn't a covert operator; his experience had been on the secret intelligence side—the recruitment and management of agents. The culture of spy-running shared nothing with the covert derring-do of the cowboys. Down this meandering road we eventually reached the tough subjects—assassination, drug experiments on unwitting subjects, the overthrow of governments—and having talked about everything else these retired intelligence officers found there was generally something unclassified to say about the tough subjects, too. There was no deep trick to it: you had to want to know, you had to do a lot of homework, and you had to listen.

When the article was done I decided to do a book. By that time Helms had returned from Iran and I had several interviews with him. They were all conducted in the same way. I would arrive at his home at the appointed hour and he would be standing on the front stoop, waiting. We would talk in his study. I recorded the interviews and if he wanted to say something off the record he would ask me to turn the machine off. Colleagues sometimes described Helms as cool, distant, or enigmatic, but I found him full of pungent opinion and frank in saying what he thought about the people he had worked with, the things he had been asked to do, and the nature of the intelligence business. He could be irritated and he could be angry, but I never found him to be petty. He had a kind of naturalist's interest in how Washington worked and could be extremely interesting about the power of congressional committees, the attention span of presidents, or the strange people who sometimes scuttled in through the door as one administration replaced another.

The last interview took place at my home in New York. I had sent him a copy of the manuscript and he brought it with him. On perhaps eight or ten pages he had placed neat check marks. The hand was unmistakably his but in fact a friend had done the work of reading for error. Most of the check marks concerned minor points of fact but one involved a question of judgment. I had written that the covert operators—the field officers who paid, encouraged, and sometimes even ran paramilitary operations in far corners of the world like Tibet —were "careless" about the fate of the locals who hitched their fortunes to ours. Helms was troubled by this. He knew those people. He admitted they were sometimes forced to carry out tough decisions— walk away from allies when White House policies changed, leave them to their fate because they had no choice. But Helms did not think they were literally careless; in his opinion they did care and it was unfair to suggest they were somehow heartless and indifferent to the consequences of what they were sometimes compelled to do. In a book eventually printed at just under four hundred pages that was the only judgment with which Helms quarreled. We didn't argue about it. He said what he thought and moved on to the next check mark. Later I decided that in some sense those people were careless and I let the word stand.

In the years since the book was published we have occasionally talked. If I ran into Helms somewhere he would ask what I was working on and offer to help. Occasionally I called him with a question and from time to time went to see him for a sitdown interview— about the CIA director John Deutch, for example, and most recently after September 11. To an interview he never failed to bring handwritten notes of points he wanted to make, and sometimes he had names to suggest or documents of interest. Occasionally he telephoned to comment on something I had written. I particularly remember one such call when I had been involved in an exchange of letters with Arthur Schlesinger Jr. in the London *Times Literary Supplement*. Schlesinger, who served in the Kennedy White House and wrote a long biography of Robert Kennedy, had attacked some remark by Christopher Hitchens suggesting that President Kennedy had of course known about the CIA's plots to kill Castro. I had written to support Hitchens and admonish Schlesinger for ignoring a bushel of evidence. When Helms saw this exchange he telephoned to let me know he had not quit paying attention. "That Schlesinger," he said, "will go on defending those Kennedys until the last dog is hung."

Schlesinger wasn't the only one. The assassination of John F. Kennedy was one of the great traumatic events in American history, and the possibility that he was guilty of intending what his killer was guilty of doing was more than Kennedy loyalists were willing to admit. The sensitivity of this question explains the otherwise odd lack of conclusions in the report released by a Senate investigating committee headed by Senator Frank Church in November 1975. One question is answered definitively in the 346 pages of *Alleged Assassination Plots Involving Foreign Leaders*: the CIA made repeated and serious attempts to kill Castro (and a number of other foreign leaders as well). This fact, never shared with the Warren Commission established to investigate the President's assassination, inevitably revived the question whether Lee Harvey Oswald had acted alone. One result has been the release of additional CIA documents now totaling hundreds of thousands of pages. But at the same time the Church committee conspicuously failed to answer the obvious second question: Did authority for these plots to kill Castro come from the White House? My own answer to this question can be found in summary in the pages that follow, and in greater detail in my book on Helms published in 1979, *The Man Who Kept the Secrets: Richard Helms and the CIA*. The standard of proof is set high in such controversies, and arguing the evidence soon leaves ordinary readers behind, thereby obscuring matters of greater general significance. What reporters and scholars can learn about secret organizations like the CIA, and what the public needs to know, is not exactly what the agency did or did not do in any particular episode, but *what it is like*.

The CIA, the KGB, the British Secret Intelligence Service (SIS), and the Israeli Mossad all have distinct histories and operating styles. All of them are successful for the most part in hiding what they do, but none of them can long conceal what they are like—the sort of people they recruit, the kinds of operations at which they excel, the nature of their relationship to the government that pays their bills. What is true of individual intelligence organizations is equally true of the whole enterprise. We may argue till kingdom come whether the KGB defector Yuri Nosenko was dispatched by the Russians to further an elaborate disinformation program or came west for his own reasons as he claimed. But it does not take long for any interested student to learn that the Russians were masters of deception, often mounted elaborate provocations, ran circles around too-trusting opponents, and were fully capable of dispatching Nosenko to muddy the waters—even though, in this case, if all the facts were known, we might conclude that they had not.

Counterintelligence can be the subtlest of intelligence arts but the rest of them have an ethos too. What photo interpreters, agent handlers, debriefers, analysts of military hardware and economic trends, the officers who handle liaison with congressional oversight committees, and chiefs of station in major European capitals or Latin American backwaters do on any given day is secret, but how they do it in the broadest sense, for whom and why, is not classified information. Knowing what intelligence organizations are like is an essential tool for anyone who wants to understand what is happening in the world, especially in those arenas where war is never distant. In the wake of the awful intelligence failure which preceded the terrorist attacks of September 11, for example, it was often argued by apologists for the CIA that predicting the attacks would have required an agent in Osama bin Laden's inner circle, something no Western intelligence service could hope to achieve. It is very likely that high officials in the Bush administration believe this to be true. On its face the challenge certainly seems difficult. The members of al-Qaeda are Islamic fundamental-ists, full of hatred for the United States and Western culture, willing to die in a cause which has God's blessing. How could some CIA govern-ment yuppie with no Arabic hope to persuade a fanatic al-Qaeda operative to betray the cause?

But old hands in the agent-running business would not tell you that the CIA's failure to deliver when it counted—before September 11 —proves it can't be done. How they might go about it was described to me indirectly a few years back at the sixtieth birthday party for a retired intelligence officer named Haviland Smith. Among the guests at Smith's party was General William Odom, who held two big in-telligence jobs before retiring—first as the Army Chief of Staff for Intelligence (ACSI), followed by three years as director of the National Security Agency. I asked Odom at the birthday party how he met Smith, who had a very different sort of career.

Smith spent his working life in the CIA's Directorate for Opera-tions (previously called the Directorate for Plans), and he spent most of it in the field. He told me once that the work was hard but had its pleasures—for example, the sheer gut thrill of making a successful brush pass on the streets of Moscow while hawk-eyed KGB watchers were on every street corner trying to make it impossible. What Smith was trying to hand over, or retrieve, he did not tell me; that was clas-sified. But he made no secret of the glow of triumph that came with success. Smith was a born operator, and Odom met him while seeking advice. "When I was ACSI I talked to Haviland about Army clan," Odom told me. "It's the endless problem—should the Army be trying to run agents at all? I asked him, what makes a good case officer? Haviland said, 'Did you see that movie with Robert Redford and Paul Newman—*The Sting*?' I said yes. He said, 'That's it—*the con!*'"

In the year since terrorist attacks destroyed the World Trade Center in New York City on September 11, 2001, the United States has embarked on a full-scale war against al-Qaeda and its allies. The opening battles to remove the Taliban regime in Afghanistan were conventional in nature and did not take long. But with the establishment of Hamid Karzai at the head of a coalition government in Kabul the conventional war has been transformed into a classic intelligence war—one fought mainly with information and the political cooperation of peoples and their governments. Conventional and intelligence wars have roughly the same goal—rendering an opponent harmless—but their conduct, cost, and duration are very different. These differences are not well understood by the American people or their political leaders. Both are accustomed to thinking of war as military violence protracted until somebody yields, but in fact the American experience over the last half-century suggests there is more to war than shooting.

The course of the Second World War was determined in part by intelligence failures and successes, beginning with a series of unanticipated and devastating attacks—by Germany on France in May 1940, by Germany on Russia in June 1941, and by Japan on the United States at Pearl Harbor that December. Thereafter the intelligence triumphs were mostly enjoyed by the Allies, who successfully broke important German and Japanese codes and maintained the secrecy of the site and date chosen for the invasion of German-occupied Europe in 1944. But important as these intelligence battles were, the outcome of the war was mainly the result of overwhelming Allied military supremacy—more of just about everything used to wage a modern war. The result was the utter collapse of Hitler's Germany and the unconditional surrender of Imperial Japan, and an American assumption that future wars, if any, would be roughly the same—diplomacy until shots were fired, followed by a mighty clash of armies with only one side standing at the end.

But that is not the way things have gone. The United States has fought three wars since the victory over Hitler in 1945—in Korea, in Vietnam, and in the Persian Gulf. The Korean and Gulf wars each expelled an invader but left the enemy regimes in power, both of which have threatened the peace ever since. In Vietnam there was an unchallenged victor at the end, but it wasn't us. The United States inflicted far more casualties than it suffered in Vietnam, and it practically never lost a conventional battle, but despite this apparent success victory was never close. One reason for the American failure was the extraordinary tenacity of the other side, which suffered a million dead but kept on fighting. But a second reason, just as important in my view, is that the other side better understood the nature of an intelligence war, in which information, political organization, the ability to hide, and selective strikes are the factors that matter most. In Vietnam, the CIA was given a shopping list of tasks to perform—providing tactical intelligence support for the American military, monitoring traffic on the Ho Chi Minh Trail, organizing local armies to resist the North Vietnamese among the Montagnard tribesmen in Vietnam and the Hmong in Laos, supporting the government in Cambodia after the overthrow of Prince Sihanouk. Far down the list was the task of actually penetrating the other side, which perhaps explains why the United States never recruited even a single spy with access to the inner circles of the government in Hanoi or the National Liberation Front in South Vietnam. Hanoi and the NLF, on the other hand, successfully penetrated the South Vietnamese government, military, and society with hundreds of agents—so many that it would have been difficult for any important American official who dealt regularly with the Vietnamese to pass even a single day without speaking to a spy for the other side. This success on the part of Hanoi and the NLF was matched by creation of a tenacious and resilient political organization throughout the South which offered little target for conventional arms; US military forces could go where they chose, and stay as long as they liked, but when they moved on the NLF always reemerged, leaving the situation as before. The American inability to find, fix, and destroy "the enemy"—a failure of intelligence, not of arms— exhausted American patience in the end.

The American failure in Vietnam ought to caution the American government now, as it embarks on an open-ended war against al-Qaeda. Conventional wars against a conventional enemy can be short and decisive, especially when a fully mobilized superpower like the United States takes on a regional power like Iraq. But conventional wars grow costly and politically divisive if prolonged, and even victory can have a cost if bystanders recoil at the one-sided punishment as unjust and unfair. Intelligence wars, on the other hand, are relatively cheap in both money and blood, they are easy to sustain politically because mostly hidden, and no single failure is ever decisive. In an intelligence war both sides generally live to fight another day, something Americans hate, but had better get used to. Israel and the Palestinians have been battling in what has been in large part an intelligence war for almost forty years, and who sees an end to that? But long does not mean without end. The protracted intelligence war between Britain and the Irish Republican Army now appears to be inching toward resolution, and if the stubborn Irish can be wearied by decades of getting nowhere, then al-Qaeda too will inevitably run out of steam. The only big mistake Americans could make now would be to try to hurry the struggle to a quick conclusion.

The essays which follow all began as book reviews, and they appear here with only small changes to correct minor factual errors, to reflect the passage of time, or to replace a tin-eared word or phrase with a happier one, as it seems to me now. They address many episodes of American intelligence history, but make no attempt to settle controversies once and for all. What interested me, and what I have tried to convey, is what the intelligence business is like, and how Americans have gone about it. From this I believe we can also learn something of who we are as a people. American secret history offers ample evidence that we are full of energy, for example, but lack patience; that we are of two minds about the keeping of secrets, and sometimes spill the biggest ones; that we tend to think every problem has a technical solution, and anything can be achieved with a big enough wrench; that our respect for the opinions of mankind is a sometime thing. Understanding what we are like is not only interesting but has practical significance: the way we go about things can determine the way they turn out—in the case of wars not just who wins, but the sort of world left at the end. If we had paid more attention to this point a dozen years ago, when the previous war in Afghanistan came to an end, we might not be trapped in a new war now.

—September 18, 2002

PART ONE

I

THE UNDERGROUND ENTREPRENEUR

ON THE EVE of World War II, the United States was the world's only great power without an intelligence service. Many agencies collected information of one kind or another, some of it secretly, but no one was in overall charge of knowing what was what. This made the country something of an innocent on the international scene. One characteristic of a nation without an intelligence service is that its officials, all jealous of their own responsibilities, have a hard time seeing why it might need one. The British, probably hoping it would help the United States to see why it ought to join the war, urged President Roosevelt to create such an organization.

Roosevelt liked the idea but took his time. When he finally signed an executive order creating the Office of Strategic Services (OSS) in June 1942, following a year of heavy bureaucratic resistance, the man he chose to run the nation's first centralized intelligence agency was William J. Donovan, a hero of World War I and a well-connected lawyer who had botched a once-promising political career mainly by saying or doing the wrong thing at the wrong time. Donovan's biographers make it clear that running the OSS was the only really important public job Donovan ever had. It lasted just over three years—four if you include the preliminaries. At the end he was abruptly kicked out and his organization scattered with tepid thanks from Harry Truman by way of farewell.

But Donovan's work survived him. One of his agents, Allen Dulles, who ran the OSS in Bern, Switzerland, during the war, wrote to a friend in 1951 that where intelligence is concerned, "once one gets a taste for it, it's hard to drop." So it proved in Washington, where the collection of intelligence and the performance "of such other functions and duties related to intelligence affecting the national security as the National Security Council may from time to time direct"—the great loophole of the charter of the CIA which Donovan did so much to create—are now taken as among the assumptions of government, like collecting taxes and maintaining a standing army.

Donovan was a simple man of sturdy character, intelligent without being clever, a good boss and a bad husband, whose only ambition was to be one of the men who ran the country. The shape of his life already has an antique air. He was born in Buffalo, New York, in 1883, a poor boy with a passion to excel. He was an altar boy, a declaimer of patriotic poems with an Irish flavor, dogged at his studies, good with his fists. His mother hoped he would become a priest. He chose law. From a local college he transferred to Columbia University where he played football, ran cross-country, made influential friends, and won a public-speaking award for an oration on "The Awakening of Japan."

After receiving a law degree from Columbia, he returned to Buffalo. By 1911 he was a partner in a leading local firm. In 1912, although ignorant of horses, he joined a newly formed National Guard cavalry unit made up largely of rich young men from Buffalo's best families. With his usual doggedness he taught himself to ride and was elected captain of the troop. In 1914 he married Ruth Rumsey, a Presbyterian society girl who bore his children and kept a diary whose terse entries recorded Donovan's compulsive absence from home throughout a marriage that lasted forty-five years. Donovan cut their honeymoon short after the outbreak of the First World War. Photographs of her show a woman with a defeated expression.

Donovan had the qualities it takes to make a hero—courage, good looks, uncomplicated devotion to basic values, drive and reasonableness in equal measure, and luck. "He's a son of a bitch, but he's a game one," said one of his men after he reached France in November 1917 as a major commanding a combat battalion in the American Expeditionary Force. He trained his men hard and they thought up names for him—"Blue-eyed Billy," "Donovan Galloping Bill," "Hard-boiled Bill," and finally "Wild Bill."

On the western front in 1917 and 1918, where for many the carnage called Western civilization itself into question, Donovan retained an uncomplicated faith in the importance of victory. In a letter home to Ruth he wrote, "Your soldier man is a sentimental person, and when he is happiest he is singing some lonesome melody of home or mother." In battle he pressed forward, exposed himself to enemy fire, did more than he was required or asked to do. His year of war reminds one of the young Winston Churchill, who had a similar reckless passion to prove himself whatever the danger. "What's the matter with you?" Donovan shouted to his men when they shrank back near St. Mihiel in September 1918. "Do you want to live forever?" Donovan himself was willing to die. "I don't expect to come back," he wrote Ruth, "and I believe that if I am killed it will be a most wonderful heritage to my family."

Not only did he escape death, but he was honorably wounded as well. Even more important, he had the right comrades and audience. His parent unit was the famous "Fighting Sixty-ninth" regiment of New York City, 90 percent Irish. His adjutant was a popular poet, Joyce Kilmer, author of "Trees" and other uplifting verse, and he was killed practically at Donovan's side. On that fact alone Donovan might have built a public career. The regimental chaplain was Father Francis P. Duffy, another sentimental hero of the Great War, whose diary was widely read after it was published in 1919. Donovan was a hero of the gallant, patriotic warrior type. General Douglas MacArthur, also heavily decorated for bravery during the war, is said never to have forgiven Donovan for winning more medals than he did. But the only medal Donovan wore in later life was the Medal of Honor, a thin blue stripe with thirteen stars, the nation's highest award. Donovan won these medals on his own merit, but it was luck that made him famous for winning them.

Things thereafter did not run so smoothly. The years between the wars were about evenly divided between failure in politics and success at the law. Twice Donovan was a public prosecutor, as US district attorney for western New York in 1922, when he made abiding local enemies by raiding some of the leading private clubs of Buffalo for violations of the liquor laws, and again in the mid-1920s as chief of the criminal division of the Justice Department, where he made even more important enemies—J. Edgar Hoover, whom he opposed as the first director of the FBI, and Senator Burton K. Wheeler, whom Donovan insisted on prosecuting (unsuccessfully) on flimsy charges brought by his predecessor. Both men gave him much trouble in later years. In 1928, Donovan, a Republican, was the nation's most prominent Catholic to support Herbert Hoover against Al Smith for the presidency. It was the only time he ever picked a winner. In return for Donovan's aid, which was considerable, Hoover promised to make him attorney general, but after the election he weaseled out of it.

Twice, too, Donovan ran for public office on his own—in the fall of 1922 as candidate for lieutenant governor in New York, when the Democratic ticket headed by Smith won; and ten years later, against sound advice, for governor of New York, when Hoover's crushing defeat by FDR doomed Donovan as well. Thereafter Donovan stuck to his own law firm, based in Washington and New York, which thrived on the big clients attracted by Donovan's prominence. His fame never faded, he had many friends from his political adventures, and he was always good with reporters, who took his charm and his wink as a sign he was up to something big.

Perhaps he was. In the years between the wars, Donovan went to a great many places he had no business going, on errands no one asked him to perform. In July 1919, on a second honeymoon with Ruth in Japan, he abruptly abandoned her for a trip to Siberia with the American ambassador in Tokyo, Roland Morris, who had been asked to investigate the White regime of the tsarist admiral Aleksandr Kolchak. Donovan spent nearly two months in Siberia, at a time when human life was held about as cheap as it has ever been. What was he doing there? The four long books on Donovan's life give no simple answer. Thomas Troy and Anthony Cave Brown simply say Morris invited him. Richard Dunlop says he was on a secret mission for John Lord O'Brian, a Donovan law partner who had gone to work for Woodrow Wilson as an intelligence adviser.

In December 1935, Donovan obtained an interview with Mussolini and wangled permission for an official trip to Ethiopia, where he immediately concluded the Italians were certain to defeat the barefoot troops of Haile Selassie. Dunlop's account of this interview is clearly based on Donovan's, in which he shamelessly gives himself all the best lines. The dictator all but swoons.

How are we to explain these mysterious trips which have such an official air but no official record? Dunlop, citing no source, and giving no further details, claims Donovan was a member of an "informal intelligence network." Brown thinks Donovan may have been recruited by the British Secret Intelligence Service (SIS) in London in 1916, when he was on a mission to Europe for the War Relief Commission of the Rockefeller Foundation. His evidence is remarkably thin. In May 1940, Churchill sent the Canadian businessman William Stephenson to New York to serve as British security coordinator and to drum up American support, especially in the form of war supplies. Stephenson carried a letter to Donovan from Admiral Blinker Hall, an acquaintance of Donovan's. Dunlop writes, "Stephenson knew that Donovan had been one of the key figures in America's clandestine intelligence net for a generation." Again, Dunlop cites no source for this claim, but his book includes a foreword from Stephenson (now Sir William), who still survives and lives in Bermuda, so it may be that Stephenson told Dunlop this was the case.

But perhaps no explanation is necessary for Donovan's quasi-secret travels to the wars of his time. War is the central preoccupation of men in government and Donovan wanted to have a part in government. Nothing else much mattered to him. He was good at his profession but dropped it whenever great events beckoned. He had no interest in money for its own sake; when he was on official business he spent his own money lavishly and his income from the law was barely sufficient to cover expenses. His net estate when he died in 1959 was $38,000. (It might also be recorded that Donovan had a tin ear when it came to investments. At the height of the stock crash in 1929 his broker barely restrained him from buying more First National City Bank stock near its high of $550 a share. Later it fell to $50.) Domestic life held no charm for Donovan. He is said to have loved children, but he grew restless in their company and was always eager to be off. After the United States entered the war in December 1941 he did not again dine alone with his wife until the night of the German surrender. Instinct seems to have drawn Donovan to Siberia, Manchuria, and Ethiopia. He wanted to be in the thick of things, and in the end he got his wish.

In the spring of 1940, Donovan arranged a meeting in Washington between Stephenson and high American officials, including the secretaries of war and state. It was not then clear that Britain could survive alone against Hitler. The US ambassador, Joseph Kennedy, thought Britain was licked. Stephenson proposed that Donovan go to London for a second opinion. Several well-placed friends of Donovan urged Roosevelt to agree. In July Donovan went. His years of poking about in foreign countries, if not in foreign intelligence matters, paid off. This was his chance, and he made the most of it. At this point Donovan's personal life—so far, it amounted mainly to a footnote to the Great War, along with a sheaf of press clippings of the sort that grow yellow in the attics of forgetful children—more or less comes to an end, and the history of American intelligence in the twentieth century begins.

The Office of Strategic Services that Donovan built during the Second World War, and hoped to make permanent later, was a curious hodge-podge of an organization, with a hand in everything from which Donovan had not been absolutely barred. No one welcomed him or the OSS into the intelligence business. General George V. Strong of the Army did everything in his power to strangle the agency at birth, and, at least once, nearly succeeded. Donovan's old enemy J. Edgar Hoover along with Nelson Rockefeller kept the OSS from working in Latin America. General Douglas MacArthur refused to admit the OSS into the Pacific theater. The British SIS, cooperative in some endeavors such as counterintelligence, worked hard to subordinate the OSS in the field.

Having so many enemies meant that the OSS grew misshapenly; it was strong and active in some regions of the war, barely present in others. Its largest military undertaking, for example, was Detachment 101, which fought the Japanese in Burma, hardly the center of the war. Donovan simply found an empty spot on the map and charged into it. Elsewhere he had to sneak in. The large OSS group in Britain, engaged mainly in liaison, was forbidden to mount its own operations in Europe until D-Day. To gain access to the Continent, Donovan established a base in Algiers, inconvenient for over-the-beach operations or parachute drops into France but the best he could get. Spy nets in Europe were run from stations in Turkey, Spain, Sweden, and Switzerland, where Dulles in Bern made the reputation and developed the taste that was to keep him in, or as close as he could get to, intelligence for the rest of his life.

The OSS tried something everywhere—Donovan even established regular liaison with the NKVD in Moscow—but its achievements were erratic and its history has a curious fragmentary quality. Donovan built quickly (from scratch to ten thousand men and women by D-Day), and for the most part he built well, but at war's end he and his organization were only just beginning to get a firm notion of what intelligence was about.

Intelligence is as old as war, but it has never been accorded the honor of the military profession. The ancient Chinese military writer Sun-tzu, an illusionless man, wrote in the sixth century BC:

> Of all those in the army close to the commander none is more intimate than the secret agent; of all the rewards none more liberal than those given to secret agents; of all matters none is more confidential than those relating to secret operations. He who is not sage and wise, humane and just, cannot use secret agents. And he who is not delicate and subtle cannot get the truth out of them.

Sun-tzu had many other sensible things to say about the conduct of secret operations and the handling of agents, whom he called "the treasure of a sovereign." But as late as 1949 a Western commentator, General Thomas R. Phillips, otherwise respectful, charged Sun-tzu with advocating "the dirtiest form of statecraft with its unspeakable depths of duplicity.... [His] section on spies is truly abominable and revolting...."

Donovan was not encumbered by such moral considerations. The British tutored him on their approach and he used many of their methods, but the large organization he set up was different from theirs. Stripped to its essentials, intelligence can be defined as the systematic attempt to gain advantage through secret means. It involves four types of related undertakings: collecting information, some of it secretly; conducting hidden operations; protecting the parent agency from compromise; analyzing what has been learned. There are good reasons for putting all four activities under a single roof, but their practitioners tend to bicker and instinctively seek autonomy. During World War II the British maintained separate organizations for espionage, counterintelligence, and secret operations. Donovan took the opposite approach, and gathered as many elements of intelligence business into the OSS as he was able. The only pieces to elude him were domestic counterintelligence, jealously protected by the FBI (as it still is), and cryptoanalysis, conducted by the predecessor of the National Security Agency (NSA).

Four basic themes recur in the accounts of various OSS operations in the four books about Donovan: clandestine contacts with Germans willing to kill or overthrow Hitler in return for a separate peace with the West which might save Germany from Russia; the attempt to establish contact with partisan undergrounds (especially in Yugoslavia, France, and Italy) and to gain political influence over them by providing munitions; the friction—sometimes with rival services, sometimes with jealous bureaucracies (and their allies in the press) at home, sometimes with the sheer cussedness of weather, machines, and "things"—which made it so difficult to *do* anything; and a low, ominous undertone of trouble with or about the Russians which in retrospect seems to have pointed unmistakably toward the cold war. The rest is stories, some of derring-do and some of spies. Very few are told about the work of the OSS's research and analysis branch where such academics as Herbert Marcuse, Arthur Schlesinger Jr., William L. Langer, and H. Stuart Hughes interpreted the evidence that came to them. Indifference toward the finished product is still the chief nemesis of analysts. Many of the stories from the field are thrilling, some are sad, and a few remain puzzling and incomplete. Taken together, they offer evidence in plenty for a study of the nature of intelligence.

None of the four books discussed here makes any attempt at such a study. They are all simply accumulations—quite large accumulations, at that—of raw material. Bradley F. Smith's *The Shadow Warriors:* OSS *and the Origins of the* CIA[1] contains many useful bits from the numerous archives that he consulted, but it is dull to read. His final chapter, however, identifies the many ways in which the CIA, especially in its early years, learned the wrong lessons from the experience of the OSS. Thomas F. Troy's book, *Donovan and the* CIA: *A History of the Establishment of the Central Intelligence Agency,*[2] is a plodding institutional history, apparently written with the cooperation of the CIA; but Troy is an intelligent writer, and his book unveils much about territorial wars between bureaucracies.

Richard Dunlop was in the OSS during the war, knew Donovan well and admired him enormously, and in *Donovan: America's Master Spy*[3] he provides the best account of Donovan's life before the OSS. Unfortunately his footnotes are identified by page and line number, making them laborious to consult, and he attributes many statements to Donovan without making it clear when he stated them, or to whom. To give only one example, Dunlop describes Donovan's trip to the Pacific in the summer of 1940 during which he took off from the aircraft carrier *Enterprise* and landed at Pearl Harbor. "If we can do this," Donovan said, "the Japs can do it too." If this was really said at the time it was a prescient remark. Later, anyone could have figured it out. So when did Donovan say it? Dunlop wasn't there, and he cites no source. After a while the reader grows angry at Dunlop for continually blunting the effect of his book through such elementary errors.

Scholars will make use of all three of these books, but most readers will get all they need to know, and much pleasure as well, from Anthony Cave Brown's *The Last Hero: Wild Bill Donovan,*[4] a huge archive, somewhat haphazardly organized, of detailed cases from all the usual

---

1. Basic Books, 1983.

2. University Publications of America, 1981.

3. Rand McNally, 1982.

4. Times Books, 1982.

sources plus Donovan's own voluminous files, to which Brown was given exclusive access. Brown shows no interest in what all this means; he simply crams in the stories. The last chapter dealing with the OSS is devoted mainly to a highly detailed account of the murder of an OSS officer in Italy—an interesting story, but Brown might have given more space to the still vexing question of what the OSS did to help win the war.

Harry Truman's abrupt dismissal of Donovan and dispersal of the OSS at the end of the war suggest that he thought it a failure. Perhaps he did; he never said in so many words. This conclusion would have been wrong, although the OSS did not equal the dramatic British achievement of reading German radio traffic, referred to as Ultra. Trying to identify the OSS operations that helped to win the war is like trying to decide which tank won a great tank battle. The OSS's accomplishments seem to have been of two sorts. In the first place it helped to spread German forces thin by financing and supporting (as did the British) resistance groups all over Europe. Dozens, perhaps scores, of divisions were busy chasing partisans when they were desperately needed in France and Russia. Military historians cite in particular the long delay of the Second Panzer Division on its way to Normandy at a time when the Allied beachhead was still insecure.

German intelligence efforts were also spread thin, and for the same reason: the OSS and the SIS were everywhere. The breadth of this clandestine engagement of spies was the OSS's second major contribution to the Allied war effort. When operations are conducted on the scale of a large industry it is the gross effort that counts. The OSS got information about the Germans and made them feel watched at many points—in neutral capitals like Stockholm, Madrid, Lisbon, Istanbul, and Bern; through German periodicals and broadcast intercepts; through spy nets inside the occupied countries; and through agents inside Germany itself, many in high places, and possibly even including Admiral Wilhelm Canaris, chief of the Abwehr, one of the main German intelligence services. The Germans, in short, were observed in too many places to hide their growing exhaustion, confusion, and weakness. In these ways the OSS contributed to the dispersion of German fighting strength, and to the kinetic sense of a faltering opponent that did as much to inspire confidence in the Allies as occasional, more explicit intelligence coups which revealed what the enemy was going to do when. Ultra was the big thing, but the OSS had much to be proud of on its own despite its inevitable blunders and failures.

If the great strength of the OSS was its freedom to try anything, its great weakness was the fact that it was doing everything for the first time. Britain had many files, based in part on Ultra intercepts, and it agreed to share them with the OSS early in the war. With their aid, Brown says, James Angleton uncovered scores of Axis agents in Italy. But some operations were badly conceived or ran out of luck, and some missions were simply outwitted by the enemy. In June 1944, for example, it was discovered that an entire net of agents sent into Central Europe and Germany from Istanbul had been compromised—but compromised by whom? It is still not quite clear. The suspected agent vanished at the end of the war. Some think he was actually working for the Russians.

According to Edward Jay Epstein, in a review of Brown's book in *The New York Times Book Review*,[5] a British liaison officer with the OSS, Colonel Charles Ellis, had been working for both the Germans and the Russians throughout the war. If this is true, it might explain why many OSS operations unraveled without apparent reason. There were many dark warnings of Russian penetration at the time, but they centered on Americans active in the Communist Party before the war. Donovan insisted he would hire anyone willing to fight Hitler. At the same time he expected a postwar struggle for Europe with the Russians, and throughout the war the OSS, like the government it served, remained of two minds where the Soviets were concerned— loyal to the embattled ally, suspicious of the future rival.

---

5. January 16, 1983.

It is difficult to read the diplomatic history of the Second World War without being impressed by the sincerity of FDR and Churchill in their attempt to reassure Stalin that the West hoped to continue East–West understanding and cooperation at war's end. Stalin had two dark suspicions—that the West dawdled in mounting an invasion of Europe in the hope that Germany and Russia would finish each other off; and that the West, in the final year of the war, would strike a separate deal with Germany denying Russia the fruits of victory. Wartime diplomatic messages are filled with reassurances to Stalin that neither suspicion was true. Dulles in Bern (among others) had many opportunities to reach such separate agreements but was blocked by Washington at almost every turn, although he did manage to secure the surrender of German forces in Italy a couple of days before the formal end of the war. There is no evidence that Churchill, Roosevelt, and their principal advisers lied about these matters.

This cannot quite be said of the oss. Intelligence services, like police departments, tend to think they know what their superiors *really* want. The oss remained preternaturally alert where the Russians were concerned; it was quick to spot and trumpet the political implications of the domination of resistance movements by Communist underground organizations, and on several occasions it simply could not resist the temptation to squirrel away information about the Soviets that more or less fell into its lap. Happy accidents of this sort occurred in Sweden and Romania.

In November 1944, the oss mission in Stockholm was approached by Finnish intelligence officers with an offer to sell some 1,500 pages of material relating to Soviet codes. Donovan reported the offer to Secretary of State Edward Stettinius but was told to reject it on the grounds that Russia was an ally. Donovan could not bear to let the opportunity pass. One of the codes was used by the NKVD. In December, the oss purchased the material and forwarded it to Washington, where Donovan told the President he had acquired four military and diplomatic codes, but without identifying them as Russian. The State Department got wind of the purchase and persuaded FDR to order Donovan to hand the material over to the Soviets forthwith. Donovan cabled General P. N. Fitin of the NKVD in Moscow that the codes had been captured in Italy, that the OSS had not studied them, and that they could be picked up in Washington. When the NKVD failed to act promptly, the material was delivered to Andrei Gromyko, then the Soviet ambassador to the United States.

Anthony Cave Brown and Bradley Smith both provide brief accounts of this episode, and they suggest one of the difficulties of writing about intelligence operations. Brown apparently had access to the OSS report to the Russians and to some accompanying documents, and accepts them at face value. He has, in effect, been gulled by what amounts to a memorandum for the record. Smith did not see the OSS material available to Brown, but searched many other archives and learned about Donovan's purchase of the documents against orders. What neither writer knows, as I found from my own inquiries, is that this material was copied before it was turned over to Gromyko, that it provided the means of decoding Russian diplomatic traffic collected by the NSA's predecessor, the Signal Intelligence Service, beginning about 1938, and that this traffic, read in bits and pieces after the war, provided counterintelligence officials with an important source of evidence on the spying activities of both Donald Maclean and the industrial espionage ring that included Julius Rosenberg. Referred to in code-breaking and counterintelligence circles as the VENONA material, this accumulated traffic (which stops about 1949, when the Soviets changed their encryption methods) was still being worked on by the NSA and the CIA as late as the 1980s. I am told that a dozen or more code names of Soviet agents in the United States have still never been identified.

An episode in some respects similar took place in Romania, where an OSS team established itself in September 1944, under Frank Wisner, a rich Wall Street lawyer before the war who went on later to run secret operations for the CIA during the height of the cold war, from 1948 until he had a physical and mental breakdown in 1958. As Cave Brown describes it, the immediate goal of the OSS mission in Bucharest was to rescue nearly 2,000 Allied airmen held as prisoners of war in Romania and Bulgaria. But the OSS group stayed on after the rescue for nearly a year, the only substantial OSS mission to operate in territory controlled by the Russians. Soon Wisner began to send messages about a concerted Soviet effort to dominate the country through the Romanian Communist Party. One of Wisner's officers, Major Robert Bishop, a counterintelligence expert in the OSS's X-2 division, made contact with a secret branch of the Romanian security service.

This branch was wholly unknown to the Russians. Since 1917 its job had been to penetrate the Romanian CP. The reports of its agents, passed on to Bishop and Wisner, and then forwarded to the OSS in Washington, provided a detailed view of the secret Russian program to obtain control of the government. Another OSS source provided access to traffic between Moscow and the Soviet commander in Bucharest, Marshal Rodion Malinovsky. Beginning in late 1944, then, the OSS was actively spying on the Russians, just as the Russians were actively spying on us. The cold war was a fact long before it was a policy.

Throughout the war one of Donovan's abiding goals was to establish a permanent American intelligence service. In October 1944 he submitted a formal proposal to the President which was met by vicious bureaucratic resistance. In February 1945 the *Chicago Tribune* reporter Walter J. Trohan published accounts of Donovan's plans and of high-level charges that the new agency would amount to an "American Gestapo." Once or twice Donovan almost got approval from Roosevelt, but his chances died with the President in April. Despite many requests for a meeting with Truman, he was granted only one, on May 14, 1945, which lasted fifteen minutes. By this time Donovan had so many enemies it is hard to say who delivered the coup de grâce. On September 20, 1945, Truman signed an executive order abolishing the OSS and parceling out its assets to the departments of State and War, both of which saw the OSS as an upstart competitor. Donovan himself, by now a major general, was dismissed from active service on January 12, 1946. His wife Ruth learned what had happened when he came down to dinner, for the first time in years, in civilian clothes. During the next few years the OSS was reconstituted as the CIA to pursue the cold war in much the same way that Donovan had worked against the Germans and Italians.

After Dulles took over the agency in 1953 he honored his old chief elaborately, but did not give him anything to do. Eisenhower made him ambassador to Thailand during the last year of the French war in Indochina but Donovan quickly exhausted his private means trying to perform the job in the large way he thought appropriate, and he resigned. He collected books on espionage, a poor substitute for the real thing. In 1957 he suffered a stroke which left him mentally impaired. During his last two years he was forgetful, often depressed, silent, subject to delusions. From his apartment window he imagined he could see Russian tanks approaching across the Queensboro Bridge. His death in 1959 released a torrent of admiring eulogies.

Donovan was a kind of entrepreneur of big intelligence who dealt in global politics rather than in oil or steel. The delicacies of espionage were all very well but he wanted to *do* things. In 1953 he told an aide that Dulles had "ruined" the CIA by turning it into a reporting agency. Even though he had been cast aside, he probably knew better. Dulles's CIA was as aggressive as it could be without actually becoming a military force, and it was following the pattern Donovan himself had established. In his final chapter, Bradley Smith accurately describes the OSS's principal legacy to the CIA—a wartime spirit which stressed operations and neglected espionage and other forms of secret intelligence collection. After a period of restraint during the 1970s, the CIA revived its cowboy methods in Central America with ambitious paramilitary programs aimed at the government of Nicaragua.

Some of the OSS officers in charge of paramilitary operations came out of the Second World War with a deep distrust of behind-the-lines derring-do—which often accomplished little except to provoke brutal retaliation—but their cautions were ignored. Many high CIA officials during the 1950s tended to remember only D-Day, when European resistance movements, augmented by OSS Jedburgh teams that parachuted into France in the critical period just before the invasion of Normandy, did much to help defeat the Germans, but only at terrible cost—a cost paid mainly by the local citizens. Sufferings of this sort may be justified when a big army is on the way, but in peacetime—however tense the peace—they are futile. This point was lost on the CIA. It fought the cold war as if invasion were imminent.

One of the warriors was Frank Wisner, who was too wound up to return to the dull routines of Wall Street. Wisner ran the Office of Policy Coordination from 1948 until 1952 with only the lightest sort of supervision from the director of central intelligence. He was not much more restrained during the years between 1952 and 1958 when he was the CIA's deputy director for plans. Wisner opened his postwar career with clandestine political campaigns against the Communist parties of France and Italy. He built a huge propaganda apparatus which he called his "mighty Wurlitzer," and he established secret contact with European labor unions, peace groups, and anti-Communist intellectuals. The Russians were doing the same sort of thing; Wisner never seems to have considered the possibility that the US might have conducted some of its own efforts openly without involving intellectuals in an expanding apparatus of deception. More troubling still was Wisner's support for underground organizations throughout Soviet-occupied Eastern Europe and even in Russia itself. In the Ukraine and along the Baltic coast he backed actual shooting wars against the Russians which did not end until the early 1950s.

In his memoirs Khrushchev reports, "Later, after the war, we lost thousands of men in a bitter struggle" against the groups backed by the CIA. According to John Loftus's book *The Belarus Secret*, Wisner's allies in this enterprise included active collaborators with the Nazis. Many had been personally involved in the killing of thousands of Ukrainian Jews. Hundreds of outright war criminals were spirited secretly into the United States at Wisner's contrivance. Later he supported a plan to invade Albania which was not abandoned until many men had died.

Other enterprises of an equally doubtful sort took place during the 1950s. They seemed like a good idea at the time because war with Russia seemed imminent. Former Nazis and Nazi collaborators were considered allies of convenience, just as Stalin himself had been during the war, when Churchill had said he would accept as an ally the devil himself, if it would help to win. Wisner was short on steadiness of temperament, but otherwise he seems rather like Donovan—aggressive, confident, fascinated with the wonderful tool he was lucky enough to direct, and so enthusiastic that he often missed the point where bright ideas crossed over into lunacy. Some of his plans blew up in his face, and he became a deeply troubled man. Nothing of the sort happened to Donovan. He was the right man for the fight against Hitler and his luck was never better than when it sent him back to private life at the end of the war.

—*The New York Review of Books*, May 12, 1983

2

THE CONSPIRACY THAT FAILED

FOLLOWING THE SURRENDER of May 1945, American intelligence officers swarmed over the carcass of defeated Germany, searching for the lessons of the war. Among their reports was one compiled by US Army counterintelligence officers on "The Political and Social Background of the 20 July Incident"—the failed attempt by German military conspirators to assassinate Hitler in 1944—which concluded:

> If the plot...had succeeded it would have undoubtedly saved the lives of thousands of Allied soldiers and the victors would have found Germany and Europe in a far better condition than it is in now. On the other hand the total defeat of Germany seems a far better guarantee for world security....

Total defeat is certainly what Germany experienced. Indeed, few nations in history, perhaps only Carthage at the end of the Third Punic War, have suffered military defeat so vast and so devastating. By war's end over 7.5 million German soldiers and civilians had died, cities had been bombed flat, Hitler and many of his associates had committed suicide, while hundreds of other Nazi leaders were in custody awaiting trial for crimes against humanity and against peace. Large parcels of German territory were severed immediately—the former

Austria restored to independence, part of East Prussia and German territory east of the Oder and Neisse rivers given to the revived state of Poland. At least twelve million Germans were expelled from their homes in the east and relocated in a shrunken Germany administered by four occupying armies.

While these huge population shifts were occurring, the eastern third of the truncated country held by the Soviet Union was first stripped of industrial machinery, raw materials, and plundered artworks and later cut off entirely to form a new nation ruled in all but name by the Soviets for nearly fifty years. Much of the German population was forced to undergo a humiliating exercise in self-justification called "de-Nazification," arbitrarily and inequitably imposed, and the very word "German" seemed to become a synonym for cruelty and villainy as the full magnitude of Hitler's genocide against the Jews gradually emerged.

The Germany that resulted from this unprecedented ordeal was a whipped and beaten country, timid in international affairs, anxious to reassure its new allies that it harbored no grievances, posed no challenge, had relinquished all claim to its lost territories, would never again disturb the peace of Europe. In short, the crushing military defeat of 1945 once and for all replaced the overweening Germany of the Kaisers and the barbarous Germany of the Third Reich with a chastened state eager to be accepted as a model citizen in the European community of nations. This, presumably, was among the goals sought by the wartime Allies at Casablanca in 1943 when they solved the problem of conflicting war aims by agreeing to accept nothing short of Germany's unconditional surrender. Time enough, they felt, to decide what the war was about after it was over.

The cost of inflicting this defeat was high on all sides. But the Germans had little claim on the world's sympathy in 1945, despite their terrible losses in the last year of the war. Millions of Jews, Poles, and Russians died between July 20, 1944, and the war's end nine and a half months later, along with many thousands of British, Italians, French, Americans, Netherlanders, and others. It is difficult to know what would have followed a successful assassination of Hitler in mid-1944, but it is at the very least possible that the organized killing of Jews would have halted, that the Nazis would have been deposed, and that the war would have come to an end before the winter of 1944–1945. What is striking about several recent books on what is now generally called "the German Resistance" is the complete absence of any evidence that Allied intelligence officers who watched the conspiracy against Hitler unfold, or their policymaking superiors, ever asked themselves in a serious way whether the conspirators' success and an early end to the war might be a good thing, and ought to be encouraged.

The history of the German Resistance has been publicly known in general outline since the appearance of three books immediately after the war—two memoirs by conspirators who miraculously survived, Fabian von Schlabrendorff and Hans Bernd Gisevius, and a brief but remarkably full account published by Allen Dulles, the wartime OSS chief of station in the neutral capital of Bern, Switzerland, where he established close relations with members of the Resistance soon after arriving in November 1942.[1] Over the years scholars have added much supporting detail to the basic story, allowing us to track the various strands of Resistance activity almost day by day. This vast literature has been drawn upon by a well-known German historian of the Third Reich, Joachim Fest, for an authoritative account of the events leading to July 20, *Plotting Hitler's Death: The Story of the German Resistance*.[2] What distinguishes Fest's account is his calm

---

1. Fabian von Schlabrendorff, *Revolt Against Hitler* (London: Eyre and Spottiswoode, 1948), later expanded and reissued as *The Secret War Against Hitler* (London: Pittman, 1965); Hans Bernd Gisevius, *To the Bitter End* (Houghton Mifflin, 1947); and Dulles, *Germany's Underground* (Macmillan, 1947).

2. Translated by Bruce Little (Metropolitan Books, 1996).

and assured command of the large cast of conspirators and of the complex unfolding of events in what is probably the only example in modern European history of an organized attempt to assassinate the ruler of a state because he was evil.

Of the many circles of those who opposed Hitler during the 1930s three may be identified as central to the events of July 20—a group of religious and philosophical opponents centering on Helmuth von Moltke, a great-grandnephew of the famous nineteenth-century general, whose ancestral estate in Silesia (now part of Poland) gave the group its name, "the Kreisau circle"; the nexus of German Foreign Office and military intelligence officials around Admiral Wilhelm Canaris, commander of the Abwehr, the German military intelligence service, and his close ally in the Foreign Office, Ernst von Weizsäcker; and a loosely knit, constantly fluctuating group of civilian politicians and high-ranking military officers centering on the former mayor of Leipzig, Carl Goerdeler, and General Ludwig Beck, who resigned as army chief of staff in 1938 in protest against Hitler's planned invasion of Czechoslovakia. Throughout the war, keeping pace with events, these overlapping groups grew from a few dozen individuals at the core to hundreds.

Any attempt to understand this extraordinary ferment of resistance at the heart of wartime Germany must begin with the recognition of two facts. The first is that just about everybody who played a central role was arrested and executed after July 20, some in the final days of the war. One of the leading historians of the Resistance, Peter Hoffmann of McGill University in Canada, has estimated the total number of executions resulting from the failed assassination attempt at two hundred. Fest in his book provides brief biographies of nearly sixty plotters, many of which end laconically with the phrase "executed in Plötzensee prison on [date]." Equally important in understanding the Resistance is the second fact that the sacrifice of lives, considered narrowly, was in vain; virtually nothing the Resistance attempted either stopped or hindered Hitler in anything he wanted to do, from making war in the first place to killing the Jews.

Opposition to Hitler was evident from the day he took power in 1933 but organized attempts to kill or depose him did not begin until the late 1930s, as it became increasingly apparent that Hitler's policies were bound to bring on a catastrophic war. In September 1938 a realistic and well-organized attempt to mount a military coup under favorable circumstances never to be repeated was thwarted at the eleventh hour by the abject surrender of the British Prime Minister Neville Chamberlain to Hitler's demands for the dismemberment of Czechoslovakia. The role played by the German diplomat Adam von Trott in the fall of 1938 was described by David Astor, who remarked that "no one seems to know what happened at the British end of this tragic story."[3] The omission was made good by the British television journalist Patricia Meehan in *The Unnecessary War: Whitehall and the German Resistance to Hitler*, her thoroughly researched and well-written account of British dealings with the German Resistance, in which she records the failure of leading British officials to recognize and exploit the chance they were given to stop Hitler before war had begun.[4] The moral bankruptcy of Chamberlain's policy of "appeasement" has long been accepted; Meehan provides many painful details of the process of surrender.

In March 1938 Hitler had occupied and absorbed Austria, then immediately began shouting demands of Czechoslovakia for its ill treatment of a German minority in the Sudetenland. Alexander Cadogan, the permanent head of the Foreign Office, wrote in his diary at the time, "Czechoslovakia is not worth the bones of a single Grenadier."

---

3. "The Man Who Plotted Against Hitler," *The New York Review*, April 28, 1983, pp. 16–21.

4. London: Sinclair-Stevenson, 1992. The strength of Meehan's book is its thorough mining of British Foreign Office records, documenting the perverse attitude which dismissed information from the Resistance as unreliable because its sources were "anti-Nazi."

Chamberlain agreed. But in Germany a group of alarmed Wehrmacht officers around General Beck and General Franz Halder, who succeeded Beck as army chief of staff, feared that the invasion of Czechoslovakia secretly ordered by Hitler would lead to a general European war.

By September, as the crisis mounted toward its climax, Halder had organized a military coup to take place as soon as Hitler issued the order to invade. A Panzer division would enter Berlin under the command of General Erwin von Witzleben. The takeover would be aided by the prefect of the Berlin police, Wolf-Heinrich von Helldorf, and his deputy, Fritz-Dietlof von der Schulenburg. The generals planned Hitler's arrest and trial but some of their allies, like Canaris's deputy in the Abwehr, Colonel Hans Oster, quietly planned to have Hitler shot out of hand. When the Panzers arrived at the Reich Chancellery, where Hitler had his office, the building's huge double doors would be opened by Erich Kordt, a trusted assistant to Hitler's foreign minister, Joachim von Ribbentrop.

The conspirators knew that Hitler planned to go to war if he did not get his way in Czechoslovakia, and they believed that both the army and the people would support Hitler's overthrow if it was the only way to avoid war. The conspirators' plans depended therefore on a genuine threat of war, and that depended in turn on the fortitude of the British. To ensure that London would play its part, the chief German Foreign Office conspirator, Ernst von Weizsäcker, arranged a back-channel contact with British leaders through Erich Kordt in Ribbentrop's office, and his brother, Theo, who was attached to the German embassy in London. In September, Theo Kordt, acting on instructions from Erich Kordt, delivered by a cousin, met with Lord Halifax, the British foreign secretary, and urged the British to stand firm while hinting at the plans for a coup: "I am in a position to assure you that the political and military circles I am speaking for will 'take arms against a sea of troubles, and by opposing end them.'" But despite knowing of this and other contacts, Chamberlain, in Scotland for the annual grouse shooting, could not steel himself for the blunt public challenge the German conspirators wanted. He wrote to his advisors that if Hitler marched "a very serious situation would arise and it might be necessary then to call ministers together to consider it. But I have a notion that it won't come to that...." These are not the words of a man who needed to be taken seriously.

Fearing something of the kind, and perhaps even informed of Chamberlain's so-far closely held plan to travel to Germany and personally beseech Hitler for peace, Weizsäcker asked a well-placed Swiss friend to repeat the essence of Kordt's message, while urging the British to send to Berlin "an energetic military man who, if necessary, can shout and hit the table with a riding crop." But Chamberlain went instead, sold Czechoslovakia (and more importantly its army, then actually larger than Hitler's) down the river, and cut the ground from beneath the German generals who had justified coup plans as the only alternative to a general European war.

Halder later said: "We were firmly convinced we would be successful. But now came Mr. Chamberlain and with one stroke the danger of war was averted...." How could Halder and the others justify a coup at the very moment of Hitler's resounding triumph over the Czechs at Munich? They did nothing. Gisevius, one of the few conspirators to survive the war, later recalled that a few days after Munich a group of them "sat around Witzleben's fireplace and tossed our lovely plans and projects into the fire. We spent the rest of the evening meditating, not on Hitler's triumph, but on the calamity that had befallen Europe."[5] In retrospect it is clear that Chamblerlain was

5. Witzleben was arrested on July 21, 1944, condemned on August 8, and executed the same day in Plötzensee prison. Schulenberg was executed in Plötzensee prison on August 10, 1944. Helldorf was executed in Plötzensee prison on August 15, 1944. Oster was executed in Flossenbürg concentration camp on April 9, 1945. The Kordt brothers survived the war. Weizsäcker was tried by an American tribunal in 1949, was repudiated by English diplomats who had

firmly committed to his appeasement policy and under no circumstances would have issued the kind of order that the German dissidents wanted.

The drama was repeated the following year as Hitler made a series of stormy demands on Poland. Again German conspirators tried to urge resolution upon the British, but their warnings and message were ignored, misinterpreted, or rejected outright as tainted by their source. In January 1939 one of the anti-Hitler military officers, Colonel Gerhard von Schwerin, answered a query about German political aims put to him by the British intelligence officer Major Kenneth Strong (later chief of intelligence for Eisenhower), with two blunt words: "world domination." Hans Oster helped Schwerin arrange a visit in June to London where he urged David Astor among others to press the British government to replace its ambassador in Berlin with a military man. When Schwerin finally won an opportunity to make his case directly to leading British army and naval officers for military demonstrations to convince Hitler of British resolve—"Hitler was the only person that had to be convinced, no one else counted"—he was dismissed as too "provocative" or discounted as unreliable because he was committing treason against his own country.

At about the same time Adam von Trott, who had made many British friends while studying at Oxford in the early 1930s, urged on several of them a policy diametrically opposed to Schwerin's—further talks in hope of reaching a peaceful settlement with Hitler over Danzig and the Polish corridor. Trott's purpose was to gain time for the military conspirators to prepare their coup. But many of his friends were furious at what they took to be his support of Nazi aims and one

---

known of his prewar efforts, and largely as a consequence was convicted of crimes against the peace. In 1951, after the intervention of numerous friends, Weizsäcker's sentence was reduced to time served. Meehan examines in great detail the case against Weizsäcker, and the British reluctance fully to admit what they knew of his prewar efforts.

of them, the distinguished classicist Maurice Bowra, went so far after the war as to make a joke of his execution at Plötzensee prison, telling a friend that Trott was one of the few Nazis to be hanged.

But Trott's advice was an anomaly. Other emissaries of the conspiracy like Fabian von Schlabrendorff and Weizsäcker's Swiss friend Carl Burckhardt stressed Hitler's belief, supported by Ribbentrop, that Britain would not fight. Both Kordt brothers came to London to warn that Hitler and Stalin were approaching agreement, something Hitler very much wanted before going to war, and Weizsäcker himself in Berlin urged the British ambassador to send a general to see Hitler who could make it unmistakably clear that any attack on Poland would mean war. But while the clock ticked away during the final days of peace no words of resolution came from Chamberlain, who was fishing in Scotland and complained that "the fish would not look at a fly"; or from the foreign secretary, Lord Halifax, who had asked before accepting the job whether he could still shoot on Saturdays; or from the permanent head of the British Foreign Office, Alexander Cadogan, who was playing golf at La Touquet. The dithering continued until the end. In Germany the officers involved in the conspiracy also failed to summon the resolution to act. When the British in fact declared war on September 3 following the German invasion of Poland, Hitler was taken aback. He had expected another cheap triumph, not a general European war.

Even in the opening months of war some conspirators from the German Foreign Office and military circles continued to hope for an opportunity to overthrow Hitler and end the fighting; but Britain refused to say how it would treat a new German government, the generals now shrank from mounting a coup while their country was actually at war, and in any event the wholesale retirements and reassignments of military commanders on the outbreak of war had destroyed the delicate Resistance networks which had been ready to act in 1938.

Resistance attempts to warn Britain, France, and the Low Countries of Hitler's war plans in late 1939 and early 1940 created only suspicion and confusion as Hitler repeatedly ordered and then cancelled attacks to the west. Those at the heart of the Resistance, including Admiral Canaris and Weizsäcker, and military officers like General Wilhelm Ulex, who called the murders in Poland a "blot on the honor of the entire German people," were morally outraged by the brutality of the war's opening phase on the eastern front, but a final attempt to halt the war with British help through the good offices of Pope Pius XII in the Vatican proceeded fitfully until it was ended entirely by Hitler's string of brilliant victories in the spring of 1940.

The fall of France brought the pugnacious Winston Churchill to power, but the last thing on his mind, facing the Third Reich alone, was negotiations with Germans of any stripe. The Resistance was never a single coherent group but a constantly shifting web of conspirators, sometimes active, sometimes in retreat, who held fast to the hope that Hitler might be overthrown and Germany saved from a catastrophe. But with the notable exceptions of Admiral Canaris's deputy, Hans Oster, forced out of the Abwehr in 1943; of Canaris himself, forced into retirement early in 1944[6]; and of Weizsäcker, dispatched to Rome as Germany's ambassador to the Vatican, most of those involved in the planned coup of 1938 were still active enough by July 20, 1944, to be swept up in the arrests that followed. The conspirators all seemed to know each other and to keep rough track of each other's progress toward open opposition without ever coalescing into a single disciplined organization.

It was this core of conspirators, now loosely but customarily referred to by historians as "the Resistance," which continued in the first half-year of the war its attempts to reach out to the Allies, but

---

6. Canaris was nevertheless also arrested after July 20, 1944, and hanged, along with his former deputy Hans Oster, on April 9, 1945, in the Flossenbürg concentration camp.

Churchill for his own reasons was as implacable as Chamberlain. "Our attitude towards all such inquiries or suggestions," he instructed the Foreign Office, "should be absolute silence...."[7] One result was that British intelligence, so far as we know, was caught almost completely by surprise on July 20, 1944, when German radio began to broadcast news of Hitler's miraculous escape from a conspirator's bomb.

Several leading members of the German Resistance—especially Adam von Trott, one of the Foreign Office conspirators, and the Protestant clergyman Dietrich Bonhoeffer—sought support in the United States before the war but their influence on thinking in Washington was slight. When Allen Dulles slipped across the border of Vichy France into Switzerland in November 1942 he brought with him no preconceptions about the German Resistance and was delighted a few months later to establish clandestine contact with it through an officer in the Abwehr, Hans Bernd Gisevius, sent to Bern under diplomatic cover by Admiral Canaris for exactly that purpose. Dulles made himself conspicuously available in Bern, and Gisevius was soon followed by numerous other visitors, contacts, and full-fledged agents —figures like Eduard Waetjen, an Abwehr colleague of Gisevius; the Dutch clergyman Wilhelm Visser't Hooft, head of the World Council of Churches, who provided Dulles with a summary of the views of Adam von Trott; and the German Foreign Office clerk Fritz Kolbe, who made five trips to Bern carrying some 1,600 documents.

The extraordinary volume as well as quality of wartime reporting from Dulles in Bern has been known to scholars in general outline for

---

7. *The Berlin Diaries, 1940–1945* of Marie "Missie" Vassiltchikov (Knopf, 1986) provides a vivid portrait of the psychology of resistance circles. Vassiltchikov, a young Russian émigré working in the German Foreign Office, was a friend of many in the Resistance, especially Adam von Trott. Churchill's minute to the Foreign Office is quoted by her brother George, who edited the diaries for publication, on page 187.

years but much new detail has become available with the transfer of the Office of Strategic Services (OSS) files from the CIA to the National Archives in Washington. Over a hundred OSS documents dealing with the German Resistance have now been reproduced, in whole or in part, in an extremely useful volume, *American Intelligence and the German Resistance to Hitler: A Documentary History*,[8] edited by two German scholars, Jürgen Heideking and Christof Mauch. Their collection demonstrates that American intelligence was in close contact with the July 20 conspirators for at least six months before the assassination attempt, but had no clearer idea than their British colleagues whether to encourage enemy nationals who sought the defeat of their own side, and, if so, how to exploit them. The skeletal account of Dulles's wartime career provided by Heideking and Mauch is amplified in several chapters of John H. Waller's *The Unseen War in Europe: Espionage and Conspiracy in the Second World War*.[9] Waller is a retired veteran of American intelligence work, who began with a stint with the OSS in Cairo; his book recounts many important cases and serves as a good, although incomplete, introduction to the role of intelligence in the war, a subject which still lacks a comprehensive single-volume history.

The evolution, often erratic, of Dulles's views of the German Resistance is amply documented by Heideking and Mauch. On January 16, 1943, he cabled Washington: "It is my personal opinion that there has as yet been no serious organization of the movement." Three weeks later he is "still of the opinion that if Hitler were to disappear, the end of Germany would begin...." By November he has concluded that "75 percent or more" of the German public opposes "the Nazi regime" and the following January he confesses, "I do not understand what our policy is and what offers, if any, we could give to any resistance

8. Westview, 1996.

9. Random House, 1996.

movement." Washington's answer, like London's at the opening of the war, was no offers, no encouragement, no deals, lest Moscow catch scent of the secret talks and begin to fear a Western attempt to make a separate peace.

This was an abiding source of anxiety in Washington and London as well, and all parties had evidence for their suspicions. Moscow in the summer of 1943 established a Free Germany Committee with the aid of German generals who had been captured at Stalingrad. Described to the British and Americans as nothing more than a morale-sapping propaganda ploy, this effort remained a nagging source of concern to Western intelligence analysts, who feared a Russian attempt to foist its client committee upon the prostrate German state as the embryo of a new government, or even to negotiate directly with the Nazis. Some members of the Resistance felt help was more likely to be found in the East than the West, but most feared above all an invasion of the German homeland by the Russians, burning with zeal for revenge for the horrific slaughters carried out by the Wehrmacht and the ss in the Soviet Union, and ready to impose a Communist regime.

In the summer of 1943 and again in December Helmuth von Moltke traveled under Foreign Office cover to Istanbul, where oss agents gleaned from his remarks the outline of what might be called a grand deal—German generals in France would capitulate to the Americans and the British while "the continuance of an unbroken Eastern Front" would be maintained pending an end to the war with a de facto "condition" of no Russian occupation of German soil. An oss officer argued that no alternative to the plan conveyed by Moltke "can offer even a remotely comparable chance of ending the War in the West at one stroke, and save perhaps many hundred thousand lives...."

But in April 1944 the oss chief of secret intelligence, Whitney Shepherdson, rejected the "Herman plan," named for Moltke's oss code name, as both inherently unworkable and "unacceptable to the

Russians in the extreme," which it would obviously have been. The original OSS report of the plan had stressed both the depth of Moltke's anti-Nazi convictions and the conspirators' recognition of the necessity for the "unequivocal military defeat and occupation of Germany...." Shepherdson paid no attention to any of that and considered the plan a more or less naked attempt to divide the Allies and to allow Germany to escape the just wrath of the Russians, whose sufferings were well known. But rather than turning aside Moltke with "absolute silence," Shepherdson proposed that the OSS chief in Istanbul, Lanning Macfarland, should

> be instructed to play upon this group as a possible instrument of double agents or in any way coldly calculated to promote the success of the invasion, without any regard whatsoever for the German individuals involved, their safety, personal relations to them, or the ultimate effect upon Germany....

But it was too late for plans of that sort. Moltke had already been arrested in Germany by the Gestapo, which held him in custody until his execution in Plötzensee prison on January 23, 1945.

Moltke's arrest came as the Resistance plotters in Berlin, close to panic at the relentless approach of the Russians, renewed their efforts to plot Hitler's assassination. As their plans took shape they continued to try to reach some understanding with the British and the Americans on the treatment Germany might expect after a successful coup. Adam von Trott traveled to Turkey, Sweden, and Switzerland. On January 27, 1944, Dulles reported from Bern with news of the plot, carried to him by a young German lawyer for Lufthansa, Otto John,[10] on one of his regular trips to Madrid and

---

10. Otto John later became chief of a West German secret intelligence organization and was briefly notorious following a mysterious disappearance into East Germany in the 1950s. He

Lisbon, the first in a series of cables code-named "Breakers." "For a number of reasons," Dulles reported to Washington, "I have not talked with Zulu [British intelligence officers stationed in Bern]...at this particular time, and pending further developments I recommend that you also refrain from doing so on the basis of information in my messages." Just why Allen Dulles wanted to keep the British in the dark about reports of the plot he does not say. He seems to be implying that they were not sympathetic to the Resistance.

Throughout the following winter and spring Dulles continued to report on the goals, the organization, and the leaders of the plot against Hitler. After the OSS chief William Donovan departed Washington for the June 6 invasion of France, which he would not have missed, he was kept up to date on the progress of Breakers as reported from Bern. On July 12, conveying news from Gisevius who had just returned from a trip to Berlin, Dulles cabled, "There is a possibility that a dramatic event may take place up north...." Almost daily thereafter he reported on the various forces involved, and at last on the evening of July 20 he cabled, "The attempt on Hitler's life is, of course, the outstanding item of news this evening." But what Dulles knew about the attempt itself came exclusively from broadcast reports. Gisevius had returned to Berlin and disappeared[11]; Eduard Waetjen at the German embassy in Bern reported that the Foreign Office had not even forwarded the customary *Sprachregelung*—instructions on what propaganda line to follow in public statements. It was not until mid-September, following Otto John's successful escape to Madrid, that

---

was tried and imprisoned for espionage in West Germany after his return. The first half of his memoir, *Twice Through the Lines* (Harper and Row, 1972), deals with his role in the German Resistance.

11. After the collapse of the coup in army headquarters on Bendlerstrasse, Gisevius spent six months in hiding before he managed to escape back across the border into Switzerland. There he remained until the end of the war, polishing his memoir of the Resistance with the help of Mary Bancroft.

the OSS received a detailed firsthand report on the tragic failure of the conspirators on July 20.

After years of discussion, planning, missed opportunities, elaborate schemes for assassination that came to nothing, horror at the crimes committed by Hitler, and despair at the tightening of the noose as Allied armies closed in, the resistance finally managed to rise from farce to tragedy through the passion and the energy of one man—Claus von Stauffenberg, youngest son of minor South German nobility, whose vow at age seven was "to be a soldier and go to all the wars."

Stauffenberg's central role in the events of July 20 has long been known. He has been the subject of several previous biographies and was of course a central figure in Peter Hoffmann's authoritative and still unsurpassed *History of the German Resistance, 1933–1945*, first published in Germany in 1969.[12] The portrait there is expanded without being much changed in Hoffmann's biography, *Stauffenberg: A Family History, 1905–1944*, which discusses Stauffenberg's social and intellectual background and his crucial role in bringing renewed energy to Resistance circles in late 1943 and early 1944, when the Resistance seemed to have run aground.[13] Stauffenberg and his brothers, like many other high-minded sons of the Catholic nobility in southern Germany, at first welcomed Hitler in 1933 as a kind of purgative for the state, corrupted (as they felt) by the tumult of Weimar democracy. But their illusions that Hitler promised anything of the sort did not last long. What Stauffenberg saw as a soldier, first in Poland and then in Russia, made him a bitter foe of the Nazis. In April 1942 on the Russian front he expressed to a fellow officer his outrage over German crimes, especially the killing of Jews and the mass starvation of Russian prisoners of war. In August he told a

---

12. Third English edition, McGill-Queen's University Press, 1996.

13. Cambridge University Press, 1995.

friend, "They are shooting Jews in masses. These crimes must not be allowed to continue." At the end of September he jumped up at a meeting of military men to shout, "Hitler is responsible. No fundamental change is possible unless he is removed. I am ready to do it."

Hoffmann has been meticulous in recording every similar statement from Stauffenberg and his fellow conspirators in order to refute charges made in Britain and America immediately after the war, and often echoed by historians since, that the resistance was driven by self-interest, held no principled objection to Hitler's crimes, and sought only to avoid the calamity of defeat by replacing the Führer with real military men who might simultaneously fight to better effect and negotiate softer treatment from the Allies.

But success in killing Hitler took more than the willingness expressed by Stauffenberg in the fall of 1942. Plenty of military officers, according to Hoffmann, were willing in varying degree. What was required was access to Hitler himself, and eighteen months passed before Stauffenberg was appointed chief of staff for General Friedrich Fromm in May 1944 and thereafter began to represent the Home Army at military briefings for Hitler. In the meantime, while serving on the staff of one of Rommel's Panzer divisions in Tunisia in April 1943, Stauffenberg was terribly wounded when his car was strafed by an Allied fighter. He recovered some months later but had lost an eye, his right hand, and two fingers of his left hand. Back in Germany, Stauffenberg threw himself into Resistance plotting. He became intensely frustrated as one plan after another came to nothing, and finally determined, despite his wounds, to kill Hitler himself. On June 7, 1944, he met Hitler for the first time, found the man weak and repellent, noted that the notoriously vain Field Marshal Hermann Goering was wearing makeup, and concluded that the minister of war production, Albert Speer, was the only sane man in the room. At his second meeting with Hitler a month later Stauffenberg carried explosives but did not act; on July 15 he was fully prepared but was blocked at the last moment when the other high officers in the conspiracy got cold feet.

A third opportunity presented itself on July 20, but the previous failure had seriously compromised prospects for a successful coup and Stauffenberg knew it. "The most terrible thing," his brother Berthold said, "is knowing that we cannot succeed and yet that we have to do it, for our country and our children." Stauffenberg himself detested the thought that he would not only fail but would "go down in German history as a traitor," but his conscience prodded him onto the courier plane from Berlin to Hitler's base in East Prussia, the so-called *Wolfschanze* or Wolf's Lair. At the headquarters of the Home Army on Bendlerstrasse back in Berlin Stauffenberg's co-conspirators anxiously awaited news of Hitler's death. When it arrived they would issue orders for Operation Valkyrie, an emergency plan, actually approved by Hitler, for the army's seizure of the state in the event of a coup attempt.

When it was all over Hitler declared that only Providence could have saved him and it is not hard to see what he meant. With special pliers, designed for his crippled left hand, Stauffenberg had activated the fuse on the bomb in his briefcase, placed it beneath the round oak table close to Hitler's seat in the briefing room, then left the room on a pretext. Moments after the deafening explosion Stauffenberg thought he saw Hitler's bloody form carried from the wreckage on a stretcher and he naturally concluded the tyrant was dead. But later in the day as the conspirators tried to get Operation Valkyrie off the ground Hitler's miraculous survival was announced, the conspirators were placed under arrest, and the panicky General Fromm, fearful of what they might say under torture about his own involvement, had the principal ringleaders given a summary court martial, sentenced to death, and marched down to the courtyard to face a firing squad. There Stauffenberg was shot. His final words were "Long live holy Germany!"

That Stauffenberg should have died and Hitler lived tells the history of the Resistance in a sentence. While the coup sputtered that afternoon, Hitler, cleaned up and in a fresh uniform, met as previously scheduled with Mussolini, who had arrived on a special train. After the war one of the German generals present described to an American interrogator the mad quarreling that afternoon of Ribbentrop, Goering, and Admiral Doenitz. The interrogator's report is quoted by Waller in *The Unseen War in Europe*:

> All of a sudden the Führer leapt up in a fit of frenzy with foam on his lips, and yelled out that he would be revenged on all traitors, that Providence had just shown him once more that he had been chosen to make world history, and shouted about terrible punishments for women and children, all of them would have to be put inside concentration camps! ... Mussolini found it most unpleasant. Meanwhile more tea was served by the footmen in white gloves. ... The Führer was in a very peculiar state at the time. It was the time when his right arm began to develop tremors. He sat there almost the whole time eating his colored pastilles [medicine tablets]. He had pastilles of all kinds of colors in front of him and kept on eating them. He would be quiet for a time, and then suddenly he'd break out like a wild animal, and wanted to put everyone, women and children too, into a concentration camp. He was the one Providence had chosen!

Providence or accident—something saved Hitler. First the crippled Stauffenberg managed to activate the fuse on only one of the two bombs he had brought with him into a washroom under pretext of changing his shirt following his flight from Berlin. Interrupted by an orderly urging haste, Stauffenberg left one of his two bombs behind. The two together almost certainly would have killed everyone in the briefing room. The conspirators at Bendlerstrasse had insisted that

Stauffenberg return to Berlin to lead them. After he left the room one of the other officers, kicking Stauffenberg's briefcase with his foot, reached under the table and moved it—to the far side of the massive wooden central pedestal supporting the table. The blast was therefore deflected away from Hitler, saving his life.

At the end of the war one of the Foreign Office conspirators, Erich Kordt, who had survived in a backwater post as a German diplomat in China, described for an American intelligence officer the efforts to enlist British help in avoiding war or overthrowing Hitler between 1938 and early 1940. Initially he asked his American friend to keep this melancholy history private, explaining, "The efforts of my friends were considerable, even if all endeavors failed, and I feel I must protect them against cheap contempt which easily attaches itself to failure."

The earliest British reactions to the assassination attempt were indeed a mixture of contempt and indifference. Alexander Cadogan of the Foreign Office recorded in his diary on the following day, "Papers full of attempt on Hitler's life. Don't know what it means. Not very much, I think.... Others rather unduly excited about it. I threw a few little cold douches...." Churchill in Parliament dismissed the failed coup as simply a case of "the highest personalities in the German Reich" trying to kill each other off, and in Switzerland Carl Jung, who often passed on his reading of events to Allen Dulles, took a similar view. Moral principle, he told Dulles's colleague and mistress, Mary Bancroft, had nothing to do with it. Gisevius and Stauffenberg simply wanted what Hitler had—power. "They were like a pair of lions fighting over a hunk of raw meat."[14]

Within a few days of the failed coup the oss at last shared the Breakers material with the British and the Russians. The response of the Russians is unclear but the British seem to have been caught

---

14. Mary Bancroft, *Autobiography of a Spy* (Morrow, 1983), p. 239.

completely by surprise, despite contacts between Adam von Trott and British intelligence in Sweden in March and June 1944 and reports passed on by Otto John to British intelligence officers in Lisbon in February and early July. The mammoth six-volume official history, *British Intelligence in the Second World War*, devotes only four pages to the July plot.[15] One looks in vain for any reminder of the numerous secret contacts between German conspirators and the British Foreign Office in the years between 1938 and 1940. Surveying the scene in early 1944 British intelligence saw nothing but Hitler and his cronies. January 11: "No evidence that any faction exists within the Army... likely to overthrow the present regime...." February 18: "There is no subversive organisation." At last, on March 23, "slight evidence" of an opposition movement appears. But as late as July 6, following meetings in Stockholm between British intelligence and Adam von Trott, the Foreign Office concluded that "these people... won't act without our backing, which, if given, might gravely embarrass us later."

The official record of British surprise on July 20 is so nearly complete one's suspicions are aroused. How could the Secret Intelligence Service (SIS), desperate for information about Hitler and his government, have failed to maintain contact with the many Germans who had knocked on British doors before the war? General Hans Oster, the chief deputy to Admiral Canaris in the Abwehr, had committed conventional treason in passing on reports of Hitler's military plans to the British and the Dutch. Otto John had contacted British intelligence in Lisbon. Is it really possible the SIS had turned a cold shoulder toward these prime assets?

The answer appears to be yes. When Otto John met secretly with Rita Winsor of the SIS in Lisbon in February 1944 she told him that London had banned all future contact with the German opposition. Dulles's best agent in Bern, Fritz Kolbe, had been turned away first by

15. Volume 3, Part 2, Appendix 22, pp. 893–896.

the British as a "provocation" (just as a later Dulles triumph, the Russian defector Oleg Penkovsky, was also brushed off initially by the British on the same grounds). Noel Annan, in *Changing Enemies: The Defeat and Regeneration of Germany*,[16] a finely written memoir of his own wartime intelligence work mainly concerned with the Germans, confirms that July 20 came as a surprise to the Joint Intelligence Staff of the War Cabinet. Annan's book is a sweeping, at times brilliantly succinct, overview of British–German relations during and just after the war. There is relatively little close description of day-to-day intelligence work, but it is clear from his account that the SIS saw no raw intelligence reports predicting a coup attempt, and that it sparked no interest on high when it occurred: "In Britain the word was put out that the plotters were nationalists trying to salvage as much as possible of Germany's ill-gotten gains."

Worse still, the BBC broadcast dismissive accounts of the plot, which included the names of possible or likely conspirators. Several were promptly arrested by the Gestapo and executed. Annan calls this broadcast "an appalling misjudgement."

The British refusal to have anything to do with the opposition was almost certainly prompted, at least in part, by lingering embarrassment over the Chamberlain government's miserable failure to resist Hitler stoutly when that might have been enough to prevent the war. But something else was clearly at work as well, a conviction, shared by the Americans, that the war was too big a thing to negotiate away with some unrepresentative group of German conspirators solely because they might kill Hitler and seize hold of the government. In a frank summary of the Foreign Office's view, Annan writes, its officials "had no wish to be confronted by a group of Prussian Junkers who, they considered, would be scarcely less nationalist than the Nazis when putting forward conditions for peace." The Allies appeared to have

---

16. Norton, 1996.

concluded that it was the entire German nation that had put Hitler in power and followed him into war and crime, and it was the entire German nation that would have to be taught a lesson it would never forget.

Even some of the conspirators seem to have shared this view, however hard they struggled to avoid the calamity they had seen coming for some time. On the last page of his book Joachim Fest recounts a conversation in Berlin on July 21, 1944, between Emmi Bonhoeffer, her husband Klaus, and her brother Justus Delbrück. (Klaus was executed on April 23, 1945; Justus almost suffered the same fate two days later, but survived when a group of prisoners convinced their executioner he might be shot himself by the Red Army if he carried out his orders.) The three were clearing the wreckage of a neighbor's house.

> When they sat down to rest amid the ruins, [Emmi] asked whether the two men could draw any lesson at all from the failure of the plot. There was a momentary pause while they weighed their answer. Finally Delbrück responded in a way that captured the pathos and paradox of the resistance: "I think it was good that it happened, and good too, perhaps, that it did not succeed."

One sees why he could have said this at that moment, not knowing how many people would be killed over the next year. Germany certainly learned a lesson, and it may be argued that the whole world learned the same lesson at the same time. But by Fest's own account, 4.8 million German soldiers and civilians died between July 20, 1944, and the German surrender on May 8, 1945—"not to mention the countless casualties in other countries or the victims of Hitler's extermination policy, which continued to the very end." Is it possible that vigorous Allied support for the Resistance might have saved some or many of these millions of lives?

The question must be asked twice—first of the period before the war, when the conspirators simply urged Britain to do what all but a few historians have since agreed it should have done—threatened war if Hitler set foot in Czechoslovakia. Resolution then, when Hitler wanted a war but was still unready, almost certainly would have avoided a big war and the Holocaust alike. But later, in mid-war, what the Allies might have done to help the conspirators mount a successful coup is far from clear. The reassurance sought by Moltke in Istanbul, Trott in Stockholm, Otto John in Lisbon, and Gisevius in Bern was never offered; but the conspirators went forward anyway, convinced that the moral gesture was as important as success. As it happened, luck was against them. Only if they had been successful might the Allies have been presented with the opportunity for an armistice that would have saved millions of lives. But the failure of the Resistance and the Allies to understand each other should not surprise us; they had different goals in mind. The Resistance was trying to end the war, while the Allies were trying to win it, and they did.

—*The New York Review of Books*, January 9, 1997

3

FOUNDING FATHER

ALLEN WELSH DULLES was not the first director of the Central Intelligence Agency, or the best, certainly not the wisest, or even the most aggressive, although in that category he comes in a very close second, after William Casey, whose most extravagant secret efforts to win the cold war may be plausibly blamed on the brain tumor which killed him. But Allen Dulles probably had the deeper natural instinct for what his biographer Peter Grose,[1] echoing Kipling, likes to call the Great Game, and he was without question the most important director of the CIA in its first half-century—granting, for the moment, that the agency will finish the full fifty years without being sliced up or killed altogether by an irritated Congress.

The conduct of secret intelligence, which was Dulles's central preoccupation from his first job as a young diplomat in Switzerland during the First World War until his forced resignation from the CIA in 1961, is only part of what Kipling had in mind when he referred to the Great Game. By that he principally meant the hundred-year struggle between Russia and Great Britain for control of Central Asia, and it was a renewed contest with Soviet Russia following the Second World War for control of the entire globe that Dulles pursued with a

---

1. *Gentleman Spy: The Life of Allen Dulles* (Houghton Mifflin/A Richard Todd Book, 1994.)

patriot's devotion, an appetite for combat, and an elastic sense of the permissible.

Dulles never doubted that the fate of the world as he knew it was at stake, but Dulles was not always right. It is possible that Stalin and his successors had more modest ambitions in mind when they determined to hold on to the countries of Eastern Europe liberated by Soviet armies in 1945. As Grose makes clear in his exemplary book, the best efforts of Dulles's spies rarely succeeded in penetrating the innermost secrets of the Soviet regime. After the CIA acquired the U-2 spy plane in 1956 and spy satellites in 1960, the agency always knew what the Soviets had, and conventional intelligence efforts kept pretty good track of what the Soviets did, but often neither Dulles nor later directors of central intelligence knew what the Soviets really intended. Dulles was required to decide this question on his own.

Next to the somber granite edifice of his older brother, John Foster Dulles, who preached the anti-Communist gospel as Eisenhower's secretary of state, Allen seemed a genial friend of everyman, with his booming laugh and comfortable way of answering hard questions with a joke or a wink. He loved tennis and played as often as he could between attacks of gout and "skull sessions," talking shop with operatives in from the field. He seems to have been completely free of personal malice. But intimates knew it was only surface polish that distinguished him from his brother. Dulles unhesitatingly rose to Nikita Khrushchev's challenge in 1956 when the Russian told a roomful of Western diplomats, "History is on our side. We will bury you." The fears and alarms of the cold war seem melodramatic and overdrawn now, but the Dulles who ran the CIA during the Eisenhower years was fired by steely resolve to carry the fight to the enemy, and to prevail. Grose gives us the fight round by round in *Gentleman Spy*; whether Dulles prevailed shall be considered below.

Allen Dulles was not the only man Eisenhower might have appointed to run the CIA in 1953. Indeed one candidate was Dulles's former boss in the Office of Strategic Services during the war, William J. Donovan, called "Wild Bill" for good reason, who was bored by the law and longed for another chance at the excitements of intelligence in a great cause. But there was behind the choice of Dulles a kind of glacial weight of career, connection, and circumstance. Born in 1893 in upstate New York, son of a Presbyterian minister of modest means, Allen Dulles was the grandson of one secretary of state (John Watson Foster, who served a year under Benjamin Harrison) and nephew of another (Robert Lansing, under Woodrow Wilson), and as a young man Dulles hoped for a chance at the job himself.

His decade with the Foreign Service, beginning in 1916, gave him much experience—a year in Vienna before the United States entered the First World War, a second year spent handling political intelligence in Bern, most of 1919 with the American delegation to the Versailles peace conference, followed by a brief posting to Berlin in time to witness a right-wing military putsch suppressed after a frightening week of confusion and street violence. Among the victims were unlucky Jews beaten half to death before Dulles's eyes. During a later tour in Constantinople the talk was all of the White forces fighting across the border in southern Russia against the Bolsheviks. But back in Washington in the early 1920s Dulles got a law degree, and in 1926 he resigned from the Foreign Service for the simple reason that the job didn't pay enough. His brother Foster's law firm, Sullivan and Cromwell, did, and he joined it.

The later 1920s and 1930s for Dulles were a time of making money, keeping a hand in with the odd diplomatic assignment, persuading his brother Foster in 1935 to quit doing business in Hitler's Germany, and finding for himself a role in the coming war. To the extent Dulles ever had a private life, this was when he had it. Between his tours in Berlin and Turkey, Dulles had acquired a wife, Clover Todd, safely Presbyterian, pretty, with a taste for going deeply into things of the mind and spirit. This was not at all Dulles's style, which they both discovered after the first bloom of marriage and young children began to fade. For the rest of their fifty years together Dulles and his wife maintained diplomatic recognition but were frequently apart, often at odds, and at times lived almost as complete strangers. They had three children, including a son who lost part of his brain to shrapnel during the Korean War and has required constant supervision and care ever since. His daughter Joan saw her father cry only once, in June 1940, when the Nazis occupied Paris.

Dulles's children do not appear to have complained to his biographer but it is clear that life at home was often bleak and lonely. Dulles gave his leisure hours to many women, among them a daughter of Toscanini, a queen of Greece, and Clare Boothe Luce, the wife of *Time* magazine's founder and publisher. Whether Clover also had lovers is not quite clear; she certainly deserved them. Dulles doubtless loved his family but they did not interest him. What interested him was men, politics, position, the drama of great events, and being on the inside. Sullivan and Cromwell offered enough of each to keep the appetite keen. His heart's desire was granted at last in November of 1942, when he slipped across the border into Switzerland with a broad mandate from Donovan as the oss's man in Bern. For the next twenty months he was a prisoner in Heaven—no wife, no kids, no dull legal work, and a secret war to fight.

The reputation that made Allen Dulles the inevitable man to head the CIA in 1953 was earned in Switzerland. There he did two notable things. Very soon after his arrival he established contact with the German Resistance, a loose nexus of German radicals, conservatives, and conscience-driven Protestants united only by courage and opposition to the crimes of Hitler. When some of them organized a plot on Hitler's life, Dulles reported to Washington on their halting progress toward the failed attempt of July 20, 1944. Making contact with the underground opposition in a police state was a major covert achievement, exceeded only by Dulles's success in keeping their exchanges secret despite the scrutiny of German intelligence, which knew his identity from the day he arrived, placed agents in his household, and at one time was even reading his secret cables to Washington. At the end of the war Dulles wrote and published a short book on the Resistance called *Germany's Underground*, still an important source on their hopes and mostly tragic fate. But good Germans were not a hot property in 1947, and the book could hardly be given away.

Dulles's second triumph in Bern was to negotiate the surrender of German military forces in Italy before the end of the war. Grose is particularly good here, as elsewhere, at providing a crisp account of a complex episode. What made this one especially delicate was Stalin's suspicion of his allies. Having precipitated the war himself by agreeing to a nonaggression pact with Germany in August 1939, Stalin was keenly alert to the danger that Churchill and Roosevelt might reach a separate peace with Hitler and leave Russia to face Germany alone. When the Americans, abiding by their agreements to the letter, informed Stalin of the initial contact with General Karl Wolff in February 1945, Dulles's task was immensely complicated. He succeeded eventually in the negotiations for surrender, but not until May 2, only a few days before the war ended generally.

Dulles got plenty of things wrong during the war; he was far too credulous, for example, about the so-called "Bavarian redoubt," where Hitler allegedly planned to fight on from an impregnable fortress in the German Alps. Hitler had no such plans and stayed in his bunker. But Dulles got the big things right when they counted most. His contact with the Resistance offered a doorway into the mood of the German elite—a growing sense of impending defeat, held in check by fear of the Gestapo. Knowing that Germans felt trapped and helpless gave Washington confidence that victory was only a matter of time—a confidence, everything considered, as useful as an extra ten divisions. Ending the war in Italy a week early saved the Allies hundreds and perhaps thousands of casualties. With the exception of the code-breakers at Bletchley Park, no intelligence operation of the

Second World War achieved more than did Dulles's tiny office in Bern, staffed with a miscellany of Americans stranded in Switzerland by the war. What Dulles did he did largely by himself. Continuing secrecy about most of the details only polished the luster of his feats. After the war he lobbied patiently for a national intelligence service, and urged that all secret activities be housed under a single roof. He was willing to work quietly in lesser jobs when others were put in charge, and was undeniably, irresistibly, and conspicuously available when Eisenhower wanted a spy chief to support an aggressive foreign policy pledged to roll back communism.

Gentleman Spy has an unusual history. Grose inherited a partly written and thoroughly researched manuscript which had been started and then abandoned a decade earlier by Richard Harris Smith, author of an early history of the OSS. Smith had interviewed scores of old CIA hands during the early 1970s and had completed a long account of Dulles's years in the agency, when a Senate investigating committee under Senator Frank Church began to release an exhaustive series of reports in 1976. Smith felt he would have to rework all he had written in light of the new material but found it impossible to resume the task.

Eventually a new publisher recruited Grose to "complete" the book, but while some sections still show the influence of Smith's earlier work this is still very much Grose's book. Smith's thousand pages, filled with operational detail, have been largely thrown out by Grose, who has instead written a genuine life—a biography which sticks closely to the man, his character, and the influence on history that was truly and uniquely his, not simply the work of the agency under his command. What emerges is a portrait of Allen Dulles as one of the architects and early commanders of the cold war, a man whose profound self-confidence gave a vigorous pugnacity to American foreign policy for a decade.

Europe was the prize fought over during the cold war, but by the time Dulles became director of central intelligence in 1953 Europe was no longer the principal battleground. The division of the continent mapped by the Iron Curtain was too dangerous to cross, a fact recognized by the Russians at the end of the Berlin blockade and by the Americans, with some internal self-questioning, and even anguish, after the popular anti-Communist uprisings were suppressed in Berlin in 1953 and Hungary in 1956. The CIA under Dulles had hoped and even prepared for rebellion in the East, and had actually organized Hungarian resistance forces; but when the moment arrived, and any serious attempt to help rebels defeat Soviet tanks would have demanded American tanks, realism prevailed. The battlegrounds of the cold war thereafter moved to the third world, where actual combat by covert warriors and proxy armies could be safely conducted—that is, without threatening the interests of an opponent so obviously vital that full-scale war was bound to result.

The principal campaigns of the CIA under Dulles form a kind of silent coda to whatever was agitating the White House and John Foster Dulles at any given moment—the propaganda war with the Soviets; the "immoral" (in Foster's view) neutralism of Indonesia and India; Soviet ambitions in the Middle East, where oil, Israel, and European allies all tugged American policy in different directions; revolutionary movements in Africa, Central America, and Cuba; and Soviet military programs which might threaten American reliance on nuclear deterrence.

This last probably burned up more calories of human energy in argument than all the others combined. The general public, horrified by the escalating levels of nuclear weaponry, never quite grasped what was at stake in the dispute over "deterrence"—whether the United States could sanely threaten to defend Europe with atomic and hydrogen bombs. Defense budgets hinged on the answer to that question. Whenever the Soviets "caught up" in the development of strategic weapons, deterrence required another upward spiral in the arms race, at staggering cost, with a corresponding increase in the danger that a failure of deterrence—that is, an outbreak of war—would more or less destroy the world. Grose provides a standard account of the beginning of this intelligence war, when the U-2 spy plane and satellite reconnaissance were brought into play. But about the ceaseless quarreling between the CIA and the Pentagon over the extent and purpose of Soviet military programs, Grose has very little to say. There are several reasons for this. For one thing, the discussion grows lethally boring once the central question of suspense—Would the arms race end with destruction of the world or not?—has been resolved by events. But just as important is the fact that White House officials and directors of central intelligence for the most part trusted aides to tell them what mattered most—what it would cost to "stay ahead."

Much has been written about the covert adventuring of the Dulles years, especially the successful overthrow of governments in Iran (1953) and Guatemala (1954). In both cases the argument for overthrowing them revolved around the danger of "Soviet footholds" in the Middle East (thus threatening Western oil supplies and the Suez Canal) and Central America (ditto the Panama Canal). But Grose is quick to point out the importance of commercial interests—nationalization of British oil companies by Iran and of banana plantations in Guatemala owned by the United Fruit Company, a client, not incidentally, of the law firm of Sullivan and Cromwell. These are twice-told tales, but Grose has added new information and unfolded the stories with clarity and dramatic verve.

Also good are Grose's accounts of the CIA's bungled attempt to overthrow the government of Indonesia in 1958, which came undone when an American pilot on a secret bombing mission was shot down and captured;[2] and of the agency's success in obtaining a copy of

---

2. The Indonesian operation is the subject of a 600-page documentary history issued by the State Department in 1994. It added new details to the story told by Grose but without altering it fundamentally. The study was the first to incorporate CIA documents in accordance with a law passed in 1991.

Khrushchev's secret speech in 1956 denouncing Stalin's crimes. It has long been generally known to have come from the Israelis, but the means by which it did so—through the circle of former Soviet political prisoners close to the Polish leader Wladyslaw Gomulka—have never been laid out with the detail Grose provides here. And there is much else besides, from Dulles's deft handling of the Red-hunting forays of Senator Joseph McCarthy, to the slow unfolding of the disaster of the failed invasion of Cuba at the Bay of Pigs, which ended Dulles's career.

Grose has a firm sense of the manner in which the operation to get rid of Castro, started under Eisenhower, cast all doubts aside and grew until it reached behemoth size. The thousand men who went ashore in April 1961 were far too many for the nucleus of a long-term guerrilla army—Fidel Castro himself began with fewer than a score—but far too few to beat Castro's huge army and militia, backed up by the overwhelming support of the Cuban people. How intelligent men convinced themselves that there was promise in this mad endeavor has been described before, but the disaster offers a lesson about the limits of "covert" action, and Grose tells it well.

With perhaps one exception. It seems to me that Grose has thrown up his hands too soon in his attempt to trace the history of CIA plans to assassinate Castro. This episode has proved unexpectedly difficult for historians, Grose now included, for reasons which have more to do with the public pain of John F. Kennedy's own murder and the literary energy of the late President's friends than they do with the inevitably spotty written record. The plots to kill Castro and other foreign leaders were the subject of an entire volume of the Church Committee Report on intelligence activities in the late 1970s. Just who bears ultimate responsibility for undertaking these efforts, however, the committee never quite spelled out. Kennedy's colleagues all heatedly denied he had ever approved, or for that matter known about, the efforts to kill Castro; and the Church Committee discovered no hard evidence proving that he did know.

Kennedy's secretary of defense, Robert McNamara, neatly laid out the dilemma posed by the record: on the one hand, he told the Church Committee, the CIA was a highly disciplined institution and so far as he knew it had never undertaken a single important measure without proper authority; but on the other hand McNamara certainly knew of no plan to kill Castro and he was morally certain President Kennedy didn't either. "I just can't understand how it could have happened," he said. "I understand the contradiction that this carries with respect to the facts."

To resolve this contradiction Peter Grose proposes resort to the "Thomas à Becket defense," prepared for monarchs with telltale drops of blood leading to their door and named for the British archbishop murdered in the twelfth century by agents of King Henry II, who had wished aloud for someone to free him of this troublesome cleric. CIA officers all told the Church Committee that "bad words" like assassination were never uttered in the same sentence with Castro's name, and that the subject was discussed with high officials in muffled manner, with delicate obliquity and airy circumlocution. "It may well be," Grose suggests, "that Kennedy, new to the job and confused by Allen's manner, simply did not understand what Allen thought he was communicating." In short, it was all a muddle: Kennedy never said do it, and the CIA never went off on its own.

American public life has been agitated by three questions of this kind in the last twenty years: Did Kennedy know about the plots to kill Castro? Did Richard Nixon know about the Watergate cover-up? Did Ronald Reagan know about Iran-contra? Those who find these questions too deeply baffling for mere men to hope to answer will perhaps be content to join Grose, who has elected grace over rigor on this point, and let it go. In fact there is a great deal of evidence about Kennedy's knowledge of the CIA plots and much of it is not at all ambiguous. If we press the question it is not in order to judge Kennedy but because it tells us two things about the CIA, true about other intelligence services as well, which are fundamental to understanding the agency's role in American politics.

The first is that the CIA works for the president. The second is that the CIA attempts to keep its covert actions secret. When they become known, effort is made to ensure they cannot be attributed to the United States. When the United States is obviously the author, the CIA protects the president by taking the blame. This is what is meant by "plausible deniability." But the concept has a flaw. When the CIA has really done something awful on its own, the responding fury of the office of the president is unmistakable and unrestrained. But when the agency is only falling on its sword in time-honored fashion, then the president's men treat the alleged excess with great gentleness, in the manner of McNamara saying with the sweet candor of a boy next to an empty cookie jar, "I just can't understand how it could have happened."

Kennedy was plenty angry about the embarrassing failure at the Bay of Pigs, but he was also man enough to admit he could have said no. Many of his aides wanted to chastise Dulles with a public flogging but Kennedy made a point of treating him with great courtesy, partly because one never burns all bridges to the man who knows your secrets, but also because a sense of personal decency was part of the President's character. Dulles was so bucked up by Kennedy's reassurance he allowed himself to hope he might stay on for another couple of years. The decent interval Kennedy had in mind was much shorter. In August, Dulles returned from the White House to tell an assistant, "I've been fired."

Dulles's life ticked on for another eight years, but his career was over, saving one further episode. After Kennedy was assassinated Dulles was appointed to the Warren Commission to investigate the crime. One of his first acts was to submit to his fellow commissioners a book arguing that American assassins were all lone nuts. It is probable he believed this. It also meant the commission had no need to know about the CIA plots to kill Castro, and Dulles made sure it didn't.

Allen Dulles did not lack for critics during his decade in power. The best informed were two old friends from the war years, diplomacy, and the Council on Foreign Relations, Robert H. Lovett and David Bruce, both princes of the establishment who were asked to study the CIA's covert action programs in 1956. Their report is still classified but Grose obtained extensive excerpts from Arthur Schlesinger Jr., who found a copy in Robert Kennedy's papers. Far from congratulating Dulles on his success in confounding America's enemies, the Lovett-Bruce report registers alarm and dismay:

> The CIA, busy, monied and privileged, likes its "kingmaking" responsibility.... There are always, of course, on record the twin, well-born purposes of "frustrating the Soviets" and keeping others "pro-Western" oriented. Under these, almost any [covert] action can be, and is being, justified.... Should not someone, somewhere in an authoritative position in our government...[be] keeping in mind the long range wisdom of activities which have entailed our virtual abandonment of the international "golden rule," and which, if successful to the degree claimed for them, are responsible in a great measure for stirring up the turmoil and raising the doubts about us that exist in many countries of the world today?

The well-financed, aggressive, "kingmaking" secret intelligence organization answerable to the president alone, which alarmed Lovett and Bruce, was Allen Dulles's contribution to the American form of government. Dulles was sometimes called "the great white case officer" for his delight in the tradecraft of spy-running, but intelligence-gathering of the traditional sort was never the favorite son in Dulles's CIA. It is doubtful any other intelligence service has ever plunged more deeply into the political affairs of sovereign neighbors, punished enemies more vigorously, paid friends more lavishly, financed secret armies

on a bigger scale, given national leaders a greater range of secret political and military weapons than the CIA as it was invented during the
Dulles years. Is this why the United States won the cold war?

We might put forward half a dozen plausible answers to this question, none of them a plain yes or no. But the moment for the attempt
has not quite arrived; too much still remains unexplored in Russian
files. What is clear is that the cold war was a war fought by other
means. Principal among them were the arms race itself and the secret
war of intelligence operatives and proxy armies. We may question
whether this war-that-never-was could have been avoided, or might
have been carried out more sensibly, or won more easily or cheaply.
These questions will be long debated by the cold war's many victims.
But there is now not much question that the secret war and the cold
war were the same thing, and that Allen Dulles did for American
intelligence what John Paul Jones did for the American Navy.

—*The New York Review of Books*, December 1, 1994

4

PHANTOM SPIES AT LOS ALAMOS

WHEN WARS END the belligerents begin to speak and write about what happened—indeed, their willingness to tell the truth is one sign that the fighting is really over. Truth-telling about the cold war took a new turn following the formal dissolution of the Soviet Union in 1991, and there has been no pause since in the flood of memoirs, documents, and declassified files published or simply opened to the public in Moscow and other capitals of one-time members of the Warsaw Pact. The Soviet murder of thousands of Polish army officers at the Katyn Forest in 1940, Stalin's agreement to let Kim Il Sung's armies invade South Korea in 1950, the crimes and triumphs of the KGB and other Soviet intelligence organizations, and a long list of other revelations, large and small, eventually will make it possible for scholars to write a true history of the cold war.

But this relentless exposure of the past is not merely useful for tidying up the record of what happened; it also helps to restore peace by feeding the public hunger for truth after decades of accusation, lies, and secrecy. "Conjecture abounds when the truth is hushed up for political reasons,"[1] said the Soviet physicist and bomb-builder Yuli Khariton in

---

1. Yuli Khariton and Yuri Smirnov, "The Khariton Version," *Bulletin of the Atomic Scientists*, May 1993.

a lecture in Moscow in 1993. "If there is no truth today, there will be myths tomorrow." But if truth heals, it also hurts, as the Poles and the Germans have discovered from secret files proving that all sorts of people—some once considered heroes of principled resistance—in fact were reporting to the police, betraying friends and allies.[2]

A painful disclosure of the kind already familiar in Europe was visited on Americans by *Time* magazine on Monday, April 18, 1994, with an eight-page excerpt from a book claiming that leading scientists involved in the Manhattan Project to invent atomic bombs—J. Robert Oppenheimer, Enrico Fermi, Leo Szilard, and the Danish physicist Niels Bohr—had served as spies for the Soviet Union during the Second World War. That evening a twenty-minute report on the *MacNeil/ Lehrer NewsHour* repeated the sensational claims without qualification or reservation and presented filmed interviews with the book's four "authors" along with archival footage of Oppenheimer and other atomic scientists, Stalin and his Politburo, the Red Army goosestepping through Red Square, and similar images of the Red menace of yesteryear. The principal "author" or "source" of these charges—we shall consider below which if either should apply—was also on camera: a shuffling, stoop-shouldered, rambling former officer of Soviet intelligence[3] named Pavel Sudoplatov, whose "special assignments" for

---

2. The case of Alger Hiss provides an example of how one "revelation" can cancel another. The Russian historian General Dmitri Volkogonov later withdrew his blanket claim that "not a single document" had been found implicating Hiss, which was originally made in a letter to a lawyer who had long struggled to vindicate Hiss, John Lowenthal. See Jeffrey A. Frank, "Stalin Biographer Offers Latest Twist in His Case," *The Washington Post*, October 31, 1992. Statements implicating Hiss in a Washington, D.C., spy ring of the 1930s are included in a confession by Noel Field, given to Hungarian intelligence officers in 1954, and described by the writer Sam Tannenhaus in "Hiss Case 'Smoking Gun'?" *The New York Times*, October 15, 1993.

3. Sudoplatov's career ended in August 1953 following his arrest as a protégé of Beria; by then the OGPU he had joined in the 1920s had gone through six name changes. In 1954 the principal Soviet intelligence service was renamed yet again as the Committee for State

Stalin and Lavrenti Beria included the assassination of Leon Trotsky in addition allegedly to managing the flow of intelligence concerning the Soviet scientific program to invent atomic bombs during and immediately after the war.

That Oppenheimer was a Soviet spy was not the most shocking of Sudoplatov's claims. A substantial literature has argued and re-argued similar charges brought in the early 1950s which prompted a formal hearing by the Atomic Energy Commission and the stripping of Oppenheimer's security clearance—not, in the end, as a spy, for which indeed there was no evidence, but as a "security risk" whose judgment could not be trusted. Even disproven charges have a way of sticking, however; when I first heard of the *Time* excerpt it struck me as possible someone really had the goods on Oppenheimer or at least some plausible facts which a reasonable person might say suggested collaboration with a foreign power. But the bald claim that Fermi, Szilard, and Bohr—especially Bohr—were Soviet spies seemed utterly incredible. It would be hard to describe to someone not steeped in the history of the time and the men why these charges are so deeply implausible; it is a bit like saying that Martin Luther King was a paid informant of the FBI or had been taking secret orders from the Grand Wizard of the Ku Klux Klan.

But sometimes incredible news is true; in a time of truth-telling one must keep an open mind. It all depends on the evidence, in this case what purports to be the memoirs of Sudoplatov in a 509-page volume, with a cluttered title page: *Special Tasks: The Memoirs of an Unwanted*

Security or KGB, the longest of its many incarnations, ending only with the dissolution of the Soviet Union in 1991. Sudoplatov never worked for the KGB per se, but I shall use that term here for simplicity's sake. Sudoplatov first emerges in the Western literature on the KGB following the 1954 defection of Nikolai Khokhlov, who was sent to Germany to murder a Ukrainian émigré. See Kokhlov, *In the Name of Conscience* (David McKay, 1959), pp. 30 ff. This was a major embarrassment for Sudoplatov, who was Khokhlov's superior, and it may partly explain why he was arrested.

Witness—A Soviet Spymaster, by Pavel Sudoplatov and his son Anatoli Sudoplatov with Jerrold L. and Leona P. Schecter, the latter two being American journalists.[4] The distinguished historian Robert Conquest has provided an enthusiastic foreword, claiming Sudoplatov's "autobiography... is perhaps the most important single contribution to our knowledge [of the Stalin regime] since Khrushchev's Secret Speech." Included are new accounts of many episodes such as the assassination of Trotsky, the arrest and murder of Raoul Wallenberg, the "Doctors' Plot" cooked up by Stalin after the war to introduce a new purge, this time mainly of Jews, and the fall of Beria after Stalin's death, when Khrushchev moved vigorously to take Stalin's place and to keep secret his own complicity in Stalin's crimes.

These are all important episodes in Soviet history. But by far the most sensational charges in the book are to be found in Chapter Seven on "Atomic Spies." The text is unequivocal:

> The most vital information for developing the first Soviet atomic bomb came from scientists designing the American bomb at Los Alamos, New Mexico—Robert Oppenheimer, Enrico Fermi, and Leo Szilard.... At first they were motivated by fear of Hitler.... Then the Danish physicist Niels Bohr helped strengthen their own inclinations to share nuclear secrets...with the Soviet Union....

These claims, if true, would suggest a degree of Communist subversion of Western science and society beyond anything charged by anti-Communist zealots in the 1950s. If the evidence cited in *Special Tasks* for atomic treason by Oppenheimer, Fermi, Szilard, Bohr, and others is solid and persuasive, then we may generally trust and make use of the book as a whole; but if not, then we must question its other claims as well.

The penetration of the Manhattan Project by Soviet spies is not in

---

4. Little, Brown, 1995.

dispute, and Soviet dependence on American bomb designs has even been conceded by scientists who helped build the first Soviet bomb, which was tested in August 1949. By far the most important Soviet atomic spy identified so far was the German physicist Klaus Fuchs, a member of the Communist Party who escaped after the rise of Hitler in 1933 to Britain, where he took his doctor's degree under another émigré, Max Born, in Edinburgh. After briefly being interned at the beginning of the war he found a job in May 1941 with yet another émigré, Rudolf Peierls, at the University of Birmingham. There Fuchs, a physicist of high ability, helped Peierls with the calculations of critical mass (the amount of fissionable material required for a bomb), which had an important part in persuading first the British, and later the Americans, to undertake a serious bomb program. The two scientists, who became very close, also made a study of probable German efforts in the field.

Following the critical mass study, submitted in June 1941, Peierls was quickly inducted into the British bomb program, and from the careful accounts we have of Fuchs's activities and confessions it seems likely that Fuchs was also privy to the most important fact—the seriousness of British and American intent.[5] But Fuchs remained a Communist as well, and sometime after the German invasion of Russia in June 1941 he made contact with a highly experienced Soviet spy, Ruth Werner, who met with him five or six times before Fuchs and a team of British scientists left for America in late 1943 to join the Manhattan Project. At his last meeting with Werner, Fuchs was given instructions for making contact in New York with "Raymond," actually an American chemist named Harry Gold, who had volunteered his services for some years to the Soviet intelligence apparat.

Fuchs arrived in the United States in December 1943 and spent the

---

5. The best account of the Fuchs case is Robert Chadwell Williams, *Klaus Fuchs, Atom Spy* (Harvard University Press, 1987).

following six months in New York City, working principally on gaseous diffusion of uranium isotopes at Columbia University. Detailed information on this work was passed on in five meetings with Harry Gold, who turned it over to the Soviet intelligence officer Anatoli Yatskov, who died in 1993. In the summer of 1944 the head of the theoretical division at Los Alamos, Hans Bethe, offered Peierls a job there and Peierls in turn asked if he might bring two British scientists as assistants, Tony Skyrme and Klaus Fuchs. By mid-August Fuchs had joined the laboratory run by Oppenheimer in the New Mexico desert, which was then embarked on a crash effort to develop what came to be known as the implosion method to detonate bombs using plutonium.

In early 1945, during a post-Christmas visit to his sister in Cambridge, Massachusetts, Fuchs delivered details of the new detonation system to Harry Gold. Further materials were passed to Gold in Santa Fe in June and September 1945. Sometime after returning to Britain in June 1946 Fuchs joined the British nuclear research station at Harwell and reestablished contact with Soviet intelligence.

In 1949 American code-breakers read a wartime Soviet cable from New York to Moscow which provided an unmistakable clue to Fuchs's espionage. He confessed to a British interrogator in January 1950, at the height of the argument among American policymakers whether to embark on a crash program to develop hydrogen bombs in response to the first Soviet atomic bomb test in August 1949. The announcement of Fuchs's arrest set off much excited commentary that the West was in peril, but within a year or two the chairman of the Atomic Energy Commission, Gordon Dean, adopted a more relaxed view, telling a congressional committee, "I don't think you would be taking too extreme a position if you said he [Fuchs] had advanced them [the Soviets] between a year and two years."[6]

---

6. *Soviet Atomic Espionage*, US Government Printing Office, quoted in Alan Moorehead, *The Traitors* (Harper and Row, 1963), p. 215.

More recently the Soviets have conceded roughly the same estimate. Retired intelligence officers and scientists who worked on the
Soviet bomb have engaged in a public squabble in the last two years
about who ought to get credit for the first bomb. In his Moscow lecture Yuli Khariton confirmed that he and his colleagues had used an
American design, stolen by Soviet spies, since speed was essential and
the Americans had proved theirs worked. But Khariton also insisted
that the team under Igor Kurchatov did much of the scientific work
on their own and came up with a superior bomb design, which soon
replaced the American model. In the heat of argument the contending
parties have released a substantial number of documents, including
secret messages of 1941 and 1942 from the British diplomat John
Cairncross (misidentified in *Special Tasks* as Donald Maclean), who
reported on early bomb discussions by the War Cabinet, and some
extensive papers by Igor Kurchatov, commenting on stolen Western
documents and listing further information he'd like to have. *Special
Tasks* conveniently reproduces a number of these documents, which
are very helpful in evaluating the text.

A number of other wartime Soviet intelligence efforts to obtain
information and documents on the Manhattan Project are known to
have taken place. Among the people used by the Soviets were a scientist named Clarence Hiskey at the Metallurgical Laboratory in Chicago,
where the first reactor designs were produced; a soldier stationed at
Los Alamos, David Greenglass, who passed crude drawings of plutonium bomb design on to his sister and brother-in-law, Ethel and Julius
Rosenberg; and the British scientist Alan Nunn May, attached to a
joint American-British heavy-water project in Canada, who provided
the Soviets with an actual sample of $U-235$. A young colleague of
Enrico Fermi in Rome in the 1930s, the Italian physicist Bruno Pontecorvo, defected to the Soviet Union in 1950 and security officials concluded he had probably been working for Soviet intelligence during
the war as well. Best known, of course, is Oppenheimer himself, who

was the target of an effort organized by a Communist Party activist in San Francisco, Steve Nelson, who dispatched confederates seeking information in the early days of the Manhattan Project. Oppenheimer rebuffed another approach from his friend Haakon Chevalier, but failed to give a full and candid account of it to security officers, eventually arousing a storm of suspicion which never died.

On a train trip from Cheyenne, Wyoming, to Chicago in September 1943 Oppenheimer confessed to General Leslie Groves, military director of the Manhattan Project, that "he had probably belonged to every Communist front organization on the West Coast."[7] Oppenheimer was married to a former Communist, was the brother of a former Communist, had conducted a love affair with a Communist, and had admittedly been approached by Communists, sent by Communists, seeking classified data about the project. But Oppenheimer insisted to Groves that he was not a Communist himself and could be trusted, and Groves believed him. Groves's chief security officer on the West Coast, Colonel Boris Pash, emphatically didn't believe him, and he refused to grant Oppenheimer a security clearance until Groves issued a written order for him to do so. Historians are in general agreement that Oppenheimer was stripped of his security clearance in 1954 primarily for his failure to support the H-bomb program enthusiastically, not because he couldn't be trusted to keep secrets.

But the record of Soviet intelligence efforts to find out about the bomb includes a recent, still unresolved, claim. In 1992 the aged Anatoli Yatskov, who has since died, claimed in a series of interviews with Michael Dobbs of *The Washington Post* that there was another major Soviet spy at Los Alamos, a physicist given the code name of Perseus. Yatskov claimed that Perseus was in contact with Soviet intelligence in 1942, more than a year before Fuchs's arrival; that the courier who

---

7. *In the Matter of J. Robert Oppenheimer* (US Government Printing Office, 1954; MIT Press, 1971), p. 159.

contacted Perseus in New Mexico was Lona Cohen, a figure of importance in other Soviet espionage cases; and that Perseus was still alive.[8] Precisely what secrets Perseus stole and when he stole them Yatskov did not say. This story set off a frenzied search for Perseus by historians and journalists, and resulted in some unpleasant moments as spotlights of suspicion were directed at aging scientists living in quiet retirement. But Yatskov's claim was too vague and provided too few clues, and Perseus remains without a name, if indeed he existed at all. This, briefly described, is the roster of known Soviet intelligence agents or assets to which we must now add the names of Oppenheimer, Fermi, Szilard, and Bohr, if the authors of *Special Tasks* can be believed.

The lives of intelligence officers involved in espionage are built around cases—either the recruitment and running, or the discovery and exposure, of agents engaged in secret work. These cases are always highly particular, and the file of even the most routine case can run to hundreds or thousands of pages. Until they are claimed by death or Alzheimer's disease, intelligence officers can usually recount their cases in painstaking, voluminous detail—just how and when the agent was spotted and recruited, what he obtained, how he was handled and looked after, when and how the case was terminated, every stage of it accompanied at the time by minute analysis and much conjecture. Years are sometimes spent in supervising a single case; every

---

8. Michael Dobbs, "How Soviets Stole US Atom Secrets," *The Washington Post*, October 4, 1992. Yatskov's claim that Lona Cohen was the contact for Perseus in New Mexico may have a bearing on the Rosenberg case; Harry Gold, in his confession to the FBI, claimed that Yatskov asked him to contact David Greenglass in Albuquerque in June 1945 because Greenglass's regular contact was unavailable. No comprehensive general history of the Soviet atomic espionage effort exists, but accounts of the different episodes may be found in Robert Lamphere, *The FBI-KGB War: A Special Agent's Story* (Random House, 1986); Philip Stern, *The Oppenheimer Case: Security on Trial* (Harper and Row, 1969); and David J. Dallin, *Soviet Espionage* (Yale University Press, 1955).

detail involving the assignment of tasks and making contact may be hashed out in committee meetings lasting late into the night. Intelligence officers joining an operation already in progress may spend weeks just reading into the case. They learn their cases backward and forward; success or failure is usually the result of details anticipated or overlooked. When an intelligence officer feels free to recount an old case the narrative can last for hours.

What distinguishes the account of atomic espionage presented in *Special Tasks* is its complete lack of the establishing and supporting details that are the signature of genuine espionage cases. When charges are made almost nothing is offered by way of circumstance, and in the very few cases where details are cited they are irrelevant, misleading, or blatantly wrong. "It is in the record," the book says, "that on several occasions they [Oppenheimer, Fermi, Szilard, and Szilard's secretary] agreed to share information on nuclear weapons with Soviet scientists." This sounds vaguely like espionage, but no prosecutor could frame an indictment without knowing what sort of agreement was reached, with whom, on which occasions, for sharing what information. If *Special Tasks* is to be taken seriously it must provide such particulars; without them the most far-reaching charges evaporate, and we are spared the spectacle of a libel case only by the Anglo-Saxon common law precept that one cannot libel the dead. "Giving secrets to the Russians" is not espionage; knowingly passing a copy of a classified document or classified information to an unauthorized person on or about a certain date is espionage.

Only two charges brought in *Special Tasks* even approach this standard for espionage, one against Oppenheimer in 1941, and a second against Bohr in 1945. The first claims that Oppenheimer told a Soviet diplomat, Gregory Kheifetz, over lunch in California in December 1941 about a letter to President Roosevelt from Albert Einstein urging a research effort to study the feasibility of making atomic bombs. It is possible but far from certain that Oppenheimer knew about this letter, written in the summer of 1940. In any event the letter contained no secrets, and was not itself an official secret. Oppenheimer had no official position with any secret program in December 1941, and the Manhattan Project did not yet exist. Lest this seem a pettifogging defense I ought to add that I do not believe the lunch ever took place, or that the authors of *Special Tasks* can provide a lucid taped or videotaped claim by the elder Sudoplatov dating or describing it.

The rest of the charges against Oppenheimer in Sudoplatov's book tend to evaporate on scrutiny. The principal ones are as follows: (1) that he deliberately recruited Fuchs to work at Los Alamos, but the huge record on the British mission establishes beyond doubt that Oppenheimer had nothing to do with bringing Fuchs either to America or to Los Alamos; (2) that he allowed Fuchs to persuade him to oppose the building of the hydrogen bomb, but the question did not come up until three years later; (3) that he allowed himself to be talked into unspecific acts of treason by his wife, Kitty, who was herself under the influence of Elizabeth Zarubin, wife of the chief Soviet intelligence officer in Washington, Vassili Zarubin; but Kitty was in Berkeley, Los Alamos, or Pittsburgh throughout the war, and there is no evidence Mrs. Zarubin left Washington until she left for good in 1944; (4) that he deliberately made secret documents available (by leaving them out on his desk at night, according to Leona Schecter on the MacNeil/Lehrer show) to a Soviet spy ("mole") he had himself placed in the Los Alamos laboratory, but no evidence including the name of the "mole" is presented to support this.

Fermi and Szilard are also charged with having arranged, in secret concert with Oppenheimer, to give secret documents to young moles they themselves placed in their several laboratories. It is separately charged that Szilard's "secretary" was working for the Soviets. In fact Szilard had no secretary, but called upon the stenographic pool at Chicago's Met Lab. The authors of *Special Tasks* appear to believe that Szilard worked at Los Alamos—he was never there during the war—and was close to Oppenheimer; in fact they met only once, in May 1945, according to William Lanouette, Szilard's biographer, and they did so in the office of General Groves.

These moles all remain unidentified, and nothing is said of when they went to work or what documents they spirited away. Leona Schecter's claim that Oppenheimer and his colleagues left documents out on their desks at night betrays a deep ignorance of the security measures prevailing throughout the Manhattan Project, which included nightly checks to see that doors and safes were locked, trash baskets were empty, and desk tops were clear. Sudoplatov as an intelligence officer would have known that any attempt to leave documents out at night would have instantly attracted the attention of security officers. The basis for Mrs. Schecter's extremely implausible claim is never made clear.

Other errors are just as glaring. *Special Tasks* alleges that Gregory Kheifetz reported in December 1941 that Oppenheimer told him he "and his colleagues were planning to move from Berkeley, California, to a new site to conduct research in nuclear weapons." In fact, the first proposal to send scientists to a remote laboratory site came nearly a year later, and the move itself did not occur until the spring of 1943. Kheifetz simply could not have sent such a report in late 1941. How then did it get into the book?

An even more troubling claim concerns Bruno Pontecorvo, the young Italian physicist who had worked with Fermi in Rome in the 1930s. Only hours after Fermi succeeded in creating the world's first self-sustaining chain reaction in Chicago on December 2, 1942, Pontecorvo is said to have reported the news to his Soviet case officer. The report was "a prearranged telephone message saying, 'The Italian sailor reached the new world.'" This story is suspect, to say the least. In the first place Pontecorvo was not in Chicago at the time of the experiment, but working as an acoustics expert with an oil-drilling rig in Oklahoma. But the account raises deeper questions of veracity as well. According to one of the best-known stories in the history of the Manhattan Project, Arthur Compton, director of the Met Lab where Fermi's experiment was conducted, telephoned James Conant, president of Harvard University, after the reactor became self-sustaining to report the success in a transparent code, which he said he invented on the spur of the moment:

> "Jim," I said, "you'll be interested to know that the Italian navigator has just landed in the new world." Then, half apologetically, because I had led the s-1 Committee to believe that it would be another week or more before the pile could be completed, I added, "the earth was not as large as he had estimated, and he arrived at the new world sooner than he had expected."[9]

In a second MacNeil/Lehrer program devoted to *Special Tasks*, prompted by protests to the first, the Schecters said Pontecorvo must have known about Compton's plan to use the phrase. This only compounds the error, since Compton himself made it clear that he did not know what he would be saying or when he would be saying it. The plain fact of the matter is that an old and familiar story found its way into what purports to be Sudoplatov's memoirs. The authors of *Special Tasks* also claim that either Pontecorvo or Fuchs delivered to Lona Cohen "a thirty-three-page design of the bomb" which had been dropped from the official report written by Henry DeWolf Smythe. But according to William Shurcliff, Smythe's manuscript, handwritten in blue ink, was given to him in the first half of June 1945 for editing by General Groves's personal science advisor, Richard Tollman. About two weeks later fifty copies of the revised report were mimeographed by Shurcliff and circulated for comment. Shurcliff told me that he handled the report at every stage from original manuscript

---

9. Arthur Compton, *Atomic Quest* (Oxford University Press, 1956), p. 144.

through its final version printed shortly before its release a week after Hiroshima. Only a few sentences were added or altered, and nothing was dropped. Whatever crimes may have been committed by Fuchs and Pontecorvo, the delivery of this imaginary thirty-three-page document was not among them.

The most specific of all the charges brought in *Special Tasks*, and the most shocking if true, claims that Niels Bohr gave secret information in the fall of 1945 to Y. P. Terletsky, a young Russian physicist who was also working as an intelligence officer. Terletsky allegedly laid out plans for the first Soviet nuclear reactor and told Bohr they couldn't seem to make it work. In *Special Tasks* Sudoplatov is reported as saying:

> I met with Terletsky in 1993, just before he died. He recalled that at first Bohr was nervous and his hands trembled, but he soon controlled his emotions. Bohr understood, perhaps for the first time, that the decision that he, Fermi, Oppenheimer, and Szilard had made to allow their trusted scientific protégés [i.e., the "moles"] to share atomic secrets had led him to meet agents of the Soviet government.

Nevertheless, according to the book, Bohr explained how Fermi had achieved success, pointed to a spot on the plans laid out by Terletsky, and said, "That's the trouble spot."

We have only Sudoplatov's word (if the book quotes him accurately) for what Terletsky told him. But a twenty-nine-page account in Russian, dictated by Terletsky before his death, flatly contradicts the story in *Special Tasks* on every detail suggesting that Bohr engaged in a secret effort to aid the Soviet bomb program.[10] In particular, Terletsky

---

10. I am indebted to David Holloway of Stanford University for a copy of Terletsky's account, cited in Holloway's history of the Soviet atomic weapons program, *Stalin and the Bomb: The Soviet Union and Atomic Energy, 1939–1956* (Yale University Press, 1994). In

said nothing whatever about laying out blueprints for a Soviet reactor; nor did he claim that Bohr pointed out "the trouble spot" (which is scientifically ridiculous on its face).

Bohr's son, Aage, himself a winner of the Nobel Prize in physics, has recently issued a statement about the Terletsky story in *Special Tasks*, saying he attended the meeting in question. When Terletsky raised "some technical questions concerning atomic energy," the elder Bohr referred him to the recently released official report by Henry DeWolf Smythe on the military uses of atomic energy. Aage Bohr adds that the Danish, British, and American authorities were all informed of the visit, a claim confirmed by a letter of November 7, 1945, to General Groves from the British embassy in Washington. This letter was written *following* the first approach to Bohr by a member of the Danish Communist Party, Mogens Fog, but *before* Terletsky's visit to Bohr.

> Bohr recently received a friendly letter from Professor [Peter] Kapitza in Moscow. This was followed some days later by a visit from a Danish friend of Bohr's who stated that a Russian scientist was visiting Denmark and had a secret letter to Bohr from Kaptiza which he had orders to deliver to Bohr under conditions of absolute secrecy so as to ensure that no other government would have been aware that the meeting had taken place.
>
> Bohr replied that he would gladly receive the letter but that it was quite impossible for him to have any secrets from his British and American friends.[11]

In his tape-recorded account Terletsky mentions the ubiquitous

---

writing this review I also benefited from conversations from many others who write about the history of nuclear weapons, including Priscilla McMillan, Gregg Herken, Stanley Goldberg, William Lanouette, and Richard Rhodes.

11. Manhattan Engineering District files, M 1109, File 11, Item F, National Archives.

security officers who followed him about Copenhagen at the time of the Bohr visit, and confirms that he returned to Moscow with nothing of use beyond a copy of the Smyth report, given to him by Bohr. Indeed, Bohr seems to have gathered most by way of intelligence from their conversation: he asked many questions about his friend Kapitza, and others, equally awkward, about the Soviet physicist Lev Landau, a colleague of Kapitza's who had previously been arrested by Beria.

The claims of espionage by Oppenheimer, Fermi, Szilard, and Bohr are not only contradicted by known facts[12] and unsupported by collateral detail but they are contradicted as well by Igor Kurchatov's letters and reports printed as an appendix to *Special Tasks*. With two modest exceptions, these documents were all published in Russia in 1992. The book says Sudoplatov was in charge of handling documents about atomic energy obtained by Soviet intelligence, and that he briefed Kurchatov on everything that had been learned on or shortly before March 7, 1943. Kurchatov's six-page response, addressed to another Soviet official on March 7, together with a second letter of March 22, makes it clear, however, that Kurchatov had been shown only intelligence documents obtained in Britain (where Fuchs had been active since at least early 1942); that Kurchatov thought Enrico Fermi was still working at Columbia University in New York; that he did not know of Fermi's successful reactor experiment in Chicago three months earlier, or even what sort of reactor it was; that he knew nothing of work at Los Alamos or Oak Ridge; that he was familiar only with American documents which had been openly published; that he was not sure whether the Americans had a bomb program

---

12. In an article in *The Wall Street Journal*, published on May 11, 1994, Edward Teller rejected the charges against Fermi, writing, "I never detected—not even in revealing side remarks—any tendency in Fermi to be anything but critical of communism and the Soviet Union. Fermi was apolitical. But he simply and clearly opposed the Stalinist nightmare even more than he opposed Mussolini."

under way; and that he (like other leading scientists in Britain, the United States, and Germany) had independently figured out how reactors might be used to make a new fissionable material (plutonium).

By mid-summer 1943 Soviet intelligence had apparently obtained a large batch of American documents, but these appear to have been part of a National Academy of Sciences study completed before the United States entered the war. The first document showing Soviet knowledge of the location of laboratories at Oak Ridge, Hanford, and Los Alamos is dated February 28, 1945, and is apparently based entirely on information obtained from Klaus Fuchs. In a letter of April 7, 1945, a few months after Fuchs delivered documents to Harry Gold in Cambridge, Massachusetts, about the design of plutonium bombs, Kurchatov refers to "the implosion method of activating the bomb, which we found out about *only recently....*" [my italics].

In short, genuine documents about the Soviet bomb program demonstrate that the alleged Oppenheimer-Fermi-Szilard conspiracy to pass secret atomic documents to Soviet intelligence could not have delivered anything before the summer of 1943, or anything about current research before early 1945. Even then, Soviet knowledge was very sketchy; Oak Ridge, for example, was not expected to be fully functional until 1948. These genuine documents refer almost entirely to materials obtained from Fuchs, and make no reference to the sort of high-level intelligence that ought to have been available from Oppenheimer, Fermi, and Szilard. The account of atomic espionage printed in *Special Tasks* is an unrelieved mess—contradictory, often incoherent, riddled with error, and unsupported in its major claims that the leading scientists who are named committed espionage. Behind the many small falsities there appears to be a big one: on May 5, 1994, in Moscow the Russian Foreign Intelligence Service, successor to the KGB, punctured the book's principal balloon when it issued a statement saying that, far from being in charge of atomic intelligence during the war, "Pavel Sudoplatov had access to atomic problems during a relatively brief period of time, a mere twelve months, from September 1945 to October 1946...." This, if confirmed, would make hash of the Schecters' claim in their introduction that it would be "impossible for anyone other than Sudoplatov, who supervised their efforts, to put the full story together." But before historians and biographers attempt the laborious task of deciding whether any of these things really happened, they should first address the more basic question of whether Sudoplatov actually said they happened.

As soon as we inquire who wrote *Special Tasks* we begin to sense the problem. The book has more authors than a Hollywood movie with script trouble; four names are listed in the copyright notice, the Sudoplatovs, father and son, and the Schecters, husband and wife. In their introduction the Schecters have claimed the book was built from "transcripts of twenty hours of taped reminiscences" and "a first draft [prepared] for Pavel Anatolievich's confirmation and approval." The elder Sudoplatov reminisced in Russian; we must assume the transcript was in Russian, and presumably the "first draft," purporting to be Sudoplatov's words, was in Russian. But no translator is credited. How did this book get from Russian to English?

The Schecters have declined a request to deliver to this reviewer the Russian "originals" on which *Special Tasks* is presumably based, saying they will eventually be given to the Hoover Institution at Stanford University. But a five-page transcript of a videotape prepared for journalists suggests the nature of the difficulty the Schecters must have faced in putting the book together. We must imagine that these passages, chosen for publicity, are as good as it gets, but the elder Sudoplatov's remarks have a rambling, confused, inexact, slippery quality. None clearly supports or justifies the charges brought in the book. An excerpt will give the feel of the whole:

Answer [from the elder Sudoplatov]: The first reports were from Grigory Markovich Kheifetz. There were Oppenheimer's plans for the atomic bomb, and the development of his work into industrial areas.

Question [the younger Sudoplatov]: When was that?

A: This was approximately 1942 and '43. Again in '43, were the results of Fermi's experiments received from Pontecorvo. Here I would like to underline to you all the time that we are talking not about these comrades; comrades, that's an old way of speaking. These scientists were not our agents. Lord save us. We're not talking about that. An agent is someone under your command. They were not under our command. Not one of these people.

Q: But they passed material to you?

A: We received material all the same. But it wasn't from agents that we received materials. We received materials from people who were fearful of the spread of the atomic plague, people who were worried about the future of the world.... In 1944 we received from Szilard material about his work at Los Alamos. This was very important, and received with great approval and interest by our scientists: Kurchatov, Alikhanov, Kikoin.... Don't forget one thing I want to specify: not every scientist communicating with our workers overseas was one of our agents. We didn't have to recruit anyone into a network of agents....

Q: Do you remember the pseudonyms used in the telegrams that we looked at yesterday?

A: Charles is Fuchs, Star is Szilard. [According to the book "Star" was also used as a code name for Oppenheimer, for Oppenheimer and Fermi jointly, and for "other physicists and scientists in the Manhattan Project...."]

Q: And Mlad, another source, is Pontecorvo?

A: I think so. Yes. These weren't people who could be bought.

Q: But they gave you information in written form?

A: Sometimes they gave us information in written form when we asked for it. They gave it in written form. These were people who liked the Soviet Union very much....

Q: What is known about the relationship between Oppenheimer and Fuchs?

A: Well, what is known is that they worked together first of all, and Oppenheimer valued Fuchs highly as a physicist....

Q: Did Oppenheimer know about Fuchs's sympathies to the Soviet Union?

A: Maybe Oppenheimer knew about his feelings, and this may have made them closer to some degree. But of course we're not talking about his knowing there was a connection to Soviet espionage. Soviet espionage was never mentioned.

How twenty hours of this stuff was transformed into *Special Tasks* is a question with no reassuring answer. It is impossible to distinguish Sudoplatov's real memories, however confused by age and years, from the Schecters' own research and general editorial tidying up. If *Special Tasks* were truly Sudoplatov's autobiography, a found object like a manuscript washed ashore in a bottle, then we ought to expect a phalanx of editorial warnings from the Schecters urging extreme caution. Standard editorial practice, after all, would have been to check the book against the published record, to consult historians and surviving participants, and to lay out the book's numerous textual problems frankly before the reader with an injunction to proceed with care. Instead, the book was hurried secretly into print in the manner now reserved by publishers for sensational revelations. No catalog announcement was made, no advance copies, so far as I know, were read by experts in the field, no bound galleys or early copies were sent to reviewers. A sudden avalanche of finished books came into the bookstores to coincide with a media blitz—in this case, *Time* magazine and the *MacNeil/Lehrer NewsHour*, which both abandoned all accepted journalistic practice by treating what amount to unsupported charges as proven. The result is widespread public acceptance of claims that Oppenheimer, Fermi, Szilard, and Bohr were spies for the Russians, which no amount of debunking in reviews like this one can ever hope to erase.

But the greatest danger of a book like *Special Tasks* is that it can poison the stream and cast into disrepute the entire effort to coax forth the true history of the cold war. Many other books drawing on secret files and the memories of old men have already emerged from Moscow, and others are planned. The Soviets had a gift amounting to genius for intelligence work and espionage; indeed, one principal source of the failure of the regime was its tendency to rely excessively on secret information and hidden manipulation. Questions of loyalty and allegiance were often raised during the cold war, and many have not been settled yet. One must keep an open mind, because sometimes the incredible news is true.

But not this time.

—*The New York Review of Books*, June 9, 1994

5

THE PLOT THICKENS

THE REVOLUTIONARY CERTITUDES of the young Jay Lovestone—born Jacob Liebstein in Lithuania in 1897—have a bizarre, antique ring now, only a decade after his death. Lovestone became a citizen and changed his name in 1919, the year he helped to found the American Communist Party. A tireless political infighter and street debater, he was ferocious with opponents—for example, the writer John Reed, famous for his firsthand account of the Russian Revolution, *Ten Days that Shook the World*, whom Lovestone attacked as "the so-called proletarian who lives on a sumptuous estate in Westchester." Reed was dead within a year, buried in the Kremlin wall and added to the calendar of Communist saints. Lovestone's road would have more twists and turns, but not yet. In a speech in Chicago, the center of the Russian-born, Russian-speaking radicals who dominated the new party, Lovestone celebrated "the inestimable progress made by the Communist Party of Russia." Spouting this sort of stuff seems craven now, but in 1923 Lovestone like many others still sounded full of ingenuous hope and high spirits:

> The Communist spirit has given tongue to the tongueless millions.... The sun never sets on the lands where Communist hearts beat in unison.... The Soviet government stands today as the granite foundation of the Communist system.

Illusions of this magnitude don't die in five minutes. Twenty years later a young machinist for the army, training for duty overseas, bought the Communist romance entire and confided to his wife in a letter that he had "been reading a lot of books on the Soviet Union. Dear, I can see how farsighted and intelligent those leaders are. They are really geniuses, every one of them.... I believe that every time the Soviet government used force they did so with pain in their hearts...."

But instead of being shipped to the European theater, as he expected, the young machinist was transferred in the fall of 1944 to the high desert of New Mexico, where he was enjoined to secrecy and put to work making parts for models of a new kind of bomb. The geniuses in Moscow knew about this project, referred to it in secret communications as "ENORMOZ," and authorized Alexander Feklisov, a Soviet intelligence officer attached to the consulate in New York City, to attempt to recruit the machinist as a spy. The pitch was made by the machinist's brother-in-law, already a spy for the Soviets, who, using the third person, wrote for Feklisov a report in December 1944 describing how a first discussion had gone:

> ...Julius [the brother-in-law] inquired of Ruth [the machinist's young wife] how she felt about the Soviet Union and how deep in general her Communist convictions went, whereupon she replied without hesitation that, to her, socialism was the sole hope of the world and the Soviet Union commanded her deepest admiration.... Julius then explained his connections with certain people interested in supplying the Soviet Union with urgently needed technical information it could not obtain through the regular channels and impressed upon her the tremendous importance of the project in which David [the young machinist, husband of Ruth] is now at work.... Ethel [Julius's wife and David's sister] here interposed to stress the need for the utmost care and caution in informing David of the work in

which Julius was engaged and that, for his own safety, all other political discussion and activity on his part should be subdued.

Feklisov passed on this report to Moscow, where a predecessor of the KGB filed it away (page 16 of Volume One of File 86191). Some fifty years later Alexander Vassiliev, a former officer in the KGB, retrieved the document, along with a great deal of other material quoted in *The Haunted Wood: Soviet Espionage in America—The Stalin Era,*[1] one of a number of recent books about Soviet espionage in the United States in the 1930s and 1940s, some (like *The Haunted Wood*) written with the cooperation of Soviet intelligence authorities, and some not. Vassiliev's co-author (it is not clear how the writing was shared out) is Allen Weinstein, best known for his previous book *Perjury: The Hiss-Chambers Case*, first published in 1978 and revised in 1997. The title comes from a poem of W. H. Auden, "September 1, 1939," in which the "haunted wood" is the arena of conflicting loyalties where left and right, Communist and fascist, East and West prepared the ground for the Second World War. Weinstein picked his title and began planning his book twenty years ago, then set the project aside.

Waiting was a good idea; the collapse of Soviet communism and the end of the cold war cracked open the door into the Soviet intelligence archives and made available documents which have illuminated and sometimes even definitively settled many old controversies about the guilt or innocence of people accused during the 1950s of having spied for the Soviet Union—the Rosenbergs, Julius and Ethel; their colleagues Al Sarant and Joel Barr, who disappeared when the Rosenbergs were arrested and surfaced decades later in the Soviet Union, where they were respected scientists living under new names; the State Department official Alger Hiss and his wife, Priscilla; the Treasury

---

1. Random House, 1999.

Department official Harry Dexter White, who died of a heart attack
shortly after being accused; numerous officers of America's wartime
intelligence agency, the Office of Strategic Services (OSS), including
Duncan Lee, a close friend and associate of the OSS chief, William
Donovan; Hiss's fellow State Department official Lawrence Duggan,
who committed suicide (maybe) shortly after being questioned by the
FBI; Lauchlin Currie, an aide to President Franklin Delano Roosevelt
who moved to South America in 1950 and later renounced his US
citizenship; and many, many others.

Most denied, some stoutly, some with a shrug, that they had ever
spied for the Soviet Union, but a few confessed, like Ethel Rosenberg's
brother, David Greenglass, who successfully bargained for immunity
for his wife, Ruth; Elizabeth Bentley, who went to the FBI in 1945 and
described in detail her work as a courier for Soviet intelligence officers
running nets in New York and Washington; and, most notoriously of
all, Whittaker Chambers, who pointed the finger at Alger Hiss.

Many of the documents quoted in *The Haunted Wood* are supported or confirmed by Soviet cables sent to Moscow by Soviet intelligence officers at the time. Beginning in 1946 code-breaking predecessors
of the National Security Agency (NSA) managed to decrypt wartime
cables sent mainly from the New York consulate to General Pavel
Fitin, the chief of the Foreign Intelligence Directorate in Moscow.
Eventually over two thousand of these cables were read, sometimes in
whole but more often in part, revealing an espionage assault on the
United States of stunning scope and alarming success. Over the years
the code-breaking effort was given many code names by the Americans—JADE, BRIDE, DRUG, and (in 1961) VENONA, the name that
stuck. The word has no meaning. When the VENONA project was
finally ended in 1980 many thousands of cables collected during the
1930s and 1940s were still unread, and slightly more than half of the
349 persons given cryptonyms by the KGB remained unknown. But
even those identified included agents seeded throughout the federal

government in Washington, in large corporations and universities, on newspapers and magazines, and in the principal laboratories which built the first atomic bombs.

The immense intellectual task of reading the Soviet traffic, consisting of five-letter groups encrypted with a technique called "the one-time pad," is described in VENONA: *Decoding Soviet Espionage in America*, a history of the project recently published by two leading scholars of American communism, John Earl Haynes and Harvey Klehr.[2] The Soviet cables for the most part concerned basic housekeeping questions involved in the running of spies, and they alerted Moscow authorities what to expect in the full reports sent by the slower but more secure means of the regular diplomatic pouch. Nevertheless, the cables often provided enough corroborating evidence—travel plans, the pregnancies of wives, professional associations, and the like—to identify the cryptonyms of agents, once messages could be read.

It was slow going at first but by the summer of 1947 enough material had been decrypted to interest counterintelligence officers of the FBI, and a year later a Soviet spy handling FBI documents in the Justice Department, Judith Coplon, was identified and arrested on the basis of VENONA decrypts. She was convicted twice in federal court but both convictions were overturned on appeal. Like other cases based on leads obtained from VENONA materials, Coplon's prosecution made no mention of Soviet cables, in court or out, in the hope of keeping the breakthrough secret from the Russians. It is now known that this hope was vain; in the spring of 1950 investigators identified an officer in the Armed Forces Security Agency (AFSA), William Weisband, as a spy for Moscow—possibly the individual referred to in VENONA traffic as "Link." He was never prosecuted but the assumption at the time that he had warned the Soviets about VENONA is confirmed in

2. Yale University Press, 1999.

The Haunted Wood by Soviet documents, including one from 1948 which credits Weisband with delivering "a large amount of very valuable documentary material concerning the work of Americans on deciphering Soviet ciphers...."

Within a few years VENONA material had put the counterintelligence sleuths of the FBI and the British Secret Intelligence Service (SIS) on the trail of many Soviet spies, including the British diplomat Donald Maclean ("Homer" in the VENONA traffic), whose defection to the Soviet Union deeply implicated his friend Kim Philby (possibly "Stanley"); the German physicist Klaus Fuchs, who had been part of the British team working on the atomic bomb at Los Alamos; Harry Gold ("Goose," "Arnold"), a courier identified by Fuchs; David Greenglass ("Caliber," "Bumblebee"), whose confession eventually sent his sister and brother-in-law, Ethel and Julius ("Antenna," "Liberal") Rosenberg, to the electric chair; Theodore Alvin Hall ("Mlad"), another Los Alamos physicist, who was never prosecuted and remained unknown to the general public until declassification of the VENONA project in 1996; Frank Coe ("Peak") and Solomon Adler ("Sachs"), Treasury officials both of whom moved to China and died there; and —in a typical chain of identifications—Amadeo Sabatini ("Nick"), who implicated Jones Orin York ("Needle"), who told the FBI in April 1950 enough about his meetings with an agent for the Soviets he knew as "Bill" to allow identification of William Weisband, thus closing the circle. It was then that Weisband was fired by the Armed Forces Security Agency, and the Soviet ability to monitor the VENONA project came to an end.

Like cable traffic in general the VENONA messages were short and to the point to minimize the chore of encrypting and decrypting communications. They do not offer the sort of long, explicit, circumstantial accounts of spying activity required for an open-and-shut case. Of all those accused of spying for the Soviets, Alger Hiss put up the stoutest defense, convincing many in the 1950s that he had been slandered by Whittaker Chambers and thereafter maintaining a position of sorrowing innocence until the day he died. The case has long ceased to have any importance to counterintelligence investigators, but the political battle over the original charges, concluding with a perjury conviction and jail term for Hiss, had a major part in the anti-Communist fervor referred to generically as "McCarthyism," after the Wisconsin Senator Joseph McCarthy, who raised the issue to fever pitch with a charge in 1950 that hundreds of Communists were harbored within the government.

As a spy-hunter McCarthy was a complete failure. His elastic numbers, never the same two days running, were much derided at the time; he never found even a single genuine Communist in the government; none of those he named recklessly during his hour on the stage was ever proved to have been a spy; and none of them appear in the VENONA traffic or the documents published by Weinstein and others. A rough-and-tumble demagogue of a certain raffish charm, McCarthy never really understood the chapter and verse of Communist spying, much less the subtler play of left–right ideological struggles, which tempted many liberals of the time to deny overheated right-wing charges of subversion with counterclaims that the "Red Menace" was all being trumped up by the FBI.

In the heat of the moment, when Chambers's charges had first become public, leading officials like Dean Acheson and President Truman had both defended Hiss, a position they would soon know enough to regret. But those regrets they kept mainly to themselves, and Hiss posed for years as the archetype of persons unjustly charged in what was criticized as a Republican witch-hunt. Still, despite McCarthy's failure to back up his charges he managed to flourish for a time in a climate of suspicion that Hiss wasn't the only Soviet spy with a claque of defenders and that the government was hiding something. At the same time, counterintelligence professionals knew McCarthy was thrashing around in the dark, but many of them also knew directly or through the grapevine that the FBI was in fact trying to identify hundreds of cryptonyms.

The cryptonyms of some Soviet spies appear dozens of times in the VENONA traffic, but not so with Hiss. The primary reason is that Hiss was part of a network run by the Chief Intelligence Directorate of the Soviet military (GRU), while the VENONA traffic consists almost entirely of KGB cables. But investigators concluded that the "Ales" mentioned in a decrypted cable of March 30, 1945, was in fact Hiss. Described as "the leader of a small group of the NEIGHBORS' probationers"—i.e., the GRU's agents—Hiss was said by the KGB author of the cable to have been spying "continuously since 1935." Following the Big Three conference at Yalta a month earlier, the March 30 cable reported to KGB headquarters, "Ales" (Hiss) stopped off in Moscow where he "and his whole group were awarded Soviet decorations" by Andrei Vyshinsky, Stalin's chief prosecutor at the show trials of the 1930s.

Investigators believed that "Ales" was Hiss because he had stopped off in Moscow on his way home from an official trip to Yalta; other evidence showed that Hiss began spying for the Soviets in 1934, and he was believed to have been working for "the NEIGHBORS"—i.e., the GRU. In any event, the March 30 cable is not proof that Hiss was a spy, just useful supporting evidence. Whether Hiss is mentioned in other VENONA cables still unread is of course unknown, and no GRU intelligence files about Hiss or any other spy have been released. But much additional evidence about Hiss's involvement with the Soviets has turned up since the voluminous and explicit claims by Whittaker Chambers and Elizabeth Bentley in the 1940s, claims which no serious scholar of the subject any longer dismisses.

In the mid-1930s, when the Soviet spy networks were being organized in Washington and New York, the GRU and the KGB occasionally crossed wires and approached the same people as potential spies. One such imbroglio occurred in April 1936, when Alger Hiss attempted to recruit a State Department officer named Noel Field on the eve of his departure for an important conference in London. In a report to Moscow, the KGB agent Hedda Gumperz Massing, who was herself busy recruiting both Noel Field and Lawrence Duggan, another State Department official, gave a long and detailed account of the Hiss–Field conversation in which she referred to Hiss by name since of course she did not know his GRU code name. Hiss was soon in hot pursuit of Duggan as well. Allowing the agents of one service or net to learn the identities of those in another breaks one of the cardinal rules of espionage tradecraft, and the frequency with which it happened among Soviet spies in the US helps to explain the rapid collapse of the whole effort once Bentley and Chambers began telling the FBI who and what to look for.

But in 1936 the Soviets were still trying to maintain compartmentalization, and Hedda Massing's boss, the illegal *rezident*, or station chief, Boris Bazarov, warned Moscow that a catastrophe was brewing. In a document quoted in *The Haunted Wood*, with true names inserted in brackets in place of code names, Bazarov described something akin to a French farce:

> The result has been that, in fact, [Field] and Hiss have been openly identified to [Lawrence Duggan]. Apparently [Duggan] also understands clearly [Gumperz's] nature. And [Gumperz] and Hiss several months ago identified themselves to each other. Helen Boyd, [Duggan's] wife, who was present at almost all of these meetings and conversations, is also undoubtedly briefed and now knows as much as [Duggan] himself.... I think that after this story we should not speed up the cultivation of [Duggan] and his wife. Apparently, besides us, the persistent Hiss will continue his initiative in this direction.

The persistent Hiss soon acquired a KGB code name of his own ("Lawyer") and appears in other KGB reports from the US, including one from yet a third Soviet spy-runner, Itzhak Akhmerov, who reported in May 1936 that

> a brother organization's worker connected with [Hiss] knew [Gumperz] well.... This brother worker, whom we know as "Peter" [in fact, Joszef Peter, a Hungarian working for the GRU as handler of the Hal Ware group in Washington, which included Hiss]...at one of his rare meetings with [Gumperz] told the latter: "You in Washington came across my guy [Hiss].... You better not lay your hands on him...."

Soviet spy networks can be nightmarishly difficult to map out. Information is always partial, case officers come and go, there are many names and code names (often more than one of the latter for each spy), their paths cross in unexpected ways, some play vital roles for years, others appear and disappear like a mouse peeking from a hole in the wall until it sees a cat. Soviet nets of the 1930s are especially difficult because the names that made the biggest news at the time (Hiss, Chambers, Rosenberg) may have been only relatively minor players, while others, barely glimpsed in the documents and confessions which chance brought to the FBI, may have been central. Above all, the Soviets were astonishingly active, aggressive, and successful; the 349 cryptonyms extracted from the VENONA traffic—most standing for agents or "trusted contacts" but some referring only to targets of interest—may be matched by as many more in the unread traffic, and the GRU cables of the same period, still almost entirely unread, might contain as many more again.

The long-version field reports sent by diplomatic pouch, not to mention the actual raw files themselves, in their row upon row of metal shelves, filling floor upon floor of the vast Russian secret service headquarters in huge high-rise buildings of numbing monotony in the Moscow suburb of Yasenevo, must describe a still-vaster web of contact, probe, retreat, and connection as intricate as the arteries, veins, and capillaries that carry blood throughout the human body. But once one has said that, which is roughly equivalent to having said that the task of writing a comprehensive history of Soviet espionage is beyond fallible man, it is nevertheless true that anyone who wants to know what Hiss and his friends were up to can find a rich, convincing, and vivid report in *The Haunted Wood* and VENONA. If many questions remain only partially answered there is yet enough to allow us to conclude clearly and simply that while the excesses of McCarthyism may be fairly described as a witch-hunt, it was a witch-hunt with witches, some in government, some not.

The espionage prosecutions of the early 1950s led to the execution of Julius and Ethel Rosenberg, sent a handful of other spies to jail for varying periods, and prompted another handful to disappear into the Communist world to escape arrest. But most of the Soviet spies active in the United States in the 1930s and 1940s, even if they were identified, suffered nothing worse than surveillance, questioning by the FBI, or the loss of a job. Many other people, entirely guiltless, were subjected to a great deal more.

Because the KGB had actively recruited agents from the ranks of the American Communist Party, a pall of suspicion fell over the radical left generally and many hundreds of people who had never told the KGB so much as the time of day found themselves hounded by self-appointed watchdogs, blackballed from work in Hollywood or academia, hectored by congressional committees, and pressed under threat of contempt charges to reveal the names of friends, fellow travelers, and chance acquaintances who had been members of the Communist Party, or only transient supporters of "left-wing causes" like an end to the lynching of blacks in the American South or the defeat of fascist armies during the Spanish Civil War.

This broader assault upon the American left—what most historians and people who lived through it mean by the term "McCarthyism"—

really was a witch-hunt, and it had little effect on the success of Soviet spying in America. That had already been brought to an end by the Soviets themselves following the discovery that American code-breakers were reading the VENONA traffic and the confessions of de-fectors like Elizabeth Bentley, Whittaker Chambers, and the Soviet GRU spy Igor Gouzenko in Canada. The rule of thumb in spying is better safe than sorry; when an operation is compromised the spy-runners cut their losses and write off everything connected to it. By the middle of the 1950s the Soviet Union was essentially without clandestine assets in the United States; friends everywhere had been replaced by friends nowhere.

In the remaining decades of the cold war, nevertheless, the Soviets recruited a great many new spies, some of them brilliantly successful like Aldrich Ames, but they never again achieved the breadth and depth of penetration of American society and government of the 1930s, so far as we know. But even with this proviso, always important, what we know now includes the extraordinary wealth of operational detail contained in six cases of notes and files brought out of Russia in 1992 by the British Secret Intelligence Service with a retired KGB archivist named Vasili Mitrokhin. Born in 1922, Mitrokhin joined the KGB in 1948 and after foreign assignments with the First Chief Directorate was transferred in 1956 to the archive where he spent the rest of a quiet life handling files and moving down an entirely solitary road toward a kind of principled inner resistance and exile.

In 1972 Mitrokhin was given the job of packing up First Chief Directorate files in the KGB's Moscow headquarters, a massive turn-of-the-century building called the Lubyanka, and shipping them to the KGB's new quarters in Yasenevo. Over a ten-year period he personally checked some 300,000 files, each devoted to a separate case and some running to many volumes. But missing, Mitrokhin discovered, were nine volumes on the fate of Communist Party leaders, KGB officers, and foreign Communists living in Russia during the Stalin years. These volumes had been destroyed in the early 1960s on the orders of Nikita Khrushchev.

Distressed by what he had learned of the nature of the Soviet regime, and perhaps fearing further efforts to rewrite history by purging the files, Mitrokhin began to take notes on the documents which passed through his hands—strictly forbidden, of course, and highly dangerous. These he took home and hid under the mattress in his Moscow apartment; then he transferred them to a dacha in the countryside, and finally, in 1992, he carried them with him by train to one of the Baltic countries where he, his family, and his six cases of materials were picked up by the British SIS.

"Case" is an elastic word. It can refer to anything from an ordinary case of wine to a crate as big as an old-fashioned steamer trunk. But on the evidence of *The Sword and the Shield: The Mitrokhin Archive and the Secret History of the KGB*, written by the well-known historian of British intelligence Christopher Andrew with the help of Mitrokhin's materials, the Russian was lugging some very big boxes.[3] This is not Andrew's first exploration of Soviet intelligence history: in 1990, with the assistance of an earlier Soviet defector to the British, Oleg Gordievsky, Andrew published a 775-page tome which seeded a comprehensive account of the KGB and its predecessors with nuggets of new material provided by Gordievsky.[4] The new book does the same thing again but with substantially more nuggets, returning to the early days of the Cheka in the 1920s and marching forward, case by case and country by country, to Mitrokhin's retirement from the KGB in 1984.

One strength of *The Sword and the Shield* lies in the fact that the narrative is based almost entirely on new material from the Soviet

3. Basic Books, 1999.

4. Christopher Andrew and Oleg Gordievsky, KGB: The Inside Story (HarperCollins, 1990).

archives, enriching stories long familiar to cold war scholars. With few exceptions, what Mitrokhin brought was the bare skeletons of cases and operations—names, dates, places, and code names— invaluable raw material for counterintelligence analysts, but impenetrable by ordinary mortals. Andrew incorporates the new Mitrokhin material into a brisk, useful, and comprehensive history of Soviet intelligence activity which, as a book, has only one serious flaw: it is printed in minuscule type more usually found in the listing of ingredients on bottles of patent medicines, which is made even more laborious to read by the narrow gutter and margins of the page. The 135 pages of notes and bibliography in the back of the book are in type smaller still and will require the assistance of a magnifying device by all but the very young. Presumably this economy saved the publisher a few bucks, but it was a signal disservice to an important book which will be consulted by scholars for many years to come.

By the universal but coarse measure of the significance of a book on espionage—the number of spies exposed—*The Sword and the Shield* set something of a record. Chief among those exposed was Melitta Norwood, code-named "Hola" by the KGB when she was recruited in Britain in 1937. Now eighty-seven years old and living quietly in the London suburb of Bexleyheath, the unrepentant Norwood worked for the British Non-Ferrous Metals Research Association in London in the 1940s, where she had access to important technical information on the construction of atomic bombs. Reference to Norwood is also made by Weinstein and Vassiliev in *The Haunted Wood* under the code name "Tina," which appears as well in a VENONA cable of September 1945. Neither "Tina" nor another British spy reporting on atomic matters, "Eric," is identified by Weinstein and Vassiliev. Beginning in 1942 "Eric" was handled by the Soviet intelligence officer Vladimir Barkovsky, and much of the ten thousand pages of material "Eric" provided actually consisted of photostatic copies of American atomic research reports which the

British had obtained just as Barkovsky and the Soviets did—by stealing them from an ally (the United States).

At a dinner in Moscow in 1997 Barkovsky, at eighty-four frail, diminutive, and short of breath, told a table of eight (which included me and my friend Joe Finder) that he was a mechanical engineer by training and was completely at sea during his first meeting with "Eric," who plunged directly into a discussion of atomic cross-sections. Barkovsky tried to beg off, promising another meeting with an intelligence officer who knew physics. But "Eric" refused, insisted Barkovsky was the man for him, and told him to obtain a copy of *Applied Nuclear Physics* by Pollard and Davidson and study it. ("I still have it," said Barkovsky.) Gently pressed for additional details about "Eric," whom he did not name, Barkovsky demurred. "I am forbidden by Article Nineteen," he explained, referring to the Official Secrets Act. So far as I know, "Eric" remains unidentified.

The identification of Melitta Norwood made the biggest noise in the press when Andrew's book was published in 1999, but she was not alone. Other spies brought to light, partially or fully, were "Hunt," a spy recruited by Norwood but still unidentified by British authorities; "William," a trade union official who worked for the Russians in the 1970s; the British policeman John Symonds, who served as a roving agent for the KGB; and the American Robert Lipka, a clerk for the National Security Agency now serving an eighteen-year prison term for spying for the Soviets in the 1960s. Numerous others, revealed in Mitrokhin's notes and known to authorities, are identified by Andrew only with code names—long lists of code names. Sometimes Andrew notes that they cannot be identified "for legal reasons," like "Grum," a "leading Irish Communist" approached by the KGB in 1977, and the French journalists called "Nant," "Veronique," "Jacqueline," and "Nancy" by their Soviet case officers. "A majority of both agents and trusted contacts" on another list of thirty Soviet agents active in the United States in the 1970s, Andrew says in a footnote, "are identified by name." Are the authorities preparing to pounce? Andrew does not say, leaving the guilty parties to fret and worry, if they are still alive.

The real importance of Andrew's book is not to be found in the three-day wonder of uncovered spies, however, but in the sheer weight of accumulated detail which reveals a madly compulsive Soviet over-reliance on clandestine means for conducting its foreign policy, maintaining social and ideological control at home, and acquiring the technological infrastructure of a modern state. For decades it all seemed to work, until Mikhail Gorbachev began to tinker with the system, hoping to breathe the pink back into the wheezing body of communism. He might have addressed his efforts to the waxen cadaver of Lenin with greater success. The anti-Soviet hostility of client states in Eastern Europe, the alienation of ordinary Russians from the Communist regime, a position in the world based entirely on military might, and the reality of a barely functioning economy helpless to compete in world trade were the reverse of the coin—an illusion of monolithic control and legitimacy on one side, police and mirrors on the other.

The Sword and the Shield relates the dark history of the Soviet obsession with inner resistance and foreign enemies. Few nations have ever been subjected to such ferocious and generally effective methods of domestic control, and none has gone further to suppress what was true. But of some charges, Andrew says, the Soviets must be presumed innocent. "There is no evidence in any of the files examined by Mitrokhin," he writes, that Yuri Andropov, the KGB chairman who stopped at almost nothing to destroy Solzhenitsyn and Sakharov, played any role in the attempt to assassinate Pope John Paul II in Rome in May 1981. Nor, Andrew says, do Mitrokhin's six cases of notes suggest that major Soviet spies in the United States and Britain remain undiscovered.

We may, therefore, reasonably conclude that now, a decade after the collapse of the Soviet Union, we have before us roughly the whole story. Detail remains to be filled in but, Andrew suggests, what has long appeared to be the case really is the case—the romantic allure of the great social experiment in Communist Russia ran aground soon after the end of the Second World War, and the role of the Soviet Union in the world for the remaining decades of the cold war depended on a vast military and intelligence effort aimed abroad, at the price of stagnation and impoverishment at home.

The evidence for the scale of that effort is amply documented in *The Sword and the Shield*, but the explanations for its initial success and ultimate failure are more easily seen in the other books here under review. When Alexander Feklisov returned to Moscow after the war, he attributed his success with the atomic spies Ruth and David Greenglass to the fact that "they are young, intelligent, capable, and politically developed people, strongly believing in the cause of communism and wishing to do their best to help our country as much as possible." Also "politically developed" was Theodore Alvin Hall, a young physicist who volunteered to spy for the Soviets in November 1944 (exposed in the VENONA traffic but never prosecuted); Morris Cohen, recruited by the KGB in Spain in 1938 and described by one of his case officers as "exceptionally honest, developed, politically literate"; and members of the spy nets in Washington who "are reliable compatriots, highly developed politically."

But "politically developed" did not mean innocent. The brilliant "illegal" (that is, an agent without official diplomatic cover) Arnold Deutsch, who helped to recruit and run the notorious British spies known as the "Cambridge Five," expressed a kind of contempt for the rich young American Michael Straight, who was recruited by Anthony Blunt in the late 1930s. Straight, Deutsch reported, "sometimes behaves like a child in his romanticism. He thinks he is working for the Comintern [the semipublic worldwide organization of Communist Parties dominated by the Soviet Union], and he must be left in this delusion for awhile." What "politically developed" really meant was the capacity to believe that Moscow was always right. The State Department official Lawrence Duggan, a romantic in the manner of Straight, proved in 1937 that politically he was still developing when he told his case officer, Norman Borodin, that he

> cannot understand events in the USSR...the disclosure of Trotskyite-fascist spies in almost all branches of industry and in the state institutions embarrass him enormously. People he has learned to respect turn out to be traitors to their motherland and to the socialist cause...all this seems to him a "remote, incomprehensible nightmare."

Duggan wanted to know what would happen to him if the secrets he was turning over to the KGB crossed the desk of one of these spies for the British and the Germans. A spy in the KGB "seems...impossible, but two months ago the same could have been said about the nine [arrested Soviet] generals.... He repeats again and again: he cannot understand it, he is embarrassed, he cannot sleep."

What was really happening to Duggan, of course, was political development in the wrong direction. He was "embarrassed" because the Moscow charges of Trotskyite conspiracy were in fact preposterous. As the Great Terror deepened, Duggan became elusive and difficult; in time he quit spying but never entirely broke with the Soviets and apparently never admitted to himself the true nature of the regime he had served. The FBI and the Soviets were both pressing hard in late 1948, and it is impossible to be certain whether he jumped from his sixteenth-floor office window or was thrown out. Either way, it was a lack of political development that killed Duggan.

The first generation of ideologically committed Soviet spies for the most part never wavered in their loyalty to Moscow during Duggan's "nightmare"—the Moscow Trials which publicly accused, convicted, and condemned old Bolsheviks by the score, heroes of the revolution all. But the leading figures accused of conspiracy with Leon Trotsky to murder Stalin, overthrow the regime, and betray Russia to capitalists in Britain and Germany were only the first selective harvest of victims in what became one of the great political cataclysms of history. Leading members of the Communist Party were the first to go (and the first to be rehabilitated by Khrushchev in 1956), but they were followed by countless thousands of officials at all levels of Soviet society, and then by millions of ordinary people, all charged with entirely imaginary crimes. How many of the victims were executed (typically with a bullet behind the ear in a prison basement) and how many died of overwork, disease, and hunger in the labor camps can never be known, but the total number of dead was many millions.

Barkovsky told us in Moscow that one reason a relative youth like himself got such a plum job running spies in London, away from the wartime deprivations of Moscow, was the fact that the ranks of older, more experienced intelligence officers had been stripped to the bone by arrest and execution. Among them were at least ten KGB officers who had served in the United States in the 1930s and were recalled for arrest, a summons most obeyed despite knowing what awaited them at home. Others, like the New York station chief Gaik Ovakimyan and Jacob Golos, the case officer who managed Elizabeth Bentley, saved themselves by the simple expedient of putting off return through one excuse after another until the worst of the purge was over.

But more typical was the fate of Theodore Stephanovich Mally, a Hungarian captured by the tsarist armies during World War I and freed by the Bolsheviks, who recruited him to the Communist cause and a career in the running of spies. Mally remains a shadowy figure even to scholars of Soviet espionage. He performed his most important job during the two years (1935–1937) he spent handling the Cambridge Five in London. William E. Duff, a retired foreign counterintelligence specialist for the FBI, took an interest in Mally's career and fate and set himself the task of documenting his life, a huge effort that took Duff from Mally's birthplace in Hungary, to Paris and London where he served, and finally back to Moscow where he disappeared from view in November 1937. Much of Mally's life is still unknown, but the character of the man emerges clearly in Duff's wonderful book *A Time for Spies: Theodore Stephanovich Mally and the Era of the Great Illegals*, which recounts the life of an ordained priest who traded the Church of his youth for the New Jerusalem promised by the revolution.[5]

In Paris in 1937, summoned back to Moscow for reasons he understood perfectly, Mally tried to explain his decision to submit to Elizabeth Poretsky, whose husband had worked for Soviet intelligence in Spain. It wasn't complicated really, he said. He felt guilty. During the Russian Civil War he had taken part in wholesale massacres of civilians; the memory of the crying of the women and the children continued to haunt him. Later he participated in the arrest of peasants for trifling offenses during the great famine of the early 1930s. The sentence for stealing a small bag of potatoes: execution. "I could not bear to live in the Soviet Union any more," Mally told Poretsky. "I had to run away somewhere...." His refuge was London, where he ran spies, Kim Philby among them, to serve the country he had fled. Like many others, Mally had given his life to serve the cause; now his services were no longer enough, and the Party wanted his life. "Don't you see that I must go back to be shot? Shall I hide now also?"

Poretsky did not see that at all. She was trying to save the life of her husband, Ignace Reiss, also threatened with arrest and execution. In this she failed; the Soviets hunted him down in Switzerland and left his body by the roadside. But Mally, as Duff relates, went back to Moscow. The cooperation of former KGB officers helped Duff to establish the outline of Mally's final year. After many months of interrogation during which he was "beaten"—that was all Duff could

---

5. Vanderbilt University Press, 1999.

learn: he was "beaten"—Mally was convicted of spying for Germany at a trial he did not attend, and where he had no lawyer to represent him. The sentence on September 20, 1938, was death; and the execution, as was Soviet custom with other tortured yet loyal agents, was carried out on the same day in a basement execution cell of the Lubyanka.

Much additional information on Mally's career can be found in *The Crown Jewels: The British Secrets at the Heart of the KGB Archives,* a history of Soviet operations in Britain in the 1930s and 1940s by the prolific writer on intelligence history Nigel West, with the assistance of Oleg Tsarev, a former KGB officer who is well known to all writers with an interest in Soviet intelligence services.[6] The KGB's foreign department assigned many intelligence officers to serve in both Britain and the United States, and the rich account provided by West and Tsarev of the recruiting of the Cambridge Five also touches on the career of Michael Straight, along with those of other Americans later active in Washington and New York. It also includes new information on the cases of Ignace Reiss and Walter Krivitsky, whose defections began the unraveling of Soviet intelligence networks and ultimately led to the American spy scandals of the 1950s. But while West and Tsarev help to explain how the KGB fabricated a charge of spying for the Germans against Mally, they fail to convey the fatalism and guilt which made him return to Moscow for a bullet in the back of his head.

Mally went back, Lawrence Duggan committed suicide or was murdered, the Rosenbergs went to the electric chair rather than confess, Alger Hiss spent the last fifty years of his life denying that any of it had happened at all. Jay Lovestone, on the other hand, was smart enough to get the picture. His faith that communism spoke for the tongueless millions came under strain as soon as he ran into Stalin. In 1929, in Moscow with a ten-man delegation seeking an end to Stalin's

6. Yale University Press, 1999.

meddling in the direction of the American Party, Lovestone very nearly became an early victim of the Lubyanka. "For scabs," Stalin said when Lovestone refused to accept a Comintern decision, "there is plenty of room in our cemeteries." But Lovestone managed to slip out of the country.

Back home he and ninety followers, henceforth excoriated as "Lovestoneites," were expelled from the Party. For a dozen years he tried to build an alternative to the CP-USA but he had no money, his Independent Labor League never had more than five hundred members, and his faith in the cause withered away. When Whittaker Chambers told Lovestone in 1938 that he had been invited to Moscow to receive a decoration, Lovestone told him: "You've been decorated twice before. This is one decoration you don't need." Lovestone broke first with Stalinism, then with communism after Stalin's judicial murder of Bukharin and betrayal of the Spanish Loyalist cause, finally with Marxist class analysis when it tried to argue that Hitler's war was only a quarrel among imperialists.

But Lovestone's whole life was politics; he could not live without a cause, and he found one in 1944 when George Meany of the American Federation of Labor gave him a job running the AFL foreign department and an open mandate to support the free democratic trade union movement wherever it was threatened. Half-hidden behind the scenes, for thirty years Lovestone and his ally Irving Brown fought the Communists around the globe, backed by Meany and funds supplied by the CIA.

That much has been public knowledge for years. What Ted Morgan brings to the story in *A Covert Life: Jay Lovestone: Communist, Anti-Communist, and Spymaster*[7] is a rich and detailed account, filled with unfamiliar characters and new material, of Lovestone's break with communism, his central role in preventing a Stalinist takeover of

7. Random House, 1999.

European labor unions following World War II, and his relations with "the fizz kids" (Lovestone's term) at the CIA—the director from 1953–1963, Allen Dulles; the chief of clandestine operations, Frank Wisner; and above all the chief of counterintelligence, who personally handled "the Lovestone account," James Jesus Angleton. "The fizz kids" were hyperactive in the 1950s and 1960s and they caused much harm—overthrowing governments in Iran and Guatemala, organizing the invasion of Cuba at the Bay of Pigs, intervening in a sometimes blundering way in the politics of countries like Italy and France. But the CIA also slipped secret funds to political parties, cultural institutions, and labor organizations that were hard-pressed by Soviet-controlled organizations flush with "Moscow gold." The CIA bitterly resented Lovestone's independence, always anathema to an intelligence organization, but Lovestone was on the payroll for twenty years, and by Morgan's account it got value for money.

Morgan's is one of the most important and original books in many years about American politics, about the politics of communism in the middle decades of the century, and about the role of the CIA in the political struggles of the cold war. But Morgan's book does not simply get all that straight; it is also a delight to read, leavened by Lovestone's pungent character and the astonishing liveliness of some of his colleagues—his sometime girlfriend and political operative Pagie Morris; his agents in Europe and the Far East; the former OSS chief William Donovan; the enigmatic and driven Angleton; and a whole host of others who enjoyed Lovestone's loyalty and friendship or endured the lash of his combative wit. Morgan has a great talent for narrative, and his longish book does not read long. In his lifetime Lovestone got one great thing right, and he got it right early enough to help do something about it—Soviet communism was a threat to free institutions and ordinary human values and given an inch would take a yard. Lovestone also got one thing wrong—the date when communism ran out of steam. He missed that by a couple of decades and spent the last part of his life worrying that a new generation was too naive to recognize the threat. Lovestone's old age was neither temperate nor attractive. But what he got wrong was smaller than what he got right and Morgan's book is a fine corrective to the many books written on the assumption that everything important was done by officials in Washington and Moscow.

Traditional historians have been slow to tackle the secret side of history. At the top of the list of important factors either slighted or missing entirely, in Christopher Andrew's view, is SIGINT—intelligence jargon for signals intelligence, which means broadcast communications of all kinds, but most importantly encrypted communications that code-breakers have managed to read. The best-known examples are ULTRA (the British success in reading German machine-generated codes during World War II), MAGIC (the American success in reading Japanese naval communications), and VENONA. Andrew argues that SIGINT and other aspects of intelligence activity are overlooked partly because of "over-classification of intelligence archives"—that is, the addiction to secrecy, common in all countries but fanatically defended especially in Britain—and partly because of "what psychologists call 'cognitive dissonance'—the difficulty all of us have in grasping new concepts which disturb our existing view of the world." Just what Andrew means by "cognitive dissonance" here is not entirely clear, but I think he means that historians, like other people, don't like to admit that they have been wrong.

The history of McCarthyism offers a fine example of dogged persistence in the defense of old interpretations, which fail to be integrated into the story of what we have learned about Soviet espionage since the end of the cold war. After all his bluster, McCarthy himself never found any spies, but Chambers, faced with Hiss's libel suit, made charges of espionage that have turned out to be true. Not all the victims of McCarthyism were harmless idealists of the left.

It is the Hiss case in particular which is central to the unfolding of what came to be called McCarthyism, and to the tortured treatment of it by many historians now. An important factor in the escalation of McCarthyism from an aberration to a genuine crisis of democracy was the denial (mostly by the left), and the furious response to that denial (mostly by the right), of what was characteristic of many Soviet spies of the 1930s and 1940s—they were of the left generally, they supported liberal causes, they defended the Soviet Union in all circumstances, they were often secret members of the Communist Party, they were uniformly suspicious of American initiatives throughout the world, they tended to be contemptuous of American democracy, society, and culture, and, above all, their offenses were too often minimized or explained away by apologists who felt that no man should be called traitor who did what he did for the cause of humanity. Once the dust of the big spy scandals settled, however, the KGB concluded that it had been a ghastly mistake to recruit agents from Communist Party ranks, and they quit doing it. But the fact that some Soviet spies could in part be identified by their politics, and the embarrassed denial of that fact by liberals who shared some of their political goals, helped turn a spy scandal into a searing schism in American political life which has not entirely healed yet, fifty years later.

It is difficult to realize now just how deeply the assumptions of both left and right penetrated American society during the McCarthy years. I still remember the night when Julius and Ethel Rosenberg were executed. I have to look up the day and year—Friday, June 19, 1953—but the moment itself is vivid. I was a Boy Scout, twelve years old, attending a regular troop meeting in the gym of the Siwanoy School in Pelham, New York. Sing Sing prison, where the Rosenbergs were scheduled to be executed at eight o'clock, was also in Westchester County and the whole troop—twenty or thirty kids—believed that so much power would be drained by the electric chair that the lights in the gym would dim. The moment came and went but the lights did not dim. For a few moments we believed they had been spared, but word soon circulated from a radio report that they died on schedule.

I regret to say that none of us, at twelve and thirteen, saw anything wrong with executing genuine atom spies. But I remember very clearly that several of my friends "knew" the Rosenbergs were innocent. This was not something they heard from their parents, believe me. They knew it the same way I knew that the atomic bomb had been invented in a secret laboratory beneath Yankee Stadium. At a certain point in my teens, after I began to take an interest in politics, I discovered that now I also "knew" the Rosenbergs were innocent, just as I "knew" that Alger Hiss had been unfairly accused by the repugnant liar Whittaker Chambers and unjustly sentenced to jail. These were never important, bedrock beliefs to me—just features of the political landscape, facts I had breathed in, things I "knew."

Years later, as a young reporter for the United Press in New York City in the late 1960s, I had occasion to call Alger Hiss on the phone. There had been some development in his efforts to rehabilitate himself—a court had said yes or no, I no longer remember the details. But I remember something curt and irritated in his voice which nevertheless conveyed the pain suffered by an innocent man wrongly accused. He sounded like a man running out of patience with the world for taking so long to grasp the truth of his innocence.

A few years later I read Allen Weinstein's *Perjury*. The experience was something of a shock. The case was not even hard. What Whittaker Chambers had claimed was true, and it was convincingly and obviously true by the time Hiss went to jail for perjury. Hiss's denial, and his persistence in it for decades, and his support in it by so many otherwise smart people, was one of the great intellectual contortion acts of history. The evidence now, following the publication of VENONA and *The Haunted Wood*, is simply overwhelming. What it shows is that Hiss was one of a number of young, brainy, overexcited converts to communism hurrying about Washington in the 1930s recruiting others to serve "real, existing Socialism" in the Soviet Union for high-minded reasons which should not have survived the opening days of the Moscow Trials, but somehow did.

No "Hiss file" has been released by the Russians, but he is one of the established cast in the routine communications of Soviet spy-runners—his name or code name turns up in many documents quoted in *The Haunted Wood*. What continues to astonish and bewilder me now is why Hiss lied for fifty years about his service in a cause so important to him that he was willing to betray his country for it. The faith itself is no problem to explain; hundreds of people shared it enough to do the same, and thousands more shared it who were never put to the test by a demand for secrets. But why did Hiss persist in the lie personally? Why did he allow his friends and family to go on carrying the awful burden of defending that lie?

The huge volume of material recently published about Soviet espionage, in which Hiss of course plays only a minor supporting role, is not just interesting, as all secrets are interesting, at least for the day of their first publication. It also has important implications for the history of the century, and for the failure of the Soviet experiment which almost spanned it. But more narrowly it helps to explain the crisis of McCarthyism, which was fueled not only by the discovery of spies but by the denial of spies. The plain fact is that the Russians were running a good many spies in the United States in the 1930s and 1940s, that they recruited them from the ranks of the left, that they ran them to steal secrets, and that when they got caught at it they went to ground and waited for a better day.

Of course some on the left had no illusions—former Communists like Lovestone and Richard Rovere, and former Trotskyites and ADA liberals, such as Arthur Schlesinger Jr., as well as labor leaders such as Walter Reuther and David Dubinsky. But many on the American left were slow and grudging in admitting first the truth and then the significance of any given spy case. Some attacked all efforts to peel open the extent of the problem as a witch-hunt, and bitterly resisted the inference that it never could have happened if the social idealism of the 1930s had not been hijacked by Moscow.

Once the new evidence is frankly faced no one can write the history of McCarthyism and the early cold war without taking into account that the hunt for spies was based on the fact that there were spies—lots of them; that those spies began with an idealism shared by a significant minority of the American people; and that the defensive response of many American liberals not only was wrong on the facts, but also exacerbated the suspicions of the right, making it easier for demagogues to argue that progressive causes and treason somehow went hand in hand.

Some of the historians who claim the McCarthy era for their territory have been slow to take up this necessary task. Whenever they read the slightest suggestion that they have been sitting on their hands too long they fly into collective action, sizzle the phone lines with faxes and e-mails, and draft a public letter claiming that the offending book or essay is filled with errors too numerous and profound to mention, and protesting furiously that they are being asked to hand Joseph McCarthy a posthumous victory. Maybe the old claims that it was all a witch-hunt were wrong on some minor factual matters, they concede, but at that time, in that climate, under those pressures, with those enemies, it was not wrong to be wrong.

They should relax. Facing the facts won't kill us. The ordeal of McCarthyism was only in part about Reds under the bed. It was also about the extraordinary success of the Soviets in penetrating America's government; we know a lot about it now that we didn't know at the time, and we should get on with figuring out why things unfolded as they did before the Russians further thicken the stew by telling us who was hiding behind the other half of those 349 cryptonyms.

—*The New York Review of Books*, May 11, 2000

6

THE RIDDLE INSIDE THE ENIGMA

"THE THREAT" WAS James Jesus Angleton's preferred term for the Soviet Union during his twenty years as chief of the CIA's Counterintelligence Staff. He did not distinguish between the country itself and the Soviet Union's Committee for State Security, the KGB, and its allied intelligence services in Eastern Europe. Angleton was a convinced man, and for a dozen years, until his forced retirement in 1974, he had the intelligence services of the West tied up in knots trying to prove that the chief instrument of "the threat" was deception on the grand scale. This deception consisted of a twin effort to penetrate and ultimately to control Western intelligence services, and to divide and disarm the West politically through agents of influence and the artful manipulation of events and appearances. For years, to take a notorious example, Angleton claimed that the apparent split between the Soviet Union and China was a brilliantly conceived act of deception. How the Soviets planned to exploit this deception was something Angleton never spelled out exactly; he never spelled out anything so far as I know. But he suspected the worst—not surprise attack and nuclear war, but a kind of slow chipping away at the independence of Soviet neighbors in ever-widening circles.

That puts it more baldly than Edward Jay Epstein does in his book *Deception: The Invisible War Between the KGB and the*

CIA,[1] a richly suggestive but ultimately inconclusive work, which comes closer than Angleton himself ever did to laying out his case for the dark view of Soviet intentions. The book is important in two ways: as a contribution to the biography of Angleton, perhaps the most interesting and certainly the most divisive figure in the history of American intelligence; and as an argument for thinking twice before accepting Mikhail Gorbachev's glasnost as evidence that the cold war is over. It is the result of ten years of the author's elliptical conversations with Angleton before his death in May 1987, of Epstein's exceptional lay expertise in the history of postwar counterintelligence, and of much reflection on Sun-tzu's fifth-century BC classic *The Art of War*. It was Angleton who suggested Sun-tzu's book to Epstein when he wanted to know what use KGB deception could be in a world armed with nuclear weapons—a characteristically circuitous answer.

But it is a very good suggestion. Unlike Angleton, Sun-tzu is very much to the point. "All warfare is based on deception," he says.

> Therefore, when capable, feign incapacity; when active, inactivity. When near, make it appear that you are far away.... Anger his general and confuse him. Pretend inferiority and encourage his arrogance. Keep him under a strain and wear him down.

Epstein implies, but does not quite say, that this is a good description of the strategy that may lie behind the face Russia is presenting to the world under Gorbachev—a weak country at the end of its economic tether, eager to renounce its dark past, ending political repression at home, experimenting with democracy, pulling back from foreign adventures, weary of the burden of arms, anxious for trade, ready to join the family of nations. In a remarkable speech in London in April 1989 Gorbachev shared his concerns with the world: the environment,

---

1. Simon and Schuster, 1989.

drugs, AIDS, terrorism, human rights, the danger of nuclear war—it was all there, everything the West has been longing to hear. "The world community stands at the crossroads of two policies," he said. "One...is a policy of force. It is rooted in the past. The other policy...[is based upon] the world's integrity and interdependence. The priority of universal human interests is its imperative." It is hard to argue with that. Is it all an elaborate trick?

Epstein has been thinking about counterintelligence for so long that he has learned to answer broad historical questions the way the professionals do—with a chain of evidence based on intelligence cases. This is not the way scholars of the Soviet Union would traditionally go about it, but Epstein's book, like Angleton's career, must stand or fall on his reading of these cases. The problem for a layman like Epstein is that the raw data for the solution—accepting for the moment that there is or can be a solution—lies in two vast collections of information, one in the files of the CIA, the other in Moscow, neither available to laymen. What Angleton knew came mainly from Soviet-bloc intelligence services and what Epstein knows comes mainly from Angleton and other American intelligence officers. It comes down in the end to what people say, and how we judge what they say. What Angleton says, and how we judge what he says, are central to the argument for grand deception.

Angleton's career in the intelligence business began during the Second World War, when he joined the Office of Strategic Services (OSS) and was assigned to the X-2 or counterintelligence branch of the OSS in London. The best account of these early years is to be found in Robin Winks's *Cloak and Gown*, a fascinating and useful omnium-gatherum of information about intelligence built around short accounts of the careers of four Yale men who worked for the OSS, including Angleton, class of 1941, and the literature professor who recruited him, Norman Holmes Pearson, who also worked for X-2 in London. There Pearson was privy to the dramatically successful

British "deception operation," which controlled all German agents in Britain under the direction of the "xx" or "Double-Cross" Committee. Pearson referred afterward to counterintelligence as "the Queen on the board" in the great intelligence game. In London for a time Angleton worked alongside and got to know H. A. R. ("Kim") Philby, the Soviet agent who crossed his path on later occasions, to Angleton's subsequent embarrassment.

Winks provides a good portrait of the young Angleton in London and later in Italy where he was chief of x-2 by the end of the war. (Before attending Yale, Angleton had spent much of his youth in Italy, where his father was the representative of the National Cash Register Company.) When the oss was disbanded in the fall of 1945 Angleton stayed on in Italy with a caretaker unit, and then transferred to the newly created CIA in Washington in 1948.

Any history of Angleton's obsession with the deeper strategems of Soviet intelligence must begin with Philby's two-year tour of duty in Washington from late 1949 until his abrupt recall, demanded by the CIA, after the disappearance of the British diplomats Guy Burgess and Donald Maclean in May 1951. After Philby's own defection in 1963, Angleton sometimes hinted he had known Philby's true allegiance all along, but the truth is that Angleton was late to catch on. In Paris in 1952 he assured an American diplomat, James McCargar, that there was no reason he shouldn't see Philby in London, adding, "I am still convinced that Philby will one day be the head of the SIS"—the British Secret Intelligence Service. During Philby's tour in Washington Angleton, like many other CIA officers, had lunch with him often and shared secrets. He knew nothing of Philby's most important task in the United States—to be the liaison with the FBI and Armed Forces Security Agency officers handling the super-secret interception of encoded Soviet messages, called VENONA.

These messages, and especially a sheaf of cables from September 1945, painstakingly read with the aid of a partially destroyed Soviet code book picked up on a battlefield of the Russo-Finnish war of 1939–1940, were studded with the cryptonyms of many Soviet agents, some still unidentified. Among them were references to "Homer," soon established as Maclean, and "Stanley," Philby's own code name. Philby showed astonishing aplomb as the investigation closed in, but what impressed Angleton most, when he reflected on it later, was the deft Soviet exploitation of a perfect intelligence loop, allowing them to monitor a dangerous investigation day-by-day through an agent on the inside. VENONA pretty much unraveled the Soviet intelligence nets that had been established between the wars, but Philby's position at the closing of the loop allowed the Soviets to minimize the unraveling's effect.

Angleton's chief rival for control of counterintelligence in the CIA in the early 1950s was William King Harvey, a former FBI agent, who wrote a memo to the agency's director, General Walter Bedell Smith, shortly after Burgess and Maclean disappeared arguing that Philby was also a spy—the basis for Smith's demand to the British that Philby be recalled. But Harvey was transferred to Berlin in 1953, and a year later Angleton was appointed to run the new Counterintelligence Staff, the position he held for the rest of his career. It was the job of the CI Staff to protect the integrity of CIA intelligence operations by serving as a kind of internal guidance module, keeping track of who's who and what's what in espionage activities in order to insure that information gathered from spies had not been poisoned at the source—in short, that it was not the product of deliberate Soviet attempts to deceive. Keeping spies out of the CIA was the job of the Office of Security.

Angleton eventually built a staff of three hundred, but he had no agents in the field, had no authority to place bugs or telephone taps, ran no foreign operations. What he did have was unparalleled access —copies of all cables to and from the CIA's Deputy Directorate of Plans (DDP), of intercepted communications of exchanges with the counterintelligence staffs of allied services, of the debriefings of Soviet defectors. His main activity was to analyze this ocean of information about Soviet intelligence operations for the telltale signs of manipulation and interference that would betray Soviet control. He concluded that nearly but not quite all Soviet defectors were "dispatched"—sent to deceive—and that in most cases defectors generated by CIA officers in the field were "bad," or run by the other side.

But that wasn't the worst of it. All intelligence services attempt to "muddy the waters" through the use of deception, double agents, the release of importantly false information concealed within a bouquet of the trivial but true, and so on. Angleton convinced himself that Soviet intelligence revealed a deeper plot to send defectors who would support each other's bona fides and back up "bad cases" generated in the field. A penetration agent or mole within the targeted service—an undiscovered Philby, say—would then "close the feedback loop," allowing the Soviets to monitor and adjust their operations, and gradually gain control of what the target service "knew" about the Soviets. The enterprise would be a replay of Britain's "Double-Cross" operation during World War II. But this time around, control of intelligence would be used by the Soviets for a broader purpose—to color what Western governments "knew" about Soviet political intentions, and thereby manipulate the Western response.

This fearful vision didn't come to Angleton all at once. It dawned on him slowly, over a period of years, as he watched cases unfold from his position of unparalleled access. Perhaps the very first seed of suspicion was planted by the extraordinary case of Michal Goleniewsky, an intelligence officer in the Polish Urad Bezpieczenstaw (UB) who sent an anonymous letter to the American embassy in Switzerland in March 1958. Goleniewsky sent fourteen letters to his CIA contact before defecting in Berlin in December 1960, and many Soviet spies in Britain and Germany were arrested as a direct result of his leads. But of the fourteen letters the one with the deepest consequences reported Soviet knowledge of a West German plan to "pitch," or attempt to recruit, the Polish intelligence officer Jan Switala in Bern.

The result was instant consternation at the CIA. Just three weeks earlier agency headquarters at Langley, Virginia, had cabled approval for an attempt to recruit Switala by the CIA officer Tennent ("Pete") Bagley in Bern, posing as a West German. Only three CIA officers knew about the operation directly; drop copies of the cable had gone routinely to the DDP and to Angleton. This was an unmistakable sign that something was badly awry. Investigation failed to find the leak but the doubt remained—there was a mole inside the CIA.

Penetration is the nightmare of intelligence services. As chief of the CI Staff Angleton compiled over the years about one hundred "serials" —collections of material on unresolved intelligence cases accompanied by his own comments indicating where Soviet penetration had taken place. Many "serials" were based on cryptonyms in the VENONA intercepted messages, including about a dozen identified as OSS officers working for or at least known to the Soviets.[2] Other "serials" referred to CIA operations in which there had been signs ("manifestations") that the Soviets had been able to interfere, always a possible sign of penetration. The Goleniewsky case became a prominent fixture in Angleton's serials, especially after signs began to appear that the Soviets had caught on to his defection within six weeks and used him to feed information to the CIA in later letters, "correcting" some of his earlier information.[3] The entire case went completely haywire a few years later when Goleniewsky, by then living in New York City,

2. One of these had been identified by collateral information in the traffic as probably referring to Donald Downes, the subject of one of Winks's portraits in *Cloak and Gown*. The FBI investigated Downes and remained suspicious of him, but it is just as likely his name and movements were known to the Soviets through a World War II operation in New York City that Downes undertook for the OSS with a German, Wolfgang von zu Putlitz, a wartime lover of Anthony Blunt who was also a friend of Philby's and almost certainly a Soviet agent.

3. One of these letters, dated 1961, claimed that the Ukrainian émigré leader Stefan Bandera, who had recently been murdered in Munich, had been poisoned at lunch by a Soviet agent. Bandera's lunch partner on that date had been an assistant to Reinhard Gehlen, chief

publicly claimed to be the son and rightful heir of the last Russian tsar, Nicholas II.

But even while the case was unfolding Angleton had growing suspicions that Goleniewsky had been unreliable from the beginning, and that the spies he uncovered were deliberately handed over by the Soviets for reasons of their own. Inevitably, the Polish branch of the DDP and the case officers who dealt with Goleniewsky in the field disagreed—the beginning of bad blood between the CI Staff and the rest of the clandestine service.

Soviet deception in such activities was just business as usual. Angleton's grand vision took its final form only after the defection in December 1961 of Anatoli Golitsyn, a KGB officer already known to the CIA from debriefing an earlier defector, the KGB officer Peter Deriabin, who had switched sides in Vienna in 1954. Golitsyn had spent a number of months going over KGB files on NATO in Moscow before being assigned to Finland, where he defected to the US, but he brought no names of agents, only clues. He said, for example, that the KGB possessed specific NATO documents; that the KGB had obtained full transcripts of the CIA's debriefing of Deriabin; that a KGB friend, Anatoly Gromov, remembered that he had once recruited a homosexual Canadian ambassador to Moscow. Golitsyn had looked at a lot of paper and he had a lot of alleged clues, some of which pointed to a CIA mole.

But Golitsyn had something else to offer as well—a report that the KGB was interested in something much bigger than run-of-the-mill cases, however successfully pursued. Following the Burgess-Maclean disaster of 1951, Golitsyn said, he had proposed that the KGB pay more attention to Washington than to London. He even claimed to

---

of the West German intelligence service. This is a classic case of muddying the waters. For as suspicion of Gehlen's assistant began to grow, the case was unexpectedly cleared up after the real murderer, the KGB agent Bogdan Stashinsky, defected to Berlin, in August 1961.

THE RIDDLE INSIDE THE ENIGMA

have spoken to Stalin of his plan. In 1958, he said, the KGB had been reorganized and had adopted a long-term plan to penetrate and deceive Western intelligence services. He predicted that since he knew about the plan, the Soviets would dispatch two phony defectors to discredit his reports.

In June 1962 the perfect candidate appeared—the KGB officer Yuri Nosenko, the son of a famous Soviet admiral. Nosenko offered himself to the CIA in Switzerland and delivered many clues to the identities of Soviet agents in perhaps ten hours of conversation with the CIA official Peter Bagley, who had gone to Geneva to debrief him. Bagley was of course thrilled with the results, but back in Washington Angleton convinced him that he had been gulled. When Nosenko defected in January 1964, Bagley and the Soviet Division assumed from the start he was sent by the KGB to deceive the CIA, not least in his claim that the Soviets had made no use of Lee Harvey Oswald for intelligence purposes, and therefore could not be charged with involvement in the Kennedy assassination.

Thereupon followed an extraordinary three-year interrogation of Nosenko, which is blandly referred to in documents as "hostile"— too pale a word for Nosenko's harsh treatment, during which he was kept in total isolation and held naked in a brightly lit room. Nosenko's case has never been resolved. His story contained many holes, but he insisted to the end that he was acting on his own. At the end of 1967 his treatment finally eased, and he was eventually resettled in the usual manner, paid for his agony, and taken on by the CIA as a consultant. Some CIA officers remain convinced that he lied, others that he was disgracefully mistreated—the details are too many and convoluted to unravel here.[4] For our purposes Nosenko's case is

---

4. The first account of Nosenko's case to appear in print can be found in an earlier book by Epstein, *Legend: The Secret World of Lee Harvey Oswald* (McGraw-Hill, 1978). Many additional details are in David Martin, *Wilderness of Mirrors* (Harper and Row, 1980).

important because his defection appeared to confirm Golitsyn's prediction, and thereby lent support to his many other claims.

By all accounts Golitsyn was a proud, difficult, combative man, and he quarreled heatedly with the Soviet Division debriefers who demanded that he provide more details. In March 1963 he insisted on going to England, where he quickly established a close relationship with the British Secret Intelligence Service—so close the SIS allowed him to see raw files in the hope that they would prod his memory. In August he returned to Washington and insisted that he had now remembered enough to pinpoint Soviet agents inside the CIA. But this time he refused to have anything to do with the Soviet Division. Angleton's CI Staff took over the handling of Golitsyn, and Angleton himself—who had never been to Russia, knew no Russian, and never knew a Russian other than Golitsyn—fell under Golitsyn's spell. As Epstein quotes Sun-tzu:

> He who is not sage and wise, humane and just, cannot use secret agents. And he who is not delicate and subtle cannot get the truth out of them.

Subtlety was Angleton's passion, and his delicacy in "eliciting" leads from Golitsyn brought them up by the bucketload. In a sense Angleton and Golitsyn were made for each other. In the intelligence business the phenomenon of "falling in love with your agent" is well known. No one ever fell harder than James Angleton.

But all defectors sense at once that they are loved for a season only; when they have no more to tell they are gently dropped. It is a sign of Golitsyn's genius that he found a way to make the marriage last. Angleton was ready to see a deeper pattern behind Soviet intelligence activities and Golitsyn confirmed his darkest fears. He insisted that his deep knowledge of the KGB ethos would allow him to sniff out traces of Soviet interference if he were only allowed to go through the files of agency personnel and operations. This ought to have set off warning bells. The conventional wisdom of counterintelligence stresses that what defectors know is precious only so long as it is uncontaminated by other information. They are quick learners as a rule, soon sense what their interrogators want, and will plunder every available source in order to deliver. Abandoning caution, Angleton gave Golitsyn unprecedented access to the files, and Golitsyn delivered.

Golitsyn's "methodology," soon notorious throughout the CIA's clandestine service, can be best seen at work in the search for moles within the CIA. On his return from England Golitsyn said that moles would be found at the CIA's Berlin base, where many cases had turned out badly over the years. He identified one by his alleged Soviet cryptonym—"Sacha," the diminutive for Alexander. A Pole was involved, whose name began with K. Two candidates were quickly found—a contract officer and translator from the Russian, and a regular CIA officer who had been in charge of technical support throughout Europe. Both were shipped to other posts although both denied they were agents. But Golitsyn's claims didn't stop there. The real purpose of the "agents," he said, had been to compromise their superiors, who had of course been recruited in turn. Angleton's suspicions fell upon two veterans of the CI's Soviet Division, Richard Kovich and David Murphy, who had handled the "agents" implicated by Golitsyn. Nothing was said to them, but their careers went quietly awry: Kovich was shipped off to Latin America; and Angleton even went so far as to warn a French intelligence chief that Murphy, newly appointed to run the CIA's Paris station in the late 1960s, was a Soviet agent. The blight of Golitsyn's "methodology" ruined other CIA careers as well.

Golitsyn's leads and Angleton's growing confidence that he had grasped the pattern of Soviet efforts—"the logic of penetration," which he explored in frequent conversations with his sole Russian— created a decade of turmoil in Western counterintelligence. One of

Golitsyn's leads suggested high-level Soviet penetrations in France, but when French counterintelligence officers tried to explore the subject with Golitsyn they quickly found that every French official they mentioned was marked down as a Soviet agent by the officers from Angleton's office who sat in on the interrogation. Another lead precipitated a bitter controversy when Angleton personally told the head of one Norwegian agency—wrongly, as it turned out—that the secretary of the man who ran another agency was working for the Soviets. Following on Golitsyn's leads, Angleton told the British SIS that the British Labour Party leader Hugh Gaitskell, who had just died, had probably been murdered by the Soviets in London in order to advance their own man, Harold Wilson, who was by then prime minister. Like so many of Golitsyn's leads, it trailed off to nothing, but the damage done in Britain was enormous.

Golitsyn's leads, backed up by VENONA intercepts, for example, convinced Angleton that Averill Harriman, the former governor of New York, ambassador to Russia, and Lyndon Johnson's negotiator with the North Vietnamese in Paris, was a Soviet agent.[5] Angleton also believed that American journalists were working for the Russians and the Romanians (which amounted to the same thing, in Angleton's view), and for a time he took seriously Goleniewsky's report—a product of his later years, passed on to the British after his claim that he was heir to the tsar—that Henry Kissinger had been recruited by the Russians in Germany shortly after the war.

But it took two other claims of Golitsyn's to push Angleton over the edge. First was Golitsyn's view, mentioned earlier, that Chinese–Soviet enmity was a hoax to lull the West, a conviction Angleton carried to the grave, despite the astonishment of Chinese and Soviet experts who

---

5. In VENONA cables the Soviets variously referred to Harriman as "the keeper of the Big House" and "capitalist." One cable reported that Alger Hiss ("Ales"), on a World War II trip with Harriman, had secretly been given an award in Moscow.

politely grilled Golitsyn on the subject in meetings referred to by skeptics as "the flat earth conference."

Perhaps more important was Golitsyn's inspired claim that buried within the KGB was a secret KGB, a tiny group that alone knew the details of the master plan. No one from the inner circle ever left the Soviet Union, and no Soviet diplomat who knew what they were up to was allowed out of the country either. Thus no case conducted by the CIA in the field and no defection of a KGB officer abroad could clear up the mysteries because only one person with knowledge of the secret KGB had ever managed to escape—Golitsyn.

Summarized briefly, Angleton's inventory of suspicions has an air of delirium, and it seems scarcely credible that they were the chief concerns of Western counterintelligence for a decade. Argued singly, his cases sounded questionable but interesting. But taken as a whole, they implied that Western intelligence services were a plaything in the hands of KGB puppeteers. The result was an atmosphere of distrust and personal bitterness, strained relations with allies, and a growing paralysis of CIA efforts to recruit agents to give information about the Soviet Union. By the late 1960s the CI Staff was shutting down virtually every case originating in the field; furious case officers, never told what had gone wrong, began requesting transfers out of the Soviet Division. Those who remained found ways to slip around the CI Staff, built files of their own, and broke the rules by discussing cases with each other. Finally a Soviet Division officer, Leonard McCoy, convinced CIA Director Richard Helms that Angleton's suspicions were crippling the agency. Internal suspicions were destroying morale. The only way to resolve the doubts inspired by Golitsyn was to find some new defector with fresh information, but the CI was blocking every effort.

Reorganization followed, in which Soviet Division officers were all let go on the theory that a new staff could not have been penetrated. The new division chief, David Blee, eventually paid a call on Angleton for "the briefing." I have heard such briefings described many times.

They are all the same—Angleton in his office behind a desk piled high with paper, chain-smoking the cigarettes that would kill him, the window blinds drawn down behind him. This is the Angleton of legend—a tall, stooped man with a basement pallor, who drew the metaphors for his trade from his hobbies, fly-fishing and orchid growing. He could be eloquent about the sexual lives of plants, the brilliant stratagems by which insects were lured to carry pollen.

In his youth, at Yale in the late 1930s, literature had been his great love, especially the poetry of Eliot and Pound. Now he worked on the subtlest texts of all—the deception buried in cases as elusive as a difficult poem. His discussion of Soviet intelligence cases going back to the 1920s and 1930s made a finely linked construction, but the way in which he connected the cases was hard to follow. Almost any detail might bring an abrupt switch in his account from one case to another —a name, a place, a date, a bit of operational craft. So it went. At each critical juncture Angleton would only raise his eyebrows—as if to say, don't you see? It was up to his listeners to spell it out: if A then B, which can only mean C—was that it?

Some intelligence professionals like to toy with the uninitiated, but never Angleton; no man ever took the burden of knowledge more seriously. He was trying to tell you, but some inner restraint—some combination of temperament and devotion to secrecy—prevented him from doing so directly. It was more or less clear that Angleton felt the Soviets had spun a monstrous web to further, and at the same time to conceal, their deeper purposes in the world, but just how that web was put together, what those intentions were, how Angleton knew it was so—at that point you were on your own, with only Angleton's body language as guide. Blee got the full treatment. At the end of three or four hours with Angleton he asked, "Is that it, Jim?" Angleton said, "That's it, Dave, you see the pattern, don't you?" But Blee didn't see the pattern. He felt Angleton had lost his way in a maze constructed of mirrors.

A lot of CIA people concluded that Angleton was crazy. There may be something to this. The range of his suspicions does suggest paranoia, but this diagnosis was hard to establish because Angleton was always in control of the evidence. He never cleared skeptics for the information that would prove his case. To me he seems to have suffered a radical loss of the ability to live with uncertainty. When World War II was over, the spy-runners on our side, Angleton included, got a chance to find out who had been running whom. But the cold war went on and on, and the mysteries compounded. Small wonder if this never-ending uncertainty proved too much. But the explanation may be simpler. Angleton was intellectually proud; he was slow to make up his mind, but once he had done so he stuck to it. So far as I know, Angleton never admitted that he had been wrong about anything, to anybody.

Edward Jay Epstein of course cannot know if Gorbachev is only carrying out the grand deception predicted by Golitsyn nearly thirty years ago. He is not so much convinced by Angleton's case as he is swept along by it, intrigued by it. Epstein can be an able analyst, quick to spot the flaws in an argument, but he makes no attempt to weigh Angleton's case in *Deception*. What animates him is only the fragile possibility that it might all be true. A kind of intellectual playfulness is characteristic of all of Epstein's books. His account of Lee Harvey Oswald in *Legend*, for example, builds a circumstantial, inferential case that the Soviets had every reason to take and retain an intelligence interest in Oswald. But did they? Epstein never says. He has dug up the Nosenko case in a masterful job of reporting, but he tells this story in order to heighten the mysteries that remain, not to resolve any.

In *Deception*, Epstein argues that Soviet intelligence likes to play games, that it has mounted sizable deception operations in the past, that the Soviet Union has habitually misrepresented itself, that it may have systematically hidden the accuracy of its missiles through technical deception, that governments and their officials are frequently

THE RIDDLE INSIDE THE ENIGMA

led astray by what they want to believe, that Western belief in Soviet weakness is mainly based on what the Soviets say about themselves, and that Sun-tzu says this is the way to lull enemies and win wars without fighting. With evidence to support it this would provide an outline for a plausible interpretation of current events. But like an inverted pyramid, it rests on an infinitesimal point, Golitsyn's lonely claim that the KGB laid a plan for just this sort of grand deception thirty years ago. We've got only Golitsyn's word for it.

Of the many defectors since Golitsyn came to Washington, none has ever backed up his claims that a secret KGB is engaged in grand deception. Lacking proof, Angleton's argument—the heart of his murky briefings—fell back on close analysis of the cases in which Golitsyn was involved. If he were right about Nosenko, for example, one had to entertain the possibility he was also right about the KGB policy of grand deception. As chains of reasoning go, this one was fragile. A better test is the case of China, but how can one reasonably argue that the last twenty years of Chinese–Soviet relations have all been orchestrated to lull the West?

In the counterintelligence world nothing just happens, but in the real world a great deal does. A secret arm of government may slip a phony piece of paper into a sheaf of the real, but Golitsyn and Angleton were arguing something altogether different—that none of the paper is real, the defectors are all phony, the secret intelligence is all disinformation. The *real* real world is a handful of men in the bowels of Moscow, pulling strings. We have heard such stuff about the Freemasons, the Sanhedrin, the Anti-Christ in Rome, even the Trilateral Commission. Angleton, in my view, properly deserves the charity of a medical excuse, but what's Epstein's excuse? He has an obligation to the reader to pass some sort of judgment on these wild claims, but gives us nothing of the kind.

In the end Angleton himself fell under suspicion. Nothing ever came of it, but the men who worked alongside him finally lost patience with him, wearied of his secrecy and suspiciousness. They forced him to retire, drastically cut back his office to a staff of eighty or so, and rewrote the CI charter. For a time Angleton was convinced that these changes had been masterminded by Philby in Moscow; he even suspected the CIA director who fired him, William Colby, was a Soviet agent. He quit saying it before he died, but I very much doubt he quit thinking it. He spent his unreconstructed final years fly-fishing, raising exotic flowers, and giving occasional interviews to writers who found it difficult to pin down just what he was trying to tell them. He told Epstein he was still trying to work out some of the finer points, but Epstein's book makes a convincing if unintentional case that Angleton was on the wrong track.

More facts about the Russians won't get us anywhere in understanding Angleton's conspiracy theories. We must look at the man himself. His fearful vision has a pathological cast—nothing was the way it seemed, enemies were everywhere, only Angleton had the key, skeptics had secret motives, he had figured it all out for himself, the world was doomed if it failed to heed his warnings. This is not the intellectual style of a man in charge of his reason. But I am not a clinician, and Angleton's personal history is still largely a blank, so it is only surmise when I say that somewhere inside Angleton there seems to have been a small boy facing a big secret in lonely terror.

—*The New York Review of Books*, August 17, 1989

7

THE BLOODLESS WAR

FOR THOSE WHO like their history built on dates it may be said that
the cold war began sometime during the eight weeks between the formal surrender of the German armies on May 8, 1945, which ended
the Second World War in Europe, and July 4, 1945, when the Soviet
military authorities first allowed American organizations to set up
shop in Berlin. For an exact date we might choose May 17, on which
day, according to *Battleground Berlin: CIA vs. KGB in the Cold War*,[1]
a fascinating and important account of the opening campaigns of the
secret cold war waged by the CIA and the KGB, the OSS officer Frank
Wisner passed on to Washington the report of three men he had un-
officially slipped into the occupied city in the hope of "establishing
contacts in an area which will shortly be denied to us"—that is, to
commence spying on the Russians.

Berlin by agreement was to be divided into four zones of occupation but the devastation of war had obliterated landmarks, leaving a
maze of erratically marked streets blocked with rubble. The first thing
American commanders wanted to know was where their writ ended
and that of the Russians began, but this required precisely the sort
of information—details of military units and strength designated in

---

1. David E. Murphy, Sergei A. Kondrashev, and George Bailey (Yale University Press, 1997).

military intelligence documents by the term "order of battle" (OB)—which the Russians by precept and temperament kept secret. By summer's end the central question of the cold war may be said to have been posed: When, if ever, would the Soviet army go home? Within a year the initial OSS efforts to establish a working map of occupied Berlin had escalated into a full-scale intelligence war—nets of half-trained agents hastily recruited by the OSS and its successor organization, the Strategic Services Unit (SSU), to gather the raw data for a Soviet OB were being arrested wholesale by Soviet counterintelligence officers whose efficiency began the long American education in how to run a secret intelligence service.

For nearly fifty years the intelligence war to gather and to deny information centered on the military strength of opposing armies, initially in Germany, later across the world—where stationed, how much, of what sort, for what purpose? Around these central questions proliferated a host of secondary questions about intentions in Washington and Moscow, political alliances, the control of territories, the development of weapons, and the operations of clandestine organizations struggling to learn the secrets of opponents and protect their own. All the subsequent accretions of layered operational minutiae in the conduct of the secret cold war may be traced back to these basic questions surrounding the planting of Soviet armies in the heart of Eastern Europe, a fact much like the grain of sand at the heart of a pearl.

The cold war lasted so long (from, let us say, May 17, 1945, until November 9, 1989, when the Berlin Wall came down), was so expensive, and at moments threatened catastrophe on so vast a scale that it pleads for some overarching explanation matching in magnitude the cost and danger. Many have been offered. Of course, there is no right answer, just varying ways of trying to talk about what obsessed us. One explanation that seems to match the deeper rhythm of the cold war, a kind of half-century inhale-exhale, can be found in the formulation, once a staple of every introductory course on geopolitics, of

Sir Halford Mackinder (1861–1947), who lived barely long enough to hear the cold war named. In a paper read to the Royal Geographical Society in England in 1904, and further refined in an influential book of 1919, *Democratic Ideals and Reality*, Mackinder said the pivotal issues of international politics all revolved around geography, and might be summarized in the maxim: "Who rules East Europe commands the heartland; who rules the heartland commands the world island; and who rules the world island, commands the world."

The cold war began with the half-hidden friction of two armies which met in Berlin. It spread outward to arenas of conflict ever farther afield, much in the manner of armies testing each other's flanks, until something like an unbroken line circled the globe. Three outbreaks of intense local war—in Korea, Vietnam, and Afghanistan— never became general, but the scale of the confrontation proved to be more than the Soviet Union could finance indefinitely. The end of the cold war came where it began, in Berlin, with abandonment of the wall erected to maintain the Soviet army planted in the heart of Europe.

Long treated as a symbol of the East–West conflict, the Berlin Wall turns out to have been genuinely central. Without it the German Democratic Republic (GDR) could not have survived, for the East Germans would have left in large numbers for the West. And with the fall of the GDR the Soviet army found itself the unwelcome guest of a reunited Germany with which it was not at war. What could the Soviets do? They accepted a large bribe and went home. This, roughly, is the political setting of *Battleground Berlin*, which retells in detail, much of it new, the ways in which Soviet and American intelligence services fought their secret, bloodless war, from its beginning in the ruins of Berlin until the night in August 1961 when the Soviets quit pretending there was anything voluntary about the division of Germany, and the wall went up.

At the height of the cold war there were as many as eighty different intelligence organizations operating more or less independently in

Berlin, but the principal adversaries were four—the Americans in the CIA's Berlin Operations Base (BOB) established by Allen Dulles in the leafy Berlin suburb of Dahlem; the KGB residency included in the vast complex housing Soviet military headquarters in the East Berlin district known as Karlshorst; the East German Ministry for State Security (the Stasi) in Normannenstrasse; and the local offices of the West German Federal Intelligence Service (BND) principally based in the town of Pullach near Munich in southern Germany. But all four—the Americans, Russians, and East and West Germans—were each represented by numerous other police, intelligence, and investigative organizations operating more or less independently and occasionally bumping into one another in the dark.

Across this crowded and bewildering landscape *Battleground Berlin* charts a straight-line course, sticking largely to the central episodes of the intelligence war and citing other players only as they intrude into the major operations of the Americans and the Russians. What's most unusual about the book is the fact that its three authors served on opposing sides in Berlin during the early years of the cold war, sometimes ran operations against one another, and have worked hard to extract documents from the notoriously tight-fisted archivists at the CIA and the Russian Foreign Intelligence Service, successor to the KGB.

Sergei A. Kondrashev was a long-time intelligence officer in the KGB, at one time headed the German Department, and retired as a lieutenant general. David E. Murphy had a similar career with the CIA, was chief of the Berlin Operations Base in the late 1950s, and later ran Soviet operations for the agency as a whole.[2] George Bailey

2. Murphy's name may be familiar to some readers as a figure in the Great Mole Hunt of the 1960s, when claims of a KGB spy in the CIA by the defector Anatoli Golitsyn led to the CIA's counterintelligence chief, James Jesus Angleton, to loony excesses of suspicion, discussed in the previous chapter. When Murphy was appointed chief of station in Paris in 1968 Angleton personally told the chief of a French intelligence service that Murphy more probably than not was a Soviet spy. See note 4 for references.

was a linguist (Russian, German, and Czech) who served with the Fifth Army Corps under General Clarence Huebner as it entered Germany in 1945 and later joined the CIA at its base in Munich. Since leaving the agency in the late 1950s he has lived and worked in Germany. All three of the authors have deep operational experience in the intelligence war.

But despite a serious effort at evenhandedness, *Battleground Berlin* remains essentially an American book; it's not entirely clear just who wrote what, or even if any sections were completely or substantially written by the Soviet co-author, Sergei Kondrashev, but the book's tone, moral judgments, and historical point of view are unmistakably American. It is not pugnacious; indeed it is generous. But this is the opening segment of a story of a political minefield successfully traversed, of war averted, of a country reunited, of a Soviet attempt to redraw the map of Europe which failed in the end; a story, in short, of what can only be called a stunning American success.

But it didn't look that way in the beginning. At first the Soviets had everything their own way in the secret war. BOB didn't get its first Russian speaker until the arrival in 1947 of George Belic, born in Russia in 1911, a veteran of US Naval Intelligence who was recruited for the interim SSU by Allen Dulles's successor in Berlin, Richard Helms. But while Belic was trying to organize an agent-recruiting effort among Russians stranded in Displaced Person camps the Soviets were crushing political opposition throughout their zone, laying the foundations for a docile client regime, and recruiting spies wholesale for coverage of the American, British, and French zones. In the early 1950s the Soviet secret services were joined in the field by the East German Ministry for State Security with its foreign intelligence branch, eventually called the Hauptverwaltung Aufklärung (HVA), headed from 1952 until his retirement in 1986 by Markus Wolf.

Probably the biggest problems facing the Americans not only at the beginning but throughout the cold war derived from the deep experience of the Soviets in collecting intelligence and running operations, dating back to the conspiratorial origins of the Bolshevik regime, and the extraordinarily tight social control maintained within the Soviet Union and the client states it established throughout Eastern Europe. The CIA referred to Soviet-bloc countries as "denied areas" because it was all but impossible to work there without the protections of diplomatic cover. American attempts to dispatch illegal agents into Russia proper met with uniform failure; the handful of successful Soviet agents were almost all walk-ins who volunteered, not the fruit of recruitment efforts. Allied services in West Germany were thoroughly penetrated by Soviet and East German agents, and American operations against the East often turned out to be controlled by the other side.

It is still much too early to tot up a realistic score for the recruitment of spies in the cold war; some important and dramatic successes of the Allies during World War II remained secret for decades after the shooting stopped. But even a tentative, preliminary accounting does not look good for the West. Among the major early disasters were Soviet recruitment of leading counterintelligence officers in the British Secret Intelligence Service (the notorious Kim Philby); in the German Office for the Protection of the Constitution, a rough equivalent of the American FBI, whose chief in 1954, Otto John, disappeared into the East for more than a year; and in Reinhard Gehlen's BND, where Heinz Felfe slipped into Pullach in 1951 and virtually dominated BND's Soviet counterintelligence operations by the time of his arrest in 1961.

Almost as damaging, in its way, was the case of George Blake, the Dutch-born British intelligence officer recruited by the KGB in a North Korean prisoner of war camp. Blake was personally handled for a time by Sergei Kondrashev in London, where Blake delivered among numerous other documents the minutes of a CIA–SIS conference on plans for what came to be known as "the Berlin tunnel"—an ambitious scheme to tap into Soviet military communications cables in

East Berlin which eventually recorded 443,000 conversations over a period of eleven months and eleven days, ending in a blaze of headlines following Soviet "discovery" of the tunnel on April 22, 1956.

This daring plan had been dreamed up and pushed through principally by the legendary William King Harvey, the former FBI agent who joined the CIA in the 1940s, helped uncover Kim Philby, and later ran the notorious Operation Mongoose, which included the CIA's multiple plots to assassinate Fidel Castro of Cuba. References to Harvey's pungent character and aggressive operational style are salted throughout *Battleground Berlin* and it is clear that the book's CIA authors, David Murphy and George Bailey, like and admire Harvey even when they cannot wholly approve of him.

Blake's betrayal of the Berlin tunnel beautifully captured the baffling ambiguity which can attach to intelligence operations. The rewards for the KGB were many—the quiet satisfaction of knowing what an opponent is up to; the brownie points for keeping the Kremlin informed; the demonstration of professional discipline in allowing Harvey's diggers to go forward in order to protect the secret of the asp in the enemy's bosom; the guilty pleasure of knowing that the KGB's bureaucratic archenemy, the GRU, was spilling its secrets over tapped lines; and perhaps—Kondrashev and his sources do not say— the operational advantages to be gained by manipulating cases through disinformation spoonfed to opponents giddy with their windfall of secrets. If Kondrashev had written this section of *Battleground Berlin* he might be forgiven for concluding that Blake blew the tunnel, Harvey and the CIA were snookered, and the army of translators and analysts back at CIA world headquarters were only spinning their wheels.

Murphy and Bailey think not. Maybe the KGB knew what was afoot even before the first CIA shovel touched earth, but so what? The tunnel went forward all the same; the KGB never warned Soviet military authorities, who chatted away without suspicion, and during the year the tape recorders were running the take was rich. According to Murphy and Bailey, "more than 350" officers in Soviet military intelligence were identified from conversations over twenty-five lines used by the GRU; "several hundred" Soviets were identified who worked for the supersecret "Ministry of Medium Machine Building," cover name for the Soviet nuclear weapons establishment; the CIA learned of and closed down a similar KGB operation to tap a US cable near Potsdam, and so on. The inventory provided is a long one, prompted, doubtless, by long-fermenting irritation at claims that everything picked up by the tunnel was just gossip and trivia. But the heart of the take was not specific secrets; it was a feel for the size and the preoccupations of the Soviet military, its plans for building East German and Polish military forces, and a deep sense of the web of communications which forms the central nervous system of an army.

Murphy and Bailey make their point nicely, but still—Blake knew. On the Allied side of the ledger are many small agents and defectors who betrayed the secrets of the East, but there is only one big one described in *Battleground Berlin*—Colonel Pyotr Popov, an intelligence officer for the GRU who volunteered to work for the Americans in Vienna on January 1, 1953. The first information sought from any defector was knowledge of plans for war, if any. Next on the list was knowledge of Soviet spies within Allied services, if any. But unlike the first question, the second rarely had a clear or definitive answer. Despite the sacred principles of compartmentalization and the "need to know," intelligence officers are curious, gossiping types, eavesdroppers and deskpeekers; they all carry a wealth of information in their heads. Debriefing them thoroughly can take months or even years, and the tiniest of clues can sometimes lead to big discoveries. The Russians and the Americans agree in considering Popov a major conduit of secrets, but the enduring interest of the case centers on the question of his arrest in Moscow on February 18, 1959.

There are two versions of what happened. The first says George Blake, attached to the SIS office in Berlin, learned of Popov's existence after Popov contacted the British there early in 1956, or later, in the spring of 1957, when one of his reports—"an intelligence bombshell" —described the contents of a frank speech by Marshal Georgy Zhukov. Soviet war plans, Zhukov said, called for reaching the English Channel on the second day of hostilities, a remark certain to attract excited attention in the West. Murphy and Bailey say the speech went to the SIS station in Berlin, where it must have been seen by Blake, and consequently must have been passed on to the Russians—thereby revealing a leak in Soviet military headquarters and providing the KGB spy-hunters with their first clue that something was amiss.

The problem with this theory is that Blake, in his memoir *No Other Choice*, insisted he had nothing to do with Popov's report, and Kondrashev backs him up. The former KGB officer says that the leak of the Zhukov speech did direct suspicion at Popov, who had been in the audience when Zhukov spoke, but he insists that the first clue (the fact the Americans and British knew about the Zhukov speech) came from a "friendly service." Blake and Kondrashev might both be lying as part of some deep operational game, or they might not.

Anyone interested in just how complex a counterintelligence case can become should read the fourteen pages in which *Battleground Berlin* lays out the intricate web of what was known to whom, through which channels, as the KGB's Valentin V. Zvezdenkov closed in on Popov, and the CIA later tried to figure out what had gone wrong. To say that the case was "watched closely" or "analyzed carefully" fails to convey the intensity with which each nuance of an unfolding case may be examined and weighed. The point at all times is to know what is really happening, who is really in control, what is true. As early as the spring of 1958 there were signs of a troubling KGB focus on Popov. A known Russian spy-hunter was reassigned to Popov's group. "More sinister," Murphy and Bailey write, "was the sudden interest taken in Popov by Lt. Col. Dmitry Fyodorovich Sknarin, who was responsible for counterintelligence...." Usually content to socialize with Popov's group, he suddenly began to take part in their volleyball games. "It isn't enough that they have informers among us," said one of Popov's buddies; "he even comes to observe us himself!"

Popov's last meeting with his handlers in Berlin took place on November 10, 1958. He was heading back to Moscow but seemed unworried; the biggest question on his mind was what to take home in the way of presents. The following February he was arrested, but for more than eight months Popov continued to operate under Soviet control, communicating more or less normally with his CIA handlers as it became increasingly clear things were definitely not right.[3] In October 1959 the game was ended with the noisy arrest of Popov and his CIA handler on a Moscow bus. There were many possible reasons for this long delay but the obvious one, chewed over at length by the CIA, would have been the KGB's desire to muddy the waters to obscure precisely how and when they discovered Popov was a traitor. The implication, of course, was that the means was one they might use again— Blake, for example, or even the ghastly possibility that the KGB had a mole at the heart of the CIA. *Battleground Berlin* wisely declines to enter this corner of the swamp, but only a few years after Popov's

---

3. It is worth noting here that the months during which Popov was strung along correspond to a similar period in the career of Oleg Penkovsky, another GRU spy for the CIA who was photographed by the KGB meeting a handler in Moscow in January 1962 but not arrested until September. In the Penkovsky case conventional wisdom says the KGB was watching him during those months, but not running him. If the conventional wisdom is wrong, and Penkovsky—like Popov—was under Soviet control during those months, we may need to look for a different explanation why Penkovsky failed to warn the CIA of Khrushchev's plan to put missiles into Cuba that fall. See Jerrold L. Schecter and Peter S. Deriabin, *The Spy Who Saved the World* (Scribners, 1993), my comment on the book in Chapter Nineteen, and an exchange of letters in *The New York Review*, June 24, 1993.

loss, counterintelligence analysts in the CIA shop run by James Jesus Angleton argued that the mole hypothesis was the right one.[4]

But if the Soviets in Berlin proved themselves masters of the intelligence game, frequently confounding the deepest ploys of the Allied intelligence services and seeding spies on an industrial scale throughout Germany, they ultimately failed in a deeper sense. This failure was rarely articulated and never grasped entire at the time, but it has become obvious since the end of the cold war that the Soviets fundamentally erred in depending so heavily on clandestine means of control and manipulation. "The most frightening aspect of the Cold War in Berlin," write the authors of *Battleground Berlin*, "was how poorly informed the Soviet leaders were...."

The fault lay in Moscow. Despite its record of success in the field the KGB was often ignored by the Politburo in the Kremlin. All intelligence agencies sometimes deliver unwelcome advice and find themselves frozen out of policy debates in response, but Moscow's dismissal of the KGB went deeper. On at least three occasions—when Stalin blocked Western access to Berlin by road and rail in 1948, when he gave Kim Il Sung permission to invade South Korea in 1950, and when Khrushchev allowed East Germany to split Berlin with a wall in 1961—the Soviet Union acted in a provocative and impetuous fashion without ever asking the KGB for its best guess about how the Western Allies would respond.

All three of these bold strokes ended badly for the USSR—the Berlin blockade with Stalin's surrender, the Korean War with the rearmament

---

4. The Great Mole Hunt has inspired a five-foot shelf of books ideal for rainy afternoons. Readers curious about the episode might consult Edward Jay Epstein's *Deception: The Invisible War Between the KGB and the CIA* (Simon and Schuster, 1989), discussed in Chapter Six; David C. Martin, *Wilderness of Mirrors* (Harper and Row, 1980); Tom Mangold, *Cold Warrior: James Jesus Angleton: The CIA's Master Spy Hunter* (Simon and Schuster, 1991); and David Wise, *Molehunt: The Secret Search for Traitors That Shattered the CIA* (Random House, 1992).

of Germany, and the Berlin Wall with an implicit confession to the world that the only way to keep the citizens of the socialist East at home was to lock them in. The first two might plausibly be dismissed as tactical errors resulting in tactical defeats, but the last—the lengthening shadow of the Wall—gradually stripped away every shred of legitimacy for the puppet regime propped up by the Soviets in East Berlin.

The Berlin Wall was fifteen years in coming, but the reason for it was implicit from the first moment German citizens were required to present papers as they crossed from the East to the West. The problem was a simple one: life was better in the West, at first a little better, then a lot better, finally so much better that some found it worth the risk of death. Both sides had been more or less equally devastated by Allied bombing and the last-ditch fighting demanded by Hitler as foreign armies closed in, but with peace, reconstruction in the West soon commenced, investment poured in, and the economy began to recover and eventually to boom, while in the East industrial machines were looted by the Soviets, war damage was left untouched once the streets had been cleared of rubble, the necessities of life were in short supply, opposition parties were outlawed, anti-Communist leaders were arrested, jobs were hard to find and poorly paid, and protest was repressed by the vast police apparatus referred to as "the Stasi."

According to Murphy and Bailey, the Gestapo of Nazi Germany at its peak had one police official for every 10,000 citizens. By the late 1980s the ratio in East Germany was one police official for 200. Little wonder that from day one the unhappy people of the East began to vote with their feet, decamping west in relentlessly increasing numbers—nearly 200,000 in 1960, more than 150,000 in the first seven months of 1961. The border between the two Germanies was relatively easy to close, but Berlin was a sprawling capital city entered from the east by a delta of local streets, rail lines, and thoroughfares. Subway and commuter trains passed freely back and forth between zones. There was no way to keep East Germans out of Berlin, no way to prevent their passing into the western half of the city, and, once they were there, no way to retrieve them. The city was open by solemn agreement but continued Soviet control of the East required an end to the hemorrhage.

Over the years BOB had speculated the Soviets might try to close the border at its most porous point—in Berlin—but Murphy and Bailey make no attempt to hide the depth of the CIA's surprise on the night of August 12, 1961, when East German soldiers began to put up barbed wire along the demarcation line. It was later concluded there had been plenty of evidence; any number of defectors or border crossers could have reported the stockpiling of brick, barbed wire, cinder blocks, railroad ties, steel tank traps, and the like. But the standard questions put to refugees had failed to get the right answers. Another CIA spy in the GRU, Oleg Penkovsky, learned about plans for the Wall a few days after the decision to build was reached in Moscow on August 6, but he was unable to contact his agency handlers.

The day the wall went up, *Battleground Berlin*'s co-author David Murphy was in Washington. He was summoned by Allen Dulles, who took him to the White House for a meeting with the President to discuss problem number one—the streets full of demonstrators in West Berlin. It would have been "legal" for the US military to tear down the Wall as fast as the East Germans put it up, but the risks of starting something it couldn't finish had stayed the American hand. The Murphy-Bailey account proceeds:

> It was a full house, and one could sense the group's frustration.... The president...made sure Dulles and Murphy realized that "our writ does not run in East Berlin." It was evident that Kennedy did not wish to hear Murphy argue that the border closure was unacceptable. But he did welcome insight into the problem of West Berlin morale.... They now needed reassurance that they would not be abandoned by the United States

and its allies. This explanation apparently made sense to the president. He responded by ordering Defense Secretary Robert McNamara to augment US forces in Berlin....

The building of the Wall ended the public humiliation of Moscow and its East German client but it did nothing to reconcile the citizens of the East to their fate. Over the next twenty-three years 200 people were killed trying to scale the Wall or cross the border elsewhere, a number which only suggests the true state of affairs. Instead of attempting to kill or jail all who wanted to leave, the East German government in 1963 adopted a more inviting course—they sold them. The East German lawyer who worked out the details, Wolfgang Vogel, established a price (based on the fiction of East German costs in schooling and training those who left), and negotiated it upward from time to time. Over the years East Germany sold 33,775 political prisoners and another 215,019 citizens seeking to join relatives already in the West for hard currency payments totaling 3.5 billion deutschmarks, nearly $2 billion at current values.

This traffic, which included numerous spies for both sides—the U-2 pilot Francis Gary Powers and the Soviet illegal arrested in New York City in 1957, Colonel Rudolf Abel; the BND mole Heinz Felfe, the HVA spy Gunter Guillaume (whose arrest toppled the government of Willy Brandt in 1974), the Soviet Jewish refusnik Natan Scharansky, among a total of about 150—is related in a fine book of a few years back, *Spy Trader*,[5] by the *New York Times* reporter Craig Whitney. What especially strikes the reader is Vogel's complacency about the comfortable living he earned as a broker of souls, sure that everyone saw him as he saw himself—a kind of good Samaritan and friend of man—and even dreaming at one point that the Nobel Prize for peace was within his reach.

---

5. Times Books, 1993.

But Vogel's hallucinations pale beside those of the GDR's not-quite-last leader, Erich Honecker, who fussed and preened over arrangements for the fortieth anniversary celebration of the founding of the GDR held on October 7, 1989. The guest of honor, Mikhail Gorbachev, seized the occasion to tell Honecker the play was over: Soviet troops would no longer come to the rescue of Moscow's clients in Eastern Europe. Honecker resigned in mid-October, the Wall came down on November 9, and early in the New Year mobs broke into the headquarters of the Stasi on Normannenstrasse and plundered the files. This at least the Stasi had seen coming. In his memoirs, *Man Without a Face*,[6] the East German spymaster Markus Wolf writes that in the two months before the break-in on January 15 "highly sensitive intelligence files were destroyed...."

But not all of them. A sudden flood of prosecutions by the reunified government of Germany a couple of years later was based on leads passed on by the CIA. Just how the CIA laid hands on this material remains unknown, but Wolf has an idea. For years the bureaucrats had been "seeking to centralize records." Even Wolf's boss, Erich Mielke, chief of the Stasi, "was desperate to have me provide a central index of agents. I refused pointblank." Wolf fears his successor in 1986, Werner Grossmann, ignored his parting advice "never to put the agent files onto any kind of computer disk." This is a modern corollary of the old intelligence axiom which says if you want to keep it secret, don't

---

6. For those interested in the intelligence war this is an important work, but its usefulness is undermined by the difficulty of knowing when the language is really Wolf's, and when it is that of his co-author, Anne McElvoy, a British journalist who has also written a book about East Germany. McElvoy appears to have written in English; Wolf is fluent in English but his first language is German. There are many small errors about dates and facts certainly known to Wolf, and occasional misuse of intelligence concepts and terms, such as calling the spies Kim Philby, George Blake, and Aldrich Ames "double-agents." How these gaffes slipped by Wolf is unclear. "As told to" books ought to be written in the language of the subject, and ought to be preceded by a careful announcement of how the work was done.

write it down. The reason is obvious. A computer disk is the kind of thing a man might put in his pocket as he departs for life in the West.

Wolf himself went East; he had grown up in Moscow, had been backed by Moscow for his job as chief of the HVA, had served Moscow faithfully in the decades that followed. Moscow protected him for a year but then the Communist Party was swept from power and the Soviet Union broke up following the collapse of a coup attempt in August 1991. Wolf returned to Germany to be tried and in 1996 received a suspended sentence for a comparative misdemeanor of long ago.

But even during all those years of fraternal work on the front lines of the class war Wolf sensed that Moscow felt no respect for the HVA, the Stasi, or East Germany. In June 1953, hurrying back to his office at the time of the riots in East Berlin that first served notice that Moscow was not winning hearts and minds in Eastern Europe, Wolf was arrested by Soviet troops and locked up in a cellar with other suspicious persons. "There," he writes, "I had a few hours to ruminate on who really ran things in our part of Germany!"

But what rankled most was Moscow's habitual failure to confide. The HVA shipped information to Karlshorst by the truckload; little came back. The first word Wolf got about the Berlin tunnel came the day the Soviets dug it up; the chief of the Stasi at the time, Ernst Wollweber, picked Wolf up in a Volkswagen Beetle and they hurried to the site. Later they learned that the Soviets had known about the tunnel for a year from their spy George Blake, but gave the East Germans no warning. "For them, intelligence generally flowed in one direction only." In August 1961 he learned of the Berlin Wall from news on the radio. "My first reaction was one of pure professional fury," he writes. His agents in the West were all cut off, in effect, behind the lines. There is a simple and bitter truth here. "I still refuse to accept the judgmental stance of those who say our system was built only on the Lie," Wolf writes. But he lived with the lie every day—the pretense that East Germany was the ally, not the creature, of the Soviet Union.

Behind all the hugger-mugger of spies and counterspies recounted in rich detail in *Battleground Berlin*, and in sparer form in *Man Without a Face*, lay the original question of the cold war: When would the Soviet armies go home? Their determination to stay on created a chronic threat of war. General Zhukov's "bombshell" of 1957—plans to reach the English Channel with Soviet armies on the second day of a general war in Europe—suggests what was really on the minds of spies and their masters throughout the cold war. Western strategists believed there was only one way to stop Zhukov or his successors—with nuclear weapons. Soviet strategists believed there was only one way to guarantee that Zhukov or his successors could get through—intimidate the West from using nuclear weapons.

There is very little about this essential theme of the cold war in *Battleground Berlin*, somewhat more in Wolf's memoirs. One of Wolf's major coups was Gunter Guillaume's theft, in the summer of 1973, of a report from West Germany's ambassador to Washington saying he had been warned by Henry Kissinger and President Nixon that "without technological reinforcement to NATO the Americans could no longer guarantee a nuclear first strike against a Soviet ground attack."[7] This constituted a confession that the Soviets were on the verge of attaining a long-sought goal of Soviet policy—"decoupling" the defense of the United States from the defense of Europe. Alas, the Soviets never knew; the handler carrying the documents spotted a surveillance team and in panic dumped the secrets into the Rhine.

---

7. The language is Wolf's—or Anne McElvoy's—paraphrase of the stolen document. It confuses a "nuclear first strike" (an all-out surprise attack intended to disarm an opponent completely) with "first use" (the willingness to escalate a military conflict by using nuclear weapons, presumably in a limited way). But despite the confusion the meaning is clear: Nixon and Kissinger were telling the West Germans they could no longer absolutely depend on Washington's willingness to treat an attack on Germany as an attack on the United States.

But that was certainly the sort of intelligence the Soviets wanted. Wolf says he was often pressed by the commander of Soviet forces in East Germany:

> "You [East] Germans are so good. Can't you get us some more of the coordinates?" he would say, alluding to the exact map locations of the NATO bases, which the Soviets wanted to knock out first in any nuclear conflict. With terrifying bonhomie he would continue, "We don't need your papers. All we need are those coordinates, and we can drop a bomb on them and slice right through the West."

The KGB, along with the rest of the Soviet military establishment, departed Karlshorst for Russia in 1992. The CIA's Berlin Operations Base was officially closed down two years later. "How could the GDR, the keystone of the Soviet position in Eastern Europe, have collapsed?" ask Murphy and Bailey. Their answer is that "the Soviet treasure trove of intelligence never shaped Soviet policy as it could have," that Soviet leaders never took account of the bitter dissatisfaction of East Germans, and that the brightest idea in Karlshorst was to sit tight behind the Berlin Wall until it was too late.

But Wolf claims something more for himself and his profession, including its practitioners on the other side. "The intelligence services," he writes, "contributed to a half-century of peace—the longest Europe has ever known—by giving statesmen some security that they would not be surprised by the other side." By peace of course Wolf means an absence of war—the only sort of war the two sides had prepared to fight, which was nuclear war. In avoiding that, Wolf insists, "I had my share." This is not an extravagant claim.

—*The New York Review of Books*, October 23, 1997

8

SAVING THE SHAH

HIS IMPERIAL MAJESTY Mohammed Riza Shah Pahlevi, Aryamehr, Shahanshah of Iran, did not cut a figure as imposing as his titles in the coup which saved his throne—for a time—back in August 1953. The coup wasn't his idea. He felt himself a prisoner in his own palace, was afraid to speak his mind even outdoors, shrank in royal circumlocution from the frank urging of his twin sister, Princess Ashraf, that the time had come to act. The British had put the Shah in power in 1941, when he was just twenty-one, but had since written him off as hopelessly irresolute. A British diplomat proposed a "pendulum theory" to explain the Shah's erratic soaring and plunging. In one mood he felt as dazzling as the gorgeous medals on his royal chest; he even told a French interviewer, years later, that God, personally, told him what to do. But the Shah's sense of destiny was only wind; he might go to bed a king and wake up in self-doubt and despondency, certain all was lost. He was far from being the ideal sort of man to seize power from a popular demagogue, but there was no one else in 1953 when the British and the Americans decided that Mohammad Mossadegh was slipping into the Russian orbit, and had to go.

Of course this is not quite the way Kermit Roosevelt describes the Shah in *Countercoup: The Struggle for the Control of Iran.** Restoring

---

* McGraw-Hill, 1979 (withdrawn from publication).

the Shah to power is probably the happiest memory of Roosevelt's life, and he is the friendliest of historians. But there is no disguising the tremulous man at the heart of Roosevelt's short, interesting, but problematic account of the events which have been rankling the Iranian national pride ever since.

About five hundred copies of Roosevelt's book had reached reviewers and bookstores in September 1979 when his publisher, McGraw-Hill, threatened with a libel suit in England by British Petroleum, abruptly cancelled the book's official publication and recalled the copies which had already gone out. The entire edition of 7,500—less the few hundred beyond McGraw-Hill's reach—was then pulped, for a loss of about $1.50 a copy. Second thoughts are not often so dramatic. Roosevelt, it appeared, had run afoul of Britain's Official Secrets Act in his original manuscript when he ascribed a role in the coup to the Secret Intelligence Service. The SIS protested to the Central Intelligence Agency, which then insisted that Roosevelt remove all references to British intelligence in the published version of his book. Since the British role had been a large one—even greater than Roosevelt had been ready to acknowledge—this left a considerable gap in the story. Roosevelt solved the problem by simply substituting AIOC—the Anglo-Iranian Oil Company—for SIS. As the successor to the AIOC, British Petroleum protested. Hence the book's withdrawal, so McGraw-Hill could print a new version amending the record.

According to a source at McGraw-Hill, Roosevelt went back to the CIA, and the CIA went back to the SIS, and it was agreed all around that the best way out of the mess was to publish the first version of the manuscript, which correctly ascribed a role to the British. This time, encouraged by a book club sale, McGraw-Hill printed 15,000 copies and scheduled publication for January 1980. But after the US embassy was occupied by Iranian militants in November 1979, Roosevelt asked McGraw-Hill to hold up distribution once again, until after the hostages were freed. The new copies of *Countercoup*—

apparently identical to the first except for the naming of the SIS—then sat in a McGraw-Hill warehouse, as much the hostages of history as the fifty Americans being held in Teheran.

The CIA's role in the 1953 coup has been an open secret since the late 1950s, one of the two public "successes," along with the Guatemalan coup of 1954, habitually cited by the partisans of covert political intervention as a tool in the cold war. One heard that Roosevelt had pulled off the coup pretty much on his own, with a handful of CIA officers and a suitcase full of money. This is still the way Roosevelt describes the operation in *Countercoup*, ignoring, for the most part, the long debate over Iran in the White House and State Department, and passing lightly over the confused political events in Teheran which precipitated the coup. The little he has to say on these matters comes down to sketching in the cast of characters. His associates are also scanted; he not only changes the names, and in some cases the physical descriptions, of other CIA officers but also reduces them to little more than walk-ons. More surprisingly, Roosevelt completely omits the parts played by Frank Wisner, then Roosevelt's boss as deputy director for plans, and by Wisner's chief of operations, Richard Helms. The US ambassador to Iran, Loy Henderson, is described by Roosevelt as being prissily nervous, and the British are left shadowy in the background. They proposed the project (apparently to Roosevelt himself) in London in November 1952, and thereafter were content with a secondary role in charge of radio communications maintained through a base on Cyprus.

The story Roosevelt tells, stripped of just about all its institutional trappings, has a lighthearted air, as if two or three fellows, not long out of school, had adroitly pulled the whole thing off with a word here, a few dollars there, a little bucking up at the crucial moment. This version of events is not so much untrue as it is incomplete, offhand, and unreflective, the sort of story an old man might set down for the pleasure of his grandchildren.

Roosevelt does not make a point of it, but the CIA's coup was very much the doing of President Eisenhower and John Foster Dulles, who dismissed Mossadegh's claims as an Iranian nationalist, and chose to conclude that secret Russian influence was the source of Iran's squabble over oil with Britain, which, in fact, had balked at negotiating a new and more equitable oil concession. Eventually Iran nationalized the AIOC, the British were expelled, and Mossadegh went to Truman and Dean Acheson for support and understanding. In late 1952 State Department analysts concluded that he deserved both.

All that changed with administrations. Roosevelt had already begun to plan the coup in the last months of Truman's term, and he got an okay to go ahead from the Dulles brothers in June 1953. In July he slipped secretly into Iran by car from Iraq, set up headquarters in a private house in Teheran (other sources say the basement of the US military mission), and proceeded to line up Iranian support for a switch from Mossadegh to General Fazlollah Zahedi, who had been interned during the war by the British on suspicion of pro-Nazi sympathies. The charges appear to have been only a convenient pretext for the British, but all the same, Roosevelt and Zahedi conversed in German, since Roosevelt had "practically no Farsi." (On the evidence of his book, the only Farsi he did have was "Zindabad Shah"—"Long live the Shah.")

Roosevelt's plan for the coup was very far from later heavy-handed CIA efforts involving paramilitary operations, military rebellions, émigré armies, and the like. He proposed that the Shah simply dismiss Mossadegh, which he had a clear constitutional right to do, but which was risky because Mossadegh was more popular than the monarchy. The Shah required a great deal of coaxing; the pendulum seems to have been at the self-doubting end of its arc. Roosevelt's description of their meetings richly suggests the flattery and appeals to self-esteem he must have resorted to at the time. The royal figure he describes is virtually carved in marble; it is only between the lines, and from other sources, that we can see the wavering man of flesh and blood. But finally the Shah was convinced that a loyal military unit, led by the chief of his imperial bodyguard, Colonel Nematollah Nassiry (later head of Savak), could successfully deliver the royal firman dismissing Mossadegh and appointing Zahedi in his place.

The attempt was made on Saturday, August 15, 1953, and it failed. Mossadegh had learned of the plan through a spy in the Shah's camp —apparently a double agent trusted by the CIA—and Colonel Nassiry was confronted by a hostile military unit when he arrived at Mossadegh's official residence. The undaunted colonel bluffed his way through the troops, delivered the firman to a house servant, and even demanded a receipt before surrendering to arrest by his opponents. The following morning, Sunday, August 16, Mossadegh announced on the radio that he was taking full control of the government, in effect deposing the Shah.

At this point Zahedi was still in hiding, the Shah instantly fled the country (Roosevelt disingenuously calls it a strategic retreat), and the CIA's coup appeared to have collapsed. But three days later, a mob of Iranians, hired with CIA funds (Roosevelt says the figure was roughly $75,000, but another source claims it was much higher), marched on Mossadegh's residence and was backed up at the critical moment by a military unit. General Zahedi emerged from hiding, having been helped into his uniform by a CIA officer, Howard ("Rocky") Stone, who buttoned his tunic. Mossadegh fled over a wall at the end of his garden, and the Shah prepared to return from his two days of exile in Rome. The night of the coup, General Zahedi's son, Ardeshir (who later became something of a Washington celebrity as the Shah's ambassador), went up to Stone at a victory party and said, "We're in... We're in... What do we do now?" The Shah himself, after his return, told Roosevelt, "I owe my throne to God, my people, my army—and to you!"

On his way home, Roosevelt stopped off in London and described these events to Winston Churchill, who was in bed recovering from a stroke; the prime minister dozed off periodically during the story, but complimented Roosevelt handsomely at the end. In Washington that September, Roosevelt repeated his story for Eisenhower and the Dulles brothers. "John Foster Dulles was leaning back in his chair. Despite his posture, he was anything but sleepy. His eyes were gleaming; he seemed to be purring like a giant cat." Later, Eisenhower secretly awarded Roosevelt the National Security Medal.

The story Roosevelt tells in *Countercoup* seems to be pretty much the story he told the old adventurer Churchill, a matter of confusion, intrigue, near misses, nail-biting, sudden triumph—a salty political string-puller's yarn, rich in circumstantial detail, but so thin in context as to reduce the coup to a kind of international high jinks. This can be explained partly by Roosevelt's temperament, which still retains much of the undergraduate's enthusiasm for the exotic, the thrilling, and the faraway. He is at his most appealing describing an opium factory which he visited in 1944 as an officer in the OSS. At the center of a subterranean chamber was a huge millstone turned by a camel. Roosevelt could not imagine how the camel had been coaxed and squeezed down the narrow winding stone passage to the grinding room. A kind of golly-gee-whiz air attaches to this passage, appropriate to a traveler's tale, but jarring when it carries over into the later account of political intervention.

At first look the motives for the coup seem to have been transparent. Before the coup, British oil interests were expelled from Iran. After the coup, a consortium of British and American oil companies was invited back in, with the British getting 55 percent and the Americans dividing up the remaining 45 percent among them. It is hard for an outsider to imagine that oil could have been far from the minds of the coup's planners, but according to Richard Cottam, an academic authority on Iran at the University of Pittsburgh, oil had little to do with it. The early 1950s were years of glut in the petroleum market, and one of Mossadegh's greatest problems was to find a replacement for the expelled AIOC. So long as they didn't really need the oil, the majors were inclined to remain aloof in solidarity with the British. For one thing, they did not want to encourage the other Middle Eastern oil states to make similar demands.

Unlike Roosevelt, Cottam speaks Farsi and has followed events in Iran closely since an interest in third world nationalism first took him to Teheran as a graduate student thirty years ago. "The explanation is anti-Communism," he said in an interview. "Roosevelt and Loy Henderson both saw Communists everywhere, and found it impossible to believe there might be liberal nationalists in Iran just as there are in the West. I've read all the documents, and when they're eventually declassified you won't find any conspiracy to get Iran's oil. The basic motive was fear of Communism. It's the old story."

According to Cottam and other experts on Iran, the Tudeh Party was small, well organized, and controlled by Moscow, but it did not support Mossadegh or any other leader of the "national front," which was a loose coalition of mostly educated, middle-class Iranians in favor of modernization and hostile to the Shah's embryonic (in 1953) ambitions to restore Iran to its ancient imperial glory. Roosevelt often cites the role of the Tudeh Party as proof of Mossadegh's ties to Russia, but in fact the two were hostile and Mossadegh actually ordered the army to chase the Tudeh off the streets the day before he was overthrown. Cottam does not sentimentalize the Tudeh or attempt to minimize its conspiratorial nature and hostility to Western interests. A year after the coup, a secret ring of some four hundred Iranian army officers (many American-trained) was discovered to be under Tudeh control. But Tudeh and the national front were poles apart, and US fears of a Soviet takeover in Iran through Mossadegh were purely chimerical.

Roosevelt presumably rejects this interpretation of events, but he offers only the most casual and factually unadorned charges of Soviet–Tudeh–Mossadegh collusion to support his own view. The odd thing here is that the United States, without significant interests in Iran before the coup, should have adopted the myopic, condescending, and self-serving British view of nationalists whose most radical claim was of a right to be treated as sovereign equals. Stranger still is the fact that the United States, the world's oldest republic with a written constitution, should have thrown its support to a monarch with archaic aspirations to absolute power. This strange infatuation can only be explained by a kind of schoolboy's awe of imperial pomp and circumstance, and the air of bubbling confidence in Roosevelt's book suggests he has still not found the time, nor the occasion, to question seriously whether we supported the right side in Iran in 1953 for the right reasons. Iran was backward, foreign, and far away, and that, for Roosevelt, was reason enough to jettison that loyalty to democratic principles he would have insisted on (one hopes) as a matter of course for his own country. This carelessness made him in effect, though probably not in manner, both arrogant and cavalier.

But *Countercoup* is not a book about policy; why we did what we did does not detain Roosevelt for long. It is a book about clandestine technique, a kind of guide for covert political manipulation. Other CIA people say Roosevelt has misrepresented events in a number of ways, slighting the role of key figures, misrepresenting the positions held by some CIA employees, and minimizing both the initial failure of August 15–16 and the importance of luck in the success of August 19. One CIA officer involved in the coup has been privately circulating a seven-page critique of Roosevelt's version of events. The exact truth about what happened is of course difficult for an outsider to pin down, but even so it is clear that this was a political, not a military, undertaking. It shares nothing with the crude military approach of the United States to the Bay of Pigs, or of Russia in Afghanistan. It can be argued that Roosevelt backed the wrong horse, in the long run, but at least it was an Iranian horse. The Americans served an important role as catalyst in the coup, but we did not carry it out ourselves, and we were never in a position thereafter to back up our allies with the sanction of arms, as Russia has done in East Germany, Hungary, and Czechoslovakia. Whatever it was that Roosevelt really did, he did it with a light touch, which was for the most part unnoticed at the time.

Roosevelt has argued, in *Countercoup* and newspaper interviews, that his success in Iran fatally dazzled Eisenhower and the Dulles brothers. A second "success" in Guatemala the following year, from which that country has never recovered, led inevitably to later failures in Syria in 1957, Indonesia in 1958, and Cuba in 1961, because the Dulles brothers had grown fond of the quick and dirty approach without regard to the real strength of local allies. Covert political manipulation of the sort that worked in Iran offered policymakers the one thing they couldn't resist—their way. If foreign leaders balked at the American view of matters, the CIA could simply brush them aside. When political measures failed to do the trick, a military approach was tried instead. By superficially logical steps the handful of men working for Roosevelt in Teheran grew into the exile army of Cubans that failed at the Bay of Pigs. Roosevelt probably exaggerates his opposition to the habit of intervention; he was still around for Operation Wakcful in Syria, by then Wisner's assistant deputy director of plans, with two legendary CIA adventurers as associates, Miles Copeland and Tracy Barnes. But the ghastly failure of Wakeful, which ended with the arrest (and in many cases the execution) of the CIA's local allies, must have confirmed Roosevelt's feeling that the ingredients of a successful coup had to be at least 90 percent of native origin.

Someday an Iranian historian, writing in Farsi, will explain what happened in 1953, giving due weight to the conflict of Islamic conservatism with the forces of Westernization which somehow opened a side door to the Shah, and allowed him to rule for twenty-five years. The revolution seems to have returned Iran to square one. The Ayatollah Ruhollah Khomeini, with his brooding, evasive eyes, and President Abolhassan Bani-Sadr, in his European suits, suggest an Iranian national schizophrenia beside which the Shah was an aberration and an irrelevance. Roosevelt put his thumb on the scale the last time the balance teetered in equilibrium, and one imagines that the Washington hard-liners who want to "unleash" the CIA would like to try again. But we ought to have learned there is no such thing as fixity in political arrangements.

Memory, on the other hand, is long. No one likes to see his country prodded and pulled by outsiders who can barely speak the language. The extraordinary hatred many Iranians feel for the United States was certainly not intended or anticipated by Roosevelt and his associates, but it was their doing all the same. By its nature a coup makes a handful of friends, and a great many enemies. The Shah was an Iranian, and he ruled with an Iranian army and an Iranian secret police. It was not the dithyrambs of Nixon and Carter that kept him in power. But the coup indelibly marked the Shah as a creature of the United States, and committed Washington to his success long after his real power had eroded.

CIA people would argue that the case of Iran proves the importance of secrecy. The trouble with the argument is that it obscures the heart of the American failure in Iran, which was not gabbiness on the part of Roosevelt and Allen Dulles, proud of their "success," but a deeper misreading of Iran itself. Recent events suggest we have not figured it out yet. It is this blinkered vision that is the most disturbing quality of Roosevelt's book, something it shares with a number of other CIA memoirs. As a CIA officer, Roosevelt was given broad operational freedom, but he was not encouraged to brood on the wisdom of what he was asked to do. That was "policy," and it was jealously guarded by the White House. The result, at Roosevelt's level, was a progressive intellectual numbness, the good soldier's devotion to the task at hand. He was more adroit than some of his successors, but like them he has little appetite for the broader question of whether what we did was really a good idea.

—The Nation, April 12, 1980

PART TWO

9

AND AFTER WE'VE STRUCK CUBA?

OCTOBER 1962 WAS not August 1914 because John Kennedy had learned the lessons of Munich, which may be summarized as follows: get angry in private, think before you speak, say what you want, make clear what you're prepared to do, ignore bluster, repeat yourself as often as necessary, and keep the pressure on. Where Kennedy learned the mixture of forbearance and resolution which lies at the heart of international peace and good marriages is a mystery; his mother and father were no better at solving problems than Neville Chamberlain and Adolf Hitler. But two recent books about the Cuban missile crisis show how, in a pinch, Kennedy managed to keep a serious argument from slipping out of control.

In retrospect it seems clear that the moment of maximum danger probably came in the first two or three days of the crisis, which began with the American discovery on Monday, October 15, 1962, of unmistakable evidence that the Soviet Union was building launch facilities in western Cuba for ballistic missiles carrying nuclear warheads. But in the course of a week of intense discussions in the White House, Kennedy and his advisers gradually turned away from proposals for an out-of-the-blue bombing raid on the missile sites and settled instead for a blockade of the island (soothingly called a "quarantine") by the US Navy with an unspecified promise of further action at some future but not distant moment to ensure that the offending missiles would be "removed"—either crated up and shipped back home or, if necessary, destroyed.

It was during this week, and especially during the first few days, that the fundamental question—war or peace?—was resolved. What tilted the balance was the passage of time and the nature of the discussion among Kennedy and his advisers—not the arguments themselves, but the manner in which they were conducted. Yet this emerges only tangentially and incidentally in these two books, both of which aspire to, and achieve, a breathtaking completeness in recounting what happened. It is between the lines that we can detect the peace being preserved. But what happened comes first.

The world at large learned simultaneously about the missiles and the American response from Kennedy's speech on the evening of Monday, October 22, and immediately feared the worst. Contemporary memoirs are filled with the desperate thoughts and plans of panic-stricken citizens who felt the end was near. The story which sticks in my mind was told to me by Victor Weisskopf, whose friend the physicist Leo Szilard, carrying his worldly belongings in a single suitcase, appeared on Weisskopf's doorstep in Switzerland within twenty-four hours of Kennedy's speech and solemnly announced: "I am the first refugee of World War Three." Szilard could be forgiven his alarm. Kennedy had issued a harsh demand and was plainly ready to back it up with military force. Would Khrushchev bend the knee and slink away, or call what he had ample reason—the Bay of Pigs, the Berlin Wall—to suppose was only the young President's bluff?

The crisis in the Cuban missile crisis ended halfway into the second day—Wednesday, October 24—when a meeting between Kennedy and his advisers was interrupted by a report that six Soviet ships had stopped in mid-ocean rather than challenge the American quarantine. It took a few minutes for the news, delivered by John McCone of the CIA, to sink in. A tape recording of the meeting includes a muffled remark followed by a bark of laughter from the national security adviser, McGeorge Bundy. It was probably at that moment, according to Ernest May and Philip Zelikow, the editors of *The Kennedy Tapes: Inside the White House during the Cuban Missile Crisis*, that Secretary of State Dean Rusk had leaned over to Bundy and whispered: "We're eyeball to eyeball and I think the other fellow just blinked."[1]

The racing of the public heart did not immediately abate during the following weeks of high-level talk and breathless newspaper headlines, but from that moment, Kennedy and his advisers knew that Khrushchev and his advisers had grasped and accepted the fateful truth of the correlation of forces: while Khrushchev could have chosen global war, he did not have the means to protect his ships at sea or his military forces in Cuba. Once it was absolutely clear that Kennedy meant to do what he said—remove the missiles one way or another—Khrushchev was quick to see he had to give in.

The big secrets of the American half of the Cuban missile crisis have long been known, but what the Russians were thinking and doing had to wait for the collapse of the Soviet state. There are many surprises in *"One Hell of a Gamble": Khrushchev, Castro, and Kennedy, 1958–1964*, by Aleksandr Fursenko and Timothy Naftali,[2] especially about the weird reporting of the KGB as Russia's steadily growing support for Castro's revolution brought anxiety in Washington slowly to the boil. But two major unknowns remain: why Khrushchev decided to make such a bold gamble in the first place, and with whom, if anyone, he discussed his prompt decision to cut his losses once the quarantine was in place. Fursenko and Naftali have had access to the minutes of meetings of the Presidium, the collegial body which ran the Soviet government, but nothing recorded on Thursday, October 25, explains Khrushchev's brisk decision to quit exchanging

---

1. Belknap Press/Harvard University Press, 1997.

2. Norton, 1997.

"caustic remarks" with Kennedy. "We must dismantle the missiles to make Cuba into a zone of peace," he said, suggesting that maybe the Americans would in return "give us a pledge not to invade Cuba." In any event, it was "correct and reasonable" to back off.

Andrei Gromyko, the foreign minister, and Rodion Malinovsky, the defense minister, said little. The very same Presidium that had approved Khrushchev's proposal in April—"Why not throw a hedgehog at Uncle Sam's pants?" Khrushchev had asked—now voted to reverse itself almost without debate. When he came to write his memoirs Khrushchev claimed that Kennedy's no-invasion pledge, soon given, made the missile gamble a huge success, but his colleagues evidently didn't take the same view, and when they got rid of him in 1964, they spoke of his dangerous "adventurism."

"*One Hell of a Gamble*" tells the whole story of the Soviet–American conflict over Cuba from the moment Castro's revolution triumphed in Havana on New Year's Day 1959, through his courtship dance with the Communists, the embrace of Moscow, the repeated invasion scares culminating in the CIA-mounted failure at the Bay of Pigs, Khrushchev's decision to put missiles on the island, the American discovery of the missiles, and the crisis which prompted their removal. During all this time Cuba was consistently overshadowed by the still more volatile conflict summed up in the word "Berlin"—the crisis of Communist authority (and of Russian prestige) represented by the tide of East German refugees escaping to the West through the jointly occupied capital.

On the one hand, Western powers were committed to maintaining their presence in the divided city, as had been agreed during the war. On the other, Khrushchev threatened measures which carried a real danger of aggression if the city was not handed over to the Russians, who could then pinch off the humiliating spectacle of East Germans voting with their feet. Failure to staunch the flow in Berlin meant that eventually *all* the East Germans would leave, the state would collapse, and the Russian presence in Central Europe would stand revealed for the military occupation that it was. Almost everything Khrushchev did during the years 1959–1962 was intended to help resolve his Berlin problem. Kennedy's timidity at the Bay of Pigs, when he permitted an invasion but denied it the air support required for success, was widely believed to have encouraged Khrushchev's bullying treatment at the Vienna summit later that spring, and his gamble in August when the Russians divided Berlin, first with barbed wire and then with a wall, guard towers, land mines, and orders to shoot to kill. Throughout the Cuban missile crisis Kennedy and his advisers kept looking for the Berlin angle, the sudden move, perhaps even a Russian seizure of the city, which would confront Kennedy with the truly agonizing choice of sticking to the stated Allied policy of defending Berlin with nuclear weapons, which meant global nuclear war; or letting Berlin go, which would serve notice on America's partners that her promises were some-time things, thereby encouraging further Russian provocations, much as Munich had encouraged Hitler, with similar consequences down the road. The biggest surprise of the Cuban missile crisis for Kennedy and his advisers was not Khrushchev's willingness to take the risk, but the fact that the entire drama played out without Berlin ever coming up.

All of this, and much more, is explained in both *The Kennedy Tapes* and *"One Hell of a Gamble."* A good deal of new material about Russian intelligence during the Cold War has been published in recent years but the authors of *"One Hell of a Gamble"* were appar-ently given access to the archives on an altogether grander scale. The result is an unusually comprehensive and rich account of the inner workings of the Soviet government during a moment of crisis. The principal Soviet intelligence organizations—the civilian KGB and the military GRU—are everywhere apparent, but their role is sometimes troubling in unexpected ways. Khrushchev may have read but cer-tainly did not register a July 1960 KGB warning that only two things could really be counted on to prompt a full-scale US intervention in Cuba: an attack on the American naval base at Guantánamo or the siting of Soviet missiles on the island. Two years later, when Khrush-chev decided on the second, he seems never to have asked for a KGB opinion on how the Americans might respond. The KGB, for its part, was sometimes guilty of having a tin ear when it came to separating the intelligence wheat from the chaff. For example, a June 1960 report from the head of the KGB, Aleksandr Shelepin, addressed to Khrush-chev personally, baldly claimed: "In the CIA it is known that the lead-ership of the Pentagon is convinced of the need to initiate a war with the Soviet Union 'as soon as possible.'" Not to be outdone, the GRU reported in March 1962 that an American plan for an out-of-the-blue nuclear attack on the Soviet Union the previous September had been foiled by the Soviet resumption of nuclear testing.

Both claims are completely without foundation but Fursenko and Naftali uncover no skepticism (nor any surprise or alarm, for that matter) on the part of the Soviet leaders privy to these extraordinary reports. The Americans, too, had unruly fears. In June 1962 Robert Kennedy asked a Russian confidant whom he rightly thought to be an officer in the KGB: "Tell me Georgi, is there anyone in the Soviet lead-ership who advocates a decisive clash with the United States?" The meeting and the question were reported to Moscow by the Soviet am-bassador, Anatoly Dobrynin. A true answer would have been that Khrushchev certainly wanted a little more give, but no clash, decisive or otherwise.

As the Cuban missile sites were readied in October Khrushchev must have felt he was going to get away with it. Kenneth Keating, a Republican senator, delivered garbled warnings about Soviet offen-sive weapons in his speeches but the administration seemed uncon-cerned. In a cable to the Kremlin, Gromyko reported a certain tension during a meeting with Kennedy on October 18 but he told his boss, "The situation in general is wholly satisfactory." That weekend the GRU picked up signals of American military activity but sounded no alarm. Khrushchev was unprepared for the news that Kennedy would give an unscheduled talk on prime-time television a few hours later. He called a meeting of the Presidium to consider what the US might be planning and how Russia should respond. Fear and panic were apparent in the room. "This may end in a big war," Khrushchev gloomily observed. Malinovsky urged calm and argued against giving Russian commanders in Cuba the authority to use nuclear weapons at will, saying he thought Kennedy's talk might only be "a pre-election trick."

An American air attack at that moment—something which virtually all of Kennedy's advisers had vigorously urged only a week earlier —would almost certainly have triggered a Russian military response and things might well have progressed rapidly to the only war ever named in advance: World War Three. What saved us emerges gradually in the course of the grueling seven hundred pages of verbatim transcripts of the meetings of Kennedy and his advisers, published for the first time in *The Kennedy Tapes*.

Ernest May and Philip Zelikow have convincingly placed the White House deliberations within the political and military context of the missile crisis itself. To this they have added a brilliant account of the shared assumptions which Kennedy and his advisers brought to their discussions: what they took to be the lessons of Munich; their reading of what worked or failed during the Berlin Blockade and the Korean War; their sense of what was at stake in Khrushchev's challenge over Berlin. Above all, May and Zelikow have vividly captured the individual styles and mannerisms of the leading players and the way they reacted to each other. Rusk, McNamara, Bundy, Bobby Kennedy, and the President himself have never been better described.

That John Kennedy had installed a taping system in the White House had long been known and the missile crisis transcripts were naturally expected to unveil a whole new family of secrets about American thinking and decision-making when the world teetered on the brink. But as it turns out, there are precious few secrets in these pages and pages of material—perhaps, in the end, only one: that presidents and their advisers, when they are not under public scrutiny, communicate as much with subtle emotional signals as they do with words. How else shall we interpret the murky exchanges that go on for pages, the obsessive tongue-tied repetitions, the sentences that occasionally parse but often convey no recoverable meaning? The alleged brilliance of these men David Halberstam once called "the best and the brightest" is rarely in evidence. The discussions in the week before and the week after Kennedy's quarantine speech had none of the intellectual rigor of proper debate, nor even the rough-and-tumble but structured exchanges of the kind you hear in a courtroom. What we have is a bunch of men talking, occasionally interrupting when a colleague seems to have run aground, or interjecting a sudden insight, but otherwise calm, receptive, patient, anxious to be understood, and always alert to the subtle shifts in the mood and the wishes of the President. On the whole, the men around Kennedy treated each other with respect, never resorting to sarcasm, made no effort to score points, let everyone have his say. A family counselor sitting in on these deliberations would have beamed with approval. There were exceptions, however. General Curtis LeMay, head of the Strategic Air Command, snorted contempt for anyone with second thoughts about an all-out air assault. And there is a sharp exchange between the director of the CIA, John McCone, and Bundy, as a meeting was breaking up; had the President been there both men would probably have continued to be on their best behavior.

But the words themselves—these are the puzzle. They don't make sense the way sermons and book reviews make sense. The protagonists seem to have no difficulty following the drift, but the reader of the transcripts thirty-five years later is frequently baffled. Consider the following exchange from the transcript of a meeting on Thursday, October 18, before the discovery of the missiles has been made public. McNamara and Bobby Kennedy are discussing the relative merits of a blockade and a military attack:

MCNAMARA: At the moment I lean to the blockade because I think it reduces the very serious risk of large-scale military action from which this country cannot benefit under what I call Program Two [rapid introduction of military action]. Russian roulette and a broken alliance.

[Someone echoes: Russian Roulette.]

ROBERT KENNEDY: What are the chances that you've got to say to him: "They can't continue to build these missiles. You're going to have to keep them flying all the time?" Well, at night it looks a little different than it did the next morning.

MCNAMARA: Oh, he's not going to stop building. He's going to continue to build.

ROBERT KENNEDY: [Unclear] though, Bob?

MCNAMARA: This goes back to what you said—this type of blockade. I'm not sure you can say that.

ROBERT KENNEDY: Are you going to let him continue to build the missiles?

MCNAMARA: This goes back to what you begin to negotiate. He says: "I'm not going to stop building. You have them in Turkey. You've acted by putting the blockade on. That's done."

ROBERT KENNEDY: Then you let them build the missiles?

MCNAMARA: Then you talk.

AMBASSADOR LLEWELLYN THOMPSON: Is this on the assumption that he would run the blockade?

MCNAMARA: No, no. They have enough inside that they can continue the construction.

ROBERT KENNEDY: We tell them they can build as many missiles as they want?

MCNAMARA: Oh, no. What we say is: "We're going to blockade you. This is a danger to us. We insist that we talk this out and the danger is removed."

ROBERT KENNEDY: Right. But now they just go ahead and build the missiles.

MCNAMARA: [responding to an interjection] Overflights, definitely.

ROBERT KENNEDY: They put the missiles in place, and then they announce that they've got atomic weapons.

MCNAMARA: Sure. And we say we have them in Turkey. And we're not going to tolerate this.

ROBERT KENNEDY: What is the relationship then between the blockade and the danger?

MCNAMARA: Well, all this time Castro is being strangled.

THOMPSON: Why wouldn't you say that, if construction goes on, that you would...

MCNAMARA: Well, I might, I might. But that is a more dangerous form of the blockade.

GENERAL MAXWELL TAYLOR: What is your objection to taking out the missiles and the aircraft?

MCNAMARA: My real objection to it is that it kills several hundred Russians, and I [unclear]...

After a few more exchanges Dean Rusk finally suggests: "I think we've got to pursue this further, and, Bob, I think that perhaps we could detail Alex [Alexis Johnson] and Paul [Nitze] and Tommy [Thompson] to sketch in the body of these [unclear]—and get together as a group and..."

This exchange is elusive; its exact meaning seems to hover just out of reach. Other passages are simply incomprehensible as Kennedy's advisers converse with each other in a semi-coherent shorthand of sentence fragments, truncated questions, vague allusions, swallowed words, repetitions, deferential nods and shrugs, and miscellaneous noises of objection, assent, qualification, emphasis. There are pages so opaque and unrecoverable that it seems one could evolve a whole new perspective on spoken language as depending less on grammar and syntax than on a kind of emotional semaphore.

What becomes clear in the course of these often tedious discussions is that men in groups don't so much try to figure things out—an intellectual process depending heavily on articulation—as feel things out: to weigh what they are planning to do, and their reasons for doing it, by consulting their gut. What Kennedy and his advisers felt in the first shock of discovery at their initial meeting on the morning of Tuesday, October 16, was anger and resolution and an untroubled readiness to send the US Air Force to destroy the missiles and the launch sites, details to follow. But as the details came in, it became apparent that the hundred or so sorties at first contemplated would more likely be many hundreds or even thousands, that thousands of Russians would inevitably be killed, that at least some of the missiles were virtually certain to survive intact, and that about Russia's response and the ultimate consequences there was no telling. By the time of their second meeting on Tuesday afternoon, Kennedy's advisers and the President himself had begun to cool.

> McNAMARA: The second thing we ought to do, it seems to me, as a government, is to consider the consequences... I don't know quite what kind of world we live in after we've struck Cuba...

That idea is left hanging. There follows much back and forth of we-do-this, they-do-that. Then George Ball introduces a new phrase: "This coming in there, a Pearl Harbor, just frightens the hell out of me as to what goes beyond..."

> BUNDY: What goes beyond what?
> BALL: What happens beyond that. You go in there with a surprise attack. You put out all the missiles. This isn't the end. This is the *beginning*, I think.

Pearl Harbor was invoked from time to time over the following days, as the archetype of a sneak attack which would betray America's highest ideals and traditions, an invitation to international criticism, a bad move in the propaganda war. What was never explicitly mentioned, but seems to have been fermenting just below the level of consciousness, was the widespread American reaction to Pearl Harbor itself—the implacable fury at the killing of so many Americans and the impulse to strike back. By the afternoon of Saturday, October 20, McNamara had absorbed the point clearly and ticked it off last on his list of four advantages of a blockade over an air assault delivered without warning. This meeting was not taped; the note-taker recorded: "It avoids a sudden military move which might provoke a response from the USSR which could result in escalating action leading to general war."

Another point which nagged at the group, and especially bothered Kennedy, was the difficulty they all found in explaining why Soviet missiles in Cuba justified a confrontation, but American missiles in Turkey did not. In the end the Turkish missiles were quietly added to the price America paid for Khrushchev's removal of his own missiles in Cuba, but throughout the Kennedy group's deliberations, the question of Turkey kept resurfacing. They knew it was different but could not immediately identify why. The reason was not pinned down until Kennedy finally delivered his speech (written by Ted Sorensen) on Monday evening, October 22. Khrushchev's move did not create a danger where none had existed, Kennedy conceded; Americans were already vulnerable to Soviet ICBMs, but

> this secret, swift and extraordinary build-up of Communist missiles—in an area well-known to have a special and historical relationship to the United States and the nations of the western hemisphere, in violation of Soviet assurances, and in defiance of

American and hemispheric policy—this sudden, clandestine decision to station strategic weapons for the first time outside of Soviet soil—is a deliberately provocative and unjustified change in the status quo which cannot be accepted by this country if our courage and our commitments are ever to be trusted again by either friend or foe.

Khrushchev's response to Kennedy's speech, as reconstructed by Fursenko and Naftali, pretty much mirrored that of Kennedy and his advisers to the arrival of the missiles in Cuba: an initial bristling of anger and resolution, followed by second thoughts and cooling tempers as Khrushchev sorted out what mattered from what did not. He might have chosen war, but why? He could not win locally, in the seas around Cuba or on the island itself, and war where he was strong, in Europe, could not be contained or limited. The sensible course was to extract such concessions as he could get, and then go home.

There was a great deal of talk in the White House during the first week of the missile crisis but in the end the President made only two decisions which mattered: that he would not tolerate Soviet missiles in Cuba, and that he would say so in public before he did anything about it. If Kennedy had blustered but done nothing, or if he had blown the missiles and their Soviet crews sky-high in a sneak attack, all sorts of horrors might have followed. What *The Kennedy Tapes* offer is not more secrets—of which enough already—but the salutary example of intelligent statesmanship.

Such crises, routine at home, are rare among nations. Kennedy did not live to write his account of the lessons learned from the Cuban missile crisis, but it would probably have sounded very much like the sort of thing marriage counselors say every day to marriage partners at the breaking point: leave your anger in the office, decide what you want, if you want to make up, say so; if it's over, say that; draw the line and make it clear, set your limits, stick to your guns—all those common-sense things which Kennedy's parents, like Neville Chamberlain, got completely wrong.

—*The London Review of Books*, November 13, 1997

IO

THE HEART OF THE STORY

THINGS BEGAN TO go wrong when John F. Kennedy was murdered in November 1963, but not in the way you might think. We recovered from Kennedy's loss quickly enough, but we're still suffering from the questions left open by his death. Everybody has his own theory about the murder, some of them baroque in their conspiratorial complexity, some pugnaciously dismissive. My own theory is that Kennedy's murder marked the moment when we stopped thinking about what we might become as a nation, and started looking for whom to blame.

It is not just easy, but almost irresistible, to make fun of the Kennedy assassination skeptics with their Oswald doubles and triples, the ectoplasmic gunmen on the grassy knoll, the phantom CIA agents hovering over Oswald's shoulder, the logical proof that Oswald, the so-so Marine sharpshooter, could not have fired the fatal shots. They remind me of those arguments that Marlowe or Bacon must have written *Hamlet* for no better reason, when you got down to it, than that writing *Hamlet* must have been beyond a bumpkin of no breeding from Stratford-on-Avon. But conspiracy-spinning isn't amusing, because it isn't a game. Doubt has become the last frontier of the American dissidents, the point they will not yield. Once upon a time they believed America might transcend racism, poverty, injustice, and war; now they are hunting villains among the ecto-plasm. If that strikes you as funny, well ... it doesn't me.

I realize this is a long preamble for another book about the Kennedy assassination, but I wish it were longer still. If I had four or five issues of *The New York Times Book Review* to work with, I might lightly skim the evidence for conspiracy and give you a taste of the desert where the skeptics live. There is no water or life there, just the odd "fact" surrounded by thorns. If I could take you into that wilderness for a week or two, you might appreciate more readily what a miraculous book Priscilla Johnson McMillan has written, miraculous because McMillan had the wit, courage, and perseverance to go back to the heart of the story, and the art to give it life.

The Oswald who emerges in *Marina and Lee*[1] was a young man badly put together—erratic, lonely, proud, impatient, and violent. His ambitions were soaring, his abilities uncertain, his education limited to what he had picked up in public libraries despite the reading dis-ability called dyslexia. From the age of fifteen he considered himself a Marxist-Leninist. His "ideas" were unsophisticated, bits and pieces of naive leftism, but he treasured them the way a lonely boy might treasure his collection of baseball cards.

Often unemployed, fired from the only job he ever liked, and bored to distraction with the rest, Oswald spent hundreds of hours working on his "ideas," drawing up manifestoes and political programs, ana-lyzing the failures of Soviet society as he saw them, working in a radio factory in Minsk after his defection to Russia in 1959. His dyslexia forced him to copy and recopy everything he wrote, and even then his letters and half-finished essays were riddled with what appear to be the spelling errors of a near-illiterate.

In Russia Oswald had married Marina Prusakova. She was pretty enough, but it was her thinness that appears to have captured Oswald's

---

1. Harper and Row, 1977.

heart. Fat women reminded him of his mother, a grasping, self-centered, at times hysterical woman, all jowl and self-pitying complaint, who placed Oswald and his two brothers in an orphanage for reasons of convenience. Marina liked Oswald because he was neat and polite, because he was an American and made her girlfriends envious, and because he was the only man she had ever known with an apartment of his own. This was no small matter in overcrowded Russia. Marina's uncle, a colonel in the Ministry of Internal Affairs (MVD), had already rejected one of Marina's suitors out of hand because he had no apartment; the colonel resented Marina's presence in his home and made it clear that he certainly didn't want a nephew-in-law moving in as well.

Looked at from the outside, the marriage was a disaster from the beginning. Oswald was secretive, overbearing, and short-tempered. After he returned to the United States with his wife and young daughter in the summer of 1962, a streak of physical cruelty emerged. He horrified the Russian community of Dallas, where they moved, by the ferocity with which he sometimes beat his wife, by his cruel refusal to let Marina learn English or make friends of her own, and later, in 1963, by his threat to send her back to Russia alone.

Life with Oswald was so bad Marina frequently threatened to leave him for good, but at the same time she loved him, blamed herself for their arguments, pitied his loneliness, forgave his violence, hoped Oswald would outgrow the "ideas" that no one but he took seriously. Once, in the summer of 1963, when their relationship was strained to the snapping point, Marina found Oswald in the kitchen, sobbing inconsolably. Life defeated him at every turn; he didn't know what to do. She took him in her arms, comforted him, told him it would be all right, they would find a way. Twisted and painful as it was, Oswald's relationship with Marina was the closest to being normal of any throughout his life.

Marina was familiar enough with Oswald's "ideas" but she did not grasp his desperate readiness to act on them until April 1963. Earlier that year Oswald had ordered a pistol by mail, and later a rifle and four-power telescopic sight, in the name of "A. J. Hidell," apparently chosen because it rhymed with Fidel, the name he wanted to give the son he expected.

On Wednesday, April 10, 1963, Oswald confessed to Marina with tears in his eyes that he had lost his job in a photo studio, the only one he had ever liked. That night he failed to come home at the usual time. Marina found a note in Russian on his desk, giving meticulous instructions about how she was to live in his absence. "If I am alive and taken prisoner," the note concluded, "the city jail is at the end of the bridge we always used to cross when we went to town. . . ."

"At 11:30," McMillan writes, "Lee walked in, white, covered with sweat, his eyes glittering.

"'What's happened?' Marina asked.

"'I shot Walker.' He was out of breath and could hardly get out the words.

"'Did you kill him?'

"'I don't know.'"

The next day—half-relieved, half-disappointed—Oswald learned he had missed. Typically, he blamed his target. At the last moment, he told Marina, Major General Edwin A. Walker, U.S.A. (Ret.), a champion of the John Birch Society, had moved his head. There was a flurry of notices in the press, but no evidence turned up to implicate Oswald. Later he showed Marina the elaborate plan he'd drawn up for Walker's murder, complete with maps and photographs and a statement of Oswald's political "ideas." Marina made him burn the incriminating documents, but she kept his note of instructions and made him swear never to do such a thing again.

McMillan's description of this episode is characteristic of her book, rich in brilliant detail, passionate, and compelling. Oswald's desperate personal unhappiness before his attempt, the emotional aftershock (for one whole night he was literally in convulsions), the calm that followed, are all of a piece. They describe a man with a capacity—not reasons—for murder. McMillan's painstaking, intimate account of Oswald's last months proves one simple, important point: he was no phantom, but a man with an hour-by-hour existence like any other. If she does not know exactly why he wanted to kill Walker or Kennedy —how is one to extract a reason from the irrational?—she nevertheless demonstrates that nothing he is said to have done contradicts what we know he was. McMillan's portrait is very dense indeed. If the skeptics are to preserve their conspiracies, they will have to squeeze them into the corners of Oswald's life. McMillan achieves with art what the Warren Commission failed to do with its report and twenty-six volumes of lawyerly analysis, testimony, and supporting evidence. She makes us *see*.

Or made me see, at any rate. The skeptics, I suspect, are in no mood to be convinced. The word is already out on McMillan in buff circles: Her book can be dismissed. She is unreliable, not to be trusted. She may have been working for the "State Department"—or worse—when she had an interview with Oswald in Moscow back in October 1959. On top of that, McMillan's principal source was Marina Oswald, who was the niece of a colonel in the MVD (Marina believes he was in charge of convict labor working on timber projects in Belorussia.) How can you trust the work of someone working for the "State Department," based on information from the niece of a colonel in the MVD? At best, the buffs say, *Marina and Lee* is a fantasy; at worst, part of the cover-up.

The people who are taking this position ought to be ashamed of themselves; they are accusing McMillan of the same failings—either secret motives or ad hominem arguments—so often brought against themselves. The argument is confusingly circular: you can't trust the book because you can't trust McMillan, and you can't trust McMillan because you can't trust Marina. That follows only if you assume

Marina was a witting party to a conspiracy to kill Kennedy. If you don't believe that—and very few assassination buffs do; they look for the villains elsewhere—then her testimony is as good as anyone's else.

One skeptic who does include Marina in the conspiracy is the British solicitor Michael Eddowes, whose book, *The Oswald File*,[2] is typical in that it depends heavily on existing documents (admittedly voluminous) and offers a tortured and intricate rationale for what might be explained more simply. Eddowes believes that Oswald was actually "Oswald"—a Russian agent who impersonated Oswald in order to kill Kennedy. He offers exactly one piece of evidence for this bold conjecture, the fact that Oswald's height is given as five feet nine inches on some documents, and five feet eleven inches on others. That's it. For the rest, he simply marches his straw "Oswald" through the familiar story, occasionally pausing to reinterpret the known facts in light of his theory. (E.g., Marina and "Oswald" only pretended to fight, in order to discourage suspicion they were really in cahoots.)

Eddowes is untroubled by the fact that Oswald's mother, brothers, and other relatives never doubted that Oswald was Oswald, and even copes with the fact that Oswald's fingerprints taken while he was in the Marines in 1956 match those of "Oswald" after Kennedy's murder in 1963. A Russian agent, he says, switched files in the FBI. The only reason Eddowes thinks "Oswald" was a Russian, so far as I can tell, is that logic demands the imposture take place after the real Oswald left his family for Russia in 1959, and before the phony "Oswald" married Marina. It would be too much to ask us to believe that the switch took place without Marina having noticed.

One might raise any number of objections to this theory: Why would "Oswald's" wife and co-conspirator tell the Warren Commission about the attempt on Walker's life? Why would "Oswald" deliver a threatening letter to the FBI only days before Kennedy's murder?

---

2. Clarkson N. Potter, 1977.

Why did "Oswald" and Marina both write to the Soviet embassy, when the KGB surely knew their letters would be routinely intercepted by the FBI? Why would the Russians go to such trouble to have "Oswald" spend two years hanging around Texas in a succession of blue-collar jobs? And so on, ad infinitum. But there is only one question that really matters: Why would the Russians deliberately choose to impersonate a man with a known Russian connection, who was bound to attract the attention of American intelligence services? The idea behind imposture is to hide connections, not to reveal them.

Eddowes's book is so breathtakingly bad—woodenly written, implausible, contradictory, lacking in evidence—that a real conspiracy theorist might darkly suspect it was intended to discredit the genre. The quality of their work is generally a lot higher than that.

But are the skeptics right? Most of them now seem to believe that Oswald was at least *involved* in Kennedy's murder—a quantum jump in credence—but that others must have put him up to it. Their reasons for thinking so are severely particular, and any book dealing with the whole body of evidence and conjecture in a sober, analytical way will necessarily include more footnotes than there are stars in the heavens.

Priscilla McMillan approached her subject in quite a different spirit. From the moment she heard of Oswald's arrest—"My God!" she told a friend, "I know that boy!"—McMillan wanted to know why Oswald had killed Kennedy. Beginning in August 1964, she spent seven months talking to Marina, then wrote her book in fits and starts over the following thirteen years. It is very much Marina's story—there was apparently nothing she was unwilling to discuss—but McMillan also conducted numerous interviews with people who had known both of them.

McMillan never seems ever to have doubted for a moment that Oswald did it, or that he did it for reasons of his own. He had his "ideas"—he seems to have rationalized the assassination as a salutary shock for a complacent public—but his real motive emerges as a desperate desire to transcend the obscurity and impotence to which fate was inexorably confining him. A failure in every job he held, in danger of driving away his wife and child, ignored or condescended to whenever he brought up his "ideas," reluctantly accepted by the Russians in 1959 and rejected by the Cubans in 1963, Oswald refused to slip under with only a whimper. He killed Kennedy for the same reason he fired a shot at Walker: to prove he was there, and counted.

It is not at all easy to describe the power of *Marina and Lee*. Its texture is rich and convincing, as painful as the events it describes. It is far better than any book primarily about Kennedy, with the unsettling result that the assassination is experienced from the wrong end. McMillan follows Oswald's life with such fidelity and perception that it is *his* death which hurts in her final pages, not Kennedy's. Other books about the Kennedy assassination are all smoke and no fire. *Marina and Lee* burns. If you can find the heart to read it, you may finally begin to forget the phantom gunmen on the grassy knoll.

—*The New York Times Book Review*, October 30, 1977

11

THE MIND OF THE ASSASSIN

IF JACK RUBY had trusted the American legal system to deal with the killer of Jack Kennedy, or if he had been delayed another five minutes at the Western Union office where he'd gone to send a money order that Sunday morning, or if he had been halted at the door of the Dallas police station, or if he had been searched and his gun seized, or if his gun had been deflected and his bullet had gone two inches either way, then Norman Mailer's leviathan volume *Oswald's Tale: An American Mystery*,[1] along with many of its predecessors, would never have been written. Lee Harvey Oswald in prison for decade after decade— surfacing in the news whenever parole boards met, but otherwise forgotten, like Sirhan Sirhan, James Earl Ray, Arthur Bremer, John Hinckley—would have faded back down to size. It is Oswald dead and unexplained that excites suspicion. We needed a good long look in order to forget him.

One of the questions Oswald eventually might have answered was, Why Kennedy? The twenty-six volumes of evidence collected by the Warren Commission in its investigation of the assassination reveal nothing in Oswald's life to match Mailer's long obsession with this president. Some months before Oswald smuggled his Italian rifle into

1. Random House, 1995.

the Texas School Book Depository, he used it to take a shot at a very different target, Major General Edwin A. Walker, while he sat at his desk one night in Dallas in April 1963.

Why Walker? The retired general had been in the news. He had a small reputation as a right-wing zealot and demagogue. He lived only a bus ride away. Local newspapers reported his return from a well-publicized speaking tour a day or two before Oswald was fired from a printing company, where he held the only job he ever liked. Oswald had recently purchased the rifle by mail for $22. His marriage to Marina Prusakova was a dank hell of hurt feelings. So Oswald scouted Walker's residence, approached it by dark, fired a single shot, and then hurried home to listen breathlessly to the radio to learn if he had succeeded. He had not.

Oswald told Marina, "Look how many people would have been spared if somebody had eliminated Hitler." But Oswald could have made no serious case that Walker was really an embryonic Hitler. Walker was little more than a name to him. It would be fairer to say that Oswald was in a murderous mood and Walker happened by.

That such a blind and meaningless chain of contingency could be all the explanation offered by history for the long national trauma of the murder of John F. Kennedy is more than Norman Mailer is willing to accept without a struggle—an 828-page struggle, in point of fact. In *Oswald's Tale* Mailer argues that if we ascribe this great event to Oswald acting by himself, prompted by his own prosaic agonies, guided by luck to hit a moving target at eighty-eight yards when he had missed Walker at thirty-five, then we concede that "we live in a universe that is absurd." This Mailer is not about to do. "It...is more tolerable," he says, if we can see Kennedy's killer as "tragic rather than absurd."

So Mailer's self-appointed task in his twenty-eighth book is to provide Oswald's life with some stature beyond a few seconds of lucky shooting. Previous attempts to give Kennedy's murder a cause as big as the consequence have generally tried to dismiss Oswald as little more than a plain foot soldier—a patsy—in a dark machine of conspiracy. Mailer tells us he began his own existential errand "with a prejudice in favor of the conspiracy theorists." But despite much probing of the Warren Commission's lone-assassin version of the deed, it is pretty clear that from the outset Mailer was not really looking for, and certainly did not expect to find, phantom shooters on the grassy knoll, rogue CIA officers, KGB specialists in assassinations ("wet affairs"), anti-Castro zealots, Mafia hit men, or any of the other candidate conspirators provided by central casting over the years. What Mailer went looking for was the soul of the man who squeezed the trigger.

Oswald's Tale is two books. They are completely different in style and method. Either one of these books published alone would have been a minor affair. The two together are breathtaking in ambition and ask more than readers may be prepared to give. Let's look at them in order.

In the fall of 1959 in Moscow, the former marine Lee Harvey Oswald "defected" to Russia—that is, he made such a scene that Soviet authorities reluctantly granted his application for residence. For thirty months he lived in the Belorussian city of Minsk, where he worked (none too hard) in a factory that assembled radios, lived in a one-room apartment grand by Soviet standards, eventually learned pretty good Russian, married a Russian woman, and was watched with obsessive care by the local office of the KGB. In May 1962, after a year of struggle with Soviet and American bureaucracies, Oswald engineered his return to the United States with his new wife and infant daughter.

While the cold war lasted, this blank period of Oswald's life offered a kind of terra incognita for the plotting required by assassination theorists if their conspiracies were to be plausible. One British writer, for example, argued that the real Oswald had been replaced during the Minsk years by a Soviet look-alike who then "returned" to America, killed Kennedy, and was exposed (by the British author) only after an autopsy revealed that the dead Oswald was too tall to be the real Oswald. This bizarre tale depended heavily on the fact that investigators could not go to Russia, let alone Minsk, and nose around.

But the terra was not really incognita. A rich and vivid account of Oswald's life in Minsk was published in 1977 by Priscilla Johnson McMillan after extended conversations with Oswald's widow. Despite strong reviews (including an enthusiastic one by me), McMillan's book, *Marina and Lee*,[2] made no deep impression on the public, which was unready to recognize, much less accept, Oswald's humanity, while the professional assassination scholars darkly suspected that Marina (and perhaps even McMillan!) might be part of the plot.

It was into this still (relatively) virgin territory that Mailer entered after the collapse of the Soviet Union in 1991, armed with promises of access to one-time KGB officers and previously secret files as well as to the many former Soviet citizens who had known Marina Prusakova or Oswald during his years in Minsk. The result of six months of interviews by Mailer and his colleague Lawrence Schiller with about fifty Russians is "Oswald in Minsk with Marina," the roughly 350-page self-contained "Volume 1" of *Oswald's Tale*.

Oswald was only twenty when he arrived in Minsk. His experience of the world had been limited to a stint in the marines. He was severely dyslexic, had done poorly in school, had been moved repeatedly by his hysterically narcissistic mother throughout his childhood, fancied himself a student of Marxism, and had begun a "Historic Diary" to record his discoveries in the homeland of communism. Oswald's Russian was self-taught and rudimentary. He had no skills. He tended to fall in love with every woman who crossed his path.

The world Oswald found in Minsk was colorless, impoverished, lonely, and dull. His friends all put in six-day workweeks and went home to cramped lives in tiny apartments. They yearned for material

---

2. See Chapter Eleven.

possessions of the humblest sort, were a little awestruck at knowing an actual American, trembled when called on the carpet by "the Organs," as they called the secret police. The young men Oswald knew were all looking for girls, the women were looking for husbands, and Marina and Lee, after the twists and turns usual to courtship, found each other. Some marriages go wrong slowly over years; Marina and Lee appear to have plunged into pain and recrimination almost immediately, and while Marina thought that in some ways—sexually, for example—things gradually improved during their years together, to Mailer their marriage seems like the death of a thousand cuts.

All of this is described wonderfully well. Mailer's account adds many new characters and incidents to the story told by McMillan, but it is also distinguished by a brilliant linguistic invention, a kind of Mailer-patent Russian-English that captures Russian rhythms not only of language but also of thinking and feeling about love, work, and the ways of the world. Oswald's Intourist guide when he first arrived in Moscow in 1959 was a young woman named Rimma Shirakova. After a suicide attempt that persuaded the authorities to let Oswald stay, Mailer writes in a typical passage, "Rimma's relationship with Lee became a good deal closer. He was very much like a relative now— but not a brother, not a boyfriend, in between. He wanted to kiss her and was ready to try, but she didn't want that. She never kissed him at all, not ever.... Certainly not. She had a boyfriend.... A Russian writer said once, 'It's better to die than to kiss without love,' and good girls were of that same opinion. If she didn't love him and didn't want close relations, then she should not kiss. So she patted him on his hand. Enough. Her psychology."

The style of "Oswald in Minsk with Marina" is like a novel stripped of everything but the story. There are no cumbersome asides to track great events offstage, no boring travelogues, no Tolstoyan speculations on fate and history. What we get is Oswald plain.

In this marvelous book within a book we learn two things. The first is that Oswald was unhappy to the root. When he got what he wanted, he grew restless and angry and ruined what he had. The second contribution of "Oswald in Minsk" to the story of the Kennedy assassination is to be found in Mailer's account of the investigations of two pseudonymous officers of the KGB, whose job was to establish whether or not Oswald had been deliberately inserted into the Soviet Union by the CIA on a mission of espionage.

KGB counterintelligence officers bring no sense of humor to such questions. They investigated Oswald as if he were Trotsky returned from the dead, beginning with a meticulous examination of questions like whether Oswald was secretly fluent in Russian despite the appearance of halting incomprehension; whether he brought to his work in the radio factory a suspiciously deep knowledge of electronics; whether on outings with a local hunting club he betrayed undue curiosity about forbidden zones. The KGB watchers followed Oswald daily; his friends were interrogated; his apartment was bugged; and his conversations, consisting frequently of crazily painful quarrels with Marina, were recorded and transcribed. These domestic miseries reassured the KGB that Oswald was not in fact a master spy but a pathetic nonentity.

"Stepan," the KGB officer in charge of street surveillance of Oswald, is presented to us by Mailer in a seven-page life that is to my mind one of the greatest encapsulations of the soul of the policeman to be found anywhere in literature. "Asked one more time to give his opinion of Oswald's case," Mailer writes, "he says it proved to be 'primitive—a basic case,' because it did not involve anyone of extreme intelligence. Nor did it cost too much money. Oswald did not have a large circle of friends and was not erratic in his behavior. It wasn't as if one week he had three friends and by the following week had accumulated twenty so they had to increase their budget immediately to watch twenty people instead of three. No, this case was simple because it did not have variables, it did not fluctuate, and finally there wasn't much that really raised a lot of new questions."

The second book in Mailer's tome, "Oswald in America," is completely different. There is nothing new in it. Mailer has declined to phone up all the old witnesses with all the old questions. Instead, for his account of Oswald's slow progress toward the awful day, Mailer resorts to the record, which turns out to include not only the mountains of testimony and evidence collected by the Warren Commission but also three published books: Edward Jay Epstein's *Legend: The Secret World of Lee Harvey Oswald*,[3] which suggests without actually claiming that Oswald was part of some broader conspiracy; Gerald Posner's *Case Closed*,[4] which argues with an awesome command of evidentiary detail that Oswald did it, period; and the already mentioned *Marina and Lee*. Of the three Mailer depends by far the most heavily on McMillan's book, quoting from it scores of passages and thousands of words, for which right he paid a modest sum.

With these materials Mailer has fashioned a narrative history of Oswald's life and deeds. In style it is workmanlike and thorough. In whole chapters, Mailer writes, it will be his job simply "to guide each transcript to its proper placement on the page." Mailer the author comes to roaring life only with his "speculations," some of which set a new record even for Mailer for defying the law of gravity. Of the never-quite-explained death of one of Oswald's fellow marines in the Philippines, who died of a gunshot wound entering beneath the arm and exiting through the neck, Mailer writes that it is "an undeclared possibility" he was murdered by a man performing fellatio! And it is "not inconceivable" that that man was Oswald! For this there is no trace of a wisp of a shred of evidence. But "if" it were true, imagine what an effect it would have had on Oswald! In Mailer this sort of extravagance is a sign of irrepressible high spirits.

In soberer fashion he pauses in his narrative with irritating frequency

3. McGraw-Hill, 1978.

4. Random House, 1993.

to consider possible evidence of unseen hands. It's my guess that even the most indifferent reader has heard most of the "what abouts" before. What about the shadowy figures of Guy Banister and David Ferrie, who passed within Oswald's orbit in New Orleans? What about the Cuban woman Sylvia Odio, who says Oswald and two secret operatives visited her on a certain night in Dallas in September 1963? What about the mysterious George de Mohrenschildt, who knew Oswald, knew CIA officers, and shot himself after passing on dark hints to a writer in 1977? What about the Mafia heavies Jack Ruby knew? Like a Natty Bumppo of the political wilderness, Mailer pauses by each bent twig and bruised blade of grass, looking for signs of a passing herd of conspiratorial buffalo. None of it goes anywhere.

But the central body of the story, while familiar in outline, has lost none of its power, and Mailer draws us into its spell. From the Dallas papers, Oswald learned that the President's motorcade would pass the Texas School Book Depository, where he worked. On Thursday, November 21, the day before the assassination, he told a friend at his job that he needed to pick up some curtain rods. The friend drove him out to the Dallas suburb where Marina was staying with the children. That evening Marina rejected Oswald's plea that she move back in with him; during the night he kicked away her foot when she touched him in bed. In the morning he left money on the bureau—more than he had ever left before. He also left his wedding ring—something he had never done. He busied himself in the garage with an object wrapped in a blanket. He drove back into Dallas for work carrying his brown paper parcel of "curtain rods."

So it goes—one relentless detail pressing on another, through the killing, the arrest, the time in jail, the panic of wife and mother and brother, the terrible moment when Jack Ruby lunged through the police line and fired the single pistol bullet that denied us forever Oswald's tale as he might have told it himself.

But Mailer has not forgotten his existential errand. To the familiar story he has added a careful gloss of his own. His goal is to give Oswald an inner life commensurate with his deed, to chart the future assassin's thoughts as he sought frantically for some combination of act and stance that would express his own sense of worth. That Oswald rated this very highly Mailer does not doubt, nor does he scoff. In Oswald's own mind, Mailer suggests, the man who dressed himself in black for a portrait with his gun is a kind of "private-general." The public Oswald is as low in the formal rank of things as a buck private in the army. But the secret Oswald is a marshaler of great forces, a driver of history, a general on the level of Hannibal or Napoleon. On the eve of the private-general's apotheosis, Mailer writes, "Oswald has reached that zone of serenity that some men attain before combat, when anxiety is deep enough to feel like quiet exaltation." After the killing Oswald spent the final two days of his life in jail, "gathering in some vast multiple of all the attention he had been denied for most of his life."

At the end of his book Mailer approaches his own quiet exaltation, the moment when the evidence has been presented and the author must tell us without prevarication what he thinks it means. Mailer has Oswald firmly in mind now. The doubts have all been put aside. "Every insight we have gained of him," he writes, "suggests the solitary nature of his act."

Why Kennedy? "It was the largest opportunity he had ever been offered."

Mailer is not the first historian of the assassination to remark on Oswald's aggrandizing ego. Priscilla Johnson McMillan took the measure of the man with great precision in 1977. But Mailer is the first deliberately to treat Oswald's estimate of himself with respect. A fine title for his book, he writes, would have been *An American Tragedy*, reminding us of his hope that a "tragic" Oswald would somehow soften the blow of Kennedy's murder and thereby save us from the

despair of living in an "absurd" universe. It took courage and gen-
erosity for Mailer to conceive of this mighty rescue operation.

Does it work?

For success Mailer must draw on a reader's reserves of human
empathy here, and I am afraid mine are not quite up to the job. I was
never confused about who killed Kennedy, and the fact that Oswald
wanted attention does not make me feel better. I admire Mailer for his
effort to understand Oswald, but at some level I feel invited to place
a sympathetic arm around the killer's shoulder, and I'm not about to
do it. *Oswald's Tale* brings us right up to the pinch-lipped misery and
sour odor of the man. He brought pain to many and happiness to none.
Anger is what this makes me feel. It was an insect that brought
Kennedy down. Would to God he had popped first beneath somebody's foot.

—*The New York Times Book Review*, April 30, 1995

12

THE INTERESTING ONE

ON THE DAY his brother Jack was shot to death in Dallas, Texas, Robert Kennedy asked the director of the Central Intelligence Agency, John McCone, point-blank, if the CIA had been responsible for the murder. It is hard to know which is more remarkable—that Kennedy wasn't sure of the answer, or that he expected to hear the truth either way. McCone of course said no, and there is no evidence that Kennedy ever doubted him, but that only narrowed the list of suspects in his mind. There were several others: organized crime and crooked labor unions, both hounded by Kennedy as a Senate investigator before his brother's election, and as attorney general after it; Cubans opposed to Fidel Castro, and especially those Cubans who had gone onto the beach at the Bay of Pigs and been abandoned there; and Castro himself, who had been marked for death by Kennedy's government, who knew it, and who had warned that two could play at that game.

But behind these suspicions, never resolved, lay a still darker fear in the mind of Robert Kennedy: that he himself, if any of the four had been established as the guilty party, could not have escaped at least some measure of responsibility for arousing and stoking the anger that resulted in his brother's assassination. Kennedy had learned secrecy at his father's knee, he was not loquacious in the Irish manner, when he had something big and personal to say he fell back on quoting the greats, and he rarely brooded aloud even with his closest friends about his brother's death. But any man watched as closely as Kennedy was by rivals, journalists, and obsessive file-keepers like J. Edgar Hoover of the FBI was bound to give himself away on the things that troubled him most, and nobody was paying closer attention than President Lyndon Baines Johnson, who openly detested "that little runt" and was hated in return.

When Kennedy after much agonizing broke ranks with the administration over Vietnam, calling the war a "horror" in a Senate speech in March 1967, Johnson was instantly back at him with a poisonous leak to the *Washington Post* columnist Drew Pearson, who flatly accused Kennedy of masterminding an effort to assassinate Fidel Castro. Had Kennedy's plan "backfired against his late brother"? Pearson wondered. Was it possible the senator had been "plagued by the terrible thought that he had helped put into motion terrible forces that indirectly may have brought about his brother's martyrdom? Some insiders think so."

The question must have been a painful one. But guilt was only one of the torments which entered Robert Kennedy's life with Jack's assassination. With it also came a fatalism hard to distinguish from despair and the onset of a raw spiritual sensitivity as tender as a wound that would not heal. Tough and ruthless by common report; a good hater by his father's; single-minded and driving according to just about everybody who ever worked for him or joined him in a game of touch football, Robert Kennedy was abruptly changed in the middle of his life from one kind of man into another.

This astonishing transformation, rare in any walk of life and practically unknown among working politicians, forms the dramatic core of *Robert Kennedy: His Life*, Evan Thomas's fine biography of the Kennedy who retains the most power to unsettle and surprise.* Jack

---

*Simon and Schuster, 2000.

will always have a bigger place in the national memory than he will in its history. Teddy has the longest résumé and may have a lot more useful work in him yet. But the Robert who emerges convincingly from Thomas's skillful telling of this sad American story is a man interesting entirely in himself—for having learned to see things he had ignored, learned to feel things he had suppressed, and learned to say things he had feared to utter.

The Kennedy who changed so radically was born just late enough, and just far enough down the line, to escape the full attention of his father, Joseph P. Kennedy, who made the family's fortune, dreamed of becoming president himself, and drove his two oldest boys to succeed where he had fallen short. Money, the Roman Catholic Church, and the pack of clamoring siblings who gave him little notice and less mercy made Robert a kind of outcast as a child, tentative, withdrawn, even a bit of a mama's boy. His mother, Rose, worried in the summer of 1940 that he "does not seem to be interested particularly in reading or sailing or his stamps." As a student at Portsmouth Priory he struggled along with middling grades until his senior year, when a cheating scandal—some student got hold of an exam ahead of time—ended his career there. Exactly what happened is unclear. Kennedy departed but the record would not support a flat claim that he was kicked out. Rose wrote her older boys, off at war, that Robert "did not seem to make much headway in his classes last year; that is, he did not show any particular effort...." In any event, he would now be going to Milton Academy.

It would be hard to imagine a clearer example of Rose's way of sliding past the hard parts. She conspicuously failed to notice her husband's many mistresses, not even the actual arrival in the family's Cape Cod summer house of the movie star Gloria Swanson on Joe's arm in the summer of 1929. More astonishing was her failure to protest the abrupt removal from the family circle a dozen years later of her second-eldest daughter, Rosemary, a kind of problem child, slow, difficult, and given to explosive outbursts of anger and frustration. In the category of family secrets this dark episode resides in a class that might be called Irish gothic. Thomas does not tell us precisely what afflicted Rosemary, but it reached a critical stage in mid-1941 and Joe's remedy was drastic. Without telling anyone else in the family—and especially not the girl's mother—Joe subjected the physically blooming, twenty-three-year-old Rosemary to a prefrontal lobotomy—surgical removal of part of the brain—which all but killed her. Barely able to speak, almost catatonic, Rosemary was summarily deposited in an institution. Rose was given no explanation for her daughter's disappearance, or for Joe's flat refusal to permit visits, and she did not even press for an answer until many years later. The operation itself, Rosemary's condition, and even her existence were obscured in silence.

But tender as the subject of Rosemary was—"A mystery so strange and awful can haunt a family for generations," Thomas writes—there was one more painful still: Joseph Kennedy's failure of nerve as FDR's ambassador to Great Britain between 1938 and 1941. Long worried that a new war in Europe would be bad for American business, and fearful that his own fortune would be destroyed in the process, Kennedy wholeheartedly backed Neville Chamberlain's policy of appeasing Hitler. On a trip to Germany in the summer of 1938 Hitler's air marshal, Hermann Goering, persuaded Kennedy that the German air fleet was the world's strongest. A friendly encounter in September with the isolationist airman Charles Lindbergh further convinced him that resistance to Hitler was hopeless. The practical thought that American power, added to the balance, might help avert the war Kennedy feared somehow never crossed his mind.

In a letter to his friend Arthur Krock during the tense countdown toward war over Hitler's demands for a big piece of Czechoslovakia, Kennedy moaned that he would have to send his family home to escape the inevitable bombing, and "stay here alone for how long

God only knows. Maybe," he added, thinking of his own demise, "never see them again." Chamberlain's surrender at Munich a few days later thrilled and relieved Joe, who grabbed Rose and "kissed me and twirled me around in his arms, repeating over and over what a great day this was and what a great man Chamberlain was." But the euphoria of "peace in our time"—Chamberlain's giddy claim on his return to London—did not last long.

When war broke out in September 1939, Kennedy immediately sent his family back to America and then failed to sense the increasingly chilly British response to his repeated warnings about German might and the futility of war. Kennedy began to think of getting out. In the fall of 1940, just as German air raids on London were getting under way, Kennedy departed for America, formally resigned his post the day after FDR's reelection to a third term, and two days later gave an ill-advised, rambling, ninety-minute interview to newsmen in which he ridiculed the British cabinet and talked openly of the futility of resisting Hitler:

> I'm willing to spend all I've got left to keep us out of the war. There's no sense in our getting in. We'd just be holding the bag.... People call me a pessimist. I say, What is there to be gay about? Democracy is all done.... Democracy is finished in England. It may be here.... [England] isn't fighting for democracy. That's the bunk. She's fighting for self-preservation, just as we will if it comes to us.

The elder Kennedy tried to repudiate the interview but it was too late. The British did not conceal that they were glad to see the last of him, his relationship with FDR was permanently poisoned, and his hope of a political career was over. Worse, and more lingering, was the impression that Joe's antiwar views weren't simply foolish and naive in the manner of Chamberlain's, but had their root in funk pure and simple—a lack of the courage, principles, and resolution asked of anyone who hopes to lead.

It is hard not to conclude that his own family worried about this most, going to reckless extremes to prove they had no streak of yellow of their own. John F. Kennedy's bravery in the South Pacific, where he rescued crewmates from his destroyed PT boat, was reported within days on the front page of *The New York Times*. A year later his older brother, Joseph Jr., was killed during an almost suicidal volunteer mission to fly a planeload of explosives directly into German rocket sites on the French coast. The plan was to parachute to safety at the last moment but Joe Jr.'s plane blew up on its way across the channel. The entire family was shattered by grief, but the elder Kennedy's friend Arthur Krock thought the old man's sorrow was tinged with an extra bitter intensity by his fear that Joe died trying to prove Kennedys weren't yellow. More than once Robert went after people who hinted his father was a coward, and his visceral dislike of Lyndon Johnson was born in Los Angeles in 1960 the moment he learned that Johnson, angling for the Democratic nomination which went to Jack, was ridiculing Joe to newsmen as a "Chamberlain umbrella man"—a reference to Chamberlain's trademark umbrella, which had come to symbolize Munich and appeasement.

The life of Robert Kennedy breaks down roughly into three periods—his childhood as an overlooked kid, his years as his brother Jack's extra arm, and the last years on his own. The stretch that engages Americans now and forms the heart of Thomas's book is astonishingly brief—barely eight years, from Jack's election in 1960 to the night of the California primary in 1968. The White House stories are all interesting but mostly familiar—the pursuit of Kennedy's long campaign to destroy Jimmy Hoffa, boss of the Teamsters Union, begun when he had been chief investigator for the Senate Rackets Committee; the courtship dance with Hoover, director of the FBI, who informed the attorney general from time to time as he acquired secrets of sexual liaisons and CIA plots that could destroy the President; the back-channel negotiating with posturing segregationists like George Wallace of Alabama and Ross Barnett of Mississippi; Jack's taste for women who were trouble, like Judith Campbell Exner and Marilyn Monroe; the on-again, off-again FBI wiretapping of Martin Luther King Jr., who drove the just-tell-me-what-you-want, deal-making Robert crazy with his mountaintop orations.

Jack had casually issued a vast promissory note to the black population of America in October 1960 with a single telephone call to King's wife to commiserate about the jailing of her husband. At the time, worried about the vote in wobbly Southern states, Robert was furious. "Do you know that this election may be razor close," he shouted at the campaign aides who had suggested the call, "and you have probably just lost it for us?" Three Southern governors had promised to deliver their states—but only if Jack stood up to Jimmy Hoffa, Nikita Khrushchev, and the Reverend King.

Robert was running Jack's campaign and there wasn't an ounce of mercy in him for anybody who didn't put winning ahead of everything else. Administration was not Robert's gift; during his brother's 1952 Senate campaign, Thomas writes, there was no hiding "his failings as an organizer—his impatience, his amateurism, his predilection for going outside channels." But he was tireless, selfless, and above all single-minded, and he knew Southerners put King at the top of the hate list, above even Communists and labor organizers. But one of Kennedy's aides, Louis Martin, got around Kennedy's pragmatic objections. King was jailed, Martin said, because the judge had refused to allow bail for what came down to a misdemeanor traffic violation. "You can't deny bail on a misdemeanor," objected Kennedy. "Well they just did it," Martin said.

That night, after assuring other aides he was not going to get involved in the King mess, Kennedy changed his mind and telephoned the Georgia judge who had put King in prison. "I called him," Robert told an aide, Harris Wofford, "because it made me so damn angry to think of that bastard sentencing a citizen to four months of hard labor for a minor traffic offense." Maybe, and maybe not. Thomas writes that the call, long portrayed as an impulsive act of conscience, in fact came at the tail end of covert talks with the Georgia governor. But even so it was Robert who made the call that got King out of jail, and in the end it proved to be a brilliant political stroke—some analysts even suggest it decided the election. So what was it—pure political calculation, solving a problem that was embarrassing Southern Democrats, or the act of a man peeved at injustice? There is no clear answer; Kennedy seems to have been pulled both ways at once.

Race and civil rights took up a lot of Kennedy's time as attorney general, a job his father pressed his brother to give him and flatly insisted Robert take; but Kennedy's instinct was for compromise, the deal, working things out behind the scenes, not for the kind of moral confrontation whipped up by King in his prophetic mode. Kennedy urged patience, progress one step at a time, giving a little to get a little—not enough to satisfy King, who demanded equality, justice, and redemption. Suspicious of King, and urged on by Hoover, Kennedy authorized wiretaps on King's phone and may have okayed bugs in his hotel rooms as well. The frail justification was concern about a King adviser who had once been a member of the American Communist Party. But in truth Kennedy wanted King, the freedom riders, and the whole civil rights movement to cut a deal and go away to leave him free to concentrate on the things which preoccupied his brother —table-pounding by Khrushchev over Berlin, the worldwide challenge presented by Soviet-backed wars of national liberation, and the Communist leader of Cuba, Fidel Castro, who mocked the power of the United States and promised a domino chain of revolutions throughout Latin America.

The depth and intensity of the Kennedy brothers' obsession with

Cuba are still hard to grasp. Its origin was the humiliating failure of the CIA-backed invasion by Cuban exiles in April 1961, inherited from the Eisenhower administration, which left the President looking weak and confused. Initial fury at the agency, justified but futile, soon gave way to a redoubled national commitment to get rid of Castro— but quietly this time, with a clandestine finesse notably lacking at the Bay of Pigs. The President put his brother on a blue-ribbon panel to study the causes of the failure, and come up with a surer way to do it next time. After a decent interval the discredited parties at the CIA— Director Allen Dulles and Deputy Director for Plans Richard Bissell —were quietly removed. Replacing them were John McCone, a Republican businessman, and the career intelligence officer Richard Helms. But in the shadows, pressing hard for an aggressive new effort to get rid of Castro, was Robert Kennedy. "My idea is to stir things up," Kennedy noted to himself after a White House meeting on Cuba in November 1961; "we have nothing to lose...." In his efforts to make it happen Robert reached deeper into the heart of the American intelligence community than any other outsider, before or since.

No international issue got more attention from the Kennedys than Cuba, and the Bay of Pigs fiasco and the missile crisis that followed eighteen months later have been minutely scrutinized by historians. Robert had little to do with the invasion, but he was deeply involved in the deliberations in September and October 1962 that finally decided on a blockade of Cuba to force the Soviet Union to remove nuclear missiles which threatened two thirds of the mainland United States. Thomas accepts previously published claims that Robert was a leader of the faction that urged caution and argued against the "surgical strike" favored by the Air Force and elder statesmen like Dean Acheson, comparing it to Pearl Harbor. "My brother is not going to be the Tojo of the '60s," Robert insisted, referring to the Japanese general who brought the United States into World War II with the sneak attack on the American naval base.

But this restraint came to Kennedy only slowly, over the course of days of argument. "If we go in," he scribbled in a note to himself on the first day of the crisis, "we go in hard." Robert McNamara, the secretary of defense and by this time a close friend of Robert's, told Thomas that "RFK was a hawk in his head and his heart.... But he changed." Others noted the change as well. One of Robert's aides entered his office in the Justice Department in the middle of the crisis and, knowing nothing of the imminent showdown with the Soviet navy, said, "Something is different in here."

"I'm older," said Kennedy.

Kennedy's role throughout the crisis, and the subtle day-by-day shifts in his thinking, are documented in the transcripts of the Executive Committee meetings which argued the pros and cons of military versus political action. In addition, the release of both American and Soviet documents and the publication of numerous memoirs make this tense encounter, arguably the most dangerous of the entire cold war, one of the best-documented international confrontations in history. But Robert's leadership of the secret American effort to get rid of Castro between the Bay of Pigs and the missile crisis is a very different matter, poorly documented and only sketchily described by those with firsthand knowledge of Kennedy's insistent prodding and poking as he tried to whip the agency to attempt what it basically knew to be impossible—overthrow a well-established police-state regime with pinprick guerrilla attacks and cockamamie schemes to spark a popular revolt. In particular there is no smoking-gun evidence to flesh out Drew Pearson's charges published in 1967—that it was Robert Kennedy who played the most direct role in urging the post–Bay of Pigs efforts to get rid of Castro in the one way that would really and truly get rid of him.

But the lack of a smoking gun does not mean the evidence provided by Thomas is thin. It is not. It includes several explicit reports and a pattern of events which together strongly support claims that

Robert Kennedy knew about and pressed plans for the assassination of Castro. In October and November 1963, for example, when Robert was the driving force on the secret committees overseeing anti-Castro efforts, the CIA's Desmond Fitzgerald managed to recruit a highly placed Cuban agent named Rolando Cubela who had agreed to "eliminate" Castro. On October 11, the day the CIA first met with the Cuban, Fitzgerald telephoned the attorney general—about what the record does not say. Another CIA official—unnamed—told Thomas that Kennedy knew what Fitzgerald was doing and approved a delivery of arms to Cubela. A Kennedy aide named David Ellis, who helped come up with a plan to attach a bomb to Castro's car, told Thomas he hand-delivered the car-bomb plans to Kennedy's secretary, Angie Novello. The lawyer Joseph Califano, counsel to the secretary of the army, Cyrus Vance, during the height of the anti-Castro plotting in 1963, told Thomas he personally heard Robert discuss "knocking off Castro." Richard Helms, who had nominal control over CIA efforts to overthrow the Communist regime in Cuba, told investigators in the mid-1970s only that he was pushed hard by Robert Kennedy to "get rid" of Castro.

Later, talking with Henry Kissinger in the privacy of the White House, Helms went further. Called back from his post as ambassador to Iran to help quiet a growing CIA scandal in early 1975, Helms warned Kissinger that any serious investigation was going to dig up real dirt. "Helms said all these stories are just the tip of the iceberg," Kissinger reported later that day to President Gerald Ford. "If they come out blood will flow. For example, Robert Kennedy personally managed the operation on the assassination of Castro."

None of this evidence is ambiguous, but it still falls short of the "smoking gun" standard demanded by Kennedy's family and friends. "As my father always told me," Kennedy wrote John McCone in mid-1962, "'never write it down.'" The paper record at the CIA is mainly concerned with housekeeping details, and the minutes of the

Cuba committee meetings were selective and incomplete about the assassination of Castro. Robert Kennedy never confessed himself to anyone willing to speak clearly now, and the many keepers of the flame insist he would never have contemplated such a thing. On some questions in this world certainty is denied. Evan Thomas provides a fair summary of the evidence and concludes with a Scotch verdict—not proven. But Thomas also believes that Kennedy suffered something more than a kind of survivor's guilt following his brother's murder. "Without question," Thomas writes, "he worried that his own aggressive pursuit of evil men had brought evil upon his own house."

The great fault line in the life of Robert Kennedy was the assassination of his brother. Any man's life would be jolted by an event so violent, sudden, and final, but the effect on Robert was more than one of grief and loss, profound as both clearly were. The person he had been—right arm, door-opener, detail-man, enforcer, adviser, devoted and loyal brother—died in Dallas and was eventually replaced by a different sort of person.

The great strength of Thomas's book is the clear and unsentimental way in which he records this exchange of one way of living and thinking for another, in some ways almost the mirror image of the discarded self. An editor at *Newsweek* magazine and author or co-author of several accounts of cold war history and institutions, Thomas has a deep knowledge of the cast of characters during the Kennedy years, and especially of the CIA officials who tried to give the Kennedys what they wanted. His group portrait of Frank Wisner, Desmond Fitzgerald, Richard Bissell, and Tracy Barnes in *The Very Best Men* is probably the best single account of the kind of men who went into the intelligence business in the agency's glory days. That kind of detailed knowledge is one of the two things required for writing the life of a man like Kennedy, whose career is simultaneously public and hidden.

The other is a confident sense of the narrative line—what matters most about the life, and how it grows from personality and circumstance.

The depth and intensity of Robert Kennedy's emotional appeal for the people who wrote about him, worked for him, and lined the streets to see him is no secret. But the early books about Robert Kennedy tended to see him as a kind of secular saint, and often shrank from the darker episodes in his history. Later accounts, when more was known, were harsher, less forgiving, and tended to see him as shallow, illiberal, and opportunistic. Thomas is frank about Kennedy's failings—wiretapping King and then lying about it, the unjustified bitterness of his hatred for Lyndon Johnson, and the like—but at the same time he accepts as genuine Kennedy's identification with the ignored and the excluded. The awful wound of Jack's murder, the unraveling of Robert's persona as the devoted brother, and his search for a renewed sense of purpose and emotional commitment are the central threads of Thomas's book and give it the power to touch even readers who imagine they are long beyond any twitch of feeling for a Kennedy.

But first came the grief, expressed in all the usual ways—tears, anger, confusion, and a feeling of tremendous loss. The night of his brother's murder a friend heard him cry out, "Why, God?" Before Jack's coffin was closed for good, Robert and the dead president's wife, Jacqueline, both placed mementos inside—letters and a piece of scrimshaw from Jackie; a silver rosary and a lock of hair from Robert. For months thereafter Robert was deeply attentive to Jackie, often visiting Jack's grave with her at night in Arlington National Cemetery.

This grief did not surrender easily; he had trouble sleeping, lost weight, was listless about work, quit thinking about Jimmy Hoffa and the mob, sometimes had difficulty holding his head up or looking a dinner partner in the eye. With Jackie he discussed fate, God, and the meaning of life. On a trip to the Caribbean with her, Robert read for the first time Edith Hamilton's study of history and tragedy, *The Greek Way*. From that he progressed to the ancient Greek playwrights like

Aeschylus, marking passages like "God calls men to a heavy reckoning/For overweening pride." A lifelong reader, Robert had always been interested in the muscular part of history—the deeds of great men, battles, political struggles. Now he turned to its meaning. Along with the Greeks he read Albert Camus and other writers with more questions than answers. He was not an intellectual in the usual sense; he did not discuss, analyze, and argue with the books he was reading, but instead visited them, hunted solace in them, let them speak for him when he was overwhelmed by the imponderables of life.

The attempt to make sense of the inexplicable was one of Robert Kennedy's responses to his brother's death; a second, just as important, was a kind of compulsive courting of danger and even of death. In his copy of Emerson's *Essays* Kennedy underlined the sentence: "Always do what you are afraid to do." He had a deep contempt for anyone who in his view failed the basic test of bravery: President Johnson he thought a "coward," Nelson Rockefeller had "no guts," Chester Bowles was a "weeper." All the Kennedys played sports aggressively, skied like daredevils, but Robert after Dallas took the refusal to admit fear to a new extreme.

When Canada honored his brother by giving his name to the highest unclimbed peak in North America, Robert agreed to join a National Geographic Society expedition to climb the 13,900-foot Mount Kennedy despite a lifelong fear of heights. After scaling a stretch of nearly vertical ridge, with a six-thousand-foot drop below him if he fell, Robert told the guide he didn't want to pause for a picture—"Just get me the hell up the mountain." He later confessed he enjoyed no part of the venture. Testing himself against his own fears, ignoring danger, and taking chances were a running theme of his last years. On a white-water rafting trip in Utah he alarmed the guides when he insisted on jumping into the water and swimming through the rapids. On a cruise through the fifty-degree waters off the coast of Maine he dove overboard without hesitation when a gust of wind blew his brother's old leather bomber jacket into the water. "The captain...worried that Kennedy would drown in the icy water," Thomas writes. "He estimated that Kennedy could last no more than twelve minutes. That was about how long it took to fish RFK, blue and shaking but holding the sacred garment, from the sea."

Kennedy often wore the bomber jacket and he soon determined to take his brother's place in politics as well, going all the way to the White House; he began with a close but successful race for a Senate seat in New York. But the friends and advisers who shared his dream of a restoration all assumed that Robert's year would be 1972, after LBJ's second term. His willingness to wait had nothing to do with a sense of deference; Kennedy loathed Johnson, whom he thought of as a usurper. But challenging an incumbent of one's own party threatened disaster in November and violated all the conventional rules of presidential politics, beginning with party loyalty. So Robert Kennedy determined to stick by the rules, put aside his own rising alarm about the course of the war, and wait his turn.

The old Robert Kennedy probably would have done it, but by 1968 he had become a different person, open to different concerns, quicker to listen, less patient, more impulsive, no longer quite convinced that winning was everything. What happened next is what separates Kennedy from the host of other inspirational American politicians, from William Jennings Bryan to Adlai Stevenson, who never made it to the White House. That Kennedy was assassinated, not beaten at the polls, only partly explains the power of the story. In some sense Kennedy almost seems to have invited his fate—ignoring the cautions of family and friends, plunging into crowds, riding in open cars, challenging hostile groups. He knew he might encounter a man with a gun almost anywhere as he stumped the country, but he refused to shrink from the danger. Perhaps most extraordinary of all is the way Kennedy quit thinking in practical political terms and became an advocate of precisely those populations with the least money or power—migrant farmworkers, blacks in rural and urban ghettoes, American Indians living on reservations, the poor in Appalachia, and the young with no chance in life. Vietnam was the big issue of 1968, but what animated Kennedy was his emotional identification with the excluded, the oppressed, the impoverished.

As a senator Kennedy had been erratic. He often missed votes, was bored by the mechanics of writing laws, didn't like the politicking required to get them passed, was impatient with the endless requests of constituents for the little favors that win support and gradually make incumbents unbeatable. But after his brother's death something in Kennedy grew sensitive to questions of justice. "It is a reach," Thomas writes, "to compare Kennedy's travails as the neglected little brother to the despair of ghetto dwellers, but Kennedy seemed to feel a direct kinship with the troubled youth of any time and place." In the fall of 1965 he made a tour of Latin America and was startled and then touched by the fervor of the crowds. None shouted louder than the poor and he made a point of visiting slums. In Chile he was warned to avoid a university dominated by Communists who would shout him down and might even injure him; he went, ducked the garbage and eggs thrown at him, ignored a student who spat at him, went on shaking hands. On the second anniversary of his brother's murder he drove through a Brazilian slum crying out, "Every child an education! Every family adequate housing! Every man a job!"

By the time the three-week tour was over Kennedy had established the new pattern of his life—physically plunging into crowds, seeking out those most hostile, and promising in spite of himself what no man, no political party, no program could ever deliver: recognition, change, and justice. From migrant farmworkers in California to the black townships of South Africa, from Indian reservations to the urban wasteland of Bedford-Stuyvesant to windowless shacks where children starved in Mississippi, Kennedy during the final years of his life was drawn to exactly those people with the biggest problems and the least to offer any man running for president.

But Kennedy stuck to his plan and stayed out of the 1968 presidential race until Eugene McCarthy proved in the New Hampshire primary that a Democrat could take the nomination away from President Johnson. Cynics said he let McCarthy take the risk of testing the waters, then moved in to grab the prize; Kennedy himself insisted he hung back at first for fear he would make things worse by running—whatever he urged, Johnson would do the opposite. Either way, McCarthy proved the Democratic Party and the country were already divided and Kennedy could sit still no longer.

The campaign which followed was headlong, chaotic, expensive—Ted said it was going to cost the family $4 million—and far from certain of success. After Johnson withdrew at the end of March he threw his support to Vice President Hubert Humphrey, the man Jack had defeated for the nomination in 1960. To win Kennedy needed the backing of the party but party leaders by no means shared his passions over Vietnam, poverty, and race. Not even a clean sweep of the primaries would have guaranteed his nomination and the sweep wasn't clean—he won in Indiana but with less than half the vote, and he lost Oregon to Eugene McCarthy. "There are no ghettoes in Oregon," observed a congresswoman backing him.

But Kennedy plunged ahead anyway. He accused the Johnson administration of "calling upon the darker impulses of the American spirit"; he attacked audiences for hardheartedness toward the poor; he walked the streets of black ghettoes during the riots that followed the assassination of Martin Luther King Jr. in April. The crowds were often wild with excitement, mobbing Kennedy's car, shouting and grabbing at him, pulling off his cufflinks and even his shoes. Cooler heads warned this was playing all wrong on television; Americans were worried about riots and violence and Robert in his speeches was whipping them up. "You've got to turn it down," a worried reporter told Ted Sorensen when a black crowd in Washington almost tipped over Kennedy's car. "We can't," he responded. "It's too late."

But it wasn't crowds that threatened the life of Robert Kennedy; it was a lone man with a gun. "That could have been me," he said to a friend the night of the King assassination. Everybody connected to the campaign, everybody who knew Kennedy, everybody who read newspapers or watched television knew that Robert Kennedy was a walking target. But he refused to pull back for fear of being killed. When an aide wanted to close his hotel room blinds one night Kennedy said, "Don't close them. If they're going to shoot, they'll shoot." In a notebook he wrote down a quote from Camus: "Knowing that you are going to die is nothing." Every time he stopped his car to shake hands, or moved down onto the floor of a meeting hall, or even stepped outdoors, Kennedy placed himself in harm's way. Even when police and bodyguards learned of threats in advance Kennedy paid little attention; he knew the lone man with a gun could be anywhere.

As it happened he was standing in a hotel corridor filled with kitchen staff. Kennedy had been on his way to the ballroom of the Ambassador Hotel in Los Angeles to declare victory in the California primary but a crowd of shouting teenagers blocked the direct route. A hotel official took Kennedy and his wife another way, down through the kitchen, into the corridor where the man with the black .22 caliber pistol—he had bought a box of ammunition only that day—suddenly saw his chance. Why did he fire? He was Palestinian; a few days earlier on television he had seen Kennedy wearing a yarmulke outside a synagogue. That may have been the reason, or perhaps the gun itself was the reason.

What would have happened if he had lived, and been nominated and elected? Kennedy himself was far from sure. "If I get to be president, what can I do anyway?" he had asked his friend Richard Goodwin during the Indiana primary. "With Congress and the press, what chance do I have to make basic changes?"

None of it would have gone easily, Thomas thinks, but Kennedy would have tried. "He might have been rash, he might have tried to do too much, and he might have blundered," he writes. "Failure, in a divided country in a confused time, was probably more likely than not. Nonetheless, Kennedy's life story suggests that had he failed, he would have failed trying his utmost to lift up the poor and the weak."

Kennedy raised hopes but it stopped there. His ambitions were big but none of it happened. He wasn't nominated, he wasn't elected, he passed no important laws, he never tackled the big issues, his speeches are rarely read, and his brothers Jack and Teddy have sounder claims on the sober historian. But all the same, Bobby was the interesting one.

—*The New York Review of Books*, November 2, 2000

13

MARILYN WAS THE LEAST OF IT

MARILYN MONROE ALONE escapes untarnished from *The Dark Side of Camelot*,[1] this file cabinet of a book, in which the celebrated investigative reporter Seymour M. Hersh holds up to the available light in strict chronological order just about every report, claim, rumor, or telltale clue of precisely and exclusively those things that President John F. Kennedy, his brother Robert, his friends, assistants, confidants, lawyers, secret emissaries, faithful government servants, and, we are assured, his numerous onetime, part-time, sometime, and longtime sexual partners were united in wishing to shroud in decent secrecy forever.

Monroe is identified as one of Kennedy's lovers, but the news is old and has long since lost its power to shock. The star is not onstage for long—once again, isolated in the spotlights of the old Madison Square Garden in May 1962, Monroe sings as only a sex goddess can a steamy version of "Happy Birthday" to the President beaming nearby, as who wouldn't. Hersh has also obtained and prints a bit of text from the transcript of a stream-of-consciousness tape Monroe made for her psychiatrist: "Marilyn Monroe is a soldier. Her commander in chief is the greatest and most powerful man in the world.

---

1. Little, Brown, 1997.

The first duty of a soldier is to obey her commander in chief. He says do this, you do it. He says do that, you do it. This man is going to change our country.... It's like the Navy—the President is the captain and Bobby is his executive officer. Bobby would do absolutely anything for his brother and so would I. I will never embarrass him. As long as I have memory, I have John Fitzgerald Kennedy."

This is sad and pathetic but it is not shaming. There's a bit more of the same and then it's over. The Marilyn Monroe we have always known—beautiful, confused, smarter than you might think, and lonely as only a star can be—survives intact. But her modest walk-on role, we have been informed by weeks of highly public scandal, is very far from the full treatment Hersh originally had in mind. What Hersh had, or thought he had, or in any event persuaded ABC News for a time that he had, was a sheaf of incriminating documents—including letters, contracts, and memorandums signed by President Kennedy— which proved, or purported to prove, or if true would have proved, that Marilyn Monroe changed her mind about embarrassing the President, threatened to deface the President's image as a family man with the sensational news of their sexual affair, and was bribed to shut up only by the President's timely agreement to establish a substantial trust fund for the comfortable maintenance of her mother. There was lots more of the same, incriminating not only Monroe, in the documents allegedly left at his death by a New York lawyer who, according to his son, numbered among his private clients the President.

Hersh's sensational discoveries and their incontrovertible proof had been rumored in journalistic circles for a year or more, but when the documents were at last examined in a serious way it was discovered, as ABC infuriated Hersh by telling the world, that the trove had been fabricated. The documents had all the earmarks of an utter scam, a cynical attempt to bilk naive collectors. Why they fell for it is not hard to imagine, but what about Hersh, the Pulitzer Prize–winning investigative reporter, the man who exposed the My Lai massacre in

Vietnam, the man who first reported domestic spying by the Central Intelligence Agency? How are we to explain that to the children?

Since the Marilyn papers were exposed, Hersh and his far-too-long romance with the forgeries have been the subject of unflattering comment in news stories and magazine articles. Some might say there is a certain rough justice in the fact that the investigative journalist at last faces a little investigating. How Hersh could have let himself be dazzled will be addressed below, but in fairness it ought to be admitted here that Hersh came to his senses in time, and the sensational Marilyn Monroe documents never made it into his book. But a lot of other stuff did, and the question on the table is what to make of it.

The first thing to be said about *The Dark Side of Camelot* is that it is a reporter's book, not a historian's. What's in it is mainly Hersh's. Again and again we are told that so-and-so "said in an interview for this book" or "told me" thus-and-such or that certain documents were "obtained for this book" and are here "published for the first time." The first half-dozen times this seems boastful and aggrandizing, but we soon grow used to the litany, and it becomes clear that Hersh has done his legwork; he is not trying to smuggle things in from other books. He tells us what he's found up front, making judgment easier for reviewers and blood enemies alike. The source notes at the back can be a little cumbersome, but compared with investigative reporters who provide no source notes whatever, Hersh is standing in the choir with Edward Gibbon.

The subject of Hersh's book is what Kennedy was really like and what he really did. Advance publicity suggests this is strictly a demolition job, but in fact there is much that casts Kennedy in a favorable light or makes him human. Among the most interesting of Hersh's informants are well-known journalists like Hugh Sidey and Gloria Emerson. That said, *The Dark Side of Camelot* is mostly stuff you wouldn't want your kids to know. It contains a great deal of information about Kennedy's sexual life; his relations with the mob, especially

Sam Giancana; and what appears to have been a ready acceptance of the use of personal violence—assassination—against foreign opponents, most famously Fidel Castro. The reader will seldom be startled by Hersh's discoveries; all this has been discussed for years. But Hersh has much to add; the copious new detail often makes for painful reading, and the raw data comes from a reporter with a professional style notoriously similar to the single-minded ferocity of the wolverine, a meat eater of the north woods known among fur trappers of yesteryear for its ability to tear its way through the log wall of a cabin for a strip of bacon. If you want a considered account of the big picture of the Kennedy era you should consult a scholar like Michael R. Beschloss, the author of a definitive account of Kennedy's handling of the cold war, *The Crisis Years: Kennedy and Khrushchev, 1960–1963*[2]; or Ernest R. May, the co-editor of *The Kennedy Tapes*,[3] which relates the deliberations of Kennedy and his advisers during the Cuban missile crisis. Hersh does not write history in the usual sense of the term, but he makes life difficult for historians by digging up just enough about distressing matters so they can't honestly be ignored.

Sometimes Hersh's technique works persuasively. An example is the story of Kennedy's fling in 1963 with an East German woman named Ellen Rometsch, possibly a spy, definitely trouble. Hersh has pieced it together with interviews of Washington insiders, declassified FBI and CIA files, what lay behind contemporary news accounts, and a final, revealing quotation from Ben Bradlee's 1975 memoir, *Conversations with Kennedy.*[4]

It's only too obvious that Kennedy's rambling remarks about J. Edgar Hoover, a scandal on Capitol Hill, who was paying how much for Rometsch, the Senate investigator who loved her, were all intended

2. Edward Burlingame Books, 1991.

3. See Chapter Nine.

4. Norton, 1975.

not for Bradlee's entertainment but to prepare Bradlee's newspaper, *The Washington Post*, for some very bad news heading the President's way. "There is something incredible," Bradlee wrote in 1977, "about the picture of the President of the United States and the Director of the Federal Bureau of Investigation looking at photographs of call girls over lunch." It's not so incredible now. That lunch with Hoover was not an idle gossip session. Hoover knew about Kennedy's affair with Rometsch, and made sure the President knew he knew. Hersh has tied a great many separate strands together here to create a new, convincing, and troubling tale of a man who has lost control of his appetites and is beginning to realize he is knee-deep in the tar baby.

But other chapters are all over the place, none more so than Hersh's account of how Kennedy handled Khrushchev's reckless attempt to sneak Russian nuclear missiles into Cuba. Thirty years of vigorous historical research later, the received wisdom, with which I more or less agree, is that Kennedy found just the right mix of resolution and willingness to compromise, got Khrushchev to execute an about-face, ended the world's closest brush with nuclear war, and cleared the way for a more stable relationship.

Hersh will have none of it. Whatever Kennedy did was wrong or had a sneaky motive. He made too much of a fuss about missiles that didn't matter, he never weighed the awful possibility of a nuclear exchange (not so; see *The Kennedy Tapes*), he compromised at the end by trading United States missiles in Turkey, he kept the deal secret so he could look tough. Even a week of deliberation by Kennedy's advisers meeting as an executive committee, during which initial enthusiasm for an air assault on the missile sites gradually cooled, Hersh describes as just a clever ploy. "In one move," he writes, "Kennedy isolated those men who could lead a public charge against his stewardship of state and left them to deliberate in private, while he and his brother struggled to reap political gain from a mess that had been triggered by their obsession with Cuba." This is not wrong; it's silly.

But Hersh's account of the obsession itself, and especially of the role played by the President and his brother in the CIA's attempts to assassinate Fidel Castro, is right on the money. Ever since the investigation of the CIA by the Senate committee known after its chairman, Frank Church—an investigation set into motion by Hersh's stories in *The New York Times* in December 1974—there has been a long rearguard action by Kennedy loyalists to muddy the waters about the President's responsibility for the murder plots. Robert McNamara, who had been deeply implicated himself, carefully refrained from trying to blame the secret warriors assigned the job. "The CIA was a highly disciplined organization, fully under the control of senior officials of the Government," he told the Church Committee. But assassination, McNamara insisted, "I never heard of.... I just can't understand how it could have happened."

There was ample evidence even twenty years ago for Kennedy's role in authorizing the attempts, and for Bobby Kennedy's role in pressing the effort following the disastrous failure of the CIA-backed invasion of Cuba at the Bay of Pigs. But Kennedy loyalists have been amazingly successful in selling the McNamara line to historians. Somewhere among the winks and nods and grumbles of presidential irritation must have been born an ember of conviction among high officials of the CIA that perhaps what Kennedy actually meant, and actually wanted, when he said we have to get rid of Castro was ... getting rid of Castro! The historians Aleksandr Fursenko and Timothy Naftali, in their exhaustive history of the missile crisis, *"One Hell of a Gamble,"* typically write that the Kennedy brothers "had pushed the CIA to use whatever means necessary—including probably assassination—to remove the Castro brothers."[5]

Probably? That word of doubt sticks in the wolverine's craw, and in effect inspires Hersh to dig up additional evidence, including a

---

5. See Chapter Nine.

specific claim that the man first in charge of anti-Castro operations, the late Richard Bissell, told one of the men who helped him, William Harvey, that it was the President himself who instructed him to establish an "executive action capability" for killing foreign leaders. (Hersh's new evidence includes a modest contribution from me. Hersh asked me a year or two ago if I'd learned anything new; when I told him that a former CIA officer told me that in 1961 the President had said that a move to assassinate Castro was "already in hand," Hersh backed up the story with documents in the Kennedy library.)

According to notes obtained by Hersh, Harvey met on January 25 with a CIA scientist to discuss poisons for killing Fidel Castro, among others on the hit list. Hersh has also learned that in 1962, while the assassination efforts involving Mafia hit men were still under way, Bobby Kennedy was assigned his own operational officer in the CIA, a man named Charles Ford picked from the staff of Task Force W, then commanded by Harvey. Ford's job was to handle contacts with Mafia chiefs while traveling under the pseudonym of Rocky Fiscalini, a name (along with Ford's own) that appears in Bobby Kennedy's office logs for 1962. But what Ford actually did for Kennedy remains unknown.

Hersh provides no definitive history of the CIA's attempts to assassinate foreign leaders, a subject that is complex, factually dense, and spotted with missing pieces. But he has dug up numerous pieces of new information, many of them significant for any serious history even if they fall short of being sensational headline material. His account of the CIA's campaign makes clear what CIA officers have been stressing for twenty years—that the driving force behind the all-out effort to get rid of Castro was the blast furnace of pressure from the Kennedy brothers.

This is not shocking. The basic facts, if not all the details, have long been known by those who desired to know. But it is painful to read about assassination planning by the very man whose murder was probably the greatest single traumatic event in American history. Painful in a different way is Hersh's new material about the President's sexual life. Marilyn Monroe we can forgive, just as we would forgive Antony Cleopatra. But Hersh describes many other affairs, some casual, some extended, with named individuals. His best material comes from a woman not named but not hard to identify, who describes what it felt like to be one of Kennedy's girls from the first rush when she was a nineteen-year-old Radcliffe student (Kennedy was forty, married, and running for president) to a bittersweet, postcoital moment the evening before his inauguration, when a chance comment made it clear Kennedy had no idea that a man he was considering for a high-level job was her father. She stuck it out for another two years, kept conveniently nearby with a "make-work White House job dealing with international affairs," until a sense of being used finally persuaded her to break off. She learned two things, passed on to Hersh: that Kennedy paid serious attention only to men, and that he seduced journalists in the same way he did women. This and similar stories make poignant a remark to Hersh by Jackie Kennedy's personal secretary, Mary Gallagher, that the First Lady sometimes asked her to call the President's secretary to inquire whether his schedule permitted spending the evening with him.

But the President did not simply have affairs, according to Hersh. Several Secret Service men assigned to guard the President told Hersh he had a taste for bimbos, girls brought in off the street by friends acting as procurers; that he liked cavorting naked with such women in the White House pool, that friends often joined him, and sometimes his brothers Bobby and Teddy as well. "The high point—or low point—of Presidential partying," Hersh writes, came in December 1962 at the Palm Springs estate of the movie star and crooner Bing Crosby. Secret Service men described to Hersh a night of drunken debauchery when state policemen guarding the front of the house thought the wild cries coming from the pool might be an invasion of coyotes. The women were introduced as stewardesses from a European airline, but who they really were the Secret Service men had no idea. This single tableau, including much I have not described, manages to cast a pale and bilious light over everything that's wrong with politics, sex, California, swimming pools, drinking after dinner, and all else that slips out of control once men feel they are invulnerable.

The obvious question is: Is it true? Can we trust the reporter who fell for the Marilyn papers? Two aspects of the reporting life suggest an answer. The first is that the truth never arrives neatly wrapped. Reporters must fight for every scrap of information or confirmation, and after all the hard work casual readers may airily dismiss the result as lacking a smoking gun. Reporters dream of finding the perfect witness, who knows all and wants to tell all, or the treasure trove of documents—all that secret paper that the CIA, or the Mafia's bookkeeper, or the President's lawyer, thought was safely squirreled away. But if a reporter gets to them once in a lifetime it's a sign of divine favor. We may assume that Hersh fervently dreamed of such a coup during his five years of research. The second relevant fact is that homework gradually creates a deep feel for the subject, for the operating style of the cast of characters, for the chronology and context of events. I am sure that presented to Hersh now, the Marilyn papers would set off a hundred alarm bells.

The questions inevitably raised by Hersh's gaffe are the very sort he is accustomed to jabbing at others. Did his hopes of a big score, too long in his dreams, cloud his reporter's judgment? Or did he suffer a moment of temptation, like a saint's in the wilderness, weighing the promise of big bucks against the chance no one would ever know? Hersh has made too many people squirm to sweat that one in public. "So what's new?" he said to Robert Sam Anson of *Vanity Fair*. "Boy reporter goes down wrong path." It's the inevitable answer, perhaps, but it doesn't explain anything.

The big casualty of the Marilyn-papers fiasco is the five years of hard work Hersh put into his book. One may quarrel with his judg-ments but the man is a great investigative reporter, no lie, and when he says somebody told him something he makes it easy for doubters to check it out. Nothing in *The Dark Side of Camelot* gives off even a whiff of the dead-fish aroma of the trust fund for Marilyn's mom, but Kennedy loyalists, joined by others who just don't want to know, are using Hersh's terrible misstep to dismiss what he has dug up as trifling gossip and unsupported hearsay.

I think I can understand why. Sympathy for the late President's wife must be part of it. The world may not have known for years just how much of himself Kennedy gave to other lovers, but she did, and that is hard to contemplate. Still harder to contemplate is the image of the murdered man saying okay to murder. If Hersh is right, then what we went through on November 22, 1963, is exactly what Kennedy planned for Cuba. But if it's not true, if Kennedy had nothing to do with planning the death of Castro, if the CIA was off on its own, if Hersh's witnesses were all lying, or can be dismissed, or just ignored, then we need never ask ourselves if the President's death represents a kind of rough justice.

—*The New York Times Book Review*, November 30, 1997

PART THREE

14

SOVIET INTENTIONS AND CAPABILITIES

JOHN PRADOS'S FINE history of the intelligence wars, *The Soviet Estimate: U.S. Intelligence Analysis and Russian Military Strength*,* is certain to become a standard work in the field. It's hard to think of an important intelligence issue in the past twenty-five years that Prados does not cover: the "missile gap," Galosh, the "Talinn upgrade" problem, the A-team, B-team controversy, and other flurries of concern, over "monster missiles" and alarming holes in the ground, are all there. Intelligence professionals will consult his book to find out what's in the public domain and what's still secret. Students of the national security community will mine it for data on what we knew and when we knew it.

But ordinary readers probably won't use it at all. They will find it too hard, too dense, too filled with numbers, tables, and acronyms, too dull, too obsessive in its attempt to gather in one place every fact and echo of contention in the strategic intelligence business as they have appeared over the years in the professional literature and congressional hearings. Prados's excellent bibliography, the most comprehensive I have seen, lists hundreds of items. It is one of the curses of research in this field to read the same facts and figures over and

---

* The Dial Press, 1982.

over again. How Prados survived his ordeal in the library I do not know. It must have involved years of stupefying tedium. But the result has justified his devoted efforts. Well-thumbed copies of *The Soviet Estimate* will be at the right hand of everyone who tries to understand why the United States and the Soviet Union elected to build enough nuclear weapons to break the back of our civilization.

Prados's comprehensive book raises two great questions about strategic intelligence. First: Is it honest? And second: Why are the analysts so often wrong? The question of honesty is immediately posed by the tendency of analysts to reflect the views and budgetary hopes of the institutions they represent. In the late 1940s and early 1950s, for example, the Air Force consistently predicted a huge Russian bomber-building program. Army and Navy Intelligence just as consistently derided these alarms. When the Russians finally did unveil a new long-range bomber, at the annual May Day parade in 1954, something like panic swept the upper echelons of the American government.

The CIA's Board of National Estimates (BNE) was badly buffeted in those years by conflicting claims. In theory, its paper (the generic term for finished intelligence reports) was supposed to represent the mature conclusions of the intelligence community, after all the hard evidence had been soberly analyzed. But as a practical matter, it had to sound as worried as the officials who were supposed to read its estimates. "Our answer," said Sherman Kent, board chairman at the time, according to DeForrest van Slyk, another BNE official I met in the 1970s, "is to say nothing is going to happen in the foreseeable future, and say it in the most alarming way possible." The result of this approach was one National Intelligence Estimate (NIE) after another admitting that we were still ahead for the moment but predicting a huge Russian bomber fleet down the road.

But the Russians never produced long-range bombers in any numbers. They concentrated on missiles instead. The intelligence people were slow to catch on, at least partly because the Air Force wasn't interested in missiles. It was run in the 1950s by World War II bomber generals who liked to fly. They grudgingly funded a low-level missile-research program, largely to ensure that the Navy didn't take over the job and steal away by degrees the Air Force's strategic bombardment mission. But deep down in the Air Force there were missile colonels convinced that rocket propulsion offered a cheaper, more effective way to deliver nuclear warheads. In love with missiles, the colonels concluded that the Russians were, too. In the intelligence business, this is called mirror-imaging.

One of those colonels, Ed Hall, told me that during the Korean War, when R&D funds slowed to a trickle, he concluded that nothing would budge his Air Force superiors but fear of a Russian missile. He routinely asked Air Technical Intelligence, at Wright Field, for more information about Russian missile research, but nothing came back. If they had a missile program, we didn't know much about it. So the colonel *invented* a Russian missile—a rocket, fueled by oxygen and hydrocarbons, producing one hundred tons of thrust. He figured that they must have something of the sort in the works, and drew up the plans himself. These he gave to a buddy in intelligence, asking him to include the hundred-ton rocket in his next briefing. The buddy suffered qualms of conscience, as well he should, but finally conquered his scruples and solemnly told a group of Air Force generals at Wright Field about this latest alarming development in Russian weaponry. The ploy worked fine. Funds began to flow in the colonel's direction.

It is not hard to collect stories of this sort about the intelligence business, although few involve naked fakery to quite this degree. But it is worth remembering that the colonel was right: in fact, the Russians were hard at work on missiles even bigger than the apocryphal hundred-ton rocket, and eventually the rest of the intelligence community caught on. When they did, they panicked, as they often have, and predicted a "missile gap" within a few years. The worst horrors are always in the middle distance.

Dishonesty in the intelligence business is not personal but institutional. In effect, the analysts are advocates. The Air Force wants to build planes and missiles; the Navy wants to build ships; the Army wants more tanks and fully equipped divisions. All tend to think that the Russians see things the same way, and all "interpret" the evidence according to their own lights. The scantier the evidence—and it is always scanty at the beginning—the wilder the extrapolations. Since no one knows what the evidence means for sure, every National Intelligence Estimate is subject to negotiation, an intensely political process reflecting the realities of life in Washington, where the services all have allies in Congress, alumni associations that actively lobby, and industrial backers eager to keep the factories humming. In these circumstances, the CIA can drag its feet for only so long. For example, at the height of the controversy over the SS-9—the Soviet missile, first detected in the mid-1960s, that many suspected to be a first-strike weapon—the CIA was more or less directly ordered by Melvin Laird to remove a paragraph from the Soviet NIE that said that the Russians were almost certainly not planning to build a first-strike capability. Power, not argument, carried the day. Laird was the secretary of defense, and he simply *would not accept* the offending paragraph. This may not be what scientists call objectivity, but it is the way things work.

That leaves the second great question about strategic intelligence: Why are the analysts so often wrong? Failures of prediction are the subject of endless investigation in the intelligence community, but the solution is always the same: more and better information, processed more quickly and efficiently. Thus the committees and boards proliferate, like epicycles in a Ptolemaic cosmology. The trouble with this solution is that more and better information is not readily available. Satellite photos and communications intercepts—the two principal sources of raw data—reveal a lot about what an opponent has got or is doing at the moment but very little about what he has in mind for the future. Intelligence people never tire of saying that "you can't photograph a forward plan"—at least not from a satellite. That can be done only by a spy or a technical device planted in the right place. The truth is that we have not got, or had, many of either. This leaves intelligence people with no choice but to extrapolate from the facts as we know them.

There have been three great failures of American intelligence in the years since 1945. The first was a prediction that the Russians would build bombers like ours, and lots of them. That was the "bomber gap." The second was a prediction that the Russians would have intercontinental ballistic missiles before we did, and lots of them. That was the "missile gap." The third, beginning in the mid-1960s, was a prediction that the Russians would be content with a secure deterrent— enough missiles to give us a healthy fear of attacking them—and not try to match us in numbers or quality, much less surpass us. More particularly, it was assumed that the Russians thought about missiles as we did—as tools that might prevent a war from breaking out, not weapons for winning one. This failure is not so widely recognized, does not yet have a name, and is still the subject of much debate in national security circles. The buildup is no longer disputed, but no one is really sure whether the Russians think they could win a nuclear war or whether they are willing to risk one in the pursuit of political goals. Common sense says they'd be crazy to do so, but common sense said they really didn't need all those accurate new missiles, either.

Outside of professional circles, the intelligence community does not always command respect. Some critics see it as a fraternity of closet militarists scaring each other with shrill cries that the Russians are coming. Others assume that the estimates are in the naked service of money and power—money for the military-industrial complex and power for empire-building generals. There is some truth in both caricatures, but they still fail to explain why intelligence errors run both ways: some say the Russians are coming when they're not, and some say they aren't when they are. The CIA in particular has often been accused of an "arms-control bias." If you think that sounds fine, you begin to see the problem. A bias is a bias. The CIA can't ignore the President and his principal advisers for long, which suggests that the current NIEs reflect Reagan's alarms—if only by treating them with that servile gravitas of which bureaucracies are uniquely capable. To that extent, the agency must have swung toward Reagan's view that the Russians want military superiority. But there is a case to be made that for ten years, ending in the late 1970s, CIA analysts were amazingly slow to see a pattern in what amounted to a Russian military buildup on a stupendous scale.

At the heart of most intelligence failures is a misreading of evidence, but anybody can make a mistake. Prados catalogs many examples in his book. The troubling thing is the persistence of certain *types* of errors, which we might categorize as errors of fear and errors of hope. Behind all of them is something rarely alluded to in the estimates or the professional literature—the awesome power of nuclear weapons. Referring to it would constitute something very like a breach of etiquette, but in fact the weapons themselves have long since superseded the political differences that divide the United States and the Soviet Union. We threaten each other not politically but militarily. The magnitude of the threat beggars the routine superlatives of the language. Fear and hope are ultimately what twist the analysts this way and that. Some see the Russians preparing to pounce, and desperately warn that we must build up our deterrent. Others take a softer, more optimistic view, and look for signs that nobody means any harm, they're just like us, if we can only keep the jingoists quiet we can work things out.

As early as 1945, a number of atomic scientists saw how things would go. They described a kind of Buck Rogers global war, with missiles and bombers filling the skies. This hardware was imagined in a moment, but it took a long time to build. At the end of 1945, the

United States had a couple of dozen B-29 bombers modified to carry the huge atomic weapons of the period. The Russians, of course, had neither bomb nor bomber, and did not acquire both until the mid-1950s. It took another ten years for them to build missiles in appreciable numbers. We were ahead of them all the way and are still ahead; but finally, after thirty-five years of sustained national effort, Buck Rogers's war is a reality. All the terrible things foreseen by the pessimists have come to pass. The Russians have big, accurate missiles that might destroy ours on the ground. It took longer than the pessimists thought it would, but that seems academic now. We threaten them in the same way, and both sides are busy with technical improvements. Time to react grows ever shorter. Pershing missiles in Europe will be only three or four minutes away from Soviet silos. Some of their missiles, I have been told, are already on a launch-on-warning status. A similar American program is implicit in Reagan's plans for a huge new investment in command, communications, and control systems. Neither side wants to be caught on the ground, and both will eventually trust computers for safety. Thus it is the weapons themselves that have become the principal cause of fear and friction between the two sides. When war comes, it will almost certainly begin with an onslaught of weapons on weapons. The cities' turn will come last.

Large questions are anathema to intelligence analysts. Their paper is cautious and factual. They would not presume to tell policymakers where we are going. John Prados shares this restraint. At the end of this thorough, useful book, he notes only that the situation is a dangerous one. The historian Arnold Toynbee, at the end of a long life studying the rise and fall of civilizations, risked a bolder view. In *War and Civilization*, published in 1950, he wrote about the two great wars of the twentieth century:

> ...The most ominous thing about these wars is that they were not isolated or unprecedented calamities. They were two wars

in a series; and when we envisage the whole series in a synoptic view, we discover that this is not only a series but a progression. In our recent Western History war has been following war in an ascending order of intensity; and today it is already apparent that the war of 1939–45 was not the climax of this crescendo movement.

—*The Atlantic*, April 1982

15

THE EARS OF AMERICA

"BRUTE FORCE" IS a phrase which turns up often in *The Puzzle Palace: A Report on America's Most Secret Agency*, James Bamford's useful investigation of the National Security Agency, the largest but least known of American intelligence services.* As used by NSA officials, "brute force" refers to the method of last resort in cracking secret codes. The best method is to obtain the key to the code by stealing it, buying it, or figuring it out, but that is often impossible. A "brute force" attack simply tries out all the possible keys to a code identified through intercepted messages.

These possibilities can be very numerous. A commercial cipher with a fifty-six-bit key devised by IBM in the mid-1970s, for example, would present an inquisitive outsider with about seventy quadrillion possibilities. Large as that number is, a computer could be built with speed and capacity enough to try out every last one of them in less than a day. This helps to explain why the NSA's headquarters at Fort Meade, Maryland, is the computer capital of the world. Lieutenant General Marshall S. Carter, director of the NSA (DIRNSA) for just over four years between 1965 and 1969, told Bamford he was in charge of five

---

* Houghton Mifflin, 1982.

and a half acres of computers. Another NSA official told him that computer acreage is now about double what it was in Carter's day.

It is the scale of the NSA that impresses. According to Bamford, the NSA's main building at Fort Meade contains about 1.9 million square feet of floor space, roughly equal to the CIA's headquarters in Langley, Virginia, and the Capitol building in Washington combined. It has employed as many as 95,000 people, classifies 50 million to 100 million documents a year, produces 40 tons of classified waste per day, has up to $1 billion in contracts out at any given time, and has an annual budget of perhaps $10 billion.

Making, breaking, and protecting codes is only part of the work conducted by this vast establishment, and the smaller part at that. The larger part is collecting and analysing COMINT, SIGINT, and ELINT. COMINT and SIGINT are communications and signals intelligence—messages of every conceivable type, from ordinary commercial cables to Soviet naval communications to ships at sea. When the Soviet space capsule *Soyuz I* ran into trouble during reentry in April 1967, technicians at an NSA listening station in Turkey taped the whole awful event, from the first discussion of problems with the parachute through the cosmonaut's final farewell to his wife and a terminal scream when the capsule burned up as it plunged into the earth's atmosphere. Also included under the general heading of SIGINT are radio transmissions of a technical nature such as radar or telemetry broadcast by Soviet missiles during test flights, the principal source of American intelligence about the performance of Soviet strategic weapons. ELINT is electronics intelligence, defined as electromagnetic radiators with a nonatomic origin. (HUMINT—human intelligence collected by traditional espionage—is the province of the CIA.)

The size of the NSA budget is partly explained by the huge technical apparatus required to collect so many radio transmissions of so many different types. Here, too, the approach is one of brute force. The NSA attempts to collect all Soviet transmissions—the full daily broadcast of every conventional radio station in all the Soviet republics, every transmission to every Soviet embassy abroad, every broadcast to a ship at sea, every transmission by military units on maneuvers in Eastern Europe, the radio traffic of every control tower at Soviet airports, the radar signature of every Soviet system. (If B-52s or a new bomber are to penetrate Soviet airspace in the event of war, for example, they have got to know where Soviet air defenses are located. The NSA helps to provide the maps.)

Even when the transmissions can't be read, which is often the case, the volume of traffic itself is analyzed for whatever it might reveal. Shortly before the Berlin Wall was built in 1961, it is said, the sheer number of radio messages and the level of the codes in which they were encrypted should have indicated that something was up. In August 1968 Soviet military units on the periphery of Czechoslovakia were "lost" for several days. Apparently this was achieved by sophisticated jamming which disguised actual Soviet military radio traffic. Richard Helms, then the director of central intelligence and nominally in charge of the NSA, confessed to the President's Foreign Intelligence Advisory Board that he was much embarrassed by the failure, but assured them the intelligence community would have done better if the Soviets had been heading West.

Monitoring Soviet radio transmissions is only half the work. Since it's always possible that a code might be cracked in the future, the unread transmissions—*all* the unread transmissions—are stored, more or less forever, on magnetic tape.

The National Security Agency was established by President Truman —secretly: its official charter has never been made public—in the fall of 1952, but its true origins go back to the First World War when a State Department code clerk, Herbert O. Yardley, tried his hand at a secret message addressed to Woodrow Wilson in May 1916. He solved it within a couple of hours and immediately concluded that the British, who controlled the eastern terminal of transatlantic cables to North

America, were reading the US government's most secret diplomatic traffic. When the United States entered the war Yardley transferred to the military, founded a Code and Cipher Solution Subsection in the office devoted to military intelligence, and at the war's end was arranging liaison with the French Chambre noire, or "black chamber," a name Yardley borrowed when he was appointed to head a permanent code-breaking office in the War Department in 1919.

Yardley's initial budget was $100,000, with which he hired a staff of fifty at salaries ranging from $1,200 per year for clerks up to $3,000 for senior code-breakers. But the end of the war presented Yardley with two major problems. The first was the end of official censorship, which meant he no longer had automatic access to international cable traffic. Indeed, it was now against federal law to intercept messages, but Yardley quietly arranged with the management of Western Union and Postal Telegraph, the two major international carriers, for the Black Chamber to temporarily "borrow" messages. The two companies agreed to this illegal arrangement in the interest of national security, a precedent that was to be enduring.

Yardley's major coup during this period was cracking the Japanese diplomatic code, which allowed the US to read Tokyo's fallback position during the negotiations in 1921 to establish a fixed ratio of capital ships among the navies of Britain, the United States, and Japan. Knowing that Japanese negotiators had been instructed to accept the ten to six ratio pressed by Britain and the United States, the Western team simply sat tight until the Japanese gave in.

But this was the high point of the Black Chamber and of Yardley's career as well. His second major problem in the immediate years after World War I—indifference at high levels—was never overcome. It is war and the threat of war that turn a government's thoughts to espionage. The Black Chamber's budget was gradually reduced to $25,000 a year, most of it provided by the State Department. When Herbert Hoover's secretary of state, Henry L. Stimson, took office in March

1929, Yardley hesitated to brief him on the Black Chamber's work. When he finally did so a few months later, Stimson was appalled by the whole undertaking and ordered it to cease immediately with words about as close to immortal as any ever uttered by an American statesman: "Gentlemen do not read each other's mail."

But the end of the Black Chamber and Yardley's departure from government did not end American code-breaking efforts. The War Department established a Signal Intelligence Service (SIS) in 1930 which limped along on tiny budgets (never more than $17,400) until 1937, when the obvious approach of war brought high-level interest and funds to match. By September 1939 the staff of the SIS had grown from seven to nineteen. By December 7, 1941, it had reached 331. (The SIS had even cracked the new Japanese diplomatic code, called "Purple," and had intercepted a message that indicated war was near, but a comedy of errors delayed a warning to the US commander in Hawaii until several hours after the attack on Pearl Harbor had begun.)

By the war's end the SIS staff exceeded 10,000 and its official duties had vastly expanded to include the collection and analysis of all sorts of communications and signals intelligence. In 1949 the various communications intelligence branches were combined and named the Armed Forces Security Agency; three years later—largely as the result of high-level dissatisfaction with the AFSA's performance during the Korean War, as well as weariness with the service rivalries which drove the White House half crazy during the postwar years—the entire process of reorganization was repeated. In its present form the National Security Agency not only is bigger than the postal, telephone, and telegraph services (known as PT&Ts) of most major nations, but it draws heavily on the services of the Army, the Navy, and the Air Force as well.

James Bamford has assembled all that was known, and much that was unknown, in his history of the NSA, but the result does not make for light reading. The chapter about Yardley and a handful of stories scattered throughout the text provide the only narrative. For the rest, his book reads like a study of AT&T, with methodical lists of its directors and deputy directors, the divisions and subdivisions of the NSA, and the listening stations of various kinds scattered about the world. A great many officials are identified by name and job title. Much hardware is paraded across the page, from elaborate computer retrieval systems to giant dish antennae. Much of this material is new, gleaned from 6,000 pages of NSA newsletters and Justice Department documents that Bamford obtained under the Freedom of Information Act (and which the government, in 1982, attempted to retrieve with the claim they had been released in error). Bamford has also conducted several revealing interviews, especially with General Carter and Francis Raven, formerly in charge of reading Soviet and, later, third world communications traffic.

Bamford deserves special praise for largely avoiding the mocking, ironic, superior tone adopted by many journalists when writing about the intelligence and defense communities. These virtues add up to a considerable achievement. But that should not obscure the fact that the secrecy surrounding the NSA is still largely intact. Bamford has mapped the landscape, much as David Wise and Thomas B. Ross did in 1965 with their similar trailbreaking study of the CIA, *The Invisible Government*. Future researchers will owe Bamford a considerable debt, but they will also have plenty to do.

They might well begin with a knotty subject that Bamford never treats at length—the NSA's contribution to the national security. This is hard to gauge. Investigation of the intelligence community by House and Senate select committees in the mid-1970s for the most part mentioned only the failures and "excesses," like NSA's Operation Minaret, which maintained watch lists of about 1,680 Americans for the Bureau of Narcotics and Dangerous Drugs (BNDD), the FBI, the Secret Service, the CIA, and the Defense Intelligence Agency. Between 1967 and 1973 the NSA distributed nearly four thousand reports concerning these

Americans, but it would be hard to say what practical use they served. One director told the Senate select committee that the NSA's monitoring of international phone calls and cable traffic had helped the BNDD intercept some large drug shipments and had prevented "a major terrorist act," presumably a Palestinian attack on American Jews. Another, much larger NSA program, Operation Shamrock, intercepted just about all cable traffic entering and leaving the United States between 1945 and 1975.

This was a very large undertaking indeed. Presumably it gave the NSA access to all diplomatic cable traffic with the exception of messages hand-carried by courier. How many of these messages could have been read by the NSA is not known, but it must have been a large number. Were they useful? Bamford doesn't know, and I don't either. Officials were doubtless glad to have them, but there is no public evidence that reading other countries' secret messages has really served the American national interest. There is also no evidence that the counterintelligence arms of the FBI and the CIA were aided by NSA interceptions, or what, if anything, was done with the staggering quantities of information that must have been obtained relating to international trade in oil, grain, or high-technology equipment.

My guess is that the NSA's interception of telephone and cable messages picked up something about everything, that a lot of it fell into a nice-to-know category, and that very little of it was both critical in importance and unobtainable by other means. Whether that little is worth what it costs is impossible for an outsider to say. Officials in the national security community clearly think that it is. The only public fruits of the NSA's work are the seven thick volumes of translations published daily by the Foreign Broadcast Information Service. These are consulted by scholars and occasionally by journalists. At the moment, for example, they are a principal source of information about Iran.

There can be no question about the utility of the NSA's technical collection of radio signals related to military matters. It is well known that the verification of arms agreements, as well as general intelligence about Soviet military programs, depend all but exclusively on "national technical means," most of which are operated by the NSA. (Reconnaissance satellites are run by the Air Force under the direction of the National Reconnaissance Office. The contribution from spies run by the CIA is minuscule.) But that is only part of it. If the United States and the Soviet Union ever fight a big general war, all aspects of that war will involve intelligence of the sort collected by the NSA, from the first shots or missile launches until the final armistice or exhausted silence. The "winner"—we will not try here to settle whether there can be one—will very likely be the side with the most enduring system of "c³I," or command, control, communications, and intelligence. This is certainly the Pentagon's belief and it explains why the Reagan administration is planning to spend $18 billion on c³I over the next few years, most of it for ways to maintain or replace facilities destroyed—"stressed" in the Pentagon's term—in the course of the war.

Allied success in cracking German and Japanese codes during World War II is now well known, and the NSA's acres of computers are evidence that it hopes to do the same. But code-breaking is no longer the primary focus of the intelligence part of c³I. Modern armies emit a continual buzz and hum of radio messages and signals. The fire-control and target-finding devices of tanks and fighter planes, for example, give them away in the very process of aiding the tanks and planes to attack or to defend themselves from an enemy. Even before the ignition of a missile's rocket mortar could be picked up by infrared sensors on a satellite in geosychronous orbit high overhead, the launch order would have been suggested through radio signals. Firing a missile is not like throwing a light switch. The preparation to launch involves a blizzard of microwave transmissions.

It is the same with conventional forces. An army requires an intricate

THE EARS OF AMERICA

command web linked by radio. Mapping that web reveals where every-body is and what he's doing. But figuring these things out—finding the ways in which military units, and even weapons themselves, talk to each other—can't wait until the war begins. It has to be done in advance. This is where the NSA comes in, and why its ELINT planes and SIGINT ships have so often been attacked by target countries. The 1950s were the heyday of "spoofing"—deliberate intrusions of Soviet airspace, sometimes by formations of bombers, in order to trigger radar defenses so that they could be monitored, mapped, and identi-fied. Several US aircraft were shot down during these provocative and dangerous exercises. In 1964 the US destroyers *Maddox* and *Turner Joy* were on SIGINT missions in the Tonkin Gulf where they were apparently attacked by North Vietnamese patrol boats. The *Pueblo*, captured by North Korea in 1968, was on a similar mission.

Perhaps the most notorious of these incidents occurred in June 1967, when Israeli aircraft attacked the SIGINT ship *Liberty* cruising along the Mediterranean coast of the Sinai peninsula. The territorial limit claimed by Egypt was twelve miles, by Israel six. The *Liberty*, decks crowded with electronic gear, scrupulously remained in inter-national waters. Why was she crowding in on the battle zone? "Some-body wanted to listen to some close tactical program," Raven told Bamford, "or communications or something which nobody in the world gave a damn about...."

On the morning of the third day of the war, June 8, Israeli aircraft repeatedly buzzed the ship but made no attempt to contact her by radio. At 2 PM the aircraft returned and attacked the *Liberty* without warning of any kind, using rockets, cannon fire, and napalm. Eight US Navy men were killed outright. The ship was set afire and punc-tured by eight hundred shell holes big enough to put a fist through. At 2:24 PM three Israeli torpedo boats appeared and renewed the attack. A forty-foot-wide hole was blown in the side of the *Liberty*. Lifeboats were machine-gunned. Another twenty-four men were killed and over a hundred wounded. At 4:10 PM the Israeli government reported the attack to the American embassy in Tel Aviv and apologized. The following day an explanation was offered. The Israelis had mistaken the *Liberty* (455 feet long) for the Egyptian coastal steamer *El Quseir* (275 feet long). The US government formally accepted the apology and the explanation, and in 1980, after long negotiations, finally received $6 million in compensation for the ship (which had cost more than $30 million).

It is not hard to understand why Israel insisted the attack was a mistake, or why Washington accepted the explanation at face value, but scholars and military experts who have studied the episode mostly take a different view. For them the hard question is not whether the attack was deliberate, but why the Israelis thought it necessary. Writing in the *United States Naval Institute Proceedings* of June 1978, the naval historian Richard K. Smith concluded that Israeli military authorities, hoping to launch an attack on the Golan Heights in Syria before a cease-fire could be imposed upon them, feared that the *Liberty* was scooping up enough battlefield radio traffic to see that Israel had already won the war. According to Smith (as quoted by Bamford), the Israelis wanted to maintain the confusions natural to a rapidly unfolding campaign—what Clausewitz called "the fog of war"—in order to retain freedom of action for another few but critical days.

In the absence of definite proof Smith's view must be taken as only educated surmise. The point here is that the *Liberty*, like other "platforms" for collecting intelligence run by the NSA, really did have the capacity to gather in and process enough radio transmissions to give American authorities almost as good a view of the progress of the war, and at almost the same time, as could be obtained by the Israelis themselves. The utility of SIGINT is suggested by Israel's alleged willingness to take such drastic action against its main, indeed its only important, ally. Outsiders have sometimes criticized the NSA for its "vacuum cleaner" approach to collection, especially where the information sucked up includes the conversations and cables of American citizens. But it is precisely this omnivorousness—the "brute force" scale of collecting—that makes the NSA worth $10 billion a year to American defense planners.

Like the rest of the intelligence community, the NSA is not very good at predicting things—especially large things which come as an unpleasant surprise. It failed to predict the outbreak of the Korean War, the Chinese crossing of the Yalu River, the building of the Berlin Wall, the Soviet emplacement of missiles in Cuba in 1962, the Tet offensive in 1968, or the Soviet invasion of Czechoslovakia later that year. This list might be much extended. But the truth is that intelligence services are best at more mundane tasks—finding things, counting things, and describing things. The NSA has helped to provide US officials with a comprehensive, reliable, and extremely detailed knowledge of Soviet strategic forces. It is probably this fact which explains the willingness of Admiral Noel Gayler, the NSA director between 1969 and 1972, to support publicly the campaign to freeze nuclear weapons at current levels, rather than build the vast new systems which the Reagan administration claims are needed to "catch up" with the Russians. The focus of the NSA since its birth has been the Soviet Union. Occasionally it has gathered juicy political information—the conversations over radio-telephone of Soviet leaders traveling about Moscow in their limousines, for example. One ought not to slight such achievements. But the NSA's main job has been on a much vaster scale—to paint a comprehensive electronic portait, a kind of wiring diagram, of the Soviet armed forces.

The Soviets conduct similar operations against the West. Among other things they maintain a worldwide fleet of fishing trawlers that double as SIGINT ships. One is stationed at all times, for example, near the US missile testing site at Vandenberg Air Force Base on the coast of California, and another waits downrange near Kwajalein

Lagoon, the target area in the Marshall Islands. The Soviets also spare no pains to keep track of what the NSA is doing. A retired intelligence officer, Sam Halpern, once asked me to remove from something I had written the names of four CIA technicians who had handled secret communications traffic at a US consulate in Africa during the 1960s. He told me the Russians went to great lengths to identify Americans who had anything to do with codes, tried to recruit or blackmail them, and at times had even physically attacked and injured them in the hope that a replacement would prove an easier target. The officer insisted that the four men I had identified might be in physical danger if I published their names. When I finally admitted to myself that this could really be so, I dropped the names.

From time to time Soviet efforts of this sort are successful, as suggested in July 1982 when the British arrested Geoffrey Arthur Prime, a Russian-language translator who worked for Britain's equivalent of the NSA—Government Communications Headquarters—for nine years between 1968 and 1977. A *New York Times* story on October 24, 1982, reported that US intelligence officials were much worried about the Prime case because the NSA and GCH cooperate closely, and because Prime's job as a translator put him, and the Russians, in an ideal position to determine which of their codes had been compromised. The officials also raised the possibility that the Russians had been systematically feeding false information to the West through messages they knew we could read. Intelligence officials do not usually tell reporters of such matters. The motive in this case was clearly to pressure the British into greater candor.

The damage caused by penetration of this sort in peacetime can mostly be repaired; in wartime—or in the sort of crisis situations that can lead to war—it could be nothing short of a disaster. If the Germans had ever learned that the British at Bletchley Park were reading the daily location reports of submarines in the North Atlantic during World War II, to give only one example, the campaign to starve Britain might have gone the other way. It is in the nature of intelligence work that something very large, like the NSA, can be seriously injured by something very small—the compromise of even a single troubled employee (such as Prime), or the acquisition of a briefcase full of documents. The obsession with secrecy that follows from this fact helps to explain why the NSA is so unhappy about the publication of Bamford's book.

Frederick the Great of Prussia once said that an ordinary citizen should never know his country was at war. American policy since World War II has been to go Frederick one better, anticipating nothing but trouble from kibitzers. For thirty years the NSA, despite its size, remained happily in shadow. Bamford has given us our first good, clear look at it, and what we see confirms the impression—to my mind, at least—that the principal undertaking of our time is the preparation for war.

—*The New York Review of Books*, February 3, 1983

16

NOTES FROM UNDERGROUND

THE FOUR-ENGINE US Navy aircraft which made an emergency landing on China's Hainan island on April 1, 2001, was on a routine ELINT mission, so called for what it collected—electronic intelligence. A crew of four actually flew the plane; the other twenty Americans on board, all Navy personnel but on a mission ultimately sponsored by the National Security Agency, were there to find, identify, collect, and record a range of electronic emissions from routine military chatter on radios to the characteristic signature of Chinese defensive radars.

The NSA, with the help of the Navy and Air Force, has been doing this since the late 1940s, sometimes aggressively, and the target countries detest it. In the early days the Soviet Union shot down as many as forty American aircraft on ELINT missions, some of them deep inside Soviet airspace, killing perhaps two hundred American civilians and military men. The most recent incident, however, occurred over international waters in the South China Sea; reckless shadowing of the slow-moving, propeller-driven American EP-3E by a Chinese fighter aircraft appears to have caused a midair collision. Accident it may have been, but the message was the same as that of the Soviet shootdowns of yesteryear—back off.

But backing off is the last thing the United States is likely to do. Collecting intelligence is what great powers have learned to do instead of going to war, and the risk of war between the United States and China, not great, and at first glance crazy and unthinkable, has nevertheless been growing year by year since the collapse of the Soviet Union in 1991. The big irritant is Taiwan, over which China seeks to reassert political control. American administrations haven't ruled this out, so long as it isn't achieved by military force. But the specter of military force is very much part of the strategy used by China, which has been threatening Taiwan in symbolic ways, such as test-firing missiles near the island, and the United States has been demonstrating support in symbolic ways, such as agreeing to major new weapons sales, but not, so far, the sophisticated Aegis defense system.

What happened to the Navy's EP-3E has its symbolic side, too—the Americans were flying it up and down the Chinese coast partly to show we can't be pushed around, and the Chinese were shadowing it aggressively to show we'd better be ready for a lot of pushing. The civilian observer watching the drama unfold on CNN probably feels much like an adult watching toddlers squabble in a sandbox—what are they fighting about? Why can't they just get along?

But the making of symbolic gestures is not why the United States spends uncountable billions on ELINT flights and all the rest of the intelligence-collecting activities of the NSA. So what did the Chinese find so threatening and how did the Americans plan to use what they learned? These questions are addressed, with numerous examples and a wealth of human and technical detail, in *Body of Secrets: Anatomy of the Ultra-Secret National Security Agency from the Cold War through the Dawn of a New Century*, by James Bamford, who wrote one of the really good books about American intelligence some twenty years ago, and has now done it again.[1]

The new book revisits old ground but there is nothing tired about it. Bamford has learned some things that ought to make headlines and

---

1. Doubleday, 2001.

ignite serious argument, but the real strengths of the book are to be found in its portrait of the NSA—an institution of staggering size and capacity—and in its firm conviction that every American with enough interest in the world to read a daily newspaper ought to know what the NSA does, how it does it, and why. This may sound like elementary civics but candor about intelligence comes at a cost: the secrets uncovered by intelligence organizations are always inconvenient to somebody, and sometimes the way secrets are obtained, once it has become publicly visible, is ruled out of order. No government chooses candor if it can hide what it's up to, and without Bamford's efforts, beginning with his first book, *The Puzzle Palace*, in 1982,[2] the initials NSA would probably still stand for "no such agency."

The principal target of the National Security Agency is communication by foreign powers, and especially enciphered communications. During World War II the Allies were so successful in learning to read German and Japanese codes that some historians argue it made the difference between victory and defeat. The German navy's reliance on the Enigma code machine, cracked by British wizards at Bletchley Park, cost them the Battle of the Atlantic, and ultimately the war, just as the Japanese navy never recovered from their crushing defeat at the Battle of Midway, the fruit of American success in reading the Japanese naval code called Purple. At the end of the war, Bamford tells us in *Body of Secrets*, the Allies discovered that the Germans had also succeeded in cracking enemy codes, especially those of the Soviets transmitted by radio over a machine that broke messages into nine separate channels at one end and reassembled them at the other. The Germans read the Russian messages with a machine of their own, and once we had a copy of that machine we could begin to read Soviet back traffic —messages that had been intercepted and filed away in their coded form in the hope of just such a happy breakthrough.

---

2. See Chapter Fifteen.

Brilliant as that success was—Bamford calls it a "once-in-a-lifetime discovery" for the American soldiers who dug up the German files and equipment from beneath a cobblestone street—it was soon matched by US Army code-breakers who exploited a "bust," or procedural error, in Soviet diplomatic cables enciphered on onetime pads, which were normally unbreakable, and managed to read thousands of communications in whole or in part. Among the several hundred people disguised by cryptonyms in those messages, collectively called VENONA, were the atom spies who had betrayed important design secrets of the first plutonium bomb to the Russians.

But that, apparently, was it. Despite the immense importance attached to reading Soviet messages throughout the cold war, and the huge effort devoted to the task, the NSA never again achieved a similar breakthrough in reading an important Soviet code on a routine basis. "During the 1960s," Bamford writes, "NSA's inability to break high-level Soviet codes was becoming its biggest secret." Whole divisions of the NSA with platoons of mathematicians and acres of computers evidently tried and failed at a job which is now growing even harder. The NSA was long the silent driver in the development of computers and it still actively supports cutting-edge research—on computers, for example, that make use of living protoplasm in the manner of the human brain. But computers not only make it easier to crack codes; they make it easier to encrypt messages as well, and in the war of the code-makers and code-breakers the makers seem to be pulling ahead.

"Public encryption," as it is called—the ability of private citizens to have and use strong codes defying sophisticated attack—is something the NSA fought against tenaciously for nearly thirty years in a clandestine campaign recounted in lively detail in Steven Levy's book *Crypto: How the Code Rebels Beat the Government—Saving Privacy in the Digital Age.*[3] Early in the 1970s a handful of young computer

---

3. Viking, 2001.

wizards, distrustful of government after the hard lessons of Vietnam and Watergate, began to think of ways to preserve "privacy" in the computer age. What they meant was the ability of people to communicate without fear of the government, and what they wanted, once they started to think hard about the problem, was a means of encrypting private communication.

Levy's book follows the genesis and development of the idea of "public key encryption," brainchild of two bright and stiff-necked young mathematicians—Whitfield Diffie and Marty Hellman. Codes traditionally substitute letters according to a formula more or less complex, sometimes with the aid of machines. To read a coded message one needs the key—the formula for unscrambling the substitutions. From ancient times until the 1970s the key was always secret, held only by the sender and receiver of an encoded message. For obvious security reasons keys were frequently changed, creating a logistical problem of nightmarish difficulty for the government of a great power sending scores of thousands of coded messages to diplomats and military units all over the world. The Diffie-Hellman stroke of genius was the public key—a very large number, derived from a so-called one-way mathematical function which could be openly distributed. The first Diffie-Hellman keys were the result of multiplying two large prime numbers, a function extremely difficult to reverse. Over the following decades the original Diffie-Hellman approach was developed and refined as mathematicians created modern encryption systems which can be used to protect cell phone conversations, e-mail messages, and commerce on the World Wide Web.

How these systems actually work is complicated but not dauntingly so, and I urge interested readers to consult Levy's book. What matters here is that Diffie and Hellman began working on sophisticated codes outside the Triple Fence—Levy's term of choice for the heavily guarded, supersecret NSA. Diffie and Hellman asked no one's permission and believed they needed none. The NSA's position was, first, that code work, like certain principles of atomic physics, was born secret—classified as soon as conceived. This was such an egregious intrusion on academic freedom and the First Amendment to the Constitution that the NSA retreated to a backup claim that codes were in effect "munitions" under the law and could be denied export on grounds of national security. Because large computer software companies resisted the complexity of issuing two versions of software—a domestic program with high-level encryption, and an export version easy to crack—and because they correctly imagined foreign customers would avoid programs expressly designed to help American spies read them, public encryption was slow to develop and catch on. This Pyrrhic victory of the NSA is one reason few Americans can protect their communications and Web sites with strong encryption, and are thus too often open to invasion by hackers—or foreign information warfare experts, about which more in a moment. At the end of the millennium the NSA could still read just about all private American communications—although it was enjoined by law from doing so—while it had lost the ability to read high-level codes used by other countries, like China, Russia, and its predecessor, the Soviet Union.

The one really big and central thing the NSA was conceived and funded to do apparently never got done, but that does not mean the agency was idle or the money wasted. If we couldn't read Russian secret communications enciphered at the highest level, we could nevertheless read those of just about every other country, friend or foe, and written messages, in the electronic age, were only part of what proved interesting. Modern military forces are like vast nervous systems, linked from the loftiest general down to the lowliest private by a connective web of warning and reporting systems sometimes called C^3I—pronounced "see-cubed-eye"—command, control, communications, and intelligence. What the generals are reporting to the Kremlin or the Pentagon is important, but so is what test missiles are telling ground crews about trajectories, for example; or what sergeants in

Siberia, chatting on the phone, might reveal about the local inventory of nuclear weapons; or how many divisions of Chinese assault troops have been established along the Formosa Strait, and whether assault craft are already there or on the way. Maybe we can't read the instructions of China to its ambassadors but all the stuff we can "read," analyzed, insofar as possible, as a whole, brings us pretty close to what the Chinese leaders have on their minds. The important thing to grasp about the National Security Agency is its core belief that the best way to collect the important bits is to collect all the bits, and to understand further that it not only tries to do this—it does. All of it.

Bamford has a revealing but wearying chapter toward the end of *Body of Secrets* in which he sums up the bare facts about the NSA, telling us how many people work for the agency (38,000), eating how much soup every day (200 gallons), using how much electricity (as much as the city of Annapolis does), donating how many pints of blood annually (6,500), generating how many tons of classified paper waste each year (11,000, converted into a paper slurry used to make pizza boxes), all of it housed in how many square feet of building space (roughly a small city), surrounded by parking lots with room for how many cars (17,000). This chapter is forty-seven pages long and it essentially consists entirely of numbers intended to knock your socks off. A typical paragraph reads:

> While copies of secrets are regularly destroyed, the original information is seldom given up. Down the street from the tape library [which "may soon reach the point where all the information on the planet can be placed inside"], in Support Activities Building 2, is the NSA Archives and Records Center. Here, more than 129 million documents, all more than a quarter of a century old, are still hidden from historians and collecting dust at enormous cost to taxpayers. Even the NSA has a hard time comprehending the volume of material. "The sheer number of records

is astounding," said one internal report. A stack of them would be over nine miles tall, higher than the cruising altitude of a Boeing 747.

Bamford knows and tells us a lot about the NSA but some subjects are apparently too tough even for him. The agency's current director, Lieutenant General Michael V. Hayden, came to the NSA from a job running an "information warfare" think tank for the Joint Chiefs of Staff. Information warfare is one of the hot topics in the intelligence world. It involves the attempt to penetrate, monitor, manipulate, control, or destroy the computer-controlled operating systems of an opponent, and it is a whole lot easier to achieve when attacking unencrypted systems—which is what attackers often find in the United States, thanks to the NSA's diehard resistance to public key cryptography. Every reader of the newspaper knows that bright teenage hackers can occasionally find their way inside Pentagon computer networks, or figure out a way to crash Microsoft for a day or two. The FBI warned at the end of April 2001 that Chinese hackers protesting the loss of their plane and pilot in the EP-3E incident planned to attack American sites. One attack typical of the many that followed the FBI warning took over the Labor Department's Web site with a photograph of the missing Chinese pilot and a text reading:

CHINA HACK!
China Tianyu is here and salute a flag. The whole country is sorry for losing the best son of China—Wangwei forever, we will miss you until the end of the day.

No significant damage was done, but the Chinese government, believed to be the sponsor of the attacks, was making it clear that the United States was vulnerable.

Imagine what a really determined NSA, which is the biggest employer of mathematicians in the United States, could do to the power grid, or the air traffic control system, or the telephone switching centers of a target country. The NSA, the CIA, and other intelligence organizations isolate their sensitive computer systems with an "air gap"—there is no two-way connection to the rest of the world. But even classified systems, however well protected, are vulnerable to people like Robert Hanssen, the recently arrested FBI officer accused of spying for Russia. Hanssen was something of a computer wizard and he even wrote some of the bureau's most sensitive computer programs for compiling data.

But access to classified computers does not require a willing agent; blunders and ignorance can also open doors. Before he was pardoned by President Clinton, the former CIA director John Deutch was facing potential criminal charges for misusing an unclassified computer to handle classified data. According to investigators, Deutch's home computer had also visited "adult sites" on the Internet. Gene Poteat, the current president of the Association of Former Intelligence Officers and an information warfare innovator cited in Bamford's book, told me recently that a visit to an Internet porn site was a voyage into the unknown. The "best" ones are said to be in Russia, and many of them routinely install "applets"—miniature programs—on the computers of visitors to enhance graphics and the like. Where benign applets can go, malign applets can follow. Getting malign code into a classified computer is exactly what the air gap is intended to prevent.

The CIA's investigators said they found no evidence that Deutch's home computer had been compromised, but their worst-case nightmare was clear enough—some distracted high official, working carelessly at home, would somehow bring to the office a malign computer program concealed on a memory card. Whether the CIA, the NSA, or any other American intelligence agency has ever apprehended a "troll" program—the computer equivalent of a human mole—is unknown, but that is the kind of thing the NSA is simultaneously worrying about and trying to do. Just how wrong things can go was demonstrated on Monday evening, January 24, 2000, when the principal NSA computers crashed. The cause apparently had something to do with the Year 2000 problem, but what it was Bamford does not spell out. The result was the sort of thing information warriors dream of achieving on D-Day. For three days the NSA computers were down; information was recorded and stored, but the computers failed to sort, identify, read, interpret, or distribute any of it.

Information warfare is a new field with the potential for plenty of mischief, but Bamford gives us little beyond the concept of that potential. What he provides in *Body of Secrets* is a portrait of the agency and many accounts of the role it played in moments of crisis over the last fifty years. Like the CIA, the FBI, and the Defense Intelligence Agency, the NSA does its best to conceal what it can and does collect in order to prevent busybodies on the American public stage from trying to tell it what to look for. That right to make assignments, called tasking, is jealously preserved for the White House and other officials at the highest level, but even they are sometimes of two minds —sticking the national nose into a tense situation, then paralyzed about what to do with what it has found. Bamford tells one such story, familiar in outline but filled with new information, about the USS *Liberty*, which came to grief during the second of the Arab–Israeli wars. It would be hard to think of a better example of the ways in which intelligence gathering can generate information officials do not want to know.

The basic facts of the *Liberty* incident have long been known. Crammed with sensitive gear for picking up electronic intelligence, the *Liberty* was dispatched to the Mediterranean shores of the Sinai peninsula at the outset of the war in June 1967. Like the EP-3E impounded in China, the ship was operated by the Navy but was ultimately working for the NSA and the *Liberty*'s crew included a number of civilians segregated deep within the ship, where they picked up, sorted, and recorded SIGINT, the term of art for signals intelligence. On June 8, as the war was nearing an end, the *Liberty* was patrolling a dozen miles offshore from the Sinai town of El Arish, monitoring the radio traffic of both Israelis and Egyptians. "We want to work in the UHF [ultra-high-frequency] range," the ship's captain was told by the chief of the NSA contingent, Lieutenant Commander David Lewis. "That's mostly line-of-sight stuff. If we're over the horizon we might as well be back in Abidjan." UHF is where tactical units converse, so the *Liberty* was right up shoulder to shoulder with both belligerents. This worried the Navy but an order to pull back issued by the Joint Chiefs of Staff was delayed for sixteen hours—it had been misrouted to Hawaii—and by the time it reached the Mediterranean it was too late: the *Liberty* had already been attacked, heavily damaged, and nearly sunk by the Israelis.

Bamford delivers a fine and gripping account of this attack in which the crew suffered a devastating 70 percent casualties—34 killed and 171 wounded, some by aircraft that raked the ship with cannon fire in waves, returning again and again, the rest by torpedo boats which shot up the lifeboats on the *Liberty*'s deck—in the hope, Bamford believes, that there would be no survivors—and then fired five torpedoes at the helpless ship. Only one hit its target but even that probably would have sent the ship to the bottom if the NSA spaces in the ship had not been sealed off, trapping twenty-five NSA SIGINT collectors inside.

At about a quarter past four in the afternoon local time, two and a half hours after the first attack on the *Liberty*, the Israeli military informed the US naval attaché in Tel Aviv that the ship had been attacked by the Israeli warplanes and torpedo boats "in error." Officially, Israel has always insisted that its aircraft mistook the *Liberty* for an Egyptian vessel; the United States has always treated the attack as a baffling tragedy. But Bamford, backed up by interviews and numerous news stories in Israel and the US in the mid-1990s, argues persuasively that Israel knew the *Liberty* was an American vessel and feared the ship was recording local communications in and around

El Arish concerning the murder of several hundred Egyptian prison-ers of war by Israeli troops, something openly discussed in Israel and reported in the American press in recent years.

The White House, far from being outraged by the loss of life and the treachery of an ally, was instead more concerned, Bamford claims, that the incident might complicate American political support for Israel in the middle of a war. While the *Liberty* was wallowing helplessly off the Sinai coast, with men bleeding to death and bodies washing out through the gaping hole left by the Israeli torpedo, the Joint Chiefs of Staff ordered the American commander of the Sixth Fleet, Rear Admiral Lawrence Geis, to recall fighter aircraft that Geis had dis-patched from the *Saratoga* to find and protect the *Liberty* from fur-ther attack. Geis was predictably furious and protested directly to Secretary of Defense Robert McNamara. According to an oral history of the incident recorded in 1998 by Commander Lewis, Geis told him that McNamara's end of the conversation was at one point taken over by President Lyndon Johnson himself, who told Geis that "he didn't care if the ship sunk, he would not embarrass his allies."

Admiral Geis was not the only official to get a rude awakening about the thinking in the White House and Pentagon. While the attack was still under way, and the fate of the ship in doubt, the deputy director of the NSA, Louis Tordella, called the Joint Reconnaissance Committee (JRC) of the Joint Chiefs of Staff to remind naval com-manders that something needed to be done about the classified infor-mation and equipment on board. He was told by a staff officer on the JRC that "some unnamed Washington authorities [wanted] to sink the *Liberty* in order that newspaper men would be unable to photograph her and thus inflame public opinion against the Israelis." "I made an impolite comment about the idea," Tordella wrote the same day in a top secret UMBRA memorandum obtained by Bamford.

Wanting to know what happened was the last question on the offi-cial agenda. First was finding a way to hide or minimize the incident.

According to a State Department chronology of the affair, "Embassy Tel Aviv urged de-emphasis on publicity since proximity of vessel to scene of conflict was fuel for Arab suspicions that US was aiding Israel." By day's end a total news ban was imposed by the Pentagon, which prohibited anyone in the field from speaking about the attack, then or later. When the surviving crew members went ashore a week later on Malta they were, Bamford writes, threatened with jail if they broke silence with anyone, family and fellow crew members included. Israel agreed to pay compensation for the killed and wounded, but years of wrangling followed before Israel finally paid a token $6 million to the United States for destruction of the ship itself.

No brief summary of Bamford's account of the attack on the *Liberty* can do justice to its vivid detail and convincing array of evidence. The US Navy has rarely suffered a more devastating surprise attack in peacetime; only Pearl Harbor and the battleship *Maine* come to mind. The attack was egregious and unprovoked, and the American response weaseling, callous, timid, and dishonest. But this is a painful and embarrassing story about an ally with plenty of defenders, and Bamford can expect a vigorous counterattack. My guess is that most criticism will argue that he is somehow anti-Israeli, a charge made easier by the fact that he is, and sounds like, an angry man. Bamford is a writer of stern and bracing moral judgment, generally as willing to praise as censure, but something about the *Liberty* incident unhinges him a little, and his account is muddied at the end by a story of the killing of a journalist on the Lebanese–Israeli border in 2000. The two incidents are neither related nor comparable. Anger is best reserved for small things, cool judgment for big ones, and Bamford should have summed up what happened to the *Liberty*, so troubling in so many ways, in a calmer mood.

But that said, Bamford has done all that any journalist or historian could do, making a careful and plausible case while admitting that much remains unknown. To deepen our knowledge of this affair,

Bamford argues, Congress should attempt now the sort of exhaustive inquiry it shirked earlier, and he tells investigators exactly where to start looking—in the archives of the NSA.

The *Liberty*'s was not the only NSA crew collecting signals intelligence along the shores of Sinai on June 8, Bamford tells us. Also loitering in the area was a Navy EC-121, flying out of Athens, with SIGINT collectors picking up battlefield radio chatter in Arabic and Hebrew—referred to by the NSA as "special arabic." In the early afternoon of June 8 one of the NSA's Hebrew speakers said he'd heard something odd on the UHF channels used by Israeli naval craft—an ongoing attack on a target which appeared to be flying the American flag. Later, after returning to their base in Greece, the crewmen realized they had overheard the attack of Israeli torpedo boats on the *Liberty*. The original tapes were shipped back to the NSA, where they may presumably still be found in the archives.

Bamford has never seen the transcripts or listened to the tapes; what he knows apparently comes from interviews with the crewmen. The odds are that the tapes make explicit what the interviews only suggest, but maybe not. The only way to know would be to read the transcripts and listen to the tapes. This has been true for more than thirty years, but it is only now, after Bamford's hard digging, that a broader public can know that it is true. Whether some congressional committee will now act on Bamford's suggestion and ask for the evidence is entirely a political question, like most of the hard questions having to do with the secret collection and use of information.

Body of Secrets has something interesting and important to add to many episodes of cold war history, from the Chinese invasion of North Korea in 1950 through the early years of American involvement in Vietnam and the hijacking of the USS *Pueblo*, another Navy-operated ELINT ship seized by the North Koreans in 1968. Bamford is particularly good on the SIGINT war in Vietnam, where the NSA's interception of North Vietnamese radio traffic clearly demonstrated Hanoi's control of the war in the South at a time when journalists such as I. F. Stone were arguing that we could prove no such thing. The NSA also picked up early warnings of a major enemy offensive in late 1967 and the first weeks of January 1968 at a time when the official word in Washington was that General William Westmoreland was winning the war. The CIA's Harold Ford, writing thirty years later, generously concluded that the NSA "stood alone" in providing timely warning of the Tet offensive, which severely blood-ied American forces and marked the beginning of the end of public support for the war. But like the rest of the US military, the NSA also underestimated the power of the North Vietnamese, and even declined to make the effort required for a serious attack on high-level North Vietnamese ciphers. At the war's end, in April 1975, the unprepared agency was forced to abandon to the North Vietnamese a warehouse full of sophisticated cryptographic machines and other gear—"all in pristine condition," Bamford writes, "and all no doubt shared with the Russians and possibly also the Chinese."

The North Vietnamese, meanwhile, had been running a huge SIGINT operation against the United States with as many as 5,000 intercept operators listening in on American communications, of which far too many were transmitted in plaintext or in homemade codes. A full pic-ture of Hanoi's SIGINT operations did not emerge until long after the war but even the scattered indications of trouble described by the NSA in a secret report at the time offered "a clear, even frightening picture of Vietnamese communist successes against Allied communications."

But Bamford's stories are not confined to ancient history; he has much to say about recent events like the Gulf War of 1990–1991, which also had a SIGINT side, as do just about all episodes of interna-tional rivalry or strife. Bamford does not hesitate to judge the Ameri-can conduct of its side of the perpetual secret war, but like most of the (very few) writers who have made a profession of trying to understand intelligence organizations, he is slow to judge, and certainly does not condemn, the enterprise itself. On first encounter the intelligence business gives off a rank odor, but what the hugger-mugger boils down to is keeping your eyes open, knowing what's going on, trying to stay one move ahead as the game unfolds.

The *Liberty* apparently found out some things the other guys didn't want us to know, and the Navy's EP-3E, as of this writing still being examined on Hainan island, was trying to do the same thing. Some commentators have suggested that the Chinese held the plane and the crew for eleven days because the leadership in Beijing was divided and had not decided how to handle the matter, but to me it seems far more likely that the plane was held for the same reason Chinese fighter pilots had been dogging it through the sky, sliding up closer and closer until the Americans could recognize the pilot's face.

The danger was obvious, and it was great, and it was intended to be both—not because the Chinese national pride was offended by our routine patrols of their coastline, but because China didn't, and doesn't, want us to know all those things that spy planes suck into the memory banks of computers. As always, questions about intelligence are ultimately about freedom of action—if your opponents don't know what you're doing, they can't stop you, and if they don't know what kind of hardware backs up a threat, they're more likely to respond with caution. The American spy planes patrolling the Chinese coast expand our freedom of action, and limit China's. If Beijing could bring the flights to a halt, that balance would shift.

In the end the jostling in the air is only politics in another form. If Beijing negotiates a settlement with Taipei without recourse to force or the threat of force, it may have to concede much—things that have to do with ownership of property, human rights, free political activity, the social and economic structure of Chinese society. A threat of force, taken seriously, might convince Taipei to settle for less. With force in its most naked form—an outright military invasion of Taiwan—Beijing might escape the need to make any concessions at all. For the United States to have a voice in how things turn out, something urged by every American president since Nixon, it needs to know the state of play— not just what the Chinese are saying, but what they are actually doing, what they have to do it with, how their preparations compare to the forces arrayed against them—all those things that expensive intelligence platforms like ELINT aircraft are designed and built to monitor, identify, and collect.

And that brings us back to the exasperated questions of bystanders who feel they are watching toddlers squabble in the sandbox: Why can't these great powers get along? Why do they have to keep pushing and probing each other in these aggressive ways—cracking codes, suborning spies, stealing documents, bugging embassies, sending ships and aircraft bristling with antennae into harm's way? The answer, richly documented in Bamford's fine book, is that in international competition for power, where differences sometimes lead to war, what intelligence organizations do—all that hugger-mugger of the great game—may look like strife, but it's as close as serious international rivals ever get to peace.

—*The New York Review of Books*, June 21, 2001

17

DOING THE RIGHT THING

WHEN THE Central Intelligence Agency's secrets began to tumble out in their melancholy profusion in the mid-1970s, veterans of the agency warned that it would not be easy to put the lid back on, more questions would be raised than answered, and the process of exposure would leave the practice of intelligence in demoralized disarray. At the time, such arguments were roughly dismissed as disingenuous, motivated less by honest concern for "national security"—fast replacing patriotism as the last refuge of scoundrels—than by fear of embarrassment. But it turns out the Cassandras were absolutely right: the code-breaking computers may still be humming, the satellites clicking off their high-resolution photos, and the mighty river of paper working its way toward the National Security Council, but nothing else is the same. The intelligence community is divided and confused, just as predicted, and there is probably no better place to go for a glimpse of the awful mess than *Honorable Men: My Life in the CIA*, the memoirs of William Colby, director of the CIA from 1973 to 1976.[1]

It may come as a surprise to most readers to learn that the intelligence community blamed Colby, not nosy reporters or the congressional investigators of 1975, for the uglier revelations of those years,

---

1. Simon and Schuster, 1978.

but that is the case. Few men have suffered such dissonant reputations. The public probably remembers Colby best as the architect of the notorious Phoenix program in South Vietnam, which totted up the deaths of at least 20,000 Vietcong political cadremen; or as a peripheral Watergate figure who, in his own words, "danced around the room" to avoid giving John Ehrlichman's name to the federal prosecutors. But for CIA people, Colby is the man who may have wrecked the agency with his decision to let out the "bad secrets" concerning assassination plots, domestic intelligence programs, illegal drug-testing, and the like. While at least one segment of the public is inclined to see Colby as a war criminal, his former comrades think of him as a prig and a snitch, a turncoat (or worse) who delivered secret files by the cartload to the Pike and Church committees, who told a reporter about the CIA's illegal mail-intercept program in order to engineer the removal of an archrival, and who gave the Justice Department evidence that suggested that his immediate predecessor but one, Richard Helms, had lied to the Senate about CIA political operations in Chile. When Colby finally left the CIA early in 1976, his departure was not loudly lamented.

At first, or even third, glance William Egan Colby seems an unlikely candidate for such heated controversy. His appointment as director of central intelligence in mid-1973 seems to have been made in a fit of absentmindedness while Richard M. Nixon was busy plugging leaks in the White House levees. Certainly there was nothing inevitable about it.

For the most part Colby's years in the CIA were unexceptional, a steady climb from job to job in a manner that neither made enemies nor left much by way of anecdote among his friends. In the early 1950s he organized stay-behind nets in Scandinavia to harass Russian occupiers in the event of a third world war. A few years later, he orchestrated CIA support in Italy for the Christian Democrats and backed the "opening to the left" that brought Italian Socialists into the government, despite opposition (by the CIA's James Angleton, among others) contending that the Communists would not be far behind.

In 1959 Colby moved on to Vietnam to help gear up for the war he still feels we never should have lost. As chief of station in Saigon, chief of the Far East division in the clandestine services section of the CIA, and head of the Phoenix program, Colby spent twelve years trying to do what the French had failed to achieve before him. Vietnam absorbs the largest part of his book, as it did his life, and one is tempted to linger over his astonishing (to me) inability to notice any but the most particular causes of failure. There is something odd about a man who can cite so many weaknesses in us—a fickle US Congress, a gloomy American press, an ignorant American public, a firepower-mad American military—without ever seeming to notice that American help for Saigon was not the solution but the problem. I kept expecting Colby to conclude that we'd have done better if we had done less, but his style of postmortem is maddeningly narrow. In the end, he says, the collapse of Saigon was caused by the threat of an American aid cutoff. This is like saying that the cause of a fatal air crash was harsh impact with the ground. It will not win any awards for unraveling cause and effect.

But this is ancient history, and pretty vague history at that. If you want to know what the CIA *did* during Colby's tenure, you had better read *Decent Interval*, Frank Snepp's account of the fall of Saigon, or *In Search of Enemies*, John Stockwell's story of the ill-fated intervention in Angola.[2] The latter was a foolish and cynical undertaking of a sort that apparently held a special appeal for President Nixon and Secretary of State Henry Kissinger. In Angola, as in Chile and Kurdistan, the CIA attempted to inflate inherently weak local forces, because

---

2. Frank Snepp, *Decent Interval: An Insider's Account of Saigon's Indecent End* (Random House, 1977); John Stockwell, *In Search of Enemies: A CIA Story* (Norton, 1978).

Kissinger had the idea it would serve US interests elsewhere, mainly by convincing the Russians (as he thought) that we could still poke a stick in their eye, despite Vietnam. Stockwell's detailed account of the Angola debacle has the capacity to make you mad all over again, not so much at the way the CIA goes about its business as at the sheer institutional enthusiasm it puts into operations that amount to whims on the part of presidents and their foreign-policy advisers. The CIA just can't say no. For Colby, however, Angola was only an episode, one more embarrassment in a larger crisis of confidence that threatened to destroy the agency altogether.

From the CIA's point of view, Watergate was the foot in the door, providing congressional investigators with their first real look at the agency's paper and tables of organization. When the Senate Select Committee on Intelligence Activities began its investigation in 1975 the spell had been broken: the CIA was fair game, protected neither by mystique nor by President Gerald R. Ford. But despite Ford's retreat—he believed in secrets, but wouldn't fight to keep them—the consensus at CIA headquarters in Langley, Virginia, was for massive resistance. No one was using the word "stonewall," perhaps, but that was certainly what they had in mind.

It would have worked, as it had worked so often in the past, but for one fact: Colby had decided the time had come to surrender the bad secrets. To the amazement and horror of most of his colleagues in the CIA, he elected to cooperate with the commission headed by Vice President Nelson A. Rockefeller, and, later, with Senator Frank Church. If they would take care of the good secrets, he would hand over pretty much everything the investigators asked for. Ford and Kissinger were as opposed to this as most CIA people, and Rockefeller, a lifelong admirer of strong executives, tried in his way to tell Colby this was a whitewash they were conducting up here, not an investigation. "Bill," Colby quotes him as saying, "do you really have to present all this material to us?"

Colby felt he did, supporting his decision with two arguments. First, he felt that the practice of intelligence in America had to be subject to the Constitution, which he took to mean that it must be equally responsible to the president and Congress. The days of the Senate's automatic deference to the White House in foreign-policy matters were over. The CIA, in Colby's view, could no longer serve as the President's personal Saturday-night gun.

Second, Colby made a distinction between the "good secrets"—the names of agents, the technical details of collection systems, and so on—and the "bad secrets," which involved lapses of judgment, "excesses," and outright crimes. Colby felt things had gone too far to keep the bad secrets secret anymore, that it would be better to surrender them all at once, and it would be better for the country to know than to imagine the worst. Once the secrets were out, he said, they would not look so bad.

Colby was alone then, and he is still almost alone. His critics in the intelligence community think his approach was a mistake of horrendous magnitude—a kind of institutional suicide—because it betrayed the trust of intelligence officers and agents who acted in good faith; because it infected the world of intelligence with the posturing and hypocrisy of public men attacking the agency in public for what they might approve quietly in private; and because it exposed an enormous wealth of exact detail about the CIA to the scrutiny of hostile intelligence agencies, who are good at nothing if not the extraction of knowledge from the scantiest facts. Letting Senator Frank Church rummage about in the CIA's past, Colby's critics felt, was the functional equivalent of giving the KGB a guided tour. That these things were done was bad enough; that they were *allowed* to be done was worse, a sign of confusion, timidity, surrender, and demoralization.

But that was not Colby's worst crime, in the view of some of his old colleagues. The worst was an act so egregious and ill-advised, so destructive and disarming (in the literal sense) that CIA people will tell you in a level voice that Colby's decisions as the director of central intelligence were completely consistent with those one might expect of an enemy agent. The silence that follows this bald observation, generally delivered with direct eye contact, indicates it is intended absolutely seriously, which I take to be evidence of just what awful shape the CIA is in. What did Colby do to invite such hostility and suspicion? He junked counterintelligence.

This is a subject—alluded to but not elaborated upon in Colby's memoirs—about which two things might be said: it is complicated and it does not lend itself to clear formulation or answer, especially by outsiders. Nevertheless, here, in extreme summary, is what the argument is about:

The first job of an intelligence agency is to protect itself from penetration, lest it fall under the control of an enemy. For nearly twenty years, until Colby discharged him in 1975, counterintelligence in the CIA was in the hands of James Angleton. A man with brains, tenacity, and appetite for detail, Angleton was also characterized by a degree of intellectual arrogance that made it hard for him to admit he'd been wrong about anything, from the motives of an agent to a prediction of the weather.

Over the years, Angleton developed a profound respect for KGB scheming and devilish strategem. He detected Russian string-pulling everywhere, scoffed at just about every bit of hard-won secret intelligence as being a clever Russian plant, and argued that a long-term Russian master plan was gradually putting its agents into every government and intelligence service of the non-Communist world. Pretty soon, only Angleton would be left on "our" side. His skepticism was so deep that many of his colleagues, including Colby, concluded that he'd lost his grip and had turned into a paranoiac nut.

Angleton's argument in his own defense, according to those who have heard bits and pieces of it, is of a sort that simply cannot be summarized. One can say only that it is heavily factual in nature, that it is based on an intimate knowledge of Soviet-bloc intelligence services, that it is plausible in many particulars, that it is possible he may be completely right, and that we are never going to know. Here the awful mess cited above threatens to transcend itself, to rise to a higher plane on which it becomes the Platonic ideal of messiness, a mess of metaphysical intractability.

Bewildering to outsiders, the Angleton–Colby dispute nevertheless lies near the heart of the current disarray of American intelligence. Counterintelligence is to intelligence as epistemology is to philosophy. The problems have to do with ways of knowing, are fundamental to the discipline, and offer heavy advantage in debate to those who are skeptical of appearances. Angleton, in fact, might be called the Bishop Berkeley of intelligence, a man who insists that how we know things is a problem slipperier than it seems.

Debate of this sort does not appeal to Colby's temperament. Years of experience in the business of intelligence—although not, for the most part, on the classic agent-running end of it—convinced Colby that Angleton's obsession with counterintelligence was without profit. Tired of wrangling, Colby simply got rid of it, pretty much in the mood of Samuel Johnson, who kicked a stone and pronounced, "Thus I refute Berkeley!" Of course, Colby did not excise counterintelligence entirely; but his critics say he reorganized the life out of it.

At the heart of the current intelligence mess, then, are two questions posed by Colby: Can American intelligence be conducted successfully within a constitutional framework—that is, with a dual responsibility to both the president and the Congress? And can it safely dispense with the melodramatics of counterintelligence?

The heat with which these questions are debated in intelligence circles has to do with the fact that a "no" in either instance means Americans will pretty much have to get along without any secret intelligence service at all, as we did before World War II. I'm inclined to think Colby was right on both counts—a CIA working exclusively for the president is bound to produce as much trouble as benefit; and the KGB's master plan will turn out a Potemkin village—but both questions are very far from being settled.

Colby's book is important, a serious treatment of a serious subject, but at the same time it is flavorless. This is almost certainly not the fault of Colby's collaborator, Peter Forbath, an able writer whose recent book, *The River Congo*,[3] shows he has a fine capacity for rich narrative and evocative description, given his rein. In this instance he has been held in pretty tightly. By all accounts, including Colby's, the first version of his book set a record for soporific opacity. Forbath has rescued it from the deep camouflage of bureaucratese, but beyond that not even talent could take him.

This is partly the result of his readers' jaded appetites: we have grown used to revelations. But if Colby's book ever had any, they were excised by the CIA before publication. Even the color of men's eyes seems to have been treated as a state secret. But we are all adults now, and ought to be able to make our meals of solid, honest stuff, without condiment, if necessary. More damaging to the book, however, is the impassive, almost muffled quality to Colby's voice—the fact that he approaches his main points in a guarded manner—as well as a certain confusion of purpose. His memoirs are addressed to the public, but they are aimed at his one-time friends and colleagues, in particular Richard Helms. The title is borrowed from Helms's 1971 remark— "The nation must to a degree take it on faith that we too are honorable men, devoted to her service"—and Colby is at pains to explain why he felt compelled to tell the Justice Department that Helms might have been guilty of perjury. Helms is not likely to accept the explanation, but it shows every sign of being earnestly intended.

—*The New York Times Book Review*, May 21, 1978

---

3. *The River Congo: The Discovery, Exploration and Exploitation of the World's Most Dramatic River* (Harper and Row, 1977).

18

LAST OF THE COWBOYS

THE RUSSIANS HAVE only a walk-on part in Bob Woodward's history of the world according to William Casey. The KGB fabricated a will for Zhou Enlai, we are told; twenty-five spies were reporting to Casey's CIA from the Soviet bloc by 1984; and one of them reported the death of Konstantin Chernenko to the CIA two days before it was officially announced in the Soviet Union. This is Chernenko's sole appearance in Woodward's book *Veil: The Secret Wars of the CIA 1981–1987.*[1] The three other Soviet leaders during Casey's tenure as director of central intelligence (DCI) are cited in passing a total of eight times. Even Yuri Andropov, chairman of the KGB and thereby Casey's principal opponent in the secret war until 1982, makes only a single appearance—as one of the "three dying men" who preceded Gorbachev. There is generally a Soviet angle to Casey's preoccupations, as reported by Woodward, and the cold war provides a kind of unobtrusive background music of the sort commonly heard in elevators and supermarkets, but the "secret" wars that Casey hoped to prove we could fight and win were all conducted in the odd corners of the world, where the Russians had as much trouble with the local languages as we did.

---

1. Simon and Schuster, 1987.

Nicaragua was where Casey intended to draw the line. Like Reagan, Casey had professed to be outraged by the triumph of Marxist-Leninist regimes in Ethiopia and Angola following the American disaster in Vietnam. These Soviet successes never seemed to make a large impression on the public mind, but they were bitterly resented in that Washington netherworld where domestic politics and national security overlap. Nixon had warned that irresolution in world affairs would turn the United States into a "pitiful, helpless giant," and Casey, like Reagan, was convinced that a timid, finger-wagging Congress had brought it to pass.

The amiable Reagan seemed content to give the Russians a good verbal thumping, as he did in 1983 when he called the Soviet Union "an evil empire." He may well have known about and authorized many secret attacks during the first years of his administration, but no one has established that he did so. Casey wanted to fight, and once he got used to the fact that Reagan wasn't going to appoint him secretary of state, he determined to resurrect the salty, try-anything intelligence service that Allen Dulles had built during the 1950s with veterans of the World War II OSS, in which Casey had served. Nicaragua—which Casey, with difficulty, pronounced "Nicawawa"—was going to be the test case for a tough new American approach.

That is what Casey told Woodward and what we knew anyway from the Iran-contra hearings and many other inquiries. I would be amazed to discover that anyone reading this review had not correctly deduced that the CIA was running a "secret war" against Nicaragua commencing more or less on day one of the Reagan administration. The interesting point to emerge, not a surprise, was the extent and nature of Casey's failure. In Woodward's account, the "secret war" seems to be virtually a replay, on the wrong stage, of the hit-and-run war in France that immediately preceded the Allied invasion in June 1944. Six weeks of shooting and sabotage made a small but real contribution to the Allied landing at Normandy. The cost was high, but the effort didn't have to be sustained. Success meant planting explosives in the right place and blowing something up—not in order to destroy an expensive piece of hardware or real estate, but to deny it to the enemy at the moment when he needed it most. As a young man Casey had helped to manage the Jedburgh teams dispatched from Great Britain, and thereafter his notion of a "secret war" meant brave men with cork-blackened faces blowing up power lines in enemy territory. Or so it appears in *Veil*.

This was a bit of good luck for the Sandinistas. Things might have worked out differently if Casey's early experience had been with Tito's Partisans in Yugoslavia. There politics, not derring-do, prevailed. Success depended on clandestine control of the population, and the ability to maintain a shadow government despite years of relentless pressure from rival Yugoslav groups and the German armies of occupation. There was plenty of shooting but shooting and sabotage weren't the point. It was political organization that mattered, the popular support that allowed Tito's men to survive when the Germans were after them. In such a struggle one unarmed man can be worth more than a company with heavy weapons.

As related by Woodward, the story of what happened to the CIA in the six years Casey ran it is very much a Washington story. The narrative sticks closely to Casey's appointment calendar; we hear in considerable detail what Casey wanted and what his colleagues did to help or hinder him. An occasional side trip is made to visit the House and Senate Intelligence Oversight committees. We get the odd glimpse of George Shultz at State, Caspar Weinberger at Defense, and a dismal succession of briefcase carriers who served varying terms as Reagan's national security adviser. There are a great many interesting stories in this book—that Admiral Bobby Inman resigned as Casey's deputy, for example, because he raised objections to Casey's contra operations that Casey ignored, treating him as an "outsider." The claims about Soviet sponsorship of international terrorism in Claire

Sterling's book *The Terror Network*, which so impressed Secretary of State Alexander Haig, were apparently based in part on "an old, small-scale CIA covert propaganda operation." The study of intelligence must proceed as intelligence does itself, with such "cases," and several that Woodward reports have already been confirmed; they make *Veil* a very useful book.

But Casey dominates, and the evolution of his two obsessions—terrorism in the Middle East (which meant Qaddafi), and the Soviet presence in Central America (which meant Nicawawa)—provide the structure of Woodward's book. What was actually going on in Nicaragua Woodward makes no attempt to say, but the picture we get of the war the CIA apparently chose to run seems almost too dumb to credit.

Starting from scratch with adequate, not extravagant, funding, the CIA put together a mercenary army based on former national guardsmen, gave it some rudimentary training, supplied it with camouflage fatigues of the sort survivalists buy through mail order catalogs, and dispatched it heavily laden into those parts of Nicaragua hard to reach by taxi. There it was expected to shoot people and blow things up. The late Major General Edwin Lansdale, who ran covert operations against the Cubans for a time in the early 1960s, used to call this "boom and bang." It didn't work then either.

When the progress of the contras was inevitably slow, Casey pressed for a switch to dramatic actions closer to the cities. One result was an "air raid" on the Managua airport by a Cessna aircraft carrying two five-hundred-pound bombs. The plane crashed into the main terminal, made a mess, and killed an airport worker. This happened only a few minutes before Senators William Cohen of Maine and Gary Hart of Colorado were scheduled to arrive on a fact-finding mission. Shaken by their narrow squeak, and shocked that the dead pilot's papers tied him to the CIA, the senators asked the CIA's chief of station in Managua, and later Casey himself in Washington, what in God's name this crazy operation was intended to prove. Both men of the CIA seemed to think Cohen and Hart were angry only about their own close call.

The airport raid, like the mining of Nicaraguan harbors soon after, was apparently Casey's idea of stepping up the war—"boom and bang" in the classic mold. The CIA's only attempt to address the political aspect of the war, in Woodward's version, was the now notorious guerrilla warfare manual that recommended public execution of "carefully selected" Nicaraguan government officials. How careful could the selection be from a CIA list of suggested targets that ended with "etcetera"?

The United States has bungled operations of this sort in precisely the same way on four or five different occasions. The remarkable thing is that Casey, who considered himself a hardheaded business-man, never grasped, or at least never hinted to Woodward that he had grasped, the hopeless futility of his war, a matter of back-country ambush and random urban terrorism. A little more shooting, a little more money, and a lot less nit-picking from Congress, in his view, would do the trick. The Sandinistas would fold, the Russians would see we meant business, and the West would be saved.

Woodward seems to have listened to this nonsense on dozens of occasions without protest, which I take to be a sign of the reporter's iron stomach. It's not easy to get a director of central intelligence to sit down for an interview; use the occasion for a lecture and neither of you will learn anything. Asking questions and listening to the answers is the reporter's art. But Casey's grousing makes painful reading. His war killed people to no purpose; it squandered the nation's political energy in a fruitless repetition of old arguments; and it put the CIA through a wringer it had barely survived the first time around in the mid-1970s. But Casey seems to have died as he lived, convinced it was Congress—not the futility of trying to solve complex social and political problems through hired violence—that kept the Sandinistas in power.

That at any rate is Woodward's version of Casey's last adventure. Did it really happen that way? The intelligence business is notoriously one of managed appearance. Casey may have been a novice, but many of Woodward's other informants were intelligence officers long practiced in the art of misleading reporters. Was Woodward one of them? Did he make some of it up? The basic question of veracity was immediately raised on publication day by Woodward's account of his final hospital interview with the dying Casey at an unnamed hour on an unnamed day in the winter of 1986. This interview appeared at the end of Woodward's book, in the space normally reserved for summing up final conclusions. It was short—only nineteen words from Casey. The DCI had just had a lump of his brain surgically removed. Woodward asked if Casey knew about the diversion of funds from the sale of US arms to Iran for use by the contras. "He stared, and finally nodded yes."

Political controversies sometimes turn on loonily precise points of fact such as this one. Woodward's answer appeared not long after Congress had completed weeks of public hearings devoted largely to this very question. In every public statement Casey had always insisted he did not know about the diversion—important because he was thought to be close to President Reagan, and it was assumed that if Casey knew, then Reagan must have known, a claim the President vigorously denied. Now comes Woodward to say that Casey did know and had "told" him so.

Woodward's publication of this "interview" is a literary misjudgment of heroic proportion. Casey's nineteen words suggest his craniotomy had removed some important tissue. "Okay...better...no," he said, when asked how he was feeling. Only the left side of his mouth smiled. "Oh," was his answer to one question. "I'm gone," he said at another point. The "interview" ended when Woodward realized that Casey had nodded off. I can see how all this made some sort of sense to Woodward, steeped in the story as he was, and that he hated to lose anything so inherently dramatic as a final conversation with a dying spymaster. But the plain fact is this garble doesn't add up to anything, and the only remark of Casey's that deserves to be taken at face value is his sad admission, "I'm gone." Woodward never should have published this flimsy story as the climax of his book.

But the rest of Woodward's book seems to be of sturdier stuff. There are a great many statements of fact in *Veil*, and a great many officials identified by name. They have now had ample opportunity to call Woodward a liar, but few have troubled themselves to do so. Woodward has published hard-to-credit stories in the past which turned out to be true, like the one about Kissinger and Nixon going down on their knees to pray during the Watergate crisis. Kissinger later confirmed it. This time, Alexander Haig, campaigning in New Hampshire, confirmed a story at first given the back of the White House hand—Woodward's report that Reagan had been barely up to an hour's "work" a day at a time when the White House insisted he was fully recovered from the gunshot wound that nearly killed him in March 1981. Bobby Inman has said that conversations he is alleged to have had with Casey before he resigned did in fact take place.

For all the air of sensation that surrounded its publication, however, Woodward's central account of Casey's covert activities for the most part only adds new details to stories that have already had their day in the press. His story requires close reading. It suggests more than it claims. Woodward sticks to the order in which things happened and makes no large claims for the facts he relates. His book is truly what his colleague on *The Washington Post* Chalmers Roberts once called "the first rough draft" of history. A claim that Casey said "let's do it" is not the same as reporting that Casey in fact did it, or that it was done because Casey said so, or even that it was done at all.

Woodward is writing about matters that were intended to remain secret, and although diligence helped him to learn a great deal, that great deal is still very far from all. Only Casey is identified of Woodward's 250 sources. The rest are nameless. Scholars and historians will inevitably find this fact troubling, but it is not hard to guess who some of Woodward's sources must have been, because so much of the book turns on what a couple of dozen men thought, said, and memoed to one another. There are many detailed accounts of conversations in which only two persons were present—for example, the private meeting between Casey and the Saudi Arabian ambassador to the United States, Prince Bandar. Walking in Bandar's garden after lunch in early 1985, Casey, Woodward tells us, gave Bandar a card with a number written on it—a bank account in Switzerland. Three million dollars for a counterterrorist operation in Lebanon was to be deposited in that account. "As soon as I transfer this," Bandar said, "I'll close out the account and burn the paper."

"Don't worry," Casey assured him. "We'll close the account at once."

Who told Woodward of this meeting—Bandar? Casey? Some third party who heard it from one of the principals? A member of the staff of the Intelligence Oversight committees? There are more possibilities than at first might appear, but for the moment we have got only Woodward's word for it.

Woodward strongly suggests, but does not actually say, that this money was used to mount an attempt to assassinate Sheikh Mohammed Hussein Fadlallah, a Shia Muslim leader implicated in terrorist operations targeted on Americans. On March 8, 1985, a car bomb was detonated near Fadlallah's apartment; he escaped but eighty others died. An earlier version of this story, published in *The Washington Post* on May 12, 1985, claimed that the Lebanese intelligence service actually carried out the bombing as part of a campaign organized by the CIA, although the agency had balked at plans for a car bombing. In the earlier story Woodward also claimed that Shultz and then National Security Adviser Robert McFarlane "were chief proponents of the covert plan."[2]

---

2. See Murray Kempton's comment on this story, *The New York Review*, November 5, 1987.

Woodward's version of the story adds new details without exactly contradicting the earlier version: Shultz still backs the counterterrorist plan, the Lebanese are still involved, CIA officers still balk at a car bomb. But now Casey calls in the Saudis and meets with Bandar, in effect circumventing his own agency. An Englishman runs the operation. The Saudis betray some of the agents involved to Fadlallah in order to deflect suspicion from themselves. In the end, the Saudis bribe Fadlallah with $2 million to quit targeting Americans, and Casey is amazed how easy it was.

This story is a typical Woodward set piece—detailed, suggestive, and fragmentary. The easy part was guessing that the US had a part in the attempt on Fadlallah's life—administration officials had been promising a new eye-for-an-eye policy on terrorism, and Fadlallah was a prime suspect. The hard part, as always, was pinning the specific deed on specific American officials. Woodward has made a good stab at it, but his case would never stand up in a court of law.

Still, my guess is that Woodward's specific claims about this and other cases are solid. The larger question is whether he got the drift right, and here I am not so sure. One slant is immediately apparent: Woodward has talked to a lot of high agency officials who don't like covert operations, especially ones involving the use of local agents wearing camouflage fatigues. They're noisily public, squander people patiently recruited by the FI (foreign intelligence) types, and above all undermine the quiet, bipartisan support of Congress. Presidents like Reagan and Nixon, on the other hand, love covert operations, which are cheaper than war and more satisfying than fussy State Department white papers. It's an old argument, going back to the early 1950s when the officials who specialized in running spies and the covert operators were dragooned into a single directorate. If anyone in the agency thinks Casey was handling things just right, and the contra operation came anywhere near succeeding—and it would be amazing if there weren't —Woodward hasn't found him. The old boy network has struck again.

But it seems to me there is a second, subtler, and more important omission in Woodward's account of Casey's career at the CIA. Casey is often described as "an old friend" of Ronald Reagan, but you won't find much evidence of it in *Veil*. Casey was sure he knew what Reagan wanted, but the White House staff was divided. Casey had a hard time keeping a pipeline open. One of Reagan's speechwriters, Anthony Dolan, kept Casey informed, and William Clark, the national security adviser, was an even better source until he resigned. "Casey could get his say," Woodward reports; "he could even get a private meeting with Reagan in the White House residence. Casey played this card about twice a year." Twice a year? That hardly sounds like terms of intimacy.

In his opening pages Woodward charted the decline of Admiral Stansfield Turner's credit in the Carter White House by the coin of "access": three meetings with the President a week trailed off to one a week, then one every other week. In Washington, twice a month is the last stop before Siberia. Casey, we are told, had to send Reagan a letter to find out if the President planned to keep him through a second Reagan term. Do these two men even know each other? But eventually Casey, trying to ensure Woodward will get the point, suggests another explanation for his allegedly distant relations with Reagan. In early May 1985 he invited Woodward to share his plane back to Washington from New York. Casey railed about Reagan's failure to wring support for the contras out of Congress. "The President is uninterested," he told Woodward. "He still has his instincts, but he will not even focus on the objectives, let alone the way to get there." Then Woodward paraphrases what we are to take to be Casey's words: "Casey continued to be struck by the overall passivity of the President.... He never called the meetings or set the daily agenda. He never once had told Casey, 'Let's do this' or 'Get me that.'" This is very interesting, if true. Casey's widow, Sophia, thinks it is not. Woodward couldn't have heard all that stuff from Casey, she told reporters; he never thought the President was passive and disinterested.

Faithful to his notes, Woodward has written the version of events Casey probably would have given to the committee investigating the Iran-contra affair, if he had lived. It was Casey who wanted to revive the activist CIA, Casey who found a way to go after the terrorists in Lebanon, Casey who wanted to draw the line in Nicaragua, Casey who suggested McFarlane "explore funding alternatives [for the contras] with the Saudis, Israelis and others," Casey who was virtually Oliver North's case officer in organizing the sale of arms to Iran. Admiral Poindexter elected to take a fall in the Senate hearings, insisting he neither asked nor told the President anything about the diversion of funds to the contras. It could even be true. It appears that Casey gave Woodward roughly the same story: the secret war was his idea. That could be true, too. Reagan was by all accounts amiable, indolent, and careless of detail. Maybe he was having an afternoon nap while his loyal aides were scrounging funds for the contras. It begins to look as though the absentminded president story will never be knocked down for sure; too much evidence went into the burn bags. But I don't believe it for a minute.

The Iran-contra affair has been an agonizing ordeal for the CIA, the second in a dozen years. The central issue has been the same in both cases—the danger that an activist president, armed with a pliant CIA, might slip the leash of the Constitution. "We have a chance to establish our own foreign policy," Casey said in the fall of 1985, according to Woodward. "We're on the cutting edge. We are the action agency of the government." This was entirely true, and rightly alarming to Congress, which had already slapped down such pretensions once during the investigations of the mid-1970s. When Casey took over as director of central intelligence he found a still-chastened CIA, leery of new adventures. But presidents and DCIs will have their way, and the oversight committees can't protect the agency unless they know what's happening. They're supposed to know, but find it hard to insist on being told. Members of the president's own party don't want to undercut their man, and the rest of the committee members bend over backward to prove they're worthy of trust with the secrets in the grown-up world of war and peace. Inevitably, congressional vigilance flags. The immediate result is an implied grant of executive latitude that allows the White House its head. The ultimate result is the sort of hot water presidentially appointed security officials get into when they start to make use of the excitingly secret power that comes when they can speak in the president's name. And would they have done so entirely on their own?

Casey was the last of the OSS veterans to run the CIA, and a good thing too. One more from his mold might finish the agency once and for all. His friends will protest; they loved the activism and disdain for red tape that Casey picked up during the glory days of the OSS during World War II. But it's hard to argue with the wreckage Casey left behind. Casey's big mistake was thinking that the cold war was like the war against Hitler—one we had to win. The Russians were too tough to tackle head-on, but he hoped to turn the tide in the peripheral arenas of the world. Congress tried to impose restraint where the battle was hottest, in Central America, insisting that the CIA must spend no funds to overthrow the Sandinistas. With a straight face and fingers crossed behind his back, Casey swore to comply. Woodward refused to swallow this whopper and *Veil* cites chapter and verse of the truth behind the lie. This is no ordinary journalist's scoop; Woodward fully deserves his reputation for tenacity. But there are some things no amount of legwork can pin down, and Casey died insisting on the tallest tale of all—that Reagan didn't know.

—*The New York Review of Books*, November 19, 1987

19

THE BOTTOM LINE

THE SECRET WAR concealed within the cold war achieved a kind of climax one chilly morning in the early 1960s in the Congo, when two boats slowly approached each other along the western shore of Lake Tanganyika. These were no native dugouts, but long, sleek craft with powerful engines. Whether it was someone in the southern boat heading north or someone in the northern boat heading south who first distinguished the low diesel rumble of the approaching craft over the growl of his own I cannot say, for my informant is now dead. Nor can I say who spied the other first, or who fired first, or what was shouted in the panic and confusion as bullets were exchanged during the frantic moments before engines were revved up and the two powerful craft veered off into the mist. But I can report that the shouts of alarm that echoed over Lake Tanganyika, uttered by the hired warriors of the United States and the Soviet Union, were in both cases Cuban Spanish, mother tongue alike of the Cubans who went to the Congo to make a revolution with Che Guevara at Soviet expense and the Cubans dispatched to foil them by the intelligence agencies of America.

This brief encounter, a kind of bump in the night, summed up for my friend Sam Adams, a former analyst for the CIA, the loony quality of the secret cold war—a clash of proxies in an out-of-the-way corner of the world which was nevertheless freighted with heavy strategic significance for the policymakers of Washington. What gave Adams's story its power for me was the fact that Adams had never set foot in Africa, much less the Congo. What he loved was the stacks of secret documents that crossed his desk at the Central Intelligence Agency. A morning's work memorizing the correct pronunciation of the names of native tribes made him the house expert on the Congo. It became his job to read the Congo cable traffic every morning, and there he found the story of the battle of Lake Tanganyika. He passed it on to me a decade later with such conviction that for a year I assumed he had been in the CIA boat with the CIA Cubans looking death in the eye.

Adams's story came to my mind following the collapse of the Soviet Union in 1991, so like the disintegration of an army routed in wartime. The manner of its ending revealed some fundamental things about the cold war: it really was a war, and prosecuting it took conscious effort and resolution. The control of nations was at stake, one side lost, and the other prevailed. In every way it was like the other great political contests of history save one: there was no spasm of bloodletting at the end. Why this was so is a question intimately related to another one, also central: How important to the outcome of the cold war were the battle of Lake Tanganyika and all the other clandestine skirmishing, the spying and the counterspying, the black propaganda and hidden pulling of strings, the keeping and breaching of secrets during the forty-five years after the Soviet Union planted its armies in the heart of Europe at the end of the Second World War? In short, did the United States, which spent perhaps half a trillion dollars on intelligence since 1945, get its money's worth?

The CIA was far from alone in the secret war waged against the intelligence services of the Soviet Union and its allied states. The National Security Agency (NSA), with its code-breaking computers, dwarfs the CIA in this country, and a host of foreign services were involved in the West, especially the Bundesnachrichtendienst (BND), or Federal Intelligence Service, of Germany, and the Secret Intelligence Service (SIS) of

Great Britain. But the CIA was to the Western effort as the US Army was to the Allied landing at Normandy in 1944, first among equals and the principal source of men and money. The agency brought a crusading passion to the struggle on its founding in 1947. Disappointment and setbacks taught patience and realism to intelligence professionals, but they never lost confidence that they could handle the Russians if Congress and the press would only stay out of the way. Joseph Persico, in *Casey: From the OSS to the CIA*,[1] his fine but unfootnoted biography of William Casey, reports that an Israeli journalist once asked President Reagan's new director of central intelligence why he gave so much attention to a banana republic like Nicaragua. Casey answered, "I'm looking for a place to start rolling back the Communist empire."

This was confidence on the grand scale, and it got Casey and the Reagan administration into deep trouble. If the Iran-contra affair can be said to have had one preeminent cause it was the administration's determination to keep up the pressure on the Soviet-backed government of Nicaragua despite the Boland Amendment of July 1983 which prohibited the use of American funds to arm the contras. Congress had a hard time deciding what it wanted to do in Central America, but Casey did not. As an Irish Catholic trained in Jesuit schools, Casey had no trouble in the 1930s choosing sides in the Spanish Civil War. The way he saw it the Soviets were backing Marxists who raped nuns and killed priests. One of Casey's old friends, Leo Cherne, told Persico that Casey "was 100 per cent for Franco and 100 per cent against the Loyalists."

This strain of anti-Communist zeal, undiluted after fifty years, shocked and frightened much of the foreign-policy bureaucracy in Washington in the early 1980s when President Reagan referred to the Soviet Union as an "evil empire" and some of his aides—Paul Nitze

---

1. Viking, 1990.

and Richard Perle among others—talked of speeding up the strategic arms race in order to spend the Russians into bankruptcy. Reagan cited the practical burdens of a flood of refugees if the Communists went unchecked in Central America, but what really seems to have worried him was the Reds' slow chipping away at the "Free World." Vietnam and Cambodia were lost, Ethiopia and Angola were defended by Cuban troops, the Russians were in Kabul after one hundred years of trying; they were also sending arms to the Sandinistas, and the Sandinistas in turn were backing a revolution next door in El Salvador. But when Casey and the President talked about bankrupting the Soviets and "rolling back the Communist empire," they aroused fears of reckless provocation leading to large-scale war on the part of much of the foreign-policy establishment in Washington, the liberal press, a great many university professors, the World Council of Churches, the Democratic Congress, and me.

Only a few years later, Casey died of a brain tumor and President Reagan retired to his house in the West, but the joke is not on them. They were barely out of town when the Communist empire began unraveling. To celebrate a milestone in the historic retreat, Casey's successor, William Webster, held a little party in the CIA's headquarters in Langley, Virginia, on February 15, 1989, according to Mark Perry in his oddly titled book, *Eclipse: The Last Days of the CIA*.[2] On that day, after ten years of failure as expensive as they were humiliating, the Soviets pulled the last of their troops out of Afghanistan. A couple of years later they wouldn't even be Soviets anymore. Webster was no tiger of the cold war like Casey, but he could see the end had come. "This is a victory for America," he said, "but it is also a victory for the CIA."

It is too soon to say whether Marxism as an evangelical movement died with the Soviet state, but it is a good moment, perhaps, to

---

2. Morrow, 1992.

examine claims such as Webster's about what destroyed it. If we grant that the cold war itself was the test failed by the Soviet regime, then it follows that the secret cold war was a principal field of conflict. The torrent of intelligence books published during the early 1990s touches on many of the themes and battlefields of the secret war, starting with the first clandestine skirmishes in the Baltic and Ukraine at the end of World War II, and continuing on through the technical triumphs of overhead reconnaissance and the ten-year guerrilla war in Afghanistan. Defeat there would not have been a disaster for a healthy superpower, but the Soviet Union in the 1980s was not healthy. In this last battle of the cold war the money and the arms provided by the CIA weighed heavily in the scale.

The invasion of Afghanistan in December 1979 caught Washington unprepared. A Soviet client state in Kabul had been faltering under guerrilla attack but the CIA, preoccupied with Iran, had failed to recognize the warning signs. This amazed no one; intelligence agencies have a dismal record of predicting things that have not happened before. The Soviet attack was stunningly swift and efficient, and it was especially alarming because it broke an unwritten rule of the cold war —that the Soviets were extremely cautious about committing their own troops to battle outside Europe. But not even the hard-liners in the Carter administration suggested launching a serious attempt to drive the Soviets out again. The President simply authorized a low-level CIA program of aid to the Mujahideen rebels to make life more difficult and more expensive for the Soviets.

Backing a guerrilla war takes a hard heart. The Mujahideen—soon referred to as "the Muj"—wanted enough arms to win, but the CIA and other backers were reluctant to push the Soviets to the brink of defeat for fear of setting off a big war. The tension of managing such a conflict is well described by a former Pakistani intelligence officer, General Mohammed Yousaf, in *The Bear Trap: Afghanistan's Untold*

THE TRUTH ABOUT THE CIA

Story.[3] When Yousaf took over the Afghan bureau of Pakistan's Inter-Services Intelligence agency (ISI) in October 1983, he faced a supremely delicate problem—by providing arms to the seven Afghan political groups actually fighting the Soviets, he was in effect directing seven different wars.

The Muj had the political support of the entire Muslim world including Iran, of the United States and Britain, and of China, but when it comes to arms, business is business. Egypt, for example, sold whole warehouses full of obsolete Soviet arms to the CIA, which transferred them to Pakistan where they were divvied up for the different factions of the Muj.

The idea was to maintain the fiction that the Muj were capturing their arms from the Soviets on the battlefield. The reality was that Egypt got hard currency for worthless weapons, the CIA kept the US at arm's length from the war, and the rebels were outgunned. But Yousaf had to take what he could get, including 60,000 rifles and 8,000 machine guns of World War II vintage dug out of warehouses in Turkey, an unbelievably cumbersome Swiss antiaircraft gun which fired $50,000 worth of ammunition per minute and took twenty mules to haul around the Afghan countryside, and a British surface-to-air missile called the Blowpipe which had proved useless in the Falklands war.

What Yousaf wanted and the Muj needed was the American shoulder-fired antiaircraft missile called the Stinger. For three years the Americans held back on the grounds it might fall into the hands of terrorists. This was a sober fear; the Stinger was the perfect tool for bringing down jumbo jets loaded with passengers. But just as real was American concern that Stingers would work too well, suddenly tip the balance of power on the battlefield, and thereby invite a dangerous Soviet escalation of the war. "I had to ensure that we did not provoke

3. London: Leo Cooper, 1992.

them sufficiently to do so," Yousaf writes. "A war with the Soviets would have been the end of Pakistan and could have unleashed a world war. It was a great responsibility, and one which I had to keep constantly in mind during those years."

But eventually the Americans provided Stingers to the Muj. What decided the matter, according to a *Washington Post* article by Steve Coll in July 1992,[4] was secret intelligence information beginning in 1984 about Soviet military plans to throw more troops and weapons into the war. With American support Yousaf had been trying to "make Afghanistan their Vietnam" and it was working. The Soviets responded with a plan to win the war through sharply increased use of the KGB, elite "Spetsnaz" paratroopers, helicopters, and sophisticated battlefield communication vans. By the time the energetic commander of Soviet forces in Germany, General Mikhail Zaitsev, had been transferred to Afghanistan in the spring of 1985, the Americans were also prepared for an escalated struggle. CIA director William Casey visited Muj camps in Pakistan and backed plans to carry the war across the Amu River into the Soviet Union itself—pugnacity at a level the United States had not dared to show since the early 1950s.

But it was Stingers, not cross-border operations, that made the difference. The Muj brought down their first Soviet helicopter with a Stinger in September 1986, and over the following ten months nearly 190 of the lethal missiles were fired by the rebels with an astounding 75 percent kill rate. That was the beginning of the end for the Soviets. Afghan pilots flying the Soviet-made assault helicopters were soon overheard complaining on the radio that their Soviet "advisers" no longer dared to fly, and the Muj bottled up their opponents under virtual siege in a handful of major cities and military camps. With the failure of the Soviet offensive, Mikhail Gorbachev elected to cut his

---

4. Steve Coll, "Anatomy of a Victory: CIA's Covert Afghan War," *The Washington Post*, July 19, 1992.

losses. Just what part the Afghan disaster played in the slow-motion Soviet collapse during those years must await the work of historians with access to Soviet archives, but it is clear that the process was hurried along by the cost in blood and money of the Afghan war. The biggest share of the credit for victory goes first to the Muj who fought the war, then to the Pakistanis who stuck their necks out to back them.[5]

But the decision to use American Stingers was also important, and that in part was the direct result of "secret intelligence information," which helped to convince Washington to act before a new Soviet military campaign could get under way. *The Washington Post*'s Steve Coll, when he reported that such secret information existed, did not specify how it was obtained. I myself have heard reports, which I cannot confirm, that a high-level agent in the Soviet government was recruited by the CIA, perhaps as early as the late 1970s; that this person had access to the deliberations of the Politburo; and that his or her reports of the impulsive decision behind the invasion in 1979, followed by bitter division over how to proceed thereafter, were an important factor in the Reagan administration's willingness to risk a bigger war by taking a stand.

I write "agent," but of course the correct word might be source, if the information came from some technically sophisticated means of monitoring the deliberations of the Politburo. This is typical of the way knowledge of an important spy (or source) slowly surfaces in the public record. Journalists do not uncover spies, but only tease out, or, more often, gratefully receive, information already gathered or sur-

---

5. That such operations may later have unexpected consequences is suggested by the conclusion by Ted Koppel to a report on *Nightline*, on April 1, 1993:

> During the war in Afghanistan, the CIA and the State Department routinely facilitated trips to Afghanistan and back into the United States for members of the Mujahideen. It is more than likely that several of the men now charged with bombing the World Trade Center were once paid and supported by agencies of the US government.

mised by intelligence services. One or two vague reports suggest where something important is still to be found; later writers go back to the subject, slowly dredging up the details which guide their successors, until at some point the official keepers of secrets let the story go. Many important intelligence stories have nothing to do with spies, of course, but the most sensational revelations of the cold war have almost all been spy stories, and recent books on intelligence have tended to focus on espionage cases. Veterans of the intelligence business claim there is no substitute for human sources; the expense of recruiting agents may be immense, but an hour with a well-placed spy can be worth a year of slogging through public records, overhead reconnaissance photographs, and other technical data gathered by the bale.

The Soviet intelligence services—principally the Komitet Gosudarstvennoi Bezopasnosti (Committee for State Security), or KGB, and the Glavnoe Razvedyvatel'noe Upravlenie (Chief Intelligence Directorate of the Soviet military) or GRU[6]—had a reputation for almost occult skill in recruiting human agents. They certainly recruited a lot of them—some so sensitively placed they set off major political crises in Britain, Germany, France, and the United States. Tom Bower's recent book on clandestine British operations in the Baltic in the late 1940s, *The Red Web: MI6 and the KGB Master Coup*,[7] adds some significant detail to one major early spy episode, including a passing reference to the Finnish intelligence chief Reino Hallamaa, whose name I do not recall seeing in print before. In 1944 Hallamaa delivered 1,500 pages

---

6. I look up things like this in Leo D. Carl's *International Dictionary of Intelligence*, published by International Defense Consultant Services, Inc., of McLean, Virginia, in 1990. This is an extremely useful reference work for intelligence organizations and combatants in the cold war. Typical is a twenty-four-page list of operational code names from Operation Ajax (the 1953 overthrow of Mossadegh in Iran) to Operation Zinc (a British commando mission to Czechoslovakia during World War II).

7. Aurum, 1989.

of material, including an almost complete Soviet codebook, to the OSS station in Stockholm. This material soon reached the head of the OSS, William Donovan, in Washington, but US policy at the time was to treat the Soviets as trustworthy allies. Donovan was ordered to hand the material over to the Soviets and he did—but not before retaining a secret copy.

This is a typical backdoor entry to an intelligence story—highly particular, a little hard to follow, harder to see the point. Bower's reference to the codebook, as is often the case with disclosures of intelligence secrets, is incidental to his main story. The central subject of *The Red Web* is the provocative British operation to start a partisan war against the Soviets in the Baltic republics that were forcibly annexed by Stalin at the beginning of the Second World War. There was no shortage of Latvians, Estonians, and Lithuanians eager to die in this hopeless endeavor. The British never expected them to win, but, like the Americans during the tense years between the Berlin blockade in 1948 and battlefield stalemate in Korea in 1951–1952, they feared a big European war with the Russians might soon take place and wanted allies behind the lines when it began. The Americans ran a similar operation in Ukraine, just as hopeless, but one that still awaits a historian.

Bower tells a sad story of misplaced heroism on the part of the Baltic resisters, who were cold-bloodedly discarded by the British. Many agents were simply informed by radio that the game was over and they were on their own. The intelligence officers who ran it were old anti-Soviet hands from the 1920s and 1930s, like Harry Carr, born in Russia in 1899, the son of a British expatriate who managed a timber mill. Carr's world and his family's wealth were whisked away by the Revolution while he was at school in Britain. In 1925 Carr was working for the SIS in Riga, the world capital of espionage directed against the Bolshevik regime, when the Soviets were able to capture two of their bitterest enemies, Boris Savinkov and Sidney

Reilly, with a brilliantly executed deception operation known ever since as "The Trust." Even fifty years later CIA counterintelligence experts would cite "The Trust" in a solemn whisper as proof of the Soviet capacity for deep schemes to trick the West.

But despite watching this disaster firsthand in Riga, according to Bower, Carr fell for a similar Soviet operation in the Baltics when a KGB officer established a phony partisan band in the forests of Lithuania. We may gain a hint of how badly things went wrong from the simple fact that Carr, in the spring of 1950, was introduced to his counterpart at the CIA, Harry Rositzke, by the SIS liaison officer in Washington, Harold Adrian Russell Philby, known as "Kim" to a host of American and British intelligence officers who would spend the rest of their lives regretting every confidence shared over martinis with the infamous spy for the Russians. It was the job of the two Harrys to carry the cold war to Russia. A few months after they were introduced by Philby, the American Harry told the British Harry that the CIA had begun to suspect that the British partisans were under Soviet control. "Harry," said the British Harry, brushing these doubts aside, "I think we know our business on this one."

Such complacency was fully matched by the humiliating disaster which followed, but it was small satisfaction to the American Harry. His agents all disappeared into Ukraine. Guerrilla operations behind the Iron Curtain were over by the mid-1950s, and were never resumed until the CIA sent armed Afghani guerrillas across the Amu River. Bower, a producer of documentaries for the BBC, tells his story well, with much detail and some vividly drawn characters. There is no clearer sign of the end of the cold war than the fact that so many former British, American, and Soviet-bloc intelligence officers sat down with Bower and told him in detail about what had happened.

When we hear of the events in *The Red Web* next it will be from a scholar who has had access to the files. But it is unlikely that more detail will much change the sad story. The Soviets ran circles around these early Western operations, but the Baltic campaigns served at least one purpose all the same. Sending armed men across a rival's borders is a sign of resolution more readily believed than words. After the takeover of Czechoslovakia, the Americans and the British made it clear they would tolerate no further westward creep of the Iron Curtain, and cold war shooting thereafter took place exclusively in the third world.

But what of the Soviet codebooks discovered by the Finns and delivered to Donovan of the OSS in 1944? After the war American cryptanalysts resumed the monitoring of Soviet cable traffic, suspended during the common fight against Hitler. In the late 1940s, with the aid of the codebooks provided by the Finns, American cryptanalysts managed to break some of the KGB messages, referred to as the VENONA material, between Moscow and the Soviet consulate in New York. The best account of this still fragmentary story is to be found in *The FBI–KGB War: A Special Agent's Story* by former FBI agent Robert J. Lamphere and Tom Shachtman.[8] In the decrypted messages Soviet agents were all referred to by code names, but additional information known as "collateral"—the fact, for example, that "Homer" visited his pregnant wife in New York on a certain date—allowed some of these agents to be identified. Several of the biggest spy stories of the 1950s came directly from the VENONA material, but most of the cryptonyms have never been identified. The so-called "spy-scare" or "Red scare" of the 1950s was in some part the result of the FBI's frustration in its attempt to identify all the Soviet agents cited in the VENONA material. Since the Soviet intelligence services in the 1920s and 1930s freely recruited members of local Communist parties to serve as spies, those in, or close to, the American CP fell under a kind of blanket of suspicion.

---

8. Random House, 1986.

Lamphere's book adds much important information to the stories of Julius and Ethel Rosenberg, executed as "atomic spies" in 1951; of the British scientist Klaus Fuchs, who provided them with information from Los Alamos; and of the Soviet spy ring which included Donald Maclean, Guy Burgess, and Kim Philby.[9] What concerns Lamphere is the way these spies were identified, a story tightly classified until recent years. Fuchs confessed and Maclean, Burgess, and Philby declared themselves by defecting, but the Rosenbergs died defending their innocence. Lamphere worked to declassify the VENONA material in the hope that publication of once secret messages about the Rosenbergs would dispel public doubts about their guilt. But nowhere does Lamphere use the word "VENONA" or any of the cryptonyms of Soviet agents. A likely reason for this continued reticence is the fact that one partially decrypted message about "Stanley" may—or may not—be central to an important counterintelligence case still bitterly contested after more than fifty years.

Stanley appeared in the opening act of the secret cold war, which may be said to have begun in September 1945 with the defection in Canada of the Soviet code clerk Igor Gouzenko, who fled with a sheaf of documents and much information about Soviet spy rings. Half-forgotten now, the episode set off a major international flap at the time while the Soviets furiously accused Gouzenko of being a common thief and the Canadians debated whether to keep or surrender him. Among much other important information delivered by Gouzenko

---

9. Many loose ends of old spy stories are partially cleared up by Lamphere's book—for example, the background of the relentless security investigation of Sylvia Press, a counterintelligence analyst in the CIA, described in her fine novel, *The Care of Devils* (Beacon Press, 1958). Press was never formally charged, but she gathered that it had something to do with a male friend she had accompanied on a trip to Mexico. A CIA analyst once told me that Press's friend had turned up in the VENONA material, and Lamphere (p. 248) describes just such an incident. None of this justifies Press's hounding by CIA security officers, but it helps explain the atmosphere which made it possible.

was his report of a Soviet spy inside British intelligence—just who and where he did not know. A September 1945 KGB message, deciphered by the cryptanalysts in the summer of 1950, reported confirmation of "information from Stanley" about the Gouzenko defection. A new sentence began, "When Stanley returns from. . . ." The missing word came from the "K" section of the Soviet codebook, which had been damaged and rendered illegible on a Finnish battlefield.

In the years that followed the 1951 defection of Burgess and Maclean it was assumed by some British and American counterintelligence analysts that "Stanley" must have been Kim Philby, who fit Gouzenko's vague description and had been on a mission to Turkey at the time of the Gouzenko defection. The Russians spell Constantinople with a "K." Philby was forced out of British intelligence in 1951 and his defection a dozen years later established beyond doubt that he had been a Soviet spy. But was he Stanley?

There is no such thing as a dead case in a spy war. In the 1960s a new counterintelligence scare was precipitated by the KGB defector Anatoli Golitsyn, who tied up the CIA and the SIS in knots with claims that Soviet moles had penetrated their organization. Golitsyn and another Soviet defector, Yuri Nosenko, have been the subject of several books, most recently *Cold Warrior* by Tom Mangold, another BBC producer, and *Molehunt* by David Wise, both of which add much new detail to the affair but fail to capture the strange and elusive personality of the CIA's chief molehunter, James Angleton.[10] What's important about intelligence literature is what it tells us about international conflict, but what's interesting about it is the often obsessed cast of characters, who bring an element of human drama to otherwise abstract

---

10. *Cold Warrior: James Jesus Angleton: The CIA's Master Spy Hunter* (Simon and Schuster, 1991); *Molehunt: The Secret Search for Traitors That Shattered the CIA* (Random House, 1992). A brief explanation of the issues involved may be found in Chapter Six, on Edward Jay Epstein's *Deception: The Invisible War Between the KGB and the CIA*.

questions of policy. Angleton went mad trying to understand what the KGB was up to, but he went mad subtly, leaving room to wonder if he had not perhaps seen deeper into certain affairs than some of his critics.

But there is no question he was dotty. During the early 1960s he took as gospel Golitsyn's claim that the Sino-Soviet split was simply another deception operation in the spirit of the Trust. These were the years when Secretary of State Dean Rusk was arguing that the United States had to hold the line in Vietnam to stop "Beiping." After the war was over and the Americans had gone home it was obvious that we had fought and bled on behalf of the Chinese—the last thing they wanted was a North Vietnamese victory. Angleton, who assiduously spread doubts about the real enmity of the Chinese and the Soviets, bears some of the blame for the disaster.

Intelligence services like to hold on to their files until everybody who can explain them is decrepit or dead, so Angleton may never get the biographer he deserves. It is no discredit to Mangold or Wise to say that their well-told stories of Soviet defectors must be seen as interim reports. Wise in particular adds much new information about the devastating effect of the CIA's prolonged investigation of Golitsyn's claims. Internal investigations blighted or ended the careers of numerous CIA officials until Angleton was at last forced to retire in 1974 by William Colby—himself one of Angleton's many suspects.

But while the investigations continued old cases were reopened; Gouzenko's clues of 1945 were dusted off and the analysts hit on something truly troubling—the possibility that "Stanley" was not Philby, but the chief of the British counterintelligence service between 1952 and 1956, Sir Roger Hollis.[11] One small, perhaps vital piece

---

11. The details can be pursued in Peter Wright, *Spycatcher* (Viking, 1987), and W. J. West, *The Truth About Hollis* (London: Duckworth, 1989).

of evidence was the KGB sentence beginning "When Stanley returns from...." Here the antic God of intelligence intervened. At the same time that Kim Philby had been dispatched to Constantinople, Roger Hollis had been sent to help debrief Gouzenko in Canada, which the Russians spell with a "K."

Does any of this make a big difference? In the event of war the Soviets doubtless could have made good use of Roger Hollis at MI5, and Philby would have been an important asset as well. But how important? Philby betrayed many agents and informants, but aside from this, no one has yet shown that he gave the Soviets anything more than a secret sense of superiority. It is just as hard to establish the real importance of another famous Soviet spy, George Blake, whose autobiography, *No Other Choice*,[12] written from exile in Moscow, captures the strange naiveté of the man. Like many spies, he was caught by his interrogator, which is to say that he betrayed himself.

Blake had been active in the Dutch Resistance during the war and he joined the British SIS soon after. But in a Korean POW camp he switched sides and over the next eight years as a Soviet agent he delivered huge quantities of material to his case officers, a large part of it while stationed in Berlin. Most sensational of the secrets he betrayed was the Berlin tunnel, which made its way several hundred yards into the Soviet zone where CIA technicians tapped into telephone cables. Doubtless the Soviets were glad to know about the tunnel, which gave them an ideal opportunity to feed information to the West for their own purposes, but more important to the KGB would have been Blake's detailed information about SIS officers and their agents allowing the Soviets to monitor their adversaries. Intelligence services hold each other in close embrace; in a classic example Blake describes an SIS file he once read of the reports of British and Dutch watchers who

---

12. Simon and Schuster, 1990.

had trailed and then lost a known KGB officer named Korovin in Holland in 1953. Many heads had been scratched over Korovin's mission. It was no mystery to Blake; Korovin had come to meet him.

Even the best spies cannot survive such scrutiny for long. Eventually the British picked up information pointing to Blake, but knowing he was a spy and proving it in court are two different things. The break came when Blake's interrogator, Harold Shergold, playing the good cop in April 1961, said he understood where Blake had gone wrong—he'd been tortured by the Chinese Communists while a prisoner of war in Korea, he'd confessed he was an SIS officer, and thereafter the Soviets simply blackmailed him.

A simple denial would probably have returned Blake to the streets as a civilian. But Shergold's suggestion he'd been coerced struck Blake as monstrous. He burst out, "Nobody tortured me!... I myself approached the Soviets and offered my services to them of my own accord!" He explained that it was Karl Marx who had recruited him. There were no books in the Korean POW camp save a few texts in Russian, and *Das Kapital*, read aloud to a friend to pass the time, had convinced Blake that humanity's future was in the East. This confession led straight to jail; six years later a daring escape brought him to Russia, where, he writes in a wistful aside, "up to the 1970s one could keep up the illusion that we were moving forward all the time."

But useful as Blake may have been to the Soviets, it is hard to argue that great affairs of state turned upon his treason. A much better case can be made for the importance of what the Soviets learned from the agent they called "Homer" in the VENONA material. At the end of the war the British diplomat Donald Maclean was attached to the embassy in Washington, but he routinely met his Soviet case officer in New York City while visiting his pregnant wife, who was living there with friends. Once these facts were read by cryptanalysts in the late 1940s, it was obvious that "Homer" was Maclean. Nobody monitored the investigation more closely than Philby, the sis liaison officer in Washington; in 1951, warned by Philby of impending arrest, Maclean slipped out of Britain with his friend and fellow spy, Guy Burgess, and defected to the Soviet Union. This was the first public act in the longest-running spy case of the cold war. The spy-hunters looked for "the third man" who warned Maclean, but in 1963, just when they were about to close in on Philby, he got away. Later a fourth man was identified as the art historian Anthony Blunt, and only recently a fifth man has been named. In public, that is; the counterintelligence people had known about him for years.

Verne W. Newton, author of a carefully researched book on Maclean and Burgess called *The Cambridge Spies: The Untold Story of Maclean, Philby, and Burgess in America*,[13] has dug out of the US files a list of services that Maclean likely performed for the Soviets. In October 1945, for example, Maclean was in a position to tell the Russians about the American and British negotiating positions in a diplomatic struggle over rights of passage through the Dardanelles. A few months later he may have helped to block negotiations for an exchange of American loans for the use of British bases. In late 1946 information supplied by Maclean may have helped the Russians to force the Americans to publish figures for deployment of troops abroad, something the British had been anxious to avoid.

In one case Maclean apparently delivered on a grand scale. For a little over a year, between February 1947 and June 1948, Maclean had a "no-escort" pass at the Atomic Energy Commission (AEC) in Washington, and he used it frequently. In the late 1940s, when "the bomb" was what Washington counted on to keep Soviet armies in Europe in check, the biggest secret about American nuclear weaponry was the number of bombs we had. That number was only very slightly above zero. When Truman sent a fleet of American bombers to Britain as

13. Madison Books, 1991.

a show of force at the beginning of the Berlin blockade in 1948, no bombs were aboard—only training dummies—because there were no crews to assemble them. Verne Newton argues that Maclean knew the arsenal was empty and told the KGB; and Stalin's eerie confidence while his minions seized power in Czechoslovakia and his armies risked war by closing the highways to Berlin strongly suggests that Newton is right. Maclean's information may thus have changed history.

Another episode points in a somewhat different direction. Klaus Fuchs provided the Soviets with much technical data about bomb design which got their atomic program off to a quick start, but there is nothing like discovery of a spy to arouse fear and alarm.[14] In the fall of 1949 Fuchs fell under suspicion as the result of breakouts—i.e., decrypted passages—of the VENONA material; by November the AEC knew he had probably been a Soviet spy, a matter of some moment because the AEC was then split over whether it was worth an all-out effort to develop hydrogen bombs and Fuchs had seen all the American work on fusion theory. Word of the case began to filter through the government. By late January 1950, when Fuchs signed a confession in London and President Truman's advisers were fighting the last battles over the H-bomb, one factor in the secret debate was the troubling thought that Fuchs had told the Russians everything we knew. Among those working out the final text of Truman's decision to go

---

14. The Fuchs case is treated at length in the *The FBI–KGB War*, and is the subject of an excellent book—*Klaus Fuchs, Atom Spy*, by Robert Chadwell Williams (Harvard University Press, 1987). The German scientist Manfred von Ardenne, who worked on the Russian bomb program for a time after the war, told me that much early theoretical work had been acquired wholesale from a spy source. Later, when they both lived in Dresden, Fuchs confirmed to Ardenne that the information had come from him. For later developments in this case see Michael Dobbs's story in *The Washington Post*, "How Soviets Stole US Atom Secrets," October 4, 1992. From Anatoly Yatskov, the Russian who ran the ring of which Fuchs was a part, Dobbs learned of another Soviet spy at Los Alamos who began reporting as early as the spring of 1943. This spy, code-named Perseus, is still unidentified.

ahead was Gordon Arneson, who later wrote, "The Fuchs matter was in everyone's minds...."[15]

How much difference did it make? Fear of the Russians surely got a major boost in policymaking circles from the unfolding Fuchs case, and there is no question that fear provided the psychic energy behind the H-bomb decision. Fuchs doubtless saved the Russians time and money building their first bomb. But if the discovery that Fuchs had been a spy helped frighten the Americans into an all-out program to produce H-bombs, thereby unleashing a thirty-year arms race which bankrupted the Soviet regime in the 1980s, we may ask where was the net gain from Moscow's point of view.

Not even the most celebrated Soviet spy for the West, Oleg Penkovsky, who photographed thousands of pages of secret documents over an eighteen-month period in 1961–1962, can clearly be identified as a prime mover in a major episode of the cold war. Penkovsky is the subject of a recent book, *The Spy Who Saved the World: How a Soviet Colonel Changed the Course of the Cold War*, by the journalist Jerrold L. Schecter and the KGB defector Peter S. Deriabin.[16] The CIA released to them a vast collection of documents about the Penkovsky case under the Freedom of Information Act, making the book a virtually unique study of an agent and his handling, but the title is hyperbole all the same.

Penkovsky volunteered his services in early 1961, just about the time Nikita Khrushchev was mounting a major diplomatic and military effort to seize control of all of Berlin. The documents he photographed in Moscow included technical and training manuals which helped the United States to monitor with great accuracy the Soviets' progress in deploying nuclear missiles in Cuba in the fall of 1962. This information was extremely useful; it not only convinced the

15. Herbert York, *The Advisors* (W. H. Freeman, 1976; Stanford University Press, 1989), p. 69.

16. Scribner's, 1993.

Americans that the missiles could reach every major American city except Seattle, but it provided a timetable of just how long it would take the Soviets to get them ready.

The Spy Who Saved the World is one of the best intelligence books in recent years, filled with surprises. One is that the US State Department and American ambassadors in Moscow were extremely timid about intelligence operations, limiting the number of CIA officers attached to the embassy and initially refusing to let them deal with Penkovsky. When one weighs this along with the embassy's pathetic failure to protect its own security, thoroughly documented by Ronald Kessler in *Moscow Station: How the KGB Penetrated the American Embassy*, one finds oneself rooting for the spooks.[17]

In 1962 Penkovsky stopped providing information. Just how and why the CIA lost touch with him is not quite clear; the CIA refused to release counterintelligence files on the case, and Schecter and Deriabin do not have a good explanation for the fact that the Soviets photographed Penkovsky meeting a handler in January 1962 but did not arrest him until the following September. It was discrepancies like that one which led the British counterintelligence expert Peter Wright to argue heatedly what James Angleton only hinted—that even Penkovsky was a provocation, a controlled agent sent to deceive. Such arguments by their nature can go on forever.

What spies do is close to the heart of intelligence work, which may be defined as the pursuit of secret advantage. But it is important to remember that they work for vast bureaucracies at the service of foreign and defense ministries which consume information on an industrial scale. The history of the CIA as an institution has been much expanded by three recent books, two of them declassified CIA histories written for internal use, *The Central Intelligence Agency: An Instrument of Government, to 1950*, written by the Yale historian Arthur B.

17. Scribner's, 1989.

Darling in the 1950s,[18] and *General Walter Bedell Smith as Director of Central Intelligence, October 1950–February 1953* by Ludwell Lee Montague.[19] These leaden titles should not deceive the general reader; both books are written with intellectual vigor and a wealth of fascinating detail, and their footnotes identify many important documents for those young and patient enough to resort to the Freedom of Information Act. Darling, for example, gives a thorough account of the founding of the Office of Policy Coordination, the CIA's first covert arm, whose chief was to be named by the secretary of state and approved by the National Security Council, so long as he was "acceptable" to the director of central intelligence. Montague, in turn, gives a sometimes lurid account of the organizational stresses created by this weird flow chart, which ended a few years later in a forced marriage of the OPC with the Office of Special Operations.

Also indispensable is Burton Hersh's *The Old Boys: The American Elite and the Origins of the CIA,*[20] a portrait of a handful of men who developed a taste for intelligence work with the OSS during World War II and stayed on to fight the Russians and build the agency. No other recent intelligence book has aroused the anger of the CIA veterans as much as this one. The chief old boys, Allen Dulles and Frank Wisner, are gone, but many of their younger colleagues remain, and they particularly resent Hersh's disrespectful manner. He reconstructs several CIA failures—particularly its disastrous attempts to set up secret armies in Hungary and other parts of Eastern Europe—and his judgments are sharp and dismissive. In Hersh's account homosexuals and adulterers abound, and if anybody ever made a dumb remark or got drunk at an inopportune moment or ended up a manic depressive, Hersh is sure to have heard about it and published it. But if you want

18. Pennsylvania State University Press, 1990.

19. Pennsylvania State University Press, 1992.

20. Scribner's, 1992.

a sense of the brash confidence of the early days of the CIA, you will find much reliable information in *The Old Boys* that has seen the light nowhere else. If Hersh can be faulted it is because he gives his cast of characters hardly any of the credit they can claim for eventual American victory in the cold war.

This may sound perverse. None of the spy tales recounted in recent books seems to have provided the edge for victory; the covert warriors in blackface caused much death and havoc in Southeast Asia, Cuba, and Central America but they did the US little apparent good in any of these places. The CIA's history, moreover, is rich with failures to predict major events, among them the first Soviet atomic bomb, the North Korean and Chinese invasions in Korea, the Hungarian revolt, Fidel Castro's victory and Khrushchev's subsequent placement of missiles in Cuba, the invasion of Czechoslovakia, and the invasion of Afghanistan. Above all, the CIA failed to predict—failed even to imagine—the collapse of Soviet communism and the end of the cold war. Perry's *Eclipse* and Kessler's *Inside the CIA*[21] both discuss this failure, beginning with a great dispute among the intelligence analysts about Soviet defense spending in the mid-1970s.

The battle was joined after the Defense Intelligence Agency interrogated a defector who said the Soviets were spending 11 to 12 percent of their GNP on defense, not the 5 to 6 percent previously claimed by the CIA. One analyst, William Lee, argued that the real figure was actually as high as 25 percent. That should have told anyone paying attention that the Soviet economy was straining toward collapse, but the analysts all drew a different conclusion—that the level of Soviet military spending must mean Moscow was still trying to conquer the world. The Soviet Union was collapsing before Robert Gates brought himself to concede in public that it was even wobbling.

---

21. *Inside the CIA: Revealing the Secrets of the World's Most Powerful Spy Agency* (Pocket Books, 1954.

But these numerous intelligence failures proved less important in the end than the one thing the CIA over the years consistently got right. It is not the clandestine triumphs that justify the billions spent on intelligence—the purloined secrets, the foiled schemes, the embarrassments visited upon an opponent. It is the steadiness and pervasiveness of a kind of close contact which will unmistakably reveal an opponent's real capacities and approximate intentions. Intelligence services touch, watch, and listen to each other at a thousand points. The intimate knowledge revealed by the wrestler's embrace freed both sides from the ignorance, rumor, and outbreaks of panicky fear that spark big wars no one wants. The tensest moments of the cold war were the earliest, when the CIA depended on *Pravda*, on agents counting railroad boxcars, and on tourists with cameras in order to monitor what Stalin had in mind.

General Curtis LeMay, the commander of the Strategic Air Command in the 1950s, used to say that he did not intend to let his fleet of nuclear bombers be caught on the ground by a surprise attack. The go-order would be issued the instant he received "unambiguous strategic warning." Knowing that World War III would be the immediate result, high defense and White House officials in two administrations wanted to know just what "unambiguous strategic warning" was, and how LeMay would know it when he saw it. But this was a secret of intelligence tradecraft which LeMay did not feel free to share.

A few years ago the historian Gregg Herken spent an evening with LeMay. Thinking the general had perhaps mellowed with age, Herken made bold to ask just what sort of "unambiguous strategic warning" the general had been looking for. It was the old LeMay who snapped back: "You professors shouldn't get your balls in an uproar over that. *I* knew what it was."

The rest of the defense establishment did not share LeMay's confidence in his visceral judgments, and within a few years the intelligence agencies had found ways to pick up truly unambiguous signs of

an impending Soviet nuclear attack. How the CIA built a global apparatus which could penetrate the "denied areas" of the Soviet Union
and its allies is ably recounted in two books by Jeffrey T. Richelson,
American Espionage and the Soviet Target and *America's Secret Eyes
in Space: The U. S. Keyhole Spy Satellite Program.*[21] These make it clear
that what we knew about the Soviet Union came overwhelmingly from
what Henry Kissinger used to call "national technical means," because
it was official policy never to concede that we spied on the Russians
with satellites. It was only in September 1992, in fact, that the US
government at last admitted the existence and work of the National
Reconnaissance Office (NRO), which operates American satellites.[22]
The latest ones can look through clouds, peer sideways, see at night,
and gather information in many other technically marvelous ways.

It is probably too soon to write the history of intelligence in the
cold war. It is astonishing but true that no one has yet even attempted
to write the history of intelligence during World War II, where it was
at the very least as important as the Battle of Britain or Stalingrad,
despite the fact that most files—always excepting Britain's—have
been released. But to get them released took decades, and prying
loose the cold war files will be little easier.

When the files eventually are available, and when professional historians overcome their fear of intelligence history, they are probably
going to find that the happy outcome of the cold war depended heavily on the CIA's spies, the NRO's satellites, and the NSA's monitoring of
communications. But the edge was not the information we needed to
win in the sense that code-breaking in World War II allowed the US
Navy to defeat the Japanese in the Battle of Midway. Many small
victories and defeats in the cold war have explanations of that sort.
But what American intelligence contributed to the outcome was

21. Morrow, 1987; Harper and Row, 1990.

22. *The Washington Post*, September 19, 1992.

something quite different—the confidence that we knew what the Soviets were up to, and could afford to contain their forays while waiting for the deep change in attitude which George Kennan had predicted back in 1947. There was an element of luck of the kind sometimes called Divine Providence in the world's close scrape with catastrophe during the cold war, but official policy also had a part in getting us through.

Intelligence on the grand scale was necessary to the policy of deterrence—the belief, often derided, by me among others, that nuclear weapons could keep the peace. But it wasn't free-floating fear of nuclear weapons that made war too scary to contemplate; it was the hard-won, detailed knowledge, held by both sides, of what nuclear weapons could do, how many there were, what they were pointed at, and the certainty that they would penetrate any defense. From the emerging history of intelligence in the cold war we learn that an arms race can be stable, and Great Powers can struggle vigorously for decades without precipitating a global bloodbath, so long as both sides are good at discovering, but not too good at hiding, the secrets that really count.

—*The New York Review of Books*, May 13, 1993

20

NO LAUGHING MATTER

THE TALE OF Aldrich Ames, the CIA intelligence officer now serving a life sentence in federal prison for selling secrets to the Russians between 1985 and his arrest in February 1994, has been examined in four books crammed with true names and organizational detail—which would have been unthinkable even a decade or so ago.[1] From these varying accounts of Ames's amazing success in eluding discovery by agency counterintelligence sleuths known as "mole hunters" we may abstract eight useful axioms for understanding covert intelligence activities during the cold war.

1. What goes around comes around.

The Central Intelligence Agency was the last of the major clandestine belligerents to experience the agony and humiliation of discovering a viper in its nest. The British, French, Germans, and Russians had each in their turn been through the political trauma of having to explain how it could have happened. The names of Kim Philby in

---

1. David Wise, *Nightmover: How Aldrich Ames Sold the CIA to the KGB for $4.6 Million* (HarperCollins, 1995); Tim Weiner, David Johnston, and Neil A. Lewis, *Betrayal: The Story of Aldrich Ames, an American Spy* (Random House, 1995); Peter Maas, *Killer Spy: The Inside Story of the FBI's Pursuit and Capture of Aldrich Ames, America's Deadliest Spy* (Warner, 1995); James Adams, *Sellout: Aldrich Ames and the Corruption of the CIA* (Viking, 1995).

Britain and Heinz Felfe in Germany remain bywords for treachery to this day. But no shock was deeper than the one suffered by the Russians on June 13, 1985, when they learned that eleven trusted officials, nine of them members of the KGB or the GRU, the Soviet military intelligence service, had been spying for the Americans.

The shock was so great that the Russian government abandoned every rule of counterintelligence tradecraft and ordered the wholesale arrest of the newly discovered spies. At least ten would eventually be executed. By the end of the year the spy-runners of the CIA in turn realized they had been struck by a disaster—the Russians appeared to be arresting every American agent. The explanation could only be compromise by some ghastly technical innovation—a new Russian code-breaking capacity, a well-placed bug, or the like—or something worse still, an intelligence officer gone bad, a traitor within, a mole. In October 1986 an apologetic KGB case officer, Vladimir Mechulayev, assured his star American agent during one of their rare face-to-face meetings in Rome that he had been unable to stop the arrests, that his hands had been tied by orders from above—presumably from the Politburo and perhaps even Mikhail Gorbachev himself—but that every effort would be made to protect him by sending the CIA off on one futile chase after another. The star agent was so drunk by the end of the meeting that he forgot to return the next night as instructed for one of his many substantial cash payments—well over $2 million in all with promise of more.

"Vlad," as Aldrich Ames called his handler, was as good as his word, and Russian tactics to protect him, combined with some foot-dragging and wishful thinking by the CIA itself, no doubt gradually convinced Ames over the next eight years that God loves a sinner. But on the morning of February 21, 1994, a Monday and a holiday, Ames discovered it was not so, and the CIA was finally subjected to the common fate of cold war intelligence services—the humiliating revelation that it had been betrayed for years by a man it trusted with its most secret secrets.

2. *The guy wearing the T-shirt saying "It's me! It's me!" is the guy.*
In the hierarchy of awful things that can happen to the public
reputation of an intelligence service, the discovery of a traitor within
is bad, the discovery that he has been at it for years is worse, and
the worst of all, by far, is the discovery that he was the obvious and
inevitable candidate for suspicion from day one. Just why Aldrich Ames
left so many careless clues to his spying for the Russians remains
locked within his psychic history, but it is obvious in retrospect that
catching him should have been a routine exercise once the Soviet/East
European (SE) Division noted the sudden disappearance of its spies in
the fall of 1985.

No finger pointed at Ames before he approached the Russians in
April 1985. He was a shy and bookish sort of man, the son of a former CIA official, who had shown little talent for fieldwork during a
tour in Turkey in the 1970s; but he performed well later in New York,
where he was assigned to keep watch on two important Soviet spies
including the high UN official Arkady Shevchenko, who later defected
to the United States. Ames had a drinking problem but so did a great
many other CIA officers; he was getting a divorce and was broke but
that was not unusual either.

But Ames's style as a spy was reckless and conspicuous from the
first day, when he walked into the Soviet embassy in Washington
(which was under constant surveillance by the FBI as Ames well knew)
and offered to turn traitor for $50,000. Two months later he handed
over a sheaf of documents identifying at least eleven Soviet agents
working for the CIA and the Russians realized they had acquired a
gold mine. They paid him a fortune but otherwise handled him in
exemplary fashion; the books on Ames by David Wise and by Tim
Weiner, David Johnston, and Neil A. Lewis of *The New York Times*
provide a kind of Russian tradecraft primer in dead drops, signal
sites, and eluding surveillance.

The Russians were good at what they did. It was Ames who nearly gave the game away by making numerous large cash deposits in bank accounts in his own name; paying cash for a $540,000 house and a $50,000 white Jaguar sportscar; getting falling-down drunk while on duty; telling friends lame stories about the rich relatives of his Colombian second wife, Rosario; failing to declare the influx of cash on his IRS return; failing to report his frequent meetings with Soviet officials as was required; and failing, as was required, to report his trips out of the country. Added to this, he left letters to and from the Russians on his home computer, threw into the household trash a draft of a note to his Russian handlers, charged airline travel to secret meetings to his personal credit card, and allowed the profligate Rosario to run up $30,000 monthly credit-card and phone bills, while discussing the details of meetings with Russian agents with her over the telephone.

So conspicuous was the flush of sudden wealth in the household following the return of the Ameses from a tour in Rome in 1989 that an old friend immediately connected the money, the frosty, tense impression that Ames and his wife gave to visitors, and the arrest of the agents by the Russians in 1985. But the attention of CIA mole hunters was soon distracted and the white Jaguar remained a familiar sight in the agency parking lot for another five years.

In the history of secret intelligence this refusal to register the obvious set no precedents. Spying is high-stress work and spies both are and act like desperate men. Indeed the previously most damaging American spy in the CIA's history, Edward Lee Howard, actually told two CIA officials in September 1984 that he had recently approached the Soviet embassy with thoughts of selling agency secrets. The truth was he had already done so—but in Vienna, not in Washington. Nevertheless a year passed before the the CIA took Howard's activities seriously, and then only after the Soviet defector Vitaly Yurchenko told his debriefers in Washington—Aldrich Ames among them—that a certain "Robert" had been selling secrets to the KGB. CIA counterintelligence officials knew immediately it was Howard to whom Yurchenko referred, and after five awful days of prayer for a miracle they finally told the FBI. Howard escaped anyway. What made catching Ames difficult was not picking him out of the crowd, but knowing what would happen next.

3. *If nobody knows, it didn't happen.*

Among the many consequences of catching Ames nine years late have been the following: the departure of CIA director R. James Woolsey like a whipped dog; the shattering of numerous other agency careers in a business where longevity counts for much; the CIA's loss of control over counterintelligence (now transferred to the FBI); the establishment of a new commission to rethink everything about the CIA from its table of organization to its name; the spreading awareness within the CIA's Directorate of Operations that Ames must have divulged to the Russians virtually every name, technical capacity, and trick of tradecraft they wanted to know; public doubt that the CIA can do anything right; exposure and humiliation of the agency before a worldwide audience, including everyone who is or who might consider telling secrets to the CIA; and skepticism about the CIA's ability to catch anything less obvious than an elephant in a telephone booth.

This is typically what happens when intelligence services catch spies in their own ranks. The trouble begins when they are caught. If they are never caught there is no trouble. All interested parties in the CIA understood this back in 1985 when operations of the Soviet/East European Division began to go bad in wholesale fashion. It is the principal reason why the mole hunters took nine years to catch Ames.

4. *Secrecy magnifies.*

Secret knowledge is a classic example of a double-edged sword—it may convey great power if timely and right, or it can precipitate a disaster if late or wrong. Hitler, to give one example, depended on his intelligence services to tell him where the Allies planned to invade Europe in 1944. If the Abwehr had known that the invasion would take place in Normandy during the first week of June, and if the report had been made a month or two in advance, the battle might have gone differently. Knowing this, Allied intelligence services did everything they could to ensure the Abwehr would not learn the plans, to confuse the Germans about the true meaning of whatever they did know, to feed the Germans false clues of alternative plans, and so on. All the activities of intelligence services may be extrapolated from this model, in which one side strives to learn the intentions of the other, while its opponent works to conceal the truth. A success or failure in these efforts may be small in absolute terms, involving a handful of pieces of paper, or one tapped telephone line, or a single person with secret loyalties, while the result may be loss of a battle, a campaign, or even a war.

In an army the man upon whose actions the common fate depends will probably be a general with a public reputation earned during a long career; but in an intelligence service the person who makes all the difference at a crucial moment may be a very ordinary man— bright enough, skilled perhaps, but little more than a visitor to the world of great affairs, modestly paid, mindful of his boss, a fellow with his own ideas and a few friends and a private history of small aspirations and disappointments, just a guy, in short, not all that different from the frequently drunk, chronically broke, easily dismissed figure of Aldrich Ames.

On June 13, 1985, during a bibulous lunch at Chadwick's restaurant in the Georgetown section of Washington, D.C., Ames destroyed a network of CIA agents inside the Soviet intelligence services which had been decades in the making. The implications of the lunch, of the manila envelope he passed to his handler, of the documents it contained were all hugely magnified by the fact that the spies of one superpower in the bowels of another disappeared in a day. But the two superpowers were at peace. If they had been at war the consequences would have been vastly greater.

5. The case is never closed.

One of the spies betrayed by Ames was a general recently retired from a long career in the GRU, Dimitri Polyakov. In the early 1960s Polyakov had been stationed in New York City where he was recruited by the FBI, an episode recounted for the first time by David Wise in *Nightmover*. The FBI gave Polyakov the code name Tophat, ran him until he was recalled to the Soviet Union, and then turned him over to the CIA, which maintained intermittent contact with him over the next two decades as he went on with his career as an intelligence officer.

Students of intelligence literature are all familiar with Polyakov as half of a two-man team of FBI spies known as Tophat and Fedora. Both men gave the United States much information about Soviet missile and chemical warfare programs. Fedora also backed up the story of another Russian defector, Yuri Nosenko, who became a central figure in the ruckus raised by the gray eminence of CIA counterintelligence between 1954 and 1974, James Jesus Angleton, who drove the intelligence services of the Western world frantic with his claims that the Russians had spies everywhere and that all the defectors subsequent to Anatoli Golitsyn—who went over to the CIA in Finland in 1961—were bogus.

The first historian of this controversy was Edward Jay Epstein, who argued in his book *Legend: The Secret World of Lee Harvey Oswald*, published in 1978, that Nosenko was not a genuine defector but still a KGB agent and that Fedora's lies about him proved that both were still working for the Russians. Later Epstein expanded his argument to include Tophat. By the time Fedora (identified by David Wise as one Aleksei Kulak) died of natural causes in 1983 the FBI had reluctantly joined the CIA in concluding that both Fedora and Tophat were phony defectors, sent to deceive. The apparent goals of the KGB in sending them were not trivial; they were supposed to convince the United States that Soviet missile builders lagged behind the US in crucial kinds of technology, and especially in missile guidance, while in fact the Soviets were surging ahead of the United States, and well on their way to building a force of super-accurate, super-powerful missiles that might disarm the Americans in a single surprise attack. Believing that Fedora and Tophat were false defectors, and that the Russians were really embarked on such a course, the Reagan administration began a huge new arms buildup of its own which soon bankrupted the Soviet Union.

But now it appears that Polyakov (Tophat) was arrested along with the rest of the spies betrayed by Ames in 1985, and, like many of them, tried, convicted, and executed. Much of what he told the FBI and the CIA supported Fedora's most important claims as well. Does that mean both were genuine defectors after all? Must the CIA and historians of the cold war now go back and reinterpret all the conclusions based on the agency's assumption that Fedora and Tophat were feeding them disinformation about Soviet missiles?

The Ames case puts a toe in the door of another case as well. CIA analysts have been arguing about the bona fides of Vitaly Yurchenko ever since he slipped his CIA watcher and redefected to the Russians in November 1985. The CIA has officially insisted he was a genuine defector who changed his mind. But one reason the CIA took so long to catch Ames was the success of Russian stratagems to make the agency think that all sorts of other explanations existed for the arrest of their spies. The most plausible, for a time, was the notion that Edward Lee Howard gave them away. That claim was made by Vitaly Yurchenko. Was he sent to the US to make it?

Such cases refuse to remain closed.

6. *Something is missing from this story.*

In the history of cold war counterintelligence cases there are many examples of spies identified with the help of the reports of defectors. The control and routing of information within intelligence organizations is intended to make catching spies easier, and the analysts go on alert whenever they detect signs the other side knows something it shouldn't. But it is hard to think of a single spy of significance uncovered by either side without at least some kind of timely tip. When Ames walked into the Soviet embassy in 1985 the CIA had a huge network of spies working within the Soviet intelligence services. The Russians were stunned.

The story of the investigation that eventually led to the arrest of Ames is a classic counterintelligence story because it began with a sense that something was wrong—things were happening that couldn't happen unless the other side *knew*. But the investigation that followed took an ungodly amount of time to spot the spendthrift under the agency's nose. The investigators compiled huge dossiers of incriminating information—including (in September 1992) the fact that Ames had made large cash deposits on the same days in which he had held unreported meetings with Soviet officials. Still they failed to accuse him. What were they waiting for?

A defector. That's how it's done. A defector provides a lot of clues about time, place, and identity—generally referred to as "collateral" —and the sleuths then scrutinize his information and draw a conclusion. But first they need a defector with clues.

Did a defector finger Ames?

All of these four books describe the Ames case as a combination of CIA and FBI investigations which eventually settled on the culprit. None suggests that any important help came from defectors or spies. But one or two remarks in passing suggest that a big piece of the real story is still unreported. The most explicit of these clues is provided in *Betrayal* by Tim Weiner and his colleagues, who report that a "source" in Moscow in January 1993 delivered information that "closely matched the conclusions the investigators were drafting." Peter Maas in *Killer Spy* reports that the FBI quit poking through Ames's trash for a time in September 1993 for fear he had been put on the alert by a claim in Ronald Kessler's *The FBI: Inside the World's Most Powerful*

Law Enforcement Agency[2] that the bureau was investigating spies implicated by a former KGB "employee." Walter Pincus in *The Washington Post* reported that American officials were helped in the Ames case (1) by access to East German intelligence files (March 6, 1994), (2) by "a former communist official...in early 1993" (April 6, 1994), and (3) by "information given to the FBI by a former communist intelligence official" (October 2, 1994).

None of these claims is amplified in the four recent books on the case, but they help to explain important turning points in the investigation which would otherwise be left hanging—a CIA decision to seek the help of the FBI in May 1991, and the FBI's decision to open a criminal case against Ames in May 1993. It seems likely the mole hunters took so long to find Ames because they trusted to the time-honored method—they waited for someone to tell them.

7. *Old hands are best.*

It is part of the folklore of the intelligence world that the best counterintelligence analysts are old and gray and quiet sorts with capacious memories and a talent for fussy attention to detail and a deep respect for fact—the red socks, the preferred brand of cigarette, the crossing of a certain international border on a certain date—and above all the intuitive feel acquired from prolonged immersion in the study of an opponent. Only such prepared minds, it is believed, can exploit the chance of an investigation.

Something similar is certainly true of writing about the intelligence world. Each of these four books takes a different approach to the case. James Adams, the Washington bureau chief for the London *Sunday Times,* was first to reach the bookstores with a serviceable summary of the case. Peter Maas was next with an account of the FBI investigation which includes two things missing from the other books—the story of the pregnant FBI agent whose firm sense of Rosario's psychology

---

2. Pocket Books, 1993.

allowed the agent to predict that, handled carefully, Rosario would quickly grasp the chance to save herself by betraying her husband; and an account of the Justice Department's oddly timid reluctance to approve Rosario's arrest for fear of criticism it would be leaving the Ameses' son, Paul, with no parent to care for him.

The account by the *New York Times* team led by Tim Weiner is distinguished by some beautifully written passages, by a lucid structure that makes sense of the many complications of the investigation, and by a keen appreciation of the ways the case destroyed the career of R. James Woolsey.

But the best of the four books, everything considered, is by David Wise, because he brings to the case the deepest personal knowledge, based on thirty years of inquiry into the history and ethos of the Central Intelligence Agency. The modern study of American intelligence organizations begins with Wise's book *The Invisible Government*, written with Thomas B. Ross and published in 1965. Until that time writing about intelligence concentrated almost exclusively on alien efforts at "subversion"—how the Nazis or the Reds tried to steal the secrets of the Free World—and gave only cursory accounts of American spymasters in the hero-worshiping, Dick Tracy, G-man mode that was acceptable to the FBI and CIA. *The Invisible Government* treated the CIA as simply another branch of the American government, fair game for critical analysis and aggressive reporting.

Nightmover is Wise's eighth book on intelligence, and it is filled with the sort of detail valued by those who seriously want to know what the spooks are up to—names, dates, positions, tables of organization, summaries of cases. Some of this material—for example, Wise's account of the recruitment of Dimitri Polyakov—may not seem strictly germane to the Ames case. But Wise knows what is new and what is not, and the details of the FBI's recruitment of Polyakov, which was pushed with uncommon vigor, are too good to ignore. The essence of intelligence work is file-keeping, and the same goes for writing about intelligence. Accurate information about the subject is hard to come by and, as Wise understands, it is the details that count.

8. *This is not a joke.*

"Keystone Cops" is a phrase often invoked in writing about intelligence. The original cops tripped over their own feet on the silent screen, hit each other with their billy clubs, rammed the patrol car into fire hydrants, arrested bystanders pushing baby strollers while men in masks escaped, and otherwise demonstrated that even ten half-wits may be expected to overlook the fox in the henhouse.

There is plenty of broad farce in the CIA's handling of the Ames case, but after the laughter fades it remains a fact that the United States spends $29 billion a year for the collection of intelligence, that it has been doing so on a similar scale for nearly fifty years, and that every important episode of the cold war has a clandestine history. Throughout the last half-century the United States and the Soviet Union courted and skirted military catastrophe, often with little more to guide them than the clues provided by spies and spymasters, broadly defined, to the intentions of the other side. The spies betrayed by Ames and their predecessors were the source of information that nudged or restrained the deliberations of policymakers on both sides in subtle ways. Tracing what they knew, when they knew it, and what they did about it presents for historians a problem of recovery and reconstruction of nightmarish difficulty.

Can the addiction of governments to secrecy magnify a wretch like Aldrich Ames into a threat to the nation? Citizens blanch at the thought that questions of war and peace might really depend on the hunger of a spy's wife for a new kitchen and five hundred pairs of shoes, and historians shrink from trying to sort out the exact degree to which it is really so. This is where the Keystone Cops come to the rescue. It's easier to laugh the whole thing off.

—*The New York Review of Books*, August 10, 1995

21

WHO WON THE COLD WAR?

THE GREAT STILL-UNANSWERED question left by the collapse of the Soviet Union and the end of the cold war is what military power had to do with it. When Mikhail Gorbachev took office in 1985 the Soviet Union possessed the world's largest military establishment, including thousands of nuclear-armed missiles acquired at great expense in the twenty-some years since Nikita Khrushchev's humiliating backdown in a confrontation with the United States over Soviet nuclear forces in Cuba. The details of the surrender had been negotiated by Vasily Kuznetsov with the American official John McCloy, at the latter's home in Connecticut. "Well, Mr. McCloy," Kuznetsov said, "we will honor this agreement. But I want to tell you something. You'll never do this to us again."

Despite this plain warning, according to Robert M. Gates in *From the Shadows: The Ultimate Insider's Story of Five Presidents and How They Won the Cold War,*[1] his memoir of a life spent watching the Soviet Union for the CIA, "the Agency did not foresee this massive Soviet effort [beginning in the mid-1960s] to match and then surpass the United States in strategic missile numbers and capabilities." One hesitates even to sketch in the background of this seemingly simple

---

1. Simon and Schuster, 1996.

statement. Any attempt to explain Soviet and American nuclear policy during the cold war threatens to become overwhelmed with detail. But it is impossible for anyone to understand why so much money was spent on the arms race for so many years without making it clear why the strategists on both sides never believed for long that ten bombs, or a hundred bombs, or a thousand bombs, were "enough."

By the mid-1960s each side had nuclear forces in plenty to prevent an unprovoked attack on its cities by the other. Any such attack would have brought a devastating response. What the Soviets hoped to achieve was a level of strategic forces great enough to inhibit the United States from ever using, or threatening to use, its own nuclear weapons for any purpose except retaliation against all-out attack. As a practical matter, that would have meant no first use, which meant no threat by the US to use nuclear weapons to defend American forces in Europe in the event of a conventional military attack. This meant, in turn, that we would extend only a feeble military guarantee to our NATO allies, since our combined ground forces never equaled, or came close to equaling, those of the Soviet Union and the Warsaw Pact nations. The result of any change in US willingness to defend NATO with nuclear weapons, if necessary, would be, in Washington's phrase, "de-coupling" the defense of the United States from that of Europe.

US leaders were intensely concerned to prevent de-coupling, and they steadily assured their European allies that they would respond with nuclear weapons to an attack on Brussels just as they would to an attack on Kansas. Nuclear policy throughout the cold war always involved terrifying numbers of weapons and strategies for their use which seemed to get crazier by the decade. But readers will be able to understand why things unfolded as they did, and why policymakers debated these issues with such relentless, mind-numbing exactitude, if they will keep in mind that US policy required a credible threat—one the Soviets really believed—to use nuclear weapons in the event of purely military necessity, and especially to defend against an attack on Western Europe.

The Soviets meanwhile endeavored to establish a true nuclear standoff—a counterbalancing of forces that would make American first use "impossible": they wanted to ensure that the Americans would not use nuclear weapons first under any circumstances, even to rescue American ground forces in Europe from imminent defeat. Readers may think that point was reached years ago, and that American threats of first use in the case of a Soviet conventional attack were completely crazy; but the fact is that American planners believed these threats were credible, and the Soviets believed so, too. There is no sign that the Soviets ever doubted for a moment that the Americans could and would use nuclear weapons to protect American military forces and their European allies. So there was a standoff, but it was on American, not Soviet, terms.

It was this standoff that the Soviet Union challenged after the Cuban missile crisis, and according to Gates the all-out Soviet bid for an intimidating nuclear supremacy was not the only thing missed or muddled by the Kremlin-watchers in the CIA. The burden of military spending on the Soviet economy was at least twice as heavy as calculated in CIA estimates of the 1970s and 1980s. Moreover, ethnic minorities in "the prison house of nations" (Lenin's phrase) sincerely hated the Russians' guts, Soviet client states in Eastern Europe were seething with discontent, and Soviet adventures abroad were costing a mint and going badly. Cynical careerism had replaced communism as the state religion, and the aging members of the Politburo spent their active hours basking in the sun like pink walruses along the shores of the Black Sea.

Frequent references throughout the 1980s to these and other signs of terminal decay in the "homeland of socialism," Gates insists, are to be found in the never-ending river of paper which is the CIA's principal product. He quotes liberally, often from papers he wrote himself, to prove that the agency was on the ball. But Gates confesses he was amazed by the breakdown of the USSR and rests his defense on the entirely fair observation that virtually no one in the defense or intelligence business predicted that the Soviet Union was bound for the dustbin of history until it hit bottom.

The collapse of the Soviet Union and what the United States did to hasten its demise are the twin themes of *From the Shadows*. Gates resents the needling of critics who claim that he was among the last to see what Gorbachev was trying to do and where it was leading. But while Gates is at pains in his book to argue that Gorbachev's frantic waving of the olive branch left him skeptical and cautious but not blind, it is explaining the last half of the cold war—from the American failure in Vietnam through the Kremlin hard-liners' last-gasp coup of August 1991—that is really on Gates's mind. Of two things he is sure: the fifty-year struggle really was a war, and we won it.

Gates is not the first to make this claim, which has already sparked vigorous argument. The cold war has roots stretching back to World War I and ended, as it began, with a change of course by the man in charge in Moscow. As Gates describes the final phase the cold war was a good deal like a prizefight in which a sudden flurry of hooks and jabs in the ninth round put the big guy down on one knee for the count.

But Gates's version cannot be dismissed out of hand; "war" is not too strong a word for a quasi-military struggle which sometimes threatened to end civilization in a day, and the military and political challenges raised by President Reagan in the 1980s were not easily countered by a Soviet Union in deepening economic difficulties. The United States and the Soviet Union were indisputably toe-to-toe throughout the decades of the cold war, and the collapse of the Soviet Union resembles a military defeat in every respect save one—very little blood was shed in the final round. Gates thinks American foreign and military policy—where we drew the line, the weapons we bought to defend it—explains the way things turned out, and we cannot fairly reject the prizefight analogy unless we have a clearer interpretation to offer in its place.

Gates himself arrived on his corner of the battlefield in August 1968, when he joined the CIA's intelligence directorate as a Soviet analyst the day before Warsaw Pact armies marched into Czechoslovakia to quash a challenge to Communist rule. That confident projection of naked military power by the Soviet Union perfectly embodied the character of its policy for two coming decades, including repression of criticism at home, all-out military support for North Vietnam in its victorious war against the United States, funding of Cuban armies in Africa, deployment of a sophisticated new generation of nuclear missiles targeted on Western Europe, military and financial support for a leftist regime in Nicaragua which was actively trying to subvert its neighbors, a full-scale invasion of Afghanistan, tireless military innovation, and the bullying of world opinion to recognize and acclaim the Soviet state as legitimate. The serious question at the heart of Gates's book is how these ventures could all fail, and the state that sponsored them collapse and disappear without being forced to undergo the tragedy of a great war, which typically marks the demise of empires.

Credit for the outcome, in Gates's view, goes largely to the United States, which did three things right. First, it resisted Soviet military initiatives wherever they appeared. Once the Soviets' runaway strategic weapons program was recognized for the challenge it was, the United States embarked on modernization efforts of its own—new missiles with more warheads and more accurate delivery systems, new command and control systems which would allow the United States to fight a nuclear war by stages, and, under Reagan, an ambitious program of space-based antimissile defenses which the technologically deficient Soviets could never hope to equal. These efforts were intended to maintain a credible US threat to use nuclear weapons in the event of war, and they worked. For all the billions they devoted to strategic forces the Soviets exacted very little advantage in return. American nuclear policy in 1985, when Gorbachev came to power at the head of an impoverished state, was pretty much what it had been fifteen years earlier.

The expensive new round of American spending on strategic forces was accompanied by a willingness to challenge Soviet friends, allies, and clients on the ground in Africa, Central America, and Afghanistan. Gates has little to say about the cruelty of these proxy wars; what interests him is the fact that American support for the contras and the Mujahideen increased the financial and political pressure on the Soviet Union, already hard-pressed to meet the ballooning defense budgets of Presidents Carter and Reagan. Strategic forces are not nearly as expensive as conventional armies, but they cost plenty, and by the time Gorbachev assumed control in Moscow in the mid-1980s the Soviet budget-makers knew the well was dry. Reagan and some of his aides—especially Paul Nitze, Richard Perle, and Richard Pipes—sometimes hinted (it was not a popular policy) in the early 1980s that they were deliberately challenging the Soviets to spend themselves into bankruptcy. Gates is not quite convinced that any of them believed it, but he thinks that is in fact what happened.

Whether this is really so is hard to say. No sovereign state can go bankrupt in the usual sense of the term. But by the middle of the 1980s the Soviet economy was in crisis, spending on the military was at unsustainable wartime levels, and apparently no one in the Kremlin believed that more expenditures, tightening the belt just another notch or two, would deliver genuine military advantage at last. The US may not have spent the Soviets into literal bankruptcy—and at great cost to its own domestic economy—but it had certainly proved that it had the money and the political will to meet any Soviet challenge. The result was Gorbachev's entirely sensible decision to try something radically different.

The second thing that Americans did right, according to Gates, was to trade recognition of the frontiers of Europe for Soviet agreement to what was technically known as "Basket III" of the Helsinki Accords of 1975—that is, the free movement of people and ideas, or human rights. President Ford was vigorously criticized by conservatives for thus legitimizing Soviet rule in Eastern Europe in return for empty persiflage about human rights, which the Soviets, it was predicted, would sneer at and ignore; and President Carter was criticized just as vigorously for pressing the cause of human rights when it only irritated the Soviets, cast a pall over arms-control talks, and jeopardized growing business relationships.

But far from being an irrelevant distraction, according to Gates, Western pressure for human rights encouraged dissidents throughout the Soviet empire and alarmed Soviet leaders that their right to rule was being called into fundamental question. The Helsinki Watch groups which sprang up in Eastern Europe, and in Moscow itself, attracted merciless attention from the secret police, but jail, exile, and brutal maltreatment in "psychiatric" facilities became the subjects of a robust underground literature. Publicizing such persecution steadily chipped away at Communist pretensions that the Party's rule was based on anything besides the power of the army and police. When Gorbachev, seeking a constituency for reform, embraced glasnost, or openness, he summoned to public life a class already schooled in freewheeling debate and disenchanted with the legacy of Lenin.

The importance of the Helsinki Accords was not foreseen by the CIA or anyone else. Human rights issues were always treated by intelligence analysts and propagandists alike as a wild card in the game of international politics. The common practices of many American allies —the death squads in El Salvador or the bush justice of Jonas Savimbi in Angola or the "disappearance" of leftists in Chile and Argentina— could not easily be distinguished from the methods of social discipline imposed by the KGB. But the United States lucked into a winning hand when it agreed in 1975 to the Conference on Security and Cooperation in Europe (CSCE) meetings, which included the Soviet bloc, and wrote human rights into the final document. Gates writes:

> The Soviets desperately wanted CSCE, they got it, and it laid the foundations for the end of their empire. We resisted it for years, went grudgingly, Ford paid a terrible political price for going— perhaps reelection itself—only to discover years later that CSCE had yielded benefits beyond our wildest imagination. Go figure.

Standing up to the Soviet Union militarily, and insisting that it respect the human rights of its subjects, together pushed the system to the breaking point. Credit for the fact that it broke peacefully, without a war or a die-hard phase of red terror as the Communist Party fought for its life, belongs to the United States and to President George Bush, according to Gates, for exercising restraint during the years when Gorbachev's increasingly frantic restructuring (perestroika) could have ended in an explosion rather than a dying sigh. Bush was much criticized during this period first for failing to embrace Gorbachev's peaceful gestures and then for bending over backward to accommodate Gorbachev during the diplomatic prelude to the Persian Gulf War. Bush was accused of failing to criticize Gorbachev vigorously for his erratic and bloody attempts to hold on to the Baltic states and of continuing to support Gorbachev when he replaced reformers in his government with hard-liners.

Above all Bush was attacked by US hard-liners for his mealy-mouthed speech delivered in Kiev, capital of Ukraine, in August 1991, when the bonds holding the Soviet Union together had clearly frayed to the breaking point. Gorbachev's reforms had run out of steam and rumors of a hard-line coup were sweeping Moscow. Loss of Ukraine— breadbasket of the Soviet Union, oldest of the captive nations, loud in its demands for independence—would be the final straw for the man

Bush saw as his partner in keeping the peace. Any modest tip of the hat to Ukrainian hopes would have won Bush applause at home. He declined. To the Ukrainian Parliament, in the final weeks of the life of the "evil empire" (Reagan's phrase, a winner in Gates's view), Bush delivered a finger-wagging lecture on knowing your place: "Americans will not support those who seek independence in order to replace a far-off tyranny with a local despotism. They will not aid those who promote a suicidal nationalism based on ethnic hatred."

It was not one of the bolder moments in the history of American diplomacy. But it is hard to argue with Gates's view that Bush's policy of accommodation, understanding, and circumspection was well suited to the Soviet Union's last two years of life, when a moment's surrender to crowd-pleasing bluster or triumphalism could have sent a chill of panic throughout the Soviet state, resulting in tragic civil strife. As Gates describes him, Bush was a gentle hospice worker attending the death of the Soviet Union, mopping the brow of the fevered state and whispering words of reassurance whenever the patient motioned to rise for one last battle. Gates admires Bush, is personally grateful to him, and lays the praise on thick. But it's only fair to admit that Bush did, in fact, perform his role without a major stumble, and even did it twice—first in 1989, when the Communist governments of the Warsaw Pact collapsed, then in 1990 and 1991, when the Soviet regime followed. Gates writes:

> George Bush's contribution to the success of the "Velvet Revolutions" in 1989 was in what he did not do as well as in what he did. He did not gloat. He did not make grandiose pronouncements. He did not declare victory.... He did not threaten or glower at tense moments. He did not condemn those who were under pressure to let go the levers of power.
>
> What he did was play it cool....
>
> As the communist bloc was disintegrating, it was George

Bush's skilled, yet quiet, statecraft that made a revolutionary time seem so much less dangerous than it actually was.

Robert Gates is an unusual figure in the history of American intelligence, the first director of central intelligence (DCI) to come out of the analytical side of the organization, which had been dominated for its first thirty years by the ethos of the covert operators of World War II. Gates tells us hardly anything about his family or background, except that he was brought up in Kansas and that he was recruited for the CIA at Indiana University in 1965. But before joining the agency, which offered no escape from the draft, he spent two years in the Air Force. There his job was giving intelligence briefings to ICBM missile crews at Whiteman Air Force Base in Missouri. "This was still Curtis LeMay's Strategic Air Command," Gates notes, adding that one of his commanders thought it a "goddam outrage" that 80 percent of the missiles in his command were targeted on Russian missile silos instead of Russian cities—"I want to kill some fucking Russians, not dig up dirt." With this introduction to the world of nuclear deterrence Gates moved on to become a Soviet analyst and sometime arms-control expert for the CIA during early rounds of the SALT talks in Vienna.

But Gates's rise did not come from knowing more about the Soviets and their missiles than anyone else. He was young, well scrubbed, well spoken, bright, hardworking, reliable, loyal, discreet, and a bit of a hard-ass when it came to the Russians—just the sort of fellow who flourishes as an anonymous adviser to the fully mature egos who lead the rough-and-tumble policymaking battles of the White House. As with his predecessors Colin Powell and Alexander Haig, whose careers were likewise accelerated by White House service, the most important episodes in Gates's career "with" the CIA were actually spent across the river—on the staff of the National Security Council

(1974–1976) briefly under Nixon and then under Ford, then during the Carter administration under Zbigniew Brzezinski and David Aaron (1977–1980). He had a third stint at the NSC under Bush's national security adviser, Brent Scowcroft (1989–1991). The only extended period Gates actually spent at CIA headquarters in Langley, Virginia, was during the 1980s, most of it holding positions of ever-increasing responsibility under the notoriously activist William Casey, who arrived at the CIA as President Reagan's DCI, in Gates's words, "to wage war against the Soviet Union."

It was questions about Gates's role in Casey's war, and especially Casey's relentless campaign to maintain military pressure on the Sandinista regime in Nicaragua, that blocked Gates's first nomination to the top job in 1987, when Reagan floated his name after Casey was felled by a brain tumor. The same questions nearly blocked Gates again four years later, when his nomination by Bush was fiercely contested, mainly by fellow officers of the CIA, in four weeks of public hearings. The problem the first time was the aura of what was already being called "Iran-contra"—the host of open questions about the CIA's (and inevitably Gates's) involvement in the rogue White House operation to fund the contras in Nicaragua with money diverted from illegal arms sales to Iran. He had to face that favorite question of prosecutors unwilling to call it a day without at least an indictment for perjury, namely: What did he know, and when did he know it? In Gates's case, as it unfolded in 1991, the question was what did he know about Ollie North's illegal support for the contras and when did he know about the illegal diversion of funds.

The problem, of course, is that Gates, working for Casey, North's enthusiastic backer, was in a very good position to know about both and a great deal else besides. Gates clearly liked Casey, and the feeling was mutual; one colleague of both said Casey was stricken by "love at first sight." It was Casey who made Gates his chief of staff in March 1981, promoted him to deputy director for intelligence in January

1982, and then pushed for his nomination to replace Admiral Bobby Ray Inman (not a fan of Casey's war) as deputy director for central intelligence in April 1986.

One of the strengths of Gates's memoir is its lively portraits of the men with whom Gates worked, none described with greater energy than the restless, driven Casey, who sometimes in the heat of conversation went beyond the nervous twisting of paper clips (a trait shared with the CIA's activist architect of the Bay of Pigs invasion, Richard Bissell), even in polite company, to pick up and chew on the end of his tie. Casey wanted to carry the war to the Soviets, and Gates was his man. In September 1981 he outlined an activist program in a memo to Casey concluding, "CIA is slowly turning into the Department of Agriculture." But willing as Gates was to take a hard line toward the USSR in most parts of the globe, he never shared Casey's conviction that the most important battle was the one closest to home, in Nicaragua. "For reasons I never fully comprehended," he writes, "Bill Casey became obsessed with Central America."

The elusive quarry of investigators in the Iran-contra affair, the Moby Dick sought by Independent Counsel Lawrence E. Walsh for seven years, was the person who conceived and ran the operation. It is not my intention to sort this out here, just to observe that not only the great whale but most of the lesser whales escaped the seven-year pursuit of Captain Ahab, played by Walsh, whose three-volume, 2,500-page report includes ten pages devoted to the case of Robert M. Gates (Volume I, Chapter 16). In these pages the reader may unmistakably hear in the counsel's voice the angler's anguish over the escaped fish as he confesses he "found insufficient evidence to warrant charging Robert Gates with a crime." Without the threat of conviction and jail time Walsh could not hope to win Gates's "cooperation" in his march up the chain of command toward indictment of the eminence behind it all, whoever that might have been. But the independent counsel has the dignity of his post to consider, and limits himself to the dry observation that "the statements of Gates often seemed scripted and less than candid."

Less circumspect was Gates's onetime colleague at the CIA, Tom Polgar, a veteran of the OSS and numerous posts abroad, who had spent a lifetime in the clandestine service followed by a stint in 1986 on the Senate Select Committee on Iran-Contra. Total immersion in the details of the case convinced Polgar there was no way Gates could have held the posts of authority he did without knowing perfectly well every nuance of every detail of what was going on, an opinion Polgar felt compelled to share with the Senate Intelligence Committee at a hearing on Gates's nomination to become DCI held on September 19, 1991. If Walsh's report is a lawyer's brief on what the evidence says about the role of Gates in Iran-contra, then Polgar's testimony is the case with the bark off—a careful detailing of Gates's passage through many meetings and encounters when even the furniture, Polgar argues, must have grasped what was going on.

Polgar concluded:

> His proposed appointment as Director also raises moral issues. What kind of signal does his re-nomination send to the troops? Live long enough, your sins will be forgotten? Serve faithfully the boss of the moment, never mind integrity? Feel free to mislead the Senate—Senators forget easily? Keep your mouth shut —if the Special Counsel does not get you, promotion will come your way?[2]

More painful still were the charges brought against Gates by Mel Goodman ("one of my oldest friends in the Agency") and Harold Ford ("another old friend and colleague") that he had pressured CIA

---

2. *Nomination of Robert M. Gates*, Hearings Before the Senate Select Committee on Intelligence, September 16, 17, 19, 20, 1991, S. Hrg. 102–799, Volume I, pp. 760 ff.

analysts to exaggerate Soviet involvement in the plot to kill Pope John Paul II and in international terrorism, and that he had suppressed and ignored "signs of the Soviet strategic retreat, including the collapse of the Soviet empire."

Intelligence wars are notoriously fierce but usually hidden; this one took up days of hearings and nightly newscasts and "degenerated," in Gates's words, "into an intellectual and bureaucratic food fight." Details of the argument can be found in Volume II (740 pages) and Volume III (318 pages) of the Senate hearings on Gates's nomination. The essence of the argument is that they said he did and he said he didn't. Gates arranged for the declassification and release of numerous documents to support his case. The testimony and documents suggest that agency disputes about the Soviet Union were often heated, and that Gates pressed hard for evidence and argument when he thought analysts were wrong. But Gates's critics are far from having proved their case that he slanted estimates dishonestly to curry favor with superiors. In any event, the committee accepted his defense and his further promise to hold no grudges and run the CIA fairly. The full Senate voted to confirm 64–33 on November 5, 1991, a close victory which came just a year and a bit before he was forced to retire along with his defeated friend, George Bush.

"Did we win," Gates asks at the end of his book, "or did the Soviets just lose?"

Gates does not strike triumphalist attitudes, but he is a team player, he thinks his side deserves credit, and he makes a reasonable case that the "arms race," broadly conceived to include the clash of proxy armies in the third world, cost more money than the Soviets had. But Gates's argument really has two parts—that the failure of Soviet military, political, and economic policies (no advantage from heavy military spending, no end to the bloody and expensive war in Afghanistan, no growth of the economy) precipitated a crisis, and that Gorbachev's impetuous efforts to meet the crisis undermined so many props of state and society that collapse became inevitable. From a little distance it does not appear much different from what happened to the ancien régime in 1789 after Louis XVI called upon the Estates General to raise new taxes. More specifically, Gates believes that the failure of Soviet strategic policy, faced with a hideously expensive new round of military spending to match American programs—and especially Reagan's favorite, the Strategic Defense Initiative, or "Star Wars"—was the biggest single drain on financial resources and may be fairly considered the straw that broke the camel's back. This interpretation predictably has run into a lot of resistance, notably from Gorbachev himself, who has insisted that Star Wars was not the big problem. In an unusual meeting in Colorado in the fall of 1995 of late cold war leaders, Margaret Thatcher pressed the Star Wars case succinctly:

> There was one vital factor in the ending of the Cold War: Ronald Reagan's decision to go ahead with the Strategic Defense Initiative (SDI).... The first nation that got it would have a tremendous advantage because the whole military balance would change. So it was of supreme importance. This was a completely different level of defense. It required enormous computer capability, which he knew at the time the Soviet Union could not match. And that was the end of the arms race as we had been pursuing it. I told Mr. Gorbachev when he first visited me that I was all for President Reagan going ahead with SDI and that some of our scientists would help if needed. From that particular moment, everything was not so easy in my relationship with Mr. Gorbachev.[3]

---

3. The text of the Colorado symposium is published in *New Perspectives Quarterly* (Winter 1996).

That the Soviet Union was indeed obsessed with sdi for several years after President Reagan's speech announcing it in March 1983 is well known to students of the arms race; I myself later that year heard a well-placed Soviet official (Fyodor Burlatsky) threaten a preemptive nuclear strike against the United States if we ever tried to deploy Star Wars hardware in near space. Gorbachev himself repeatedly attacked Reagan's policy head-on during his first years in office. But in Colorado in 1995 Gorbachev told Lady Thatcher that it simply wasn't so. He said:

> The first impulses for reform were in the Soviet Union itself, in our society which could no longer tolerate the lack of freedom.... In the eyes of the people, especially the educated, the totalitarian system had run its course morally and politically. People were waiting for reform. Russia was pregnant. So the moment was mature to give possibility to the people. And we could only do it from above because initiative from below would have meant an explosion of discontent. This was the decisive factor, not sdi.

And Gorbachev is far from alone in denying the argument of Gates and others that Reagan and Star Wars won the cold war. In the United States as well many longtime critics of American reliance on nuclear weapons have been loath to conclude that military hardware tipped the balance. It is not a question ever likely to produce an exact answer, and fully nuanced, considered answers will be impossible until historians can study the official Soviet files.

But one thing is clear already—with the exception of the frantic weeks of 1989, when the Communist governments of Eastern Europe fell in rapid succession, and the autumn of 1991, when the seventeen republics of the Soviet Union all went their separate ways, the last half of the cold war, like the first, unfolded with glacial deliberation.

Gates arrived at the CIA in 1968 in what might be called roughly the middle of the war in Vietnam. Another seven years passed before the last marines left Saigon. The Soviets invaded Afghanistan in 1979 and fought the Mujahideen for ten years. Beginning at about the same time the Americans fought an on-again, off-again war against the Sandinistas in Nicaragua for ten years.

But even the slow-motion struggles of what Gates calls the "Third World War" did not unfold with quite the slow inexorability of the competition in strategic arms—that is, in delivery systems for nuclear weapons. The Soviets promptly began to make good on Vasily Kuznetsov's promise to John McCloy that the Soviets would never again allow themselves to be outgunned in a nuclear confrontation. But the CIA's experts stubbornly went on insisting for ten years that the Soviets were only trying to catch up. This was Gates's special field of expertise, and he cites the milestones on the CIA's journey toward an alarmed view of what the Soviets were trying to achieve: a special National Intelligence Estimate of 1973 ("much more aggressive Soviet Union"), a 1976 National Intelligence Estimate ("a starker appreciation"), a 1978 National Intelligence Estimate on "Soviet Goals and Expectations in the Global Power Arena" ("sobering, a cold shower").

The Soviet emplacement of multiwarhead intermediate-range missiles in Europe in 1975 was the subject of eight years of argument within NATO countries and diplomatic arm-twisting before countermissiles were put into the field. Meanwhile "modernization" programs begun under Lyndon Johnson and Richard Nixon (the "missile experimental," or MX; "multiple independently targetable re-entry vehicles," or MIRVs; the Trident submarine system; a "follow-on bomber" to the B-52; terrain-hugging cruise missiles; and on and on) made their oxcart-like progress through development toward procurement and deployment. Some of these behemoths with a gestation period measured in decades are slouching our way still. Whether these weapons were all really "necessary" was debated at the time and remains open to question. But they were all largely intended to back up the credibility of American nuclear threats, and they "worked" in the sense that, so far as we know, no Soviet leader ever doubted the credibility of those threats.

Good intelligence officers develop a sense of audience. Gates notes early that "four of the five Presidents I worked for were bored to tears by the details of arms control" and he presumes much the same will be the case with readers of his book. The arguments over Soviet military capacities and intentions were discussed in the annual series of CIA National Intelligence Estimates. They must have absorbed many years of Gates's working life, but we hear very, very little about those ancient quarrels in *From the Shadows*. But those we do hear about ought to remind us of the importance of the decision taken by the United States under President Harry Truman, as confirmed by President Dwight Eisenhower, to base the defense of the Western allies on superiority in the numbers and versatility of nuclear weapons. From scattered passages in Gates's book we may piece together one chilling story of what could have been the awful consequence.

By the middle of the Carter administration the American government had reached general agreement that the Soviets were mounting a major effort to achieve strategic nuclear superiority, including an ability to disarm the United States in a first strike. Perhaps most alarming was the discovery in the 1970s that the Soviets were rapidly improving the accuracy of their ICBMs and that more than "enough" of them were actually targeted on US missile fields in the Midwest— "enough," that is, to target each US missile with a Soviet warhead. No strategic planner would aim something as powerful and expensive as a missile at another missile unless he expected to find it there when his own arrived—that is, in a first strike. But the details are of secondary importance. It is the mood of threat and runaway growth in hardware that defines the moment.

The American response to the Russian challenge included not only new weapons of our own but a new war-fighting strategy (Presidential Directive 59). It further included hardened command and control systems, elaborate new warning mechanisms, an ever-tighter loop between early warning and any decision to retaliate. A major change in military strategy, like the moment an ocean liner begins to pull away from the dock, is a public event, impossible to hide. The Soviets knew all about it, but far from calming themselves with the reflection that after all the Americans were bound to respond eventually to the Soviet buildup, they began to fear the worst.

It was in this climate of heightened fear and apprehension late in the Carter administration that the American nuclear command and control structure was upset by a series of false alarms—erroneous reports from technical systems that an attack was under way. In the most dramatic of these episodes the North American Air Defense Command (NORAD), from its bomb-proof post deep beneath Cheyenne Mountain in Colorado, informed Colonel (later General) William Odom, military assistant to Carter's national security adviser, Zbigniew Brzezinski, that the Soviet Union had launched 220 missiles targeted on the United States.

Odom, at three o'clock in the morning, called Brzezinski, who prepared himself to notify the President in time for the US to retaliate— that is, within three to seven minutes after the Soviet launch. Soon Odom called again to confirm the bad news, adding that the revised, now-correct number of attacking Soviet missiles was 2,200—the long-dreaded, all-out, Pearl Harbor–style first strike intended to destroy American missiles in their silos. Brzezinski did not wake his wife; he was convinced everyone would soon be dead. But just before he was about to call President Carter, Odom called a third time to say it was all a mistake—someone at NORAD had loaded the computer-controlled warning system with exercise tapes used for simulating war games. Nothing to worry about! Brzezinski went back to bed.

The Soviets quickly learned of the incident and ought to have been angry that some glitch in American technical wizardry nearly destroyed their country. But they took the danger one step further, adding a paranoiac spin. "CIA later learned" (Gates's code phrase for knowledge secretly obtained) that the Soviets had concluded the false alarms were nothing of the kind, but rather part of a diabolical plan to lull Soviet watchers and lay the ground for an eventual surprise attack.

The rhetoric of the early years of the Reagan administration only exacerbated Soviet fears. Some of Reagan's closest advisers, reportedly including Vice President George Bush, had expressed public confidence that even a nuclear war would have a winner; "with enough shovels" to dig homemade shelters, one theorist suggested, most civilians would pull through. While in office, Reagan slashed domestic spending and devoted uncountable new billions to defense, especially to strategic programs. In March 1983 he delivered two speeches that made the hair rise on the back of Soviet necks; in the first he condemned the Soviet Union as an "evil empire," and three weeks later he outlined an ambitious program for building space-based defense systems, soon called Star Wars. Civilians debated whether anybody could afford such a system or whether it could ever work, but defense theorists all knew that space-based defenses were well suited only to one job—mopping up the ragged retaliatory missiles that would be fired by strategic forces devastated by a first strike. The tough talk in Washington was actually aimed at rallying Congress to support politically difficult cuts in domestic spending to free up funds for Star Wars; but the Soviets did not appreciate such nuances.

Few in Moscow took a darker view of the bomb talk than the chairman of the KGB, Yuri Andropov; according to Gates, he warned a KGB conference in 1981 that the United States was actively preparing for nuclear war. In the fall of 1983, when Andropov had succeeded Leonid Brezhnev at the head of the Soviet Union but was himself already dying of kidney disease, his fears focused on a NATO command-post exercise called "Able Archer" scheduled for early November. Its purpose was to test NATO's ability to meet a military challenge requiring a nuclear response—that is, to run through the communications drill, from warning through decision to response. Of course, no actual nuclear weapons would be involved, but the electronic signature of the exercise—the crackle of messages over wire and airwaves, what the Soviets would see and hear—would naturally look just like the real thing.

NATO and the Warsaw Pact both routinely conducted military exercises and had learned to treat them calmly, but in this case, according to Gates, other technical factors contributed to the state of alarm. The following March the British, drawing on reports from their ace Soviet spy Oleg Gordievsky, informed the Americans that the panicked Russians had seriously feared that Able Archer was no exercise but a genuine prelude to war. It was crazy—but not so crazy; this is how complex systems fail. When Gorbachev brought a new style and tone to the Kremlin a couple of years later even the CIA was relieved, "feeling," according to Gates, "that the U.S.–Soviet confrontation had gotten a bit too hot in recent years."[4]

Able Archer was about as close as the United States and the Soviet Union ever came to nuclear war accidentally, just as the Cuban missile crisis of 1962, which resulted in Khrushchev's humiliating backdown, was about as close as the two sides ever got to war in the usual way, through confrontation and miscalculation. In neither case was war all that close. The Soviets never went on nuclear alert during the

---

4. Raymond L. Garthoff, in *Detente and Confrontation* (Brookings, 1990), has argued that Soviet misperceptions went much deeper, leading them to interpret all US strategic programs of the 1970s and 1980s as a new aggressiveness preparing for war. According to Garthoff, the Soviets felt they had done nothing to trigger the American buildup; Afghanistan was "an irrelevant factor" and the new Soviet theater nuclear forces in Europe did not justify the NATO response in the 1980s. Garthoff further believes that American intelligence exaggerated the Soviet buildup. See Chapter 22, pp. 882–887.

Able Archer episode, and the 3:00 AM false alarm was not backed up by other warning systems. The computer-generated report should have been preceded by satellite detection of hot missile launches and followed by confirming radar reports; the fact that neither occurred meant that a presidential order to retaliate was never close. But those nearest misses were sobering all the same, because the commanders of strategic forces on both sides understood in their bones that nothing could stop an authorized execute order, once given, short of an act of God. "Theologians of deterrence"—another nuke-speak phrase of yesteryear—might talk of "exchanges" of thousands of warheads, but the political leaders of both sides knew that even one bomb on one city, as McGeorge Bundy once observed, would be an unimaginable catastrophe.

It is in this fact that we may locate the central paradox of the cold war, the fact that catastrophe was never far, and war was never close. In retrospect it seems clear that it was the political, not the military, relations of the United States and the Soviet Union that were unstable. The initial onset of the cold war, the "spirit of Camp David" under Eisenhower, the Berlin and Cuba crises, détente under Nixon and Kissinger, Reagan's renewed rhetorical assault on "the evil empire"—the mood of the relationship swiveled violently from one decade to the next. But the face-to-face nuclear confrontation at ever higher levels of potential destructiveness was nevertheless astonishingly stable; neither side was ever in a position to push the other around, and neither treated the military power of the other with less than sober respect.

"Is it really big enough?" the Danish physicist Niels Bohr asked J. Robert Oppenheimer in December 1943, the day he arrived at Los Alamos, New Mexico, where the Americans were secretly inventing the new bomb. Oppenheimer understood him immediately—Bohr meant, was it big enough to make war impossible? The answer to this question hung in suspense until the collapse of the Soviet Union.

Gates's account of the last half of the cold war shows the importance of luck—mostly good luck as it turned out. But if Brezhnev's successor, the hard-nosed commissar Yuri Andropov, once known as the butcher of Budapest for his part in putting down the 1956 rebellion, "had been younger and healthier," Gates writes, "the odds are great that we would still be face-to-face with the Soviet Union, still militarily powerful."

This is true, but it would not have made much difference in the long run. Andropov's brightest idea for restoring the vigor of the Soviet state was to send the KGB into the streets to round up AWOL citizens standing with their string bags in food queues instead of "working." Andropov might have kept the lid on for another few years, but the factors that precipitated the Soviet collapse under Gorbachev were not the sort simply to go away. Now that the Soviet Union has disappeared Gates, along with everybody else, can see that it was doomed to disappear. It was only a question of time.

What gave us the time was not the flurry of anti-Soviet hooks and jabs of the Reagan-Casey years, which was only cold war business as usual with a modest increase in vigor. What gave us the time was the bomb. Gates spent a big part of his working life keeping track of Soviet weaponry and making sure that the American threat to use nuclear weapons remained credible. Throughout the cold war there were many occasions, especially in the early years, when the two sides might have gone to war. Just what stopped them can never be established with certainty, but one important factor surely was fear of the consequences. Hiroshima left no mystery about that. But what would happen to that fear if the threat to use nuclear weapons were removed? Many critics (of whom I was one) believed that the arms race itself, extended over decades, would make war inevitable, but that is not the way things turned out. It is Gates's purpose to convince us that official American nuclear policy, despite the many criticisms that seemed convincing at the time, in fact helped bring the cold war to a peaceful conclusion. This is a hard point to admit for those of us who spent years defending opposing views, and it may never be established conclusively, but I believe that Gates is right.

In 1947 George Kennan, writing as "Mr. X" in *Foreign Affairs*, argued that war with the Soviet Union was not inevitable; if the United States could only "contain" the natural expansionism of the Soviet Union then the process of time would gradually alter and soften the Soviet state. Kennan often wrote in subsequent years that he did not intend an exclusively military form of containment, and that he certainly would never have proposed such a dangerous American reliance above all on nuclear arms. But time is what containment took and time is what the fear of nuclear war gave us. All other factors in the outcome of the cold war fade beside that one. So the answer to Gates's question is not the Russians, not the Americans, but the bomb. The bomb won.

—*The New York Review of Books*, June 20, 1996

22

THE BLACK ARTS

THERE ARE SECRETS and there are secrets, and it is distinguishing between the two that has challenged some of the best minds of our time—currently Senator Daniel Patrick Moynihan's—to come up with a workable commonsense approach to keeping secrets. Such an approach would grant the United States government power to remain silent about the few genuine secrets that matter, while compelling it to disgorge in reasonably good time the oceans of paper stamped "secret" solely in order to relieve officials of the awkward duty of explaining why they have done, predicted, or recommended something dumb.

What is a secret that matters? Answer: any undertaking of the state which requires for its success that it be unknown, unobserved, or unanticipated. Classic examples would be the time and place proposed for the Allied invasion of France in 1944, or Boris Yeltsin's plan to devalue the ruble. But most official American secrets—roughly six million new classified documents a year, at last count—record the conversation of the government with itself. Now that we have the actual report in hand in *Bay of Pigs Declassified*[1] we can see that the CIA's *Inspector General's Survey of the Cuban Operation*, printed

---

1. Edited by Peter Kornbluh (New Press, 1998).

in something like twenty copies and circulated in the fall of 1961 to a handful of high CIA and government officials, contained a bushel of legitimate secrets. The *Survey* was not only a devastating critique of the agency's unrealistic and even reckless plans to overthrow Fidel Castro by invading Cuba, but it served as a kind of blueprint of the CIA's Directorate of Plans and discussed frankly the conduct of a struggle while it was still under way. You could argue that the policy was unwise or unworkable, but you could hardly fault the Kennedy administration for trying to keep secret exactly where and how it went wrong in a first attempt to achieve a goal—the overthrow of Castro—to which it was redoubling its commitment.

What is a secret of convenience? Answer: any item of information which, if released, might invite nontrivial public criticism of policies, endeavors, or officials. Governments entertain rosy hopes, overlook imminent dangers, lie about their purposes, and do foolish things just as people do, and so long as these gaffes remain unknown they do not have to be explained, defended, or, sometimes most difficult of all, openly confessed. For more than twenty years, and certainly since the 1976 publication of many of the agency's darkest and most embarrassing secrets in the numerous green-bound volumes of the Church Committee Report, the *Inspector General's Survey of the Cuban Operation* has been an outstanding example of this sort of secret, too. "In unfriendly hands," wrote the deputy director of the CIA, General Charles Cabell, back in 1961, "it [the *Survey*] can become a weapon unjustifiably [used] to attack the entire mission, organization, and functioning of the Agency." Unfriendly hands have got it at last, but it took thirty-seven years, much water has since flowed under the bridge, and whatever critics might say of the "mission, organization, and functioning" of the CIA is now mainly the ho-hum stuff of graduate school seminar rooms.

The inspector general (IG) who conducted the survey, Lyman Kirkpatrick, now dead, was one of the major figures in the early history of the CIA, and his unvarnished account of the Bay of Pigs bungling, which abandoned a thousand Cubans to be captured by Castro's army and deeply embarrassed President Kennedy—Theodore Draper described the whole sorry episode as "a perfect failure"—bitterly stung the architects of the plan, CIA Director Alan Dulles and his deputy in charge of clandestine operations, Richard Bissell. Until he was stricken with polio in the 1950s Kirkpatrick had been a fair-haired boy with a shot at being named director, and many thought he orchestrated the *Survey* from his wheelchair in order to belittle his rivals and give new life to his own ambitions.

I well remember the red-faced, stuttering, snorting outrage when Bissell in an interview, furiously twisting paper clips as he spoke, described his deep sense of affront on learning that Kirkpatrick had committed the unpardonable discourtesy of giving a copy of his report (on November 21, 1961) to John McCone, Dulles's successor as director of central intelligence, before showing it (on November 24) to Dulles himself. In Peter Kornbluh's edition of the *Survey*, recently pried loose from the keepers of secrets at the CIA, we may now read that Bissell went so far in a memorandum to McCone of January 27, 1962, as to say baldly that the IG's report "constitutes a highly biased document and that the bias is of such a character that it must have been intentional." And Bissell was not alone in this belief. McCone, in a spirit of fairness, ordered that a single copy of the *Survey* be preserved in the director's office and that Bissell's own vigorous defense be appended to it so that future readers, which now include us, would not accept Kirkpatrick's attack before knowing what Bissell had to say in his own defense.

Along with Bissell's rebuttal in *Bay of Pigs Declassified*, Kornbluh has included a useful chronology and other materials. Among these is a previously unpublished interview with two Bay of Pigs planners, Jacob Esterline and Colonel Jack Hawkins. But it is the 130-page *Survey* that makes *Bay of Pigs Declassified* one of the half-dozen basic texts on the United States and Cuba in the 1960s, and that makes it required reading for anyone who wants to understand what happened to the United States after World War II.

But there comes a time in the life of any secret when it has been talked to death, and this is surely the case with the Bay of Pigs. What the *Survey* adds to the record is an intimate portrait of the CIA arguing furiously with itself, and, interesting as this can be, it is nevertheless hard to imagine that the book will get many readers not somehow professionally compelled to take an interest, such as graduate students working in the La Brea tar pits of cold war studies—the alarms, excesses, and miseries of the 1960s: Cuba, Vietnam, Czechoslovakia, "the missile gap," "mutual assured destruction," the domestic upheavals encompassed by "the civil rights movement" and "the student revolution." The ordinary citizen of a certain age begs to be delivered from yet another slog into the sticky morass.

What this says about the declassifiers at the CIA is that they have got their timing down about perfectly—nothing to be released until interest has faded away practically to zero (the Bay of Pigs), or until the participants who might usefully amend and amplify the story are dead or doddering, like the patient US Army (later National Security Agency) code-breakers who forced their way into the Soviet cable traffic of the 1930s and 1940s and deciphered the Soviet secret messages collectively known as VENONA. It's a made-up word and the principal significance now of the 2,900 messages read in whole or in part is the light they cast on a handful of notorious spy cases of the 1950s. It was VENONA that first directed official suspicions to the Rosenbergs and offered a degree of confirmation to the charges of Whittaker Chambers that Alger Hiss had been a spy for Russia.

In *Secrecy: The American Experience*,[2] an oddly disjointed book redeemed by frequent flashes of the senator's wit, Moynihan "reveals" that President Truman, who angrily dismissed Republican charges of

---

2. Yale University Press, 1998.

wholesale Communist spying within the United States, was in fact "never told of the VENONA decryptions." I put quotes around the word "reveals" because Moynihan's evidence—an FBI memo of a conversation with General Carter W. Clarke, in 1949 chief of the Army Security Agency—merely reports an interagency dispute over whether to tell "the President and Admiral Hillenkoetter" about VENONA. Clarke told the FBI that General Omar Bradley, chairman of the Joint Chiefs of Staff, "wanted . . . to make sure that the Bureau does not handle the material in such a way that Admiral Hillenkoetter or anyone else outside the Army Security Agency, [deleted], and the Bureau are aware of the contents of these messages and the activity being conducted at Arlington Hall [in Virginia, site of the early work on VENONA]."

It is a fact that the CIA was not told of VENONA at the time, but whether Truman was told then or later during his remaining fifteen months in office is not established by the memo Moynihan quotes. Presidents like to know what's going on and their advisors like to tell them. Perhaps Bradley wanted to preserve the honor and pleasure for himself. Perhaps he didn't want to confide in General Clarke. Perhaps he changed his mind on reflection later the same day. Before accepting Truman's ignorance as proven I would want to see a lot more evidence. What is certain is that the Soviet Union soon learned its cable traffic had been broken in one of two ways—from William Weisband, a Soviet spy working for the Armed Forces Security Agency who had the run of Arlington Hall; or from the intelligence officer for [deleted] who was handling liaison with American intelligence organizations in Washington, the infamous Harold Adrian Russell Philby. Among the small ironies of cold war history are the facts that Kim Philby knew about VENONA before the CIA, and that the CIA and its fraternal organizations, now routinely required to disgorge their own secrets, still faithfully protect those of [deleted], no matter how anciently acquired.

But Moynihan reveals no doubts and makes vigorous rhetorical use of General Bradley's refusal to tell Truman about VENONA:

What decisions would Truman have made had the information in the VENONA intercepts not been withheld from him?... If only he had known this—known for real, that is, from the likes of Bradley. If only political liberals had known. If only those in the universities had known.

All the bitter divisions of the McCarthy years, the exaggerated Republican charges of "twenty years of treason" and the Democratic countercharges of witch-hunting, might have been avoided, Moynihan suggests, with who knows what profound consequences. There might have been no fight to the death over who lost China, no lingering nightmares at the outset of the Kennedy administration that hands-off realism in the Caribbean and Southeast Asia would inexorably summon up new howling mobs demanding to know: Who lost Cuba? Who lost Vietnam?

Maybe, and maybe not. The VENONA documents included evidence of "Hiss's guilt," as Moynihan writes, but I very much doubt that its publication would have impressed, much less silenced, Hiss's defenders, who have proved over the years that they can explain away just about anything. The VENONA document incriminating Hiss, a translation of a Soviet cable of March 30, 1945, alleges that "Ales" had been "working with the NEIGHBORS [i.e., Soviet military intelligence] continuously since 1935" and that he "and his whole group were awarded Soviet decorations." American counterintelligence experts identified "Ales" as "probably Alger Hiss" because both passed through Moscow following the Yalta conference.

This conclusion strikes me as completely likely, and it has been amply supported by recent discoveries in the archives of the former Communist world.[3] But it would have been hard to prove what the

---

3. See, for example, *Whittaker Chambers* (Random House, 1997), Sam Tanenhaus's brilliant and exhaustive biography; the 1997 Random House edition of *Perjury: The Hiss-Chambers*

"Ales" message meant in a court of law in the 1950s, when Hiss was on trial. No witnesses would have been available to testify who wrote the document, how its claims were known to be true, what "military information" had been obtained, or even whether it represented a true copy of what had been radioed from Washington to Moscow at the time. Hiss's defenders, who claimed the FBI fabricated a typewriter to "prove" that State Department documents kept by Whittaker Chambers had been copied by Hiss's wife on the family portable, would have encountered little trouble in spinning out a conspiratorial explanation of the embarrassments of the VENONA traffic.

There is a vast gulf separating the sort of evidence a prosecutor needs for a court case and the fragmentary and ambiguous materials of uncertain provenance which may be all that counterintelligence sleuths have to work with. VENONA is full of clues—hundreds of cryptonyms of probable agents and enough bits and pieces of information to let investigators identify perhaps half of them. Moynihan did the country a service in pressing for declassification of VENONA. There is no operational reason to keep this stuff secret any longer. The men and women who conducted the extraordinary feat of breaking communications enciphered with a "one-time pad"—i.e., with a code specific to each message—deserve public recognition and thanks for their efforts, and historians of the cold war will make solid use of VENONA to help explain the nationwide panic known as McCarthyism.

But I very much doubt that prompt exposure at the time would have changed the course of events significantly, and it might have done a good deal of damage. Uncertainty is not merely a fact but a tool of intelligence. The VENONA messages were read piecemeal over many years, some as late as the 1970s. In the late 1940s and 1950s they were an important aid to FBI spy-hunters, and the fact that the

---

Case, by Allen Weinstein; and Chapter Five on *The Haunted Wood: Soviet Espionage in America—The Stalin Era*, by Allen Weinstein and Alexander Vassiliev (Random House, 1999).

Soviet Union learned that a number of its messages had been decoded was less important than the alarm which must have swept Moscow at the ghastly prospect that the American code-breakers might succeed in reading all of the traffic. Hundreds of spies and operations would have been compromised. What intelligence organizations do when discovery looms is burn paper, shut operations down, roll up agent networks, pull people back to home base, abandon safe houses and meeting places, change phone numbers and the location of message drops—in short, disappear. The point in a global conflict is not to put miscreants into jail (except *pour encourager les autres*) but to keep track of what the other guys are up to, and to give a convincing impression of always knowing a good deal more than is overtly let on. What that means, among other things, is never revealing how you know what you know. Keeping VENONA secret—from the public and, insofar as possible, from the Russians—was not Boy Scout stuff but an important part of the Great Game. Naturally at some point the secret ceases to matter but knowing when that point arrives is easier in retrospect than at the time, which explains why the CIA errs vigorously on the side of caution.

Like most books about secrecy, Moynihan's is largely concerned with secret history—things that happened wholly or in part beyond public view, why the government wanted it that way, the policies and methods used to keep secrets secret. The principal tools of the US government are the definition of treason in the US Constitution and the Espionage Act of 1917, amended in 1933 to protect American code-breaking efforts and again in 1950 to protect "national defense information," mainly the scientific knowledge involved in the design and manufacture of atomic and hydrogen bombs. The British Official Secrets Act, which grants virtually unlimited power to the government on security matters and provides for no release of certain official secrets, ever, also has its origins in the First World War.

Richard Gid Powers (who bears a noble name but is no relation of mine) has contributed a long and extremely useful introduction to Moynihan's book recounting the recent history of American popular thinking about government secrets, from the blank check of the early 1950s through the discoveries of the 1960s and 1970s—the FBI's campaign against leftists, the CIA's aggressive meddling in other countries—to the delicate modern balance of skepticism with realism one finds in the work of many recent commentators: they concede the reality of the war within the cold war but darkly suspect simultaneous government manipulation of secrecy for reasons of political advantage and corporate gain. Was Kennedy obsessed with Castro because he feared a Russian military base in the Caribbean, or worried he would be clobbered in the 1964 presidential election? Did the Pentagon want more nuclear missile submarines to protect American retaliatory capacity against a Soviet first strike, or to ensure the prosperity of the Electric Boat Division of General Dynamics in Connecticut? Who can imagine that such questions have clear and simple answers?

The meat and potatoes of *Secrecy* is to be found largely in Powers's introduction. It explains and places Moynihan's argument, which would otherwise seem half-finished. Moynihan contributes the flavor and personality of the book—a rambling history of our times, some flashes of insight ("secrecy is a form of regulation"), and a discussion of the relentless growth in Washington over the decades of the cold war of a "culture of secrecy," by which he means the habit of exaggerated classification (those six million secret documents each year), the temptation to hide failure behind a screen of bogus national security, and the all-thumbs international bumbling which comes from thinking some information too secret to share with the people making decisions. How did we know the Russians had a slew of agents operating inside the American government? How did we know a Communist victory in the Italian elections of 1948 might be followed by a Stalinist coup? How did we know Castro was a client of the Russians?

How did we know North Vietnam was running the war in the South? How did we know Allende was a Stalinist in social democratic garb? How did we know the Soviet Union was building a first-strike capability? How did we know the Sandinista government in Nicaragua was running the revolution in El Salvador? How did we know the Soviet economy was 60 percent as big as the American economy?

To these and many similar questions over the last fifty years American intelligence organizations have had secret answers, and the details, on which all depends, were very often considered too secret to share with other members of government except in the bland form of National Intelligence Estimates prognosticating X with a probability of Y based on sources with a reliability of Z. Who can make head or tail of that? Moynihan thinks a lot of dumb decisions have been made over the years by people trying to play cards with half a deck, and he is probably right.

But can excessive secrecy be blamed for the really big mistakes? The biggest of all was probably Lyndon Johnson's decision not to be the first American president to lose a war. The way things turned out tells us all we need to know about the wisdom of drawing the line in Vietnam, and it is certainly clear now that one of the principal rationales for going to war—the idea that Hanoi was doing the bidding of Red China—was just utterly wrong, no matter what the secret evidence might have said. Moynihan might argue that a vigorous public debate based on all-source intelligence in 1964 and 1965 might have convinced American leaders that Hanoi and Saigon were approaching the climax of a Vietnamese civil war of no concern to us, and Moynihan might be right.

But taking Red China out of the equation wouldn't have changed some basic facts—the fact that Hanoi was Red, too; and the fact that the United States under President Kennedy had sent more than 16,000 American troops to make sure Saigon didn't lose; and the fact that Hanoi in 1965 was about to whip Saigon's ass and send American troops scuttling for safety; and the fact that the men in the White House were all serenely certain that, as Dean Rusk expressed it at the time, when a mighty nation like the United States puts its shoulder to the wheel, that wheel is going to move. The disaster of the Vietnam War wasn't the fault of secrecy-obsessed intelligence officers putting the wrong stuff, or not enough stuff, into the briefing books. Major disasters are never the result of small mistakes and overlooked details, but of men in positions of relative safety choosing by gradual stages to postpone first the inconvenience and then the pain of failure by doubling and redoubling the number of chips pushed to the center of the table.

But the intelligence failure at the top of Moynihan's list in *Secrecy* is not Vietnam but the Soviet Union, which at one moment was challenging American might in every corner of the globe, according to supersecret information regularly provided to the White House by the CIA, and the next moment had collapsed in five kinds of bankruptcy —moral, social, political, military, and above all financial. "These were the best people we had, the CIA so-called experts," said President Gerald Ford in 1997, years after the curtain had come down and longstanding Soviet weaknesses were revealed. "How they could be so in error, I don't understand, but they were."

Moynihan has much to say about the reasons for this error, which go back to the earliest days of the cold war and reached full bloom in the 1957 report "Deterrence and Survival in the Nuclear Age," known by the name of the chairman of the committee which wrote it, H. Rowen Gaither Jr. Delivered to President Eisenhower not long after the successful Soviet launching of the world's first satellite, the Gaither Report grimly concluded that "the Gross National Product (GNP) of the USSR is now more than one-third that of the United States and is increasing half again as fast." Half again as fast, Moynihan points out, would have meant Soviet growth at a rate of 8.25 percent a year, and *that* promised a crossover point, the moment when the USSR forged into the lead with the world's biggest economy, in 1998. Talk about error.

As things turned out, the Soviet GNP in 1990, the year before the USSR's collapse, was only a third of the American GNP. In the years since that collapse the CIA and some former intelligence officers have tried to suggest they weren't really all *that* wrong but it won't wash. Moynihan has got this right; the CIA not only failed to note, much less predict, the early signs of the Soviet collapse, but for decades it persistently exaggerated the economic strength which lay behind Soviet military programs.

But what if the CIA had got the Soviet GNP numbers right? That would have had no direct or necessary effect on agency estimates of Soviet military strength, which had to do largely with existing hardware and the rate at which more was being added. Counting things—planes, tanks, ships, missile silos—is one of the things the CIA has been good at since the advent of satellites and overhead reconnaissance in the early 1960s. If the Soviet economy was only *half* the size of CIA estimates, then the percentage of it devoted to military programs was *double* the estimate. In fact, during the last two decades of the cold war, when the Soviet Union was embarked on a massive buildup of strategic missiles, the percentage of its GNP devoted to the military was at levels approaching those of World War II, and was far greater than the Pentagon's slice of the American GNP.

Why this was so—what drove the Kremlin to sacrifice so much for military power—remains a troubling and unanswered question. It may have been habit, or paranoia, or the simple result of efforts by the Soviet military to consume ever more of the pie, or it may have been the fruit of the darker intentions so often imputed by Washington hard-liners who argued that nothing would make the Russians feel safe short of global dominance. An explanation for this extraordinary Soviet effort doubtless lies hidden in the archives. But one thing is sure: the CIA, and the men it advised, would not have been reassured by the discovery that Moscow was willing to outspend Washington in preparation for war by two or three times the proportion of its available wealth. The analysts would have wanted to know why the Soviets were behaving like a nation at war, and they would not have kicked back and relaxed on being told not to worry, it's only habit, paranoia, or elbowing at the public trough.

The culture of secrecy, the routinization of secrecy, and the use of secrecy as a form of regulation discussed by Moynihan are all genuine features of the ballooning of American intelligence capacity since the end of World War II. The remedy for these excesses, Moynihan feels, is openness. As chairman of the Commission on Protecting and Reducing Government Secrecy, Moynihan led an important battle to open up government files and give the American people access to their own history. The commission's report, published in 1997, recommended an overhaul of American secrecy regulations intended to reduce the number of needless and pointless secrets in order to protect those that really mattered, and to speed the process of declassification. In theory, ten years would be the maximum life of new secrets, but secret-keepers don't give up easily; they know what they want, and they extracted from Moynihan's commission an agreement to extend classification from ten to thirty years if the custodian says it's necessary, and beyond thirty years if the custodian can show (whom?) that harm (to whom? of what sort?) will result.

This is roughly the system in place now. The custodian gets to keep the secret until he is good and ready to let it go, and the rule of thumb is that if anybody is interested, then it's too soon to let it go. My own proposal for routine declassification might be called a fifteen/thirty rule—any document retained by the government at the end of fifteen years must be released after thirty. Exceptions would be granted only after public submission to Congress of a specific request for continuance executed by the president in his own hand—place, date, request for continuance of classification of such-and-such document, generated by such-and-such agency on blank date, under authority granted to me by public law such-and-such, for an additional period of blank years on such-and-such grounds (the lengthier the better), signed in the presence of the secretary of state (name) and the vice president of the United States (name)—the whole damned thing handwritten, no typing and no auto-pens. That would open the files on schedule.

It's nice to think about, but it's not going to happen. The reason is what Moynihan's book about secrecy fails to say about secrets—what they are for.

Think of intelligence organizations as the instrument of a nation's id—the desire of a government to do certain things without having to explain, defend, or justify them. Fairness, justice, restraint, and respect for the rights of others may be important terms in the public language of international politics, but when a foreign government takes action that seems seriously hostile—when Fidel Castro nationalizes American business in Cuba, when Nikita Khrushchev puts nuclear missiles into Cuba, when Hanoi thumbs its nose at American military might, when other nations want what they want and won't ask by-your-leave—then the United States government, or any other government with its back up, may decline to turn the other cheek, may seek recourse outside the limits of official remonstrance and international law, and may attempt to impose its will in secret with methods it would never confess in public. The range of methods is wide—theft of secrets is of course a main one, but there are also slander, forgery, blackmail, bribery, sabotage, terrorism, and assassination. The black arts are called black for a reason, and their common feature is the fact they work only in secret, and exposure brings them to a halt.

Think of modern intelligence organizations as being like a modern army—huge and sprawling, bureaucratic, just about everybody involved in some sort of prosaic support activity, maybe one in ten assigned to an actual combat unit, or to clandestine activity in the field. What the 10 percent does is carefully shielded from public scrutiny, but it's what the 10 percent does that makes governments willing to pay for the whole. Following the Bay of Pigs disaster President Kennedy said he'd like to scatter the CIA to the winds, but on reflection he settled for firing Allen Dulles and Richard Bissell. Far from turning his back on secret intelligence, Kennedy drew it more intimately under White House control. No other Western leader shared Kennedy's intense interest in secret operations, with the possible exception of Winston Churchill. For a time Kennedy even considered naming his brother Bobby to run the agency, and he did put Bobby in charge of the CIA's renewed effort to get rid of Castro. Only the President's own murder brought a halt to CIA plots known to have included many plans for the killing of the Cuban leader.

Neither of the two serious investigations of the Bay of Pigs disaster begun under Kennedy—Lyman Kirkpatrick's as inspector general, and a second conducted by General Maxwell Taylor—included a reference of any kind to the assassination plots and Kennedy's closest advisers at the time still stoutly deny that the President or his brother Bobby authorized or even knew about the various attempts to poison, shoot, or blow up the leader of the Cuban revolution. The fact that many historians still elect to treat this question as open demonstrates just how secret the secret operations of an intelligence organization can be.

"The fundamental cause of the disaster," Kirkpatrick wrote in the *Survey*, "was the Agency's failure to give the project...the topflight handling which it required...." This conclusion, kept under lock and key by the CIA for decades, is clearly the self-serving argument of a man insisting he could have done the job better, and still might, given a chance. The real cause of the failure was prosaic and obvious—the impossible hope that an invasion force of a thousand might successfully defeat opposing forces of scores of thousands. Dulles and Bissell were not stupid men; they knew our Cubans couldn't beat their Cubans. What gave them confidence to go ahead were two calculations never explicitly confided to paper—the hope that Castro's murder at the outset of the invasion might panic and demoralize his government, and the hope that President Kennedy, despite his robust desire to keep the whole operation at arm's length, would be forced in the event to intervene directly with American troops to end the ghastly spectacle of the slaughter on the beach at the Bay of Pigs.

It hasn't happened yet, but Moynihan's efforts to reform the keeping of American secrets may still bring useful results—a reduction in the number of classified documents generated every year, from the mad to the merely ridiculous, and a brisker pace in the rate at which they are shipped to the open shelves of the National Archives. At the moment the pace is zero, with something like a billion pages still awaiting declassification, according to the *Secrecy and Government Bulletin* published by the Federation of American Scientists. Congress has called for a dead halt pending creation of a plan to prevent the inadvertent release of "restricted data" about nuclear weapons. If the files are declassified, working through them will usefully occupy future generations of graduate students, it will keep our history honest, it will make apparent what American policy at any given moment really was, and it will tell us, not everything that intelligence organizations may have done, but what they are *like*.

But that's it. The secrets at the heart of secrets are rarely confided to official paper or the appropriate files. The deepest secrets of all have nothing to do with the burn time of ballistic missiles, the configuration of fissionable material in nuclear weapons, or other technical matters, but rather with what presidents want, and what official agencies do to give them what they want. Those are what the ancient Chinese writer about war and statecraft Sun-tzu called "mouth-to-ear" matters.

One such surfaced recently when the Assassination Records Review Board released a two-page "Memorandum of Conversation" from the Gerald Ford Presidential Library recording some comments of Henry Kissinger on January 4, 1975, during a discussion of news stories by Seymour Hersh claiming extensive wrongdoing by the CIA. According to Max Holland, who is writing a book about the Warren Commission, Kissinger, then serving as both Ford's secretary of state and his national security adviser, had sought a blanket denial from the agency but had been informed by William Colby that some major secrets remained hidden. A former director, Richard Helms, was summoned back to Washington from his post as ambassador to Iran to fill in the details for Kissinger at a breakfast meeting shortly before Kissinger met in the White House with President Ford and Brent Scowcroft, who was taking notes.

"Helms said all these stories are just the tip of the iceberg," Kissinger said, as recorded by Scowcroft during the meeting with Ford. "If they come out, blood will flow. For example, Robert Kennedy personally managed the operation on the assassination of Castro."

The friends and defenders of the Kennedy brothers say it isn't so; but there it is on paper, written down in the heat of a government crisis, the words of a man in a position to know, recorded on the day, perhaps even within the very hour, they were uttered.

Holland and Hersh, still on the case, also learned recently the name of the CIA intelligence officer named to serve as liaison with the attorney general during the year in which he continually pressed the CIA for results in getting rid of Castro—a career intelligence officer, now dead, named Charles Ford. According to Ford's office-mate Sam Halpern, a CIA officer also assigned to Task Force W in the agency's effort to get rid of Castro, Ford traveled hither and yon about the country on Robert Kennedy's business, but there public knowledge comes to an end. Hersh's book *The Dark Side of Camelot*, published in 1998, includes some additional ancillary detail. Whether still-classified CIA files can fill out the story of Ford's work for Bobby remains unknown but it's likely, just as it is likely no one will be given free range of the files until many, many additional years have passed, if then.

Think of the CIA's files as the nation's unconscious. There you may find the evidence, like the gouges on rock where a glacier has passed, of what American leaders really thought, really wanted, and really did—important clues to who we are as a people. Does this eternal battle over access to the files make sense when few still care what happened at the Bay of Pigs? Does it matter whether we are permitted to haul up the last piece of paper to the light of day before letting it rest? There is no right answer, just personal preference: some would rather know, and some would rather not.

—*The New York Review of Books*, February 4, 1999

23

THE TROUBLE WITH THE CIA

AS THE SUN rose along the eastern seaboard of the United States on September 11, 2001, the Central Intelligence Agency was in a state of what might be called permanent medium alert to detect and prevent terrorist attacks on US citizens and property. For fifteen years the agency had entrusted this task to a Counter-Terrorism Center (CTC) at CIA headquarters in Langley, Virginia, where as many as two hundred intelligence officers gathered and analyzed information from a wide range of technical and a somewhat narrower range of human sources. For five years there had been a separate task force within the CTC dedicated specifically to the danger posed by Osama bin Laden, the Saudi-born Islamic extremist believed to have been responsible for successful attacks on US troops in Saudi Arabia, US embassies in East Africa, and the USS *Cole*, almost sunk by a suicide bomber in Aden harbor only a year before.

The CIA was not alone in its efforts to prevent terrorist attacks. The United States has not been slack in voting funds for numerous inter-agency committees, offices, divisions, centers, and task forces with substantial budgets focused on the problem of terror, but none of these special-purpose entities has a clearer responsibility for "warnings and indications" than the Central Intelligence Agency, which was established in 1947 as a direct consequence of the failure to foresee the

Japanese attack on the American naval base at Pearl Harbor. Terrorism is only one threat to American security tracked by the CIA, but the danger is not remote or abstract; the agency itself has suffered grievous losses from terrorist attacks, notably in 1983, when a suicide bomber in Beirut devastated the US embassy and killed sixty-three people, including all six members of the CIA station. Visiting at the time was a legendary CIA field officer with long experience in the Middle East, Robert Ames, whose death was confirmed by the wedding ring on a hand retrieved from the debris.

The dead chief of station was replaced by another longtime CIA officer, William Buckley, who was kidnapped by terrorists in March 1984 and beaten to death over the following year. Four years later another CIA officer from Beirut, Matt Gannon, was killed when a midair explosion destroyed Pan Am Flight 103 over Lockerbie, Scotland. Gannon's wife was also a CIA officer, Susan Twetten, daughter of the agency's chief of operations, Tom Twetten, now retired and a book dealer in rural Vermont. Other CIA officers have been murdered by terrorists, including two just outside the gates of the agency itself.

The CIA thus has a visceral as well as a theoretical understanding of what terrorism is all about. The director of central intelligence, George Tenet, has often briefed Congress during his four years at the head of the CIA on the dangers of terrorism, on the threat posed by weapons of mass destruction, and specifically on the worldwide network commanded by Osama bin Laden from his protected refuge in Afghanistan. Less than a year before September 11 Tenet told the Senate Intelligence Committee that bin Laden posed the "most serious and immediate threat" to the United States, and more recently still, probably in August or early September 2001, three foreign intelligence services separately informed the CIA that bin Laden had urged one of his four wives, who was visiting Syria at the time, to return home to Afghanistan immediately—a suggestive sign that something was in the wind.

Neither the United States government nor the CIA were snoozing at their desks as the sun rose along the eastern seaboard of the United States on September 11. Both fully understood the danger of terrorism generally and of Osama bin Laden specifically. Nevertheless, when Logan Airport in Boston and Dulles Airport outside Washington, D.C., and Newark Airport began boarding aircraft that morning, nineteen men dispatched by Osama bin Laden walked through security checkpoints as easily as they had entered and operated throughout the United States during the preceding months—encountering as little interference, and arousing as little alarm, as if the Federal Aviation Administration had never heard the word "hijacking" and the CIA had never heard the word "terrorist" or the name "Osama bin Laden." By mid-morning on September 11 there can have been few Americans who had not watched—probably over and over—the collapse of the twin towers of the World Trade Center. The reason for drawing heightened attention to this single greatest failure of American intelligence since Pearl Harbor is that no official steps have so far been taken to find out how it could have happened.

People who deal with terrorism professionally tend to think of it as doctors do diseases with no cure, or as police do crime—as an ill of the human condition to be addressed one case at a time. Paul R. Pillar, a former deputy director of the CIA's Counter-Terrorism Center, has thought about the subject long enough to have it in comfortable perspective as a problem to be managed, never solved. In a study for the Brookings Institution, published in April 2001 under the title of *Terrorism and US Foreign Policy*, Pillar argues persuasively that overexcitement is the enemy of sound counterterror practice. On some things, inevitably, September 11 has proved Pillar plain wrong; he cites, for example, "a drastic reduction in skyjackings" as a "major success story" and credits "a comprehensive security system." But most of what Pillar says holds up well, even when his commonsense approach is now tinged with irony. Put simply, his approach to managing terrorism is to proceed calmly, avoid inflating the significance of any single enemy (he includes bin Laden by name), and remember that, with coalitions, small and few is better than big and many since "limits...are set by the states least willing to cooperate." Pillar has much else to say. There is, he writes, no substitute for the local influence and expertise of foreign police and intelligence services. Bringing legal cases against terrorists takes time and dries up intelligence sources. International sanctions and resolutions work slowly when they work at all. You can't ask foreign banks to track financial transactions without providing account numbers. Military retaliation rarely hits the target intended, and for every terrorist killed two more aspire to take his place.

In the weeks following September 11 it was often suggested that really vigorous efforts freed of hand-wringing restraint—assassination of terrorist leaders, use of torture in interrogation, shutting off terrorist funds to the last penny, telling allies to cooperate or else —would solve the problem with finality. Pillar's advice is to put no hope in drastic measures but remember the current facts of life. There are limits to power, America has become a lightning rod for hatred, we can't stop people from trying to hurt us, and sometimes they will succeed.

But sensible as this advice is, it is undercut by one aspect of the attacks on September 11—their magnitude. In the counterterrorism business there has been a growing concern over the last two decades, and especially since the collapse of the Soviet Union, about the threat posed by weapons of mass destruction—what Pillar calls "the much-ballyhooed danger of chemical, biological, radiological, or nuclear terrorism inflicting mass casualties," and referred to by professionals as CBRN. In Pillar's view such dangers are real but exaggerated; CBRN weapons are difficult to get and to deliver; talking about them only convinces terrorists "how much they frighten people." For Pillar the one quality essential to "sound counterterrorist policy" is perspective, and nothing undermines it more than lurid American fears of "catastrophic," "grand," or "super" terrorism—threats whose consequences are horrifying but whose probability is low.

This would still be a sound point if not for the magnitude of the attacks on the World Trade Center, which killed several thousand people, destroyed billions of dollars' worth of property, pushed the United States deeper into recession, plunged us into a foreign war, precipitated a political crisis throughout the Middle East, and shattered the confidence of Americans that they are safe in their own homes and offices. The cost in dollars will be immense, probably many times the $30 billion annual bill for all American intelligence efforts. The psychic cost of terror cannot be measured, but it ticks up every time someone catches his breath on a plane, thinks twice about getting on an elevator to the eightieth floor, wonders what is in a package, is reassured to know that the FBI can now bug lawyers talking with their clients, or decides to move the headquarters of a Fortune 500 company out of New York City. Pillar, in short, and everybody else in his line of work, is going to have to put "catastrophic," "grand," and "super" terrorism at the top of the list because the other guys have a demonstrated ability to think and operate on the grand scale, and their efforts to obtain nuclear weapons could one day succeed.

Much about Osama bin Laden and his organization remains obscure. The son of a Yemeni-born construction tycoon in Saudi Arabia, bin Laden was one of fifty-three children and the seventeenth son, who inherited on his father's death a fortune variously estimated as $50 million or as much as $300 million. The family dynamics among fifty-three siblings are difficult to imagine, but a hint to bin Laden's character can perhaps be found in the fact that he was his mother's only child, that she was the eleventh or perhaps the twelfth wife, and that his older brothers called him "the son of the slave." This bit of information comes from Simon Reeve, a British journalist who wrote an account of the first World Trade Center bomb attack in 1993 called

The New Jackals: Ramzi Yousef, Osama bin Laden and the Future of Terrorism.[2]

After obtaining a degree in civil engineering—study that usually involves a course on "strength of materials"—bin Laden was recruited, apparently by the head of the Saudi intelligence service, Prince Turki al-Faisal, to support the Mujahideen in the war to drive the Russians out of Afghanistan. Swept away by that success, bin Laden broke with his homeland when it turned to the United States for protection after the invasion of Kuwait by Saddam Hussein, moved to Sudan, built an Islamic extremist network called al-Qaeda (Arabic for "the base"), and embarked on a campaign of terror.

Under pressure from the United States in 1996, Sudan offered to extradite him to Saudi Arabia. Fearing that bin Laden was too popular to admit back into the country, Riyadh turned down the offer—something they told the Americans only months later—and bin Laden was allowed instead to fly back to Afghanistan where old friends in the Pakistani Inter-Services Intelligence (ISI) from the anti-Soviet war put him in touch with the Taliban, a religious party strongly backed by Pakistan in the Afghan civil war.

Bin Laden: The Man Who Declared War on America,[3] a recent biography of bin Laden by the director of the Congressional Task Force on Terrorism and Unconventional Warfare, Yossef Bodansky, reports in great detail the outward facts of bin Laden's progress from a builder of hospitals and military barracks in Afghanistan to the world's most wanted terrorist. Included are the names of many obscure groups, the dates of meetings, reports of individuals getting on and off planes, financial transactions, the movement of arms—all that superstructure of corroborative information which intelligence services like the CIA build into case files. From bin Laden's own writings

---

2. Northeastern University Press, 1999.

3. Forum, 1999.

and videotaped interviews we know that he wants the United States to pull its forces out of the Muslim world, he wants the UN to end the sanctions imposed on Iraq, and he is angered by the suffering of the Palestinians at the hands of the Israelis.

But Bodansky's thorough book tells us little about bin Laden's character, the people who shaped his thinking, how he came to embrace terrorism and build links with extreme Islamicist groups throughout the world. What the CIA and other intelligence organizations somehow missed between bin Laden's return to Afghanistan in 1996 and the attacks of September 11 was the transformation of al-Qaeda from an angry group of "Afghan Arabs" into a disciplined organization with the ability to hijack four airliners at roughly the same moment and fly three of them into what the Pentagon calls "high value" targets. At the time of the simultaneous attacks on the US embassies in East Africa in August 1998, the CIA officer Milt Bearden told a reporter, "Two at once is not twice as hard. Two at once is a hundred times as hard." What does that make four at once?

The CIA's failure on September 11 inevitably raises the question of what it may be missing now. This is not primarily a question of targets and means but of goals and strategies. In the absence of a secret bin Laden position paper one can still try to make sense of the attack on the World Trade Center, and Howard Hart, a retired CIA officer who ran operations against the Soviets in the Afghan war, has recorded his take in an eight-page paper privately circulated among friends. Hart resigned from the agency in 1991 and has seen no classified information since. But drawing on twenty years of experience in the Middle East and South Asia, including operations targeted on terrorist groups, Hart believes that bin Laden is not driven by hatred but is instead pursuing an ambitious grand strategy. His ultimate goal, Hart believes, is "a 'reborn,' combative and vigorous Islam" in control of governments throughout the Arabic world.

Bin Laden's initial targets, in Hart's view, are the conservative, highly centralized, relatively weak regimes of Jordan, Saudi Arabia, Egypt, and the Gulf States, all of which drift uneasily between the allure of Western material culture and the resentments of the poor and devout, who have little access to wealth themselves and are called to reject the modern world by fiery mullahs. Next on bin Laden's list, in Hart's view, are the authoritarian, mainly secular regimes of Iraq, Syria, and Libya, whose populations have been cowed by their "savage and highly effective internal security services...."

Bin Laden has no armies to achieve these great ends; his method is the ancient strategy of the weak, using terrorism to precipitate a political crisis which can be expected to drive a deepening wedge throughout the Islamic world between the godless allies of America and the champions of Allah. In Hart's view the furious American response to the September 11 attacks was part of bin Laden's plan; he and his al-Qaeda companions expected that the US reaction would drive angry Muslims into the streets. Violent measures to suppress them would escalate a growing crisis

> until police and security forces will no longer be willing to fire on their own people, and the targeted governments will collapse. In short, a repeat of events in Iran in 1978–79. Skeptics should remember that in January 1978 no one in Iran—the Shah, his military, foreign observers, even Khomeini supporters —believed the regime could be toppled by "Islamic extremists." One year later the Shah's regime had been destroyed.

Hart watched this happen in Iran, where he arrived in the spring of 1978 to keep tabs on the growing crisis, something the CIA had avoided for years for fear of offending the Shah. The situation he found is ably described by another retired official of the CIA's Directorate of Operations, William J. Daugherty, in the Winter 2001–2002 issue of the *International Journal of Intelligence and Counterintelligence*, an indispensable scholarly journal devoted to intelligence history and policy. American policy was to support the Shah unconditionally, Daugherty writes, and following the forced exile of the Ayatollah Ruhollah Khomeini in 1965 it was taken for granted in Washington that the opposition had been crippled beyond recovery and the CIA made little effort to reach its own judgment until Hart's arrival.

Some of Hart's reports in the spring of 1978 were so pessimistic that the CIA's chief of station refused to send them on to Washington, where he knew they would arouse fury in the White House. For more than three months during the summer of 1978 the CIA labored to write up a special National Intelligence Estimate (NIE) of the strength of the Shah's government. But the estimators could never agree on what was increasingly obvious: the Ayatollah had won control of the streets and the royal palace was next. Eventually the CIA's director, Admiral Stansfield Turner, shelved the NIE because it was politically too divisive. The result: official shock when the Shah's government collapsed, and bitter enmity for the United States from the Islamic activists who seized power in Iran.

Hart makes no facile claim that things might have gone the other way if only the CIA had sent a few agents into the souks. Khomeini had divined something the CIA had missed—the deep hostility toward the Shah's regime of a devout Muslim population being pushed too rapidly into the modern world. But not even Khomeini could foresee how events would unfold, Hart claims. By late 1978 the CIA had penetrated Khomeini's inner circle, and knew that the Ayatollah's closest advisers were still preparing to settle for some kind of power-sharing compromise. Having seen the fall of one regime built on sand, Hart is convinced that bin Laden, following a strategy similar to Khomeini's in the 1970s, can do it again. Whatever happens in the current American effort to hunt him down, he says, bin Laden has now been transformed into a hero of the Arab world. If he lives his charisma will shine all the brighter; if he is imprisoned or killed, others in the al-Qaeda network will carry on in his name. "The governments of Saudi Arabia and the Gulf States are also built on sand," he says.

Hart's interpretation is not easily proved or disproved. Pakistan, once thought vulnerable to Islamic revolt, seems to have survived the present crisis without great difficulty. Most scholars think Saudi Arabia is equally secure—but that is what they thought about the Shah of Iran, too, before 1978, and the CIA at the time went on claiming his throne was not in danger almost until the day he left the country. If the war against terrorism is going to persist for years, as the secretary of defense has said, governments in control today may be in trouble tomorrow. Hart knows that official policy and a CIA anxious to please can make it hard to spot—and even harder to report—the moment things start to deteriorate. He watched it happen in Iran, and the CIA's failure on September 11 makes him worried it could happen again.

Failure is not easily confessed by the CIA. "Though we did not stop the latest, terrible assaults," George Tenet said in a statement to the agency's estimated 16,000 employees on September 12, "you—the men and women of CIA and our intelligence community—have done much to combat terrorism in the past." Failure was not a word Tenet could bring himself to utter. His executive director, A. B. "Buzzy" Krongard, came closer—a little—when he told a meeting of Washington investors in mid-October that the CIA had been worrying too exclusively about atomic bombs and other weapons of mass destruction. "Over and over again, in public testimony and private briefings, we have warned of a major attack by bin Laden," he said. "We had the scope correct. We missed the means."

Like Tenet, most of the CIA people I have talked to in recent weeks have balked at the word "failure," struggling to say it without saying it. Their reading of the event, stripped to its essence, is that no intelligence service can be reasonably asked to predict every attack mounted by a terrorist group, and that the CIA's performance is more fairly measured by what has followed—identifying the likely suspects, mounting a major investigation, calling on friendly intelligence services for help in blocking further attacks, and playing a vigorous and conspicuous role in the US military campaign to overthrow the Taliban and capture Osama bin Laden in Afghanistan. The performance of the CIA, therefore, should be measured on what an intelligence service can do—respond quickly and accurately—and not on what it can't do, no matter how good it is. By any fair measure, therefore, the CIA did not fail.

Behind this defensiveness is a lively fear of the CIA's perennial nightmare—reorganization under the prod of Congress. Like all directors of central intelligence, Tenet has done some reorganizing himself; one of the first things his friend Buzzy Krongard did as executive director was to abolish the Directorate of Administration, thereby drawing under his immediate control the former DA's five separate offices for in-house management—finance, security, personnel, and the like—long famous for their independence.

The history of the CIA is a record of constantly changing offices and lines of authority, usually to reflect shifting priorities in the White House. What the agency fears is not new decision trees but radical surgery. Until he retired a year ago Senator Daniel Patrick Moynihan openly advocated doing away with the CIA entirely as an unwieldy relic of the cold war. Other would-be reformers have suggested splitting covert action from intelligence analysis, perhaps even going so far as to give covert action to the Pentagon and analysis to the State Department—despite the fact that neither wants it.

Former director John Deutch, who ran the agency for eighteen months under President Clinton, published an article in *Foreign Affairs* in 1998 arguing that the agency's Counter-Terrorism Center should be transferred to the FBI. "Senators and congressmen all think they know what intelligence is all about," I was told by Richard Helms, who ran the CIA for six years until President Nixon sent him to Iran in 1973. "Reorganization is their main delight, but I myself don't think they're going to achieve anything by it." Most longtime intelligence professionals believe, like Helms, that basic intelligence work remains the same, however much the flow charts and diagrams are changed. President Bush appears to agree. Earlier this year he asked for a comprehensive intelligence review, still unwritten on September 11. But in the days following the attacks Bush made a point of being photographed in earnest discussion with his chief advisers— Vice President Dick Cheney, National Security Adviser Condoleezza Rice, and George Tenet. The message appeared to be clear: the President is sticking with the agency and the director he has got.

But there is a group of intelligence dissidents in Washington who think this would be a historic mistake. They argue that the CIA's failure to grasp the scope of al-Qaeda's plans reveals deep structural problems within the agency that go far beyond ordinary questions of funding and who reports to whom, and that no attempt to identify weaknesses or correct problems can go forward while George Tenet remains in charge. The criticisms come not from think tanks or bureaucratic rivals of the CIA like the FBI but from a vocal group of former intelligence officers—mostly young, mostly field officers from the Directorate of Operations (DO), mostly well-respected and destined for solid careers until they chose to leave—who believe that the CIA is in steep decline. The most vocal of these critics is Robert Baer, a twenty-year veteran of numerous assignments in Central Asia and the Middle East whose last major job for the agency was an attempt to organize Iraqi opposition to Saddam Hussein in the early 1990s— shuttling between a desk in Langley and contacts on the ground in Jordan, Turkey, and even northern Iraq.

That assignment came to an abrupt end in March 1995 when Baer, once seen as a rising star of the DO, suddenly found himself "the subject of an accusatory process." An agent of the FBI told him he was under investigation for the crime of plotting the assassination of Saddam

Hussein. The investigation was ordered by President Clinton's national security adviser, Anthony Lake, who would be nominated to run the agency two years later. The Baer investigation was only one of many reasons that the intelligence organizations resisted Lake, forcing him to withdraw his name in 1997, and clearing the way for George Tenet.

Eventually, the case against Baer was dismissed with the help of the Washington lawyer Jeffrey Smith, who served as the agency's general counsel under John Deutch. But for Baer the episode was decisive. "When your own outfit is trying to put you in jail," he told me, "it's time to go."[4]

Baer's was one of many resignations in recent years; the dissidents' portrait of the agency which follows comes from him; from Howard Hart; from another veteran DO operator and former chief of station in Amman, Jordan, named David Manners; and from others who preferred not to be identified. They have differing career histories and views but on some things they agree. The Clinton years, in their view, saw a crippling erosion of the agency's position in Washington. Its leadership is now timid and its staff demoralized. Top officials, they say, worry more about the vigilantes of political correctness than the hard work of collecting intelligence in the field. The shock of discovering Aldrich Ames in 1994 was followed by a period of destructive self-criticism.

"That was the beginning of the 'Shia' era in the agency," said Manners. He was referring to the branch of Islam, centered in Iran, which stresses the unworthiness and sinfulness of man. "We all had to demonstrate our penance," Manners told me. "Focus groups were organized, we 'reengineered' the relationship of the Directorate of Operations and the Directorate of Intelligence." This meant dropping the bureaucratic wall between the analysts and the covert operators and introducing "uniform career standards." Henceforth a year in some country where it was dangerous to drink the water would get you no farther

---

4. See Chapter Twenty-Four.

up the ladder than a year pushing paper in Langley. When John Deutch came in he appointed as chief of operations an analyst, David Cohen, who had never supervised an agent or even asked the chief of a foreign intelligence service to share information from his files. This was the era of "process action teams" which studied managerial questions like what sort of paperwork to use for agent handling. A committee of a dozen, split between case officers and analysts, might spend half a day wrestling with such questions twice a week for a year or more. "Navel gazing," Manners calls it.

In the reengineered CIA it was possible for Deborah Morris to be appointed the DO's deputy chief for the Near East. "Her husband was thrown out of Russia in 1994," said one of the dissidents, referring to James L. Morris, the Moscow station chief expelled during the Ames affair. "She worked her way up in Langley. I don't think she's ever been in the Near East. She's never run an agent, she doesn't know what the Khyber Pass looks like, but she's supposed to be directing operations —telling the operators if some pitch is a good idea."

The dissidents argue that "uniform career standards" did nothing to improve intelligence analysis but hurt field operations badly. Many DO veterans resigned and others lost heart when they saw what happened to Richard Holm, the Paris station chief who was yanked back after an attempt to recruit French officials went awry in 1995. US Ambassador Pamela Harriman fumed that whatever Holm was after, "it isn't worth the embarrassment to me." The word went forth from Langley—no more flaps, which meant don't stick your neck out, which meant safe operations or none at all. When Deutch arrived, Holm left, a harsh back of the hand for one of the agency's legendary operators. To fill the gap came a new emphasis on "reports"—the number of separate pieces of paper forwarded to Langley, whatever their quality. "What use is a Cray supercomputer at the Counter-Terrorism Center," Baer asks, "if you've got nothing to put into it?"

With the end of the cold war the agency cut back on recruiting agents, closed down many stations including most of those in Africa, and even quit accepting defectors from the old KGB in 1992—several years before the CIA uncovered Aldrich Ames and another DO spy, Harold Nicholson, less celebrated but almost as damaging, who was known around the DO as "Ranger Jim." At the same time the DO dismantled all the Counterespionage Groups, staffed mainly by "little old ladies" who knew the old cold war targets backward and forward but were no longer needed. Spies were a thing of the past; the new order of the day was to "manage intelligence relationships." In Morocco, the station chief told Baer he was crazy for trying to mount ambitious operations. "We were told to stand down," another dissident said. If you had checked the books you would have found just as many code names for secret agents, the dissidents say, but it was mainly window dressing—routine CIA informants puffed up in reports.

Along with the pullback in recruiting, the dissidents say, came a turn inward. Once operators had prided themselves on their grasp of local language and culture; now they stayed home watching American videos on TV. The CIA has long been wary of letting officers become too closely identified with any single country, language, or region; the British once called it "going native," the CIA calls it "falling in love." But the great operators in the past tended to speak languages like the natives, weren't afraid of the water, had a feel for the way national politics and culture were interconnected. That, at any rate, was what the dissidents had hoped to be when they joined the agency. Howard Hart, a graduate of the University of Arizona, was sent by the agency in 1966 to India, where he learned Urdu and Hindustani; later he added "passable German." Robert Baer learned French, German, Arabic, and the Farsi dialect known as Dari when he was stationed in Dushanbe, the capital of Tajikistan. No Dari speakers served in Dushanbe after Baer left, and the agency has since closed the station down. "Do you know how many Pashto speakers the CIA has got?" he asks, citing the language of the principal ethnic group in Afghanistan, including most of the leadership of the Taliban. "The agency will tell you some imaginary number but I am telling you none. Do you know how many were sent to learn it after the embassy bombings? None."

With the mass resignations from the DO in recent years the match between station chief and country got ever more arbitrary; one recent chief in Beijing, a dissident says, picked for the job by Deutch's executive director, Nora Slatkin, spoke no Chinese and suffered from a conspicuous skin disease which the Chinese find particularly offensive. The loss of language speakers was not limited to the agency; the National Security Agency, a dissident claims, has only one Pashto speaker—a problem solved by sending transcripts of intercepted communications to Pakistan for translation by the ISI, an organization with a long history of involvement with the Taliban and Osama bin Laden. Some intelligence officials even believe that it was the ISI who warned bin Laden to get out of Khost before American cruise missiles struck in August 1998 in retaliation for the embassy bombings.

The dissidents say that the CIA is still staffed with hard-working people of talent and dedication and that it can still do competent work. They know how vast the agency's resources are and are familiar with the technical marvels which collect intelligence. Above all, they recognize that the apparent success of the military effort in Afghanistan seems to have reassured the public that things are now going well. But all the same the dissidents insist that things have gone badly wrong at the agency. Years of public criticism, attempts to clean house, the writing and rewriting of rules, and efforts to rein in the Directorate of Operations have all conspired to make the agency insular, risk-averse, and gun-shy. So have catch-up hiring of women and minorities, public hostility that makes it hard to recruit at leading colleges, complacency following victory in the cold war, the humiliation of the Ames case, even the long economic boom which put CIA salaries farther and farther behind routine offers to recent graduates by business and industry. The dissidents don't say that all of these problems are somehow the doing of George Tenet, but they do say they have undermined the CIA's ability to follow terrorists through the streets of the Arab world. A few months ago theirs was only the opinion of a group of disaffected officials; since September 11 it ought to be considered seriously.

It is hard to find anyone in the intelligence community who dislikes George Tenet. He is an open-faced, hefty man, a reformed cigar smoker, friendly in manner, a slapper of backs and a clutcher of arms, earnest, interested, quick to take a point, and open to new ideas. "The outgoingness is a genuine gift," said Helms, who has watched many directors of central intelligence come and go. "Who else could lecture Arafat on the Middle East—up close with his hand on Arafat's lapel —and get away with it?" Tenet's confirmation in July 1997 also brought a welcome end to the revolving door on the seventh floor of CIA headquarters, where Tenet replaced Deutch, who had replaced James Woolsey, who had replaced Robert Gates, with a number of failed nominations in between. Tenet has set a recent record for peaceful tenure of the DCI's long, wood-paneled office overlooking the imposing main entrance to the building which Tenet renamed (before the last presidential election) the Bush Intelligence Center. The Bush in question is the President's father, who was director for ten days short of a year in 1976–1977 and is still remembered as the ideal intelligence consumer when he was in the White House.

The bureaucratic clout of DCIs can be measured by how often they meet with the president. With some it's practically never; with most it starts often and fades off. In the case of Tenet and the current President Bush it is reported to be every day, with the arrival of the DCI at the White House carrying the President's Daily Brief, a printed document reporting much as a newspaper might the classified intelligence take and hot issues of the moment. Trust and personal liking of this sort is rare and CIA officials, happy to have the attention of the Oval Office, don't want to mess with it.

Tenet got the job by an unusual route through a succession of staff jobs dealing with intelligence issues for congressional committees. After several years as an aide to Senator John Heinz, Tenet joined the forty-member staff of the Senate Intelligence Committee in 1985. Four years later he was appointed staff director and then in 1993 he moved to the White House, where he handled intelligence matters for the National Security Council and met John Deutch, who brought him out to Langley in 1995 as deputy director of central intelligence. Even Tenet's admirers concede he got the top job mainly because Clinton did not want to risk another confirmation failure after Lake bowed out, and Tenet had already been confirmed once by the Senate. "George is a service kind of guy," said an officer who worked with him at the agency. "He knew what congressmen wanted and needed and he dealt with the White House the same way." What is remarkable about Tenet's career is that he had no intelligence background or experience of the usual kind; his expertise was all learned in the corridors of power where the deciding question is what will fly. His largely trouble-free years at the CIA prove that he knows how to navigate the maze of a political town.

Three years ago Tenet invented a new position—"counselor" to the DCI—and hired the sixty-four-year-old lawyer and businessman A. B. Krongard to fill it. A Princeton graduate and martial arts enthusiast, Krongard had recently retired after selling his share in a Baltimore stock brokerage firm to Bankers Trust for $70 million. Last March Tenet moved Krongard up into the job of executive director, where he is in charge of managing the agency, including its secret operations, while the director deals with broader issues of policy and strategy. The dissidents say that Krongard may know how to run a financial firm and make a pot of money, and George Tenet may know how to keep out of bureaucratic fights he can't win; but neither one of them, the dissidents say, really knows in any depth what effective intelligence requires, and on-the-job training isn't enough. It is impossible for any outsider to fairly judge what the dissidents are saying—and certainly not anyone as far outside as a journalist like myself. That is a matter for some official body.

When things go awry in the intelligence business it is customary to do a damage report. The Ames damage report—a four-hundred-page document written by then CIA Inspector General Frederick Hitz—in effect cost James Woolsey his job. In 1961, by the time the agency's inspector general, Lyman Kirkpatrick, got around to writing his assessment of the embarrassing failure of a CIA-trained and -financed rebel army at the Bay of Pigs, the DCI at the time, Allen Dulles, was already gone. That disaster was big enough to get a second report from a blue-ribbon panel headed by General Maxwell Taylor. The problem wasn't simply that the rebel army got shot to pieces as soon as it crossed the beach; it was that the agency had deceived itself about the real support throughout Cuba for Fidel Castro. The agency's plan couldn't work, and Taylor's job was to make sure that never happened again.

When I began to work on this article, the first person I called was the CIA officer I have known longest, a man who went to the City College of New York during the "red decade" of the 1930s, joined the OSS during World War II, was carried over into the CIA at its birth, and worked closely with every chief of covert operations until he retired after the CIA scandals of the early 1970s. This man remains extremely active in retirement. He is a member of numerous study groups, panels, and commissions, and he rarely misses a conference on intelligence. He hates to criticize the agency he served all his life, but the failure of September 11 is not something he is ready to pass over in silence. "I don't think even Pearl Harbor matches this one," he said. "How often do you lose half a division in a day? Nothing has ever happened on this scale before. This was totally beyond anybody's beliefs or dreams. Nobody wanted to think the unthinkable."

Was anybody talking about an investigation—a postmortem to figure out what went wrong?

"I don't understand it," said my friend. "There was a little talk but then it suddenly quieted down. Not even [Senator Richard] Shelby [former chairman of the Senate Intelligence Committee]—he knows he can't raise his head. Nobody is pushing for an investigation."

Is it possible to handle the problem—whatever the problem—without an investigation?

"No."

What would an investigation require?

"You need presidential and congressional authority. You can't just do it in-house."

Could it be done while Tenet was still running the CIA?

"If he's still there everybody will know he's watching. People won't tell you the truth. Everybody will be covering his ass, protecting his boss. They try to get rid of rivals. They hide paper and destroy evidence. I've seen it. You can overcome it by being a sonofabitch but only if the top guy is gone."

There is nothing this man hates more than the way politics has torn apart the CIA over the years. I would say he about half agrees with the dissidents—not 100 percent on half of what they say, but 50 percent on all of it. But he has little sympathy for people who talk out of school, and he knows how hard it is for investigators to keep political meddlers at bay, get to the bottom of what went wrong, and fix what isn't working. He was the first one to tell me, like someone describing a jewel, that Tenet had the President's ear, which meant the agency could do its job. To give that away, take your chances with someone new, open up a whole can of worms by asking how this could have happened... Talking about it he sounds like a man facing open-heart surgery.

But?

"It ought to be done. He ought to go."

—*The New York Review of Books*, January 17, 2002

24

AMERICA'S NEW INTELLIGENCE WAR

THE FIRST TASK of any intelligence organization is to establish where danger lies. In the Arab world it is traditionally considered to lie within, where revolutionaries, religious zealots, and ambitious military officers plotting to seize power are watched and periodically arrested by the local security service, the *mukhabarat*. In Egypt and Iraq, in Jordan and Saudi Arabia it is always the same: the real interest and expertise of the secret police are concentrated on the home-grown opposition. The United States may speculate obsessively on the military programs of Saddam Hussein or on Iranian ambitions in western Afghanistan, but the Arab countries worry less about neighbors, including Israel, than they do about the contacts and travels of their own radical university students, the commanders of armored divisions in urban centers, and impassioned mullahs preaching a return to fundamental Islam. Arab secret services hold tight to what they know, and are sphinxes about the things they don't know—a source of deep frustration to American intelligence officers trying to sort out the background and contacts of the aircraft hijackers of September 11.

For a brief period last fall pained noises of discontent with the level of Saudi cooperation could be heard in Congress after the CIA and the FBI explained the difficulty of prying open Arab doors. Nothing came of it. The White House insisted all was well and American intelligence officers had nowhere else to turn. CIA officers and the FBI's legal attachés assigned to American embassies could do very little on the ground in most Arab countries before September 11; there was no knocking on doors or flashing of badges, and even now they must ask the locals. The normal drill has been to send a liaison officer stationed in Cairo or Riyadh to pay a visit to the office of his counterpart, submit his questions, and then listen to the air conditioning while the counterpart goes through a folder on the desk in front of him, choosing what to share. In this way the CIA or the FBI may learn who went to high school with Mohamed Atta, or when the former Saudi intelligence chief, Prince Turki al-Faisal, last spoke with Osama bin Laden, or whether the Saudi Istakhbarat had found earlier reason to open files on the hijackers who arrived in the United States during the year 2001 to fly commercial airliners into the World Trade Center, the Pentagon, and a Pennsylvania hillside.

In high-profile cases in the past, leading officials or even the director of the FBI or the CIA might fly in to ask for help, in which case large bustling groups might gather to process the request and its answer, but otherwise the drill was the same. Americans can't order the locals to pony up; they must ask, and it is the temperature of relations with the United States that determines whether local intelligence chiefs will be forthcoming, or instead close the folder and say they are sorry, they can find nothing of interest. Following September 11, the locals have been more forthcoming in some places, like Yemen and Pakistan, where the FBI and CIA have been working closely with police to round up al-Qaeda activists. But cooperation given on one day may be taken away on another. In an intelligence war getting and keeping the help of the locals is half the battle, and for help in that half Americans are dependent on friends in the Middle East, if any. Without that help it is difficult to know who is on the other side.

Defining and describing "the threat" was easier during the forty years of cold war with the USSR, when estimators at the CIA hammered out the *Annual Survey of Soviet Strategic Intentions and Capabilities*—the hard-fought consensus reached (or in some cases not reached) by analysts from the CIA, the Defense Intelligence Agency (DIA), and other American intelligence organizations about what Soviet Russia could do and what it planned to do. No "Soviet Estimate," as it was generally called, ever predicted imminent war, and every estimate reported a vigorous and continuing Soviet military buildup. Between those two poles debate ranged widely and was sometimes bitter and prolonged. Why, for example, were the Soviets spending so much money to improve missile accuracy? Was it pure technological momentum, or were they patiently assembling the capacity for a first strike? Why did they appear to be trying to hide the results of their tests? Was it simply the historic Russian obsession with secrecy, or were they hoping to hide a growing ability to disarm America at a stroke?

Throughout the cold war it was usually Soviet "capabilities," not Soviet intentions, that drove the estimates. Plans come and go; capabilities persist from one day, one year, one decade to the next. "The threat" was not posed by Soviet plans to influence European labor unions, curry favor with India, buy enough Cuban sugar to keep Fidel Castro afloat, encourage West German *Ostpolitik*, or sell tanks to Egypt and Syria. These were all trivial irritants compared to the real threat of huge Soviet conventional armies at the door of Western Europe, far greater than anything the NATO allies ever placed in their path, and of the Soviet Strategic Rocket Forces with a capacity to obliterate every city in North America, and finally of multiwarhead, superaccurate Soviet missiles with an ability to destroy American hardened land-based missiles and bombers on the ground, while preserving a still-vast second-strike capability threatening catastrophe if the United States chose to retaliate. What Moscow intended was neither here nor there; the threat of war might have been small on any given day but Soviet capabilities—the power of the weapons themselves—were threat enough to keep the United States and its allies on edge for decades.

In the first few years of the cold war the Americans had a tough time keeping track of Soviet military developments and deployments, but by the early 1960s, with the coming of overhead reconnaissance by ever-improving satellites, the CIA and the DIA could pretty much find, count, and describe any piece of large-scale military hardware on or near the surface of the earth. But "national technical means," as American officials called the array of expensive collecting devices and systems, of which satellites were only the best known, could not answer some questions—especially those, always lurid, about what new superweapon horrors might be on the drawing boards or in the pipeline.

The "bomber gap" of the 1950s and the "missile gap" of the 1960s, powerful drivers of American military budgets in their time, both proved illusory. The Soviets chose to save money, ignore bombers, and proceed directly to missiles; and the huge numbers of missiles feared by the CIA and the Pentagon turned out, when the first overhead photos came in, to be a relative handful of cumbersome, vulnerable brutes sitting up on their launchpads in Siberia where an American nuke might have destroyed the lot. But more information did not put an end to "threat inflation"—the tendency of interested parties in the American national security establishment to argue that some alarming new Soviet development required a corresponding jump in their own budgets.

The Air Force was a perennial offender when it came to the question of "enough." American missiles, the generals argued, were never numerous enough, or safe enough in hardened launch silos; US warheads were never certain enough to hit the Politburo men's room in the Kremlin, and were not connected enough by Command, Control, Communications, and Intelligence (c3i). But in truth everybody in Washington played the game—even the CIA, with its need for total technical coverage of the Soviet Union, and the FBI. J. Edgar Hoover had long argued that the United States could not safely permit additional

Soviet consulates unless the bureau's budget was bumped up to accommodate all those extra field agents needed to follow the Russian cooks, secretaries, and chauffeurs who were really highly trained intelligence professionals working for the KGB.

How great was "the threat" in retrospect? It's hard to say. The wheezing, alcoholic, geriatric gang who ran the Soviet Union in its last decades seemed incapable of forming and executing a coherent scheme for global struggle, but their decrepitude in some ways only made the danger more acute. The arms race had created a highly combustible situation—the new missiles really were accurate, warning systems left almost no time to gauge the reality of an attack, warfighting plans on both sides made no provision for backing down or giving up. But it is equally true that the end of the cold war was so sudden and complete that it revealed a "threat" based on smoke and mirrors—a barely functioning Soviet economy, a cynical and despairing populace with a falling lifespan, technology primitive in all but a few areas of military hardware, a worthless currency, a degraded environment, allies eager to break free.

The imaginary Russia, the bear that endangered Europe and the world, according to the British intelligence historian Rhodri Jeffreys-Jones, was dreamed up by the threat-artists of the CIA and the Pentagon, a product of "the inflationary disease in American intelligence." The problem, Jeffreys-Jones says, is an "overheated imagination," but the title of his most recent book—*Cloak and Dollar: A History of American Secret Intelligence*[1]—suggests another, simpler, older explanation: money. Cold war threat inflation was certainly about money—big budgets for the military services, big contracts for military suppliers, big contributions for campaign funds, and a never-ending Mississippi of consultant money for experts in think tanks.

Priming the military-industrial-intelligence pump with "smooth

1. Yale University Press, 2002.

talk, hyperbole, deception," in Jeffreys-Jones's view, is that familiar American figure, "the confidence man." Jeffreys-Jones has in mind the salesman and boomer—the professional spinner of dreams of opportunity, the coming thing, constant progress, eternal youth—a cross between the Duke and the Dauphin in *The Adventures of Huckleberry Finn* and Willy Loman in *Death of a Salesman*, "way out there in the blue with a smile and a shoeshine." Frances FitzGerald has argued persuasively that America's greatest pitchman for super-weapon snake oil was President Ronald Reagan, whose dream of a world made safe from missiles became a kind of national bedtime story. But the dream is still only that; no other American military program has spent more money for less result than Reagan's Strategic Defense Initiative (SDI), and the billions continue to pour out. The credit for the mad national persistence in this endeavor, FitzGerald concludes in her history of SDI, *Way Out There in the Blue*,[2] must be given to the smooth talk of the Great Communicator.

So there is definitely something to Jeffreys-Jones's notion of the intelligence con game. But having made a plausible argument that the history of American intelligence can be written as a history of succeeding scare stories, he largely abandons theory to retell a dozen episodes from American intelligence history—spying by Alan Pinkerton's detective agency during the Civil War, the surprise attack at Pearl Harbor, the career of the father of American code-cracking, Herbert O. Yardley, the Kennedy administration's obsession with Cuba, indirectly leading, as news of anti-Castro plots leaked out, to Senator Frank Church's investigation of CIA intelligence activities in the mid-1970s and a subsequent basket of "reforms."

Jeffreys-Jones argues that these reforms, although obviously intended to quiet public alarm, were more than mere window dressing. The two biggest were a requirement for on-the-record, albeit

---

2. Simon and Schuster, 2000.

secret, presidential approval of covert operations and the creation of permanent intelligence oversight committees in Congress with a right to "timely" briefing on important developments—intelligence sharing with allies, for example, or the discovery of major spies. Together these reforms signaled an end to the era of anything goes.

The structure of American intelligence history can be organized in many ways—as a succession of White House manias, for example, with the CIA frantically trying to satisfy presidential demands for information on Soviet military programs, for the overthrow of unfriendly governments in Guatemala and Iraq, or for the defeat of guerrilla movements in the Congo and Vietnam. Or as a chain of public convulsions at the sudden disclosure of crimes and horrors—plots to murder Fidel Castro, spying on Americans, dangerous drug experiments with unsuspecting humans, aid for drug smugglers, training for Latin American death squads, illegal funding for guerrilla movements.

But just as important in any effort to understand the nature of the CIA is a history of its failures. The agency was founded in response to the failure at Pearl Harbor, and it has been repeatedly shaken by similar failures to spot coming trouble ever since—the North Korean invasion of South Korea in June 1950, for example, or the intervention of China into the Korean War in November 1950, the decisive Cuban response to the CIA-mounted invasion at the Bay of Pigs, the Russian invasion of Czechoslovakia in 1968, the combined Arab attacks on Israel in October 1973, the collapse of the Soviet Union between 1989 and 1991, the Iraqi invasion of Kuwait in 1990, and—to a degree still unknown—the terrorist attacks of September 11.

CIA analysts refer to these failures as examples of the either-or, yes-no kind of estimating effort they describe as "single outcome forecasting." They have tried to replace it in recent years with a more fluid approach giving a sense of the range of possible outcomes with fuzzy numbers for the probability of the major ones. This is roughly how the US Weather Bureau goes about it; 40 percent chance of rain, total precipitation two to three inches, partly cloudy, Hurricane Betsy will approach the Florida Keys in the early morning hours, etc. Rough guesses help, but some things you still want to know for sure. On December 6, 1941, American military commanders would have liked to know that there was a 100 percent chance of a Japanese attack on Pearl Harbor the following morning, and appeals to the inherent difficulty of predicting things that have never happened before offer zero solace to those caught unprepared.

Calls for an inquiry into the lack of warning on September 11, tentatively made in the first week or so, were vigorously resisted by the White House on the understandable grounds that it was "too soon." But as time goes by it appears the White House believes it will always be too soon to make a major and serious effort to investigate the failure, especially one conducted by anything as prone to twenty-twenty hindsight, Monday morning quarterbacking, finger-pointing, witch-hunting, and playing the blame game as a public commission.

Why the White House should be so troubled by the prospect of an inquiry is growing easier to understand, as the public learns by fits and starts that President Bush was briefed by the CIA on the danger of al-Qaeda hijackings on August 6, 2001, five weeks before the attacks; that the CIA had followed two of the hijackers to a terrorist meeting in Malaysia but was slow to pass on what it knew to the FBI; that the FBI for obscure institutional reasons had resisted repeated requests by agents in Minneapolis for a Federal Intelligence Security Act (FISA) warrant to search the computer hard drive on a laptop belonging to Zacarias Moussaoui, now facing the death penalty for his alleged role in the September 11 conspiracy. The same FBI official who resisted the FISA warrant request also ignored important information on Moussaoui contributed by the French, and failed to connect the episode to the July 10 warning memo from another FBI agent in Phoenix, Arizona, claiming that terrorists might be attending flight schools in preparation for an attack. These troubling facts have been reported extensively in the press and we may expect to learn of others in a steady stream as the current, preliminary investigations in the House and Senate continue. There will be much detail that is hard to absorb, but certain warnings may light up in retrospect like neon signs.

What, exactly, was the President told in that August briefing? According to Karl Rove, a White House adviser who was with President Bush on Air Force One on September 11, security officials resisted the President's demand to return immediately to Washington. In an interview with Tim Russert broadcast on CNBC on July 13, 2002, Rove said the officials warned Bush on September 11 that other hijacked aircraft might still be in the air and they could not "guarantee the security of the airspace over Washington." When the President finally returned to Washington late in the day he pointed to the smoking Pentagon and said, "Take a close look. You're looking... at the face of war in the twenty-first century." "He needed no briefing," Rove said. "He needed no explanation.... When there was a second plane [which flew into the World Trade Center] he knew exactly what it was... that a war had been declared on the United States." It seems likely that what the President knew came at least in part from the August briefing.

It is my guess that the CIA and the FBI, the two American intelligence organizations principally involved, had a startling depth of knowledge about the terrorists, their allies, and their plans and movements before September 11. When elements of the story began to reach the public in recent months a series of officials—and most prominently Robert Mueller, director of the FBI—insisted that what they knew or could or should or might have known still wasn't enough to have saved the World Trade Center. No doubt this is narrowly true. We may trust that no one was sitting on a piece of paper with hard, specific, unambiguous information on date, time, and target. *That* officials probably could have acted on. But two things are increasingly clear: first, the principal intelligence failure before September 11 was a failure by counterterror specialists deep within the FBI and CIA to sense the shape of the plot that was unfolding—the often-cited inability to "connect the dots." But the CIA well knew something was in the works and frequently said so in the months leading up to September 11. The second great failure was the decision of the Bush administration on taking office to restudy the problem of terrorism from top to bottom, rather than pursue programs already begun under President Clinton. This lost year was the subject of a *Time* magazine cover story in the issue of August 12, 2002, describing the efforts of Richard Clarke, a Clinton holdover, to win agreement from the new national security team for an aggressive effort targeted on al-Qaeda and its refuge in Afghanistan. The principals, like Vice President Dick Cheney, National Security Adviser Condoleezza Rice, Defense Secretary Donald Rumsfeld, and Attorney General John Ashcroft, all knew that terrorism posed a real danger, *Time* reported; the problem was that all had come into office with pet programs of their own and terrorism was somewhere down the list. Before a counterterror program could be placed on the President's desk, the principals had to agree, and before they could meet their deputies had to agree. That alone took the better part of a year, with the result that before the World Trade Center was destroyed, President Bush had no chance to say yes, no, or let's look at it again. It is the fear of more stories like this one that perhaps best explains the White House resistance to an inquiry.

But sorting all that out is left for the future. What's right in front of us is troubling evidence that American intelligence organizations, and especially the FBI, have lost the ability to grasp what is failing or going systemically wrong, and the fact that they lack the will to do something about it. Problems in big government bureaus are ordinarily hidden from the general public, but in the case of the CIA and the FBI the recent discovery of spies in their midst illuminates at a stroke the extent of the trouble within.

The case of Aldrich Ames, the CIA counterintelligence analyst arrested in 1994 for spying for the Russians and now serving a life sentence, has been the subject of half a dozen books, all of which stressed the astounding lethargy of the agency's attempt to figure out what had gone wrong in 1985, when just about every Soviet spying for the Americans was suddenly yanked from the street and executed or imprisoned.[3] Counterintelligence can be a wonderfully subtle and nuanced exercise, but Ames's "big dump"—a briefcase full of names and operations simply handed to a KGB intelligence officer in a Georgetown restaurant—is not an example of it. Standard procedure would have called for a sophisticated KGB game of playing back these exposed agents against us, until they could be slipped out of view one by one in ambiguous circumstances. Instead, the Russians panicked, arrested the lot, and sent as clear a message to the CIA as any analyst could have asked for—we got 'em all, and one of your people gave them to us. It is possible to dream up other explanations for this unprecedented roll-up, and mole sleuths tried to do it, but in their guts the sleuths knew at the time that the bad news was true, and the obvious answer was the right one: somebody had sold the agency down the river.

In one of many investigations of why Ames got away with it for so long, the inspector general of the Department of Justice, Michael R. Bromwich, cited in his report the FBI's contribution to this failure—a strange combination of missed opportunities, high-level inattention, and lack of curiosity. From the beginning the FBI knew that the problem could not be laid entirely at the CIA's doorstep; most of the lost Soviet agents had been run by the agency but during the same period—1985 and 1986 —the FBI had also suffered compromised operations and lost agents of its own. Nevertheless, according to an unclassified summary of Bromwich's report released by the Justice Department in April 1997,[4]

---

3. See Chapter 20.

4. Available at the Federation of American Scientists Web page, www.fas.org.

the bureau's first investigating task force, code-named ANLACE, gradually ran out of steam and then gave up in the fall of 1987 despite
having "reached no firm conclusions concerning the cause of its intelligence losses." Worse, ANLACE said nothing about their possible relation to the CIA's losses. In short, the bureau shrugged off the question
of how this could have happened.

So it went for the next six or seven years. The bureau's investigation was not resumed until mid-1991 when a joint FBI–CIA team—
two members from each organization—again tackled the problem of
finding a mole; they gradually accumulated evidence pointing a finger
at Ames, whose conspicuous outlays of cash were hard to explain. But
despite "compelling circumstantial evidence," Bromwich writes, the
FBI members of the task force made no recommendation to open an
investigation of Ames, and FBI managers, although aware Ames was
"a top mole suspect," failed to ask for details or to press for action.
The group's report, issued in March 1993, simply concluded that
"there was a penetration of the CIA" and dropped the matter there.

Bromwich describes but does not explain this odd lack of urgency
in the face of "a catastrophic and unprecedented loss" of the bureau's
own hard-won Soviet sources, who were there one day and gone the
next in a classic roll-up. He notes simply that the bureau was slow to
take note and quick to lose interest in the problem. "Senior management" never understood, or tried to understand, the magnitude of the
betrayal and "never showed any sustained interest" even in the losses
at the CIA, despite the FBI's statutory responsibility for protecting the
nation against spies. The result was "inadequate management attention as well as insufficient resources" for the effort to explain the roll-
up. "Senior management" is as close as Bromwich comes to naming
the culpable. But he does quietly offer one tacit explanation for the
bureau's tepid response—its obligation under the law to notify congressional oversight committees of "any significant intelligence failure." The only way "senior management" could escape blame for its

failure to do so, it is clear, was to tell Bromwich that they were never told of "the scope and significance of these losses." Bromwich offers no opinion whether these denials were true.

But there's a deeper irony to Bromwich's story of missing the obvious. While he was investigating the bureau's failure to catch one spy, another was contemplating further treacheries at FBI headquarters. Did Bromwich understand what is implicit in his report—that the arrest of Aldrich Ames did not quite solve the mystery? Still unexplained were the operations that failed and the agents who were lost by the bureau's New York City field office beginning in 1985. The bureau continued to gnaw at the problem but its investigation rivaled in its slowness the groping of the CIA's search for Ames, and in the end in both cases the light bulb refused to go on until the answer was more or less handed to the investigators.

How this unfolded is still largely hidden, but recent books on the FBI, taken together, offer a rough account of what happened. It was a fine example of the old maxim of mole hunters that "spies catch spies." According to Ronald Kessler, a former *Washington Post* reporter whose recent *The Bureau: The Secret History of the FBI*[5] is the latest of many useful books he has written on intelligence subjects, it was not the analysts and sleuths assigned to solve the problem who caught Ames. Instead, one of the CIA's Russian agents-in-place—that is, a mole working for the US—provided enough operational details to narrow the investigators' focus to Ames. Code-named Avenger, this spy later defected to the West and in November 2000, Kessler writes, he helped to recruit a second source, then still inside a Russian intelligence organization, who actually obtained and hand-delivered the bulky file of another spy in the United States run by the KGB and its successor.

The best account of this extraordinary coup—and of much else— is to be found in David Wise's account of the case, *Spy: The Inside*

---

5. St. Martin's, 2002.

Story of How the FBI*'s Robert Hanssen Betrayed America.*[6] Wise—
not to be confused with David Vise, who has also written about the
case—has been writing about American intelligence for nearly forty
years, and it appears that he has never forgotten the name or lost
the phone number of a source. The nuances of Hanssen's character
do not long detain him; what interests Wise is the spy stuff—the
names, dates, personal histories, old cases, and twists of tradecraft
that give intelligence files their flavor. From the day of Hanssen's
arrest it was known that the FBI had somehow obtained the KGB file.
The challenge for everybody writing about the case has been to
explain how. The short answer, Wise tells us, is that the FBI winnowed
its list of Russian intelligence officers who might have known the
mole's identity, picked one who had retired from intelligence work to
open a business in Moscow, and then lured him to America with the
hope of a contract. How the FBI managed to go after exactly the right
man Wise admits he does not know, but they did; the Russian either
had or obtained the file, and the FBI bought it for $7 million and help
in finding a new home. The file included everything but Hanssen's
name.

In an extraordinary break with orthodox intelligence procedure
the KGB had agreed to run this second agent for two decades without
knowing who he was, and communicating solely by dead drops—the
exchange of materials left at prearranged locations. The KGB knew
the agent only as "B" or "Ramon Garcia," but it didn't take long for
FBI investigators, reading the many letters of the spy to his handlers,
and listening to a taped telephone conversation, to recognize the
cocksure, opinionated voice of the guy who poked his nose into
everything at headquarters, Robert Phillip Hanssen.

Born in 1944, the son of a Chicago policeman, and an FBI agent since
1976, Hanssen had been a queer duck all his life—socially awkward,

---

6. Random House, 2002.

smarter than a lot of people but not as smart as he thought, good with computers, a daily churchgoer with a toe-the-line, by-the-book rigidity on questions of morals and behavior. In the bureau fellow agents thought him smart but weird, and in fact he was weirder than they suspected. He had few friends, a house full of guns, a passionate fidelity to the Catholic Church and especially to the half-secret Opus Dei ("Work of God") organization, and a kinky sexual obsession which led him to e-mail nude photos of his wife Bonnie to an old high school buddy, and to post lurid but probably fictional sexual narratives about her on the Internet. (One of these is quoted in full in both David Vise's *The Bureau and the Mole: The Most Famous Double Agent in FBI History*[7] and Norman Mailer and Lawrence Schiller's *Into the Mirror: The Life of Master Spy Robert P. Hanssen.*[8]) Hanssen first gave secrets to the Russians in 1979 but quit when Bonnie caught him at it. In 1985 he contacted the Russians again by writing a letter to a well-known KGB spy handler at the Soviet embassy in Washington, Viktor Cherkashin, who had also handled Aldrich Ames.

In addition to identifying some of the same Soviet spies betrayed by Ames, Hanssen left garbage bags full of secret paper at dead drops in a park near his home—more than 6,000 pages in all, including items like the National Intelligence Program for 1987, the text of a "stealth orientation" briefing for a director of the CIA, a CIA staff study of KGB "recruitment operations" against the agency, and even the US government "continuity of government" plan. The last detailed exactly how the United States would maintain the government's ability to make decisions during an all-out nuclear war, knowledge of which the Soviets might have made devastating use.

Deciding who was the more damaging to American security—Ames or Hanssen—is an academic exercise; both turned over pretty much

---

7. Atlantic Monthly Press, 2002.

8. HarperCollins, 2002.

everything they could lay their hands on, and both were in a position to scoop up plenty. But there the similarity between the two men ends. Ames was an alcoholic, careless about covering his tracks, who thought he could hold on to his demanding wife with money. Hanssen was meticulous. He routinely checked FBI files for any sign he was under suspicion. He also broke some of the oldest rules of agent-running tradecraft, by sticking to a single dead drop, for example; he accepted money but didn't press for more, and seems to have been drawn on by an obscure psychological need to risk exposure. This waxed and waned; he cautiously quit spying in 1990 when it was clear the accelerating collapse of the Soviet Union threatened the KGB's ability to protect its agents. But around 1999, apparently missing the excitement of the game as retirement approached, Hanssen got in touch with the Russians again. "Dear friend: welcome!" the Russians replied. "We express our sincere joy on the occasion of resumption of contact with you."

But something had changed in Hanssen's personality. The old take-it-or-leave-it superiority had been replaced by a hunger for recognition, acceptance, approval—a neediness well described by two *Time* magazine veteran reporters, whose account of the Hanssen case, *The Spy Next Door*,[9] is solidly informed and lucidly written. In mid-March 2000, Elaine Shannon and Ann Blackman tell us, Hanssen wrote his handlers a rambling, disjointed letter: "One might propose that I am either insanely brave or quite insane. I'd answer neither, I'd say insanely loyal.... I have, however, come as close to the edge as I can without being truly insane.... I hate uncertainty. So far I have judged the edge correctly. Give me credit for that.... It's been a long time my dear friends, a long and lonely time." Hanssen later carefully checked the FBI's Automated Case Support system for telltale keywords, including

9. *The Spy Next Door: The Extraordinary Secret Life of Robert Philip Hanssen, the Most Damaging FBI Agent in US History* (Little, Brown, 2002).

his own name and address, trusting they would pop up if he were being investigated.

By mid-November 2000 the FBI had obtained the Russian file on "B" and within weeks the bureau had Hanssen under surveillance. If the Russians knew the Hanssen file had been lifted they failed to let Hanssen know, but he still sensed a change in the weather. In his last letter to his Russian handlers, scheduled for delivery in February 2001, he wrote that "it is time to seclude myself from active service.... Something has aroused the sleeping tiger." Minutes after depositing a bag containing the letter and seven FBI documents classified secret at the dead drop code-named ELLIS—a bridge over a creek in Foxstone Park near his home—Hanssen was arrested by FBI agents. Facing a possible death penalty, he later pleaded guilty in return for a sentence of life without parole.

All the superlatives mustered to describe the Ames case were summoned again to give a sense of the magnitude of Hanssen's betrayal. Ames eluded discovery for nine years, Hanssen for twenty-one. Ames crippled CIA efforts to spy on the Russians; Hanssen did the same to the bureau and delivered an even wider range of equally damaging secrets. But more troubling than the immediate injury was the fact that the CIA and the FBI alike, somehow paralyzed despite unmistakable evidence that both organizations had been penetrated, dawdled for many years until a spy handed them the answer.

Catching the spies should have been the beginning of a process of self-examination and renewal, but nothing of the kind has occurred. The in-house damage reports, full of detail about missed opportunities and overlooked clues, fail to explain the extraordinary inability of the CIA and the FBI to face the plain facts of failure and do something about it. This paralysis when confronted by internal problems is no minor matter, because the ready excuse of secrecy makes it difficult even for authorized outsiders—congressional committees, oversight boards of distinguished public citizens, presidential advisers—to address any problem which an intelligence organization chooses to conceal. It is as if a bank had lost millions to an embezzler year after year, but continued to block the auditor at the door.

The second job of any intelligence organization, after identifying where danger lies, is to protect its secrets. In theory the secrets are being kept from enemies so that the organization—the Federal Bureau of Investigation or the Central Intelligence Agency, say—can pursue the rest of its important work, but in practice the secrets held most tightly are those that can wreck careers, let cats out of bags, or bring a halt to operations—the secrets of failure kept from public exposure. The glacial progress of the investigations of the two most damaging spies in American secret history, Aldrich Ames at the CIA and Robert Hanssen at the FBI, may be explained in part by the queasy certainty of high agency and bureau officials that they were going to catch unshirted hell when the news got out. Of course, the longer the wait the worse the explosion, but who wants trouble today when it can be put off until tomorrow —and maybe even left to ruin the career of the next person to fill the job?

Hiding trouble seems to be part of the ethos of intelligence agencies, especially at the FBI, which rejected and denied all criticism during its half-century under J. Edgar Hoover, the strange celibate who built the bureau in his own crabbed image. "Investigation" was the mission he hid behind: he insisted the bureau only collected facts—it did not interpret them. Filed in his "Do Not File" file were the capital's most embarrassing personal secrets; when he acquired a juicy one he made sure the subject knew about it—a main reason why no president dared fire him, although several wished to, and why congressional committees rarely turned down his budget requests.

Personal survival was Hoover's first goal but the second was to protect America from the kind of internal decay which fire-and-brimstone orators of yesteryear used to call "moral pollution." For decades, as recounted in Ronald Kessler's *The Bureau*, Hoover detested all those he considered un-American—most famously godless socialists and Communists—and found ways to hound and torment them; but his deepest loathing was reserved for "sexual perverts," Negro agitators like Martin Luther King Jr., and civil libertarians who denounced the bureau's appetite for gossip, rumor, and innuendo.

Still, Hoover, who died in office in 1972, was both rigid and adaptable. When public enemies changed he did, too, and by the mid-1960s the bureau was seeking telephone wiretaps, bugs, mail covers, and especially confidential informants who could deliver intelligence about the Ku Klux Klan and the loosely organized families of Italian-American gangsters known as La Cosa Nostra ("Our Thing") or the Mafia, an old word which has no accepted translation. For years Hoover resisted pressure to go after organized crime, fearing that the bureau's special agents would be corrupted by Mafia money. But Robert F. Kennedy, United States attorney general under his brother Jack, refused to take no for an answer, and eventually the FBI began to pursue the Mafia with all the energy, and many of the same techniques, it had brought to bear in Hoover's long campaign against the American Communist Party. There used to be a joke in the 1960s that half the Communists at Party meetings were reporting to the FBI on the other half, and the joke was not far short of the truth. The Mafia was harder to penetrate but the technique was the same—find somebody on the inside, get close, and turn the screw.

Confidential informants are really the same as spies—persons with a nominal allegiance or at least access to a targeted individual or group, who are willing to provide investigators with secret information, usually in return for money or preferment. FBI agents are trained in the art of recruiting informants at the bureau's academy in Quantico, Virginia, and what they are taught is very similar to the techniques learned by CIA trainees at Camp Peary a little farther down the Virginia coast. For both organizations, rule one in agent-handling is control. Money helps, loyalty is nice, and shared ideals make every-body feel good, but the bedrock of control is fear and the purpose of control is to keep the handler and his mission on top.

Agent-running is not about making friends; it is about collecting information for the purpose of law enforcement or national security. FBI Special Agent John Connolly built a dazzling reputation in the Boston field office during the 1970s and 1980s as a consummate recruiter and handler of confidential informants who provided infor-mation used to prosecute bosses in the Italian mob, a top priority of the bureau once Hoover had finally been brought to admit that the Mafia actually existed. Connolly was a native son, born and raised in South Boston ("Southie"), where the Irish mob ran the gambling, loan-sharking, and drug business. A childhood friend of many who ended up on the wrong side of the law, Connolly was a sharp dresser who liked a good time, was easy and affable in manner, and had more brass than brains. Most important, he had a pipeline into the world of Boston mobsters and he helped his bosses make the kind of cases that get headlines.

According to Dick Lehr and Gerard O'Neill, *Boston Globe* reporters who expanded their investigative journalism on the Irish mob into an important book called *Black Mass*,[10] Connolly was for years the golden boy of high bureau officials including FBI Director William Sessions, whose troubled tenure finally ended in 1993 when President Clinton took the overdue step of firing him. In 1989, Lehr and O'Neill write, Sessions "traveled to Boston to personally congratulate the Boston agents, singling out Connolly for his handling of informants." Connolly investigated no major cases, ran no big programs, never had a desk in Washington. He collected information from confiden-tial informants. "The way you solve crime, ninety-nine percent of it,"

---

10. *Black Mass: The True Story of an Unholy Alliance Between the FBI and the Irish Mob* (Perennial, 2001).

Connolly said in a radio interview, "is when people tell you what happened. I mean, every director of the FBI has said that informants are our most important resource."

Connolly's most important resource was his fifteen-year relationship with James ("Whitey") Bulger and Stevie ("The Rifleman") Flemmi, which began in 1975 and ended, officially at least, with Connolly's retirement in 1990. Bulger, a few years older than Connolly, was the brother of William Bulger, a leading Massachusetts politician who for many years ruled the state senate and is now president of the University of Massachusetts campus in Boston. Connolly was a childhood friend of Billy's and knew Whitey, whose early life in crime progressed from robbing trucks to robbing banks before it was interrupted in 1956 by nine years in jail, served in federal penitentiaries in Atlanta, Alcatraz, and Leavenworth, where he is said to have taken part in an experimental CIA drug program using LSD. When Whitey got out of jail in 1965 his brother got him a job as a custodian in a Boston courthouse, but Whitey wanted more out of life than a broom and a janitor's pay and he soon resumed his life of crime, starting with bookmaking.

If spies catch spies, as the mole hunters like to say, then criminals catch criminals, and in 1975 John Connolly, recently transferred to the organized crime squad in the Boston field office, successfully recruited Whitey to help him catch the Mafia gangsters who were the bureau's top priority. The moment of recruitment is called "the pitch"; it involves both a request and an offer. What Connolly wanted was information that the FBI later used to put away the Angiulo brothers, who ran the rackets in Boston's North End.

But what Connolly offered was not immediately clear to others. In theory confidential informants help out because they are in a squeeze —facing indictment and a long jail term. Sometimes, in a modest way, they are paid, or they are given a pass on minor offenses that are integral to the pattern of crime they are helping to shut down. But Whitey wasn't in a squeeze, he never got paid, and his ongoing crimes were far from minor. So what lay behind this unholy pact between the FBI and an Irish mobster? What did Whitey get in return for committing the one sin Southie would never understand or forgive—talking to the cops?

Dick Lehr and Gerard O'Neill played a significant part in finding the answer to this question, beginning with a story in the *Boston Globe* in 1988 about the brothers Bulger—one a powerful and respected politician, the other a criminal. But what the reporters found still stranger was Whitey's apparently charmed life: the Boston Mafia was being pulled down by the FBI in one high-profile case after another, but nothing seemed to stick to Whitey. It was hard to explain unless somebody was protecting him. In May 1988 O'Neill was stunned during an interview when an FBI supervisor, John Morris, suddenly dumped the answer on him—James "Whitey" Bulger was an informant for the FBI, he had grown close to his handler, John Connolly, and it wasn't luck that protected Whitey from the law. A second FBI source confirmed Morris's story and the *Globe* published it in September. The bureau naturally denied the connection. "That is absolutely untrue," said Jim Ahearn, the special agent in charge of the Boston field office. "We specifically deny that there has been special treatment of this individual."

But once tugged, the thread of Bulger's special relationship with the FBI continued to unravel and in 1998, during an extended federal court hearing, the story emerged in copious and painful detail. By that time Whitey and his partner Stevie Flemmi had been indicted on federal racketeering charges. Whitey disappeared in 1995 and his whereabouts are still unknown, but Flemmi was picked up when he unwisely tried to sneak back into Boston. At trial his lawyer offered a novel defense: nothing Flemmi did during the years of racketeering covered by his indictment was unknown to the FBI, which was using him and the missing Whitey as informants, and what had been overlooked then could not be charged as crimes now. Federal Judge Mark

Wolf eventually rejected that claim and Flemmi in due course was convicted and sentenced to prison for life. But the judge's 661-page ruling on the FBI's handling of Bulger and Flemmi, backed up by 17,000 pages of sworn testimony, starkly revealed the terms of the unholy pact.

What Whitey Bulger got from John Connolly, and by extrapolation from the FBI, was immunity. It was a criminal's dream: he got rid of many personal rivals and enemies, who were investigated, wiretapped, prosecuted, and jailed by the Feds, and in return he received timely information which allowed him to quit talking on phones as soon as they were wiretapped, to move his place of operations when it came under surveillance, and above all to deal in the time-honored manner with informers when they began to tell investigators about his crimes. Whitey and the Rifleman were eventually charged with twenty-one murders, eleven of them committed while acting as informants for the FBI, and three of those removed were men who had begun to talk to the FBI.

In May 2002 John Connolly was convicted of five charges stemming from his years of dealing with Whitey Bulger. For warning Whitey of his impending indictment back in 1995, thereby allowing him to escape, and for his other crimes Connolly was sentenced to eight to ten years in a federal prison. But on nine other charges Connolly was acquitted, largely because the jury didn't want to take the word of confessed killers who had copped pleas in return for their agreement to testify. At various times during the long unfolding of this story, high FBI officials, including Director Louis Freeh, have apologized for ignoring or bending the bureau's own rules and procedures for the control and handling of confidential informants. But none have conceded or addressed a conclusion that seems obvious: Whitey Bulger penetrated and ran agents inside the FBI—Connolly, John Morris, and perhaps others still unknown—just as surely as the KGB ran Robert Hanssen. There is no precise word for Connolly's treachery in the intelligence lexicon, but what he did was familiar enough—selling secrets under the guise of buying them. The only real difference between the Hanssen and Connolly cases is that Hanssen blended into the background, like a chameleon on the forest floor, while Connolly hid in plain sight. In both cases it took the FBI twenty years to notice there was a problem, and in any but the narrowest sense the bureau has yet to address the problem behind the problem.

The twin cautionary tales of Robert Hanssen and Whitey Bulger help to explain the leaden paralysis of the FBI when it was confronted in mid-2001 with the accused terrorist conspirator Zacarias Moussaoui —an episode of sustained, almost willful refusal by high bureau officials to heed the warnings of agents in Minnesota convinced that they were investigating a subject who posed a genuine terrorist threat. When the FBI's legal attaché in Paris passed on French intelligence that Moussaoui was connected to al-Qaeda, bureau officials in Washington objected that there was no proof that the French Moussaoui and the Minnesota Moussaoui were one and the same. The agent in Paris promptly replied that there was only one Moussaoui in the Paris phone book, but that didn't satisfy Washington either. The thirteen-page letter sent to FBI Director Robert Mueller in May 2002 by the legal counsel for the Minneapolis field office, Coleen Rowley, details an evasive pattern so pronounced that agents in the Minnesota office joked that the obstruction in Washington must have come from "spies or moles, like Robert Hansen [sic], who were actually working for Osama bin Laden...."

But it is not the failure to get a legal look into Moussaoui's computer before September 11 that Rowley emphasized in her letter, which was promptly classified by the FBI although portions of it were published in *Time* magazine. More troubling, in her view, was Mueller's new strategy for dealing with terror—a flying "super squad" dispatched at the first sign of trouble by the honchos at headquarters. It wasn't the special agents in the field who had failed, but the head office. In Rowley's view a super squad wasn't the solution; it was an example of the problem—the bureau's self-protective instinct to hold things close, control every detail, admit nothing.

The cause, Rowley writes, is "a climate of fear which has chilled aggressive law enforcement action/decisions" stemming from a recent history of ruined careers following decisions that "turned out to be mistaken or just turned out badly." The refusal to seek a Foreign Intelligence Surveillance Act warrant in the Moussaoui case, Rowley suggests, was based on nothing more substantial than reluctance to be "'written up' for an Intelligence Oversight Board 'error.'..." Agents had concluded that "the safer course is to do nothing," and even Mueller's own response, Rowley argues, was essentially defensive. Within days of September 11 he issued a statement that the bureau might have been able to do something "if the FBI had only had any advance warning...." Rowley and others, fearing that the new director would soon be compelled to eat his words, immediately warned headquarters to pull back—there had been a warning and it was bound to come out. But when Mueller and other high bureau officials stuck to the no-warning story, Rowley and her colleagues "faced the sad realization that the remarks indicated someone, possibly with [Mueller's] approval, had decided to circle the wagons...to protect the FBI from embarrassment and the relevant FBI officials from scrutiny." All in all, this is gently put.

"Don't Embarrass the Bureau" had been the first commandment of J. Edgar Hoover during his long career. Rowley's memo suggests it is still at the heart of the bureau's culture thirty years after his death, but the FBI is not the only Washington behemoth to circle the wagons. Since September 11 the CIA, the Defense Department, and the White House have all been peeping cautiously over the barricades with a lively fear that they are about to catch hell. The prompt and vigorous overthrow of the Taliban, ending al-Qaeda's safe haven in Afghanistan, has done nothing to soften the President's resistance to repeated calls for some sort of commission or official inquiry to look at what went wrong before the attacks. Naturally nobody wants to take the heat for allowing nineteen men armed with box cutters to strike the mightiest blow against the American homeland since the British burned the White House in 1812, but the apprehension of those inside the circle of wagons looking out goes deeper.

Once the public insists on knowing how this could have happened, it may start to ask other difficult questions—for example, how did the huge American intelligence apparatus fail to note for so many years both the scale and resolution of terror networks and the deepening of the hate that drove them? Does a combination of better police work, tighter borders, and aerial bombing provide the right tools to win the war on terror? Do we understand how we got into this war? How will we know when the war is over and it is safe to stand down?

In 1994, the year after the first attack on the World Trade Center, the CIA officer Robert Baer was a regular commuter between the agency in Langley, Virginia, and Amman, Jordan, where his job was to find and assist Iraqi dissidents who might overthrow Saddam Hussein. When he could, he liked to break the long flight with a stopover in London, and there he often visited the Arab neighborhood which had grown up along Edgware Road. Baer had learned Arabic in Tunis in the early 1980s and his assignments thereafter took him in and out of the Arab-speaking world—Sudan, a small station in the Middle East which CIA censors would not let him name in his recent book, Lebanon, the new Counter-Terrorism Center set up in the CIA by Dewey Claridge in 1986, Jordan, northern Iraq. Baer had many jobs, but the one he assigned himself was to learn who had carried out the bombing of the US embassy in Beirut in 1983, killing scores of people, including almost the entire CIA station.

Baer's memoir of his years in the agency, *See No Evil: The True*

Story of a Ground Soldier in the CIA's *War on Terrorism,*[11] is a fine
primer on the rewards and frustrations of intelligence in the field. The
rewards are few but sweet—recruiting a good source, catching a bad
guy, winning the praise of a boss you respect. The frustrations are
many. Baer once found himself, for example, standing near some
buildings guarded by Iranian soldiers in Lebanon's central Bekaa Val-
ley. An Arab companion told him that was the Shaykh Abdallah
barracks. The windows of one of the buildings were obscured by
cardboard or blankets. Inside, chained to a radiator, his eyes covered
by a blindfold, was the CIA's chief of station in Beirut, William Buckley, kidnapped by terrorists months earlier. Sometime over the next
year he would die there. "I'll be frank," Baer writes. "My visit...was
a gross fracturing of all the rules.... It was risky and did nothing to
help Buckley or anyone else." But the frustration still burns years later;
if he had managed to get that close on his own, what might have happened if his bosses had been a little more daring?

There were many moments like that during Baer's twenty years
with the CIA. He had the born clandestine agent's love of being operational—nosing around, making contacts, asking questions, getting
in where he wasn't wanted, straining the patience of bosses, sticking
with problems after Langley lost interest. His chapters on the Beirut
bombing are dense with detail—dates, organizations, people who
knew people. "Everything in the Middle East is interconnected," he
writes. "Pull on one thread and a dozen more will come out."

In June 1987 one of these threads led to the identity of an Iran Revolutionary Guard activist named Husayn Khalil, the man in charge of
the Shaykh Abdallah barracks when Buckley was held and killed
there. Khalil in turn had worked for Azmi Sughayr, a member of an
al-Fatah security force, who had provided the spotter for the embassy
bombing—the man who watched the building and said, "Now!" In

11. Crown, 2002.

October 1987 Baer recruited an agent in Hizbollah who told him the name of the suicide bomber who actually delivered the bomb: Muhammad Hassuna. "You'll have to take my word for it," Baer writes. "Evidence doesn't get much better in the intelligence business.... The only conclusion a reasonable person could make was that a Fatah cell—with or without Yasir Arafat's knowledge—blew up the American embassy in Beirut...." Eventually Baer wrote up what he knew for CIA headquarters, but the answer he got back was one of the biggest frustrations of his career: "While the information is compelling," the CIA told him, "it is only of historical interest." Baer's report was filed, not distributed.

Baer's career ended in the mid-1990s after a squall of runaway political correctness in Washington nearly put him in jail. In March 1995 President Clinton's national security adviser, Anthony Lake, personally asked the FBI to investigate Baer for "trying to assassinate Saddam Hussein," a strained interpretation of Baer's efforts to organize political opposition among Iraqi dissidents. Although facing a charge of violating federal murder-for-hire statutes, which carried a possible death penalty, Baer unwisely followed the advice of CIA officials who urged him to talk freely with investigators and to forego his right to a lawyer. In the end the investigation came to nothing, but not without many sleepless nights wondering how his world had been turned upside down. Concluding that there was no place for him in the "see-no-evil, hear-no-evil, do-no-evil model for the new CIA," Baer resigned.

With him into private life he carried the memory of all those London stopovers in 1994, when he had strolled Edgware Road, stopping frequently in the Arab bookstores. There he checked out with troubled alarm, in rack upon rack, one cheaply printed volume after another of radical Islamic tracts—burning calls for holy war against the United States. "It didn't take a sophisticated intelligence organization," Baer writes, "to figure out that Europe...had become a hothouse of Islamic fundamentalism." But the CIA station in London had no Arabic speak-ers, and in any event Americans were barred from operations in Britain to track down the organizations behind these calls for war on the Great Satan. The agency had been shutting down or cutting back stations all over the world and the officers who remained "spent most of their time catering to whatever was in fashion in Washington at the time: human rights, economic globalization, the Arab–Israeli conflict."

Stopping September 11, in Baer's view, should have begun right there on Edgware Road in 1994, when any observant man with even a smattering of Arabic could have told the supergrades back in Lang-ley that big trouble was brewing for the United States and the place to start checking it out was right there in London.

After September 11, of course, it was checked out, and what the investigators discovered, according to Jane Corbin, a reporter for the BBC, was a nexus of Islamic radicalism so dense that they began refer-ring to it as "Londonistan." Zacarias Moussaoui, it was learned, had spent time in Britain, had quarreled bitterly about jihad with the mul-lah of a Brixton mosque, and had several contacts—by phone, and face-to-face in a private home—with an aspiring British-born suicide bomber who had given himself the name of Abdul Ra'uff. In Corbin's book *Al-Qaeda: The Terror Network that Threatens the World*,[12] she describes the chain of evidence that identified Ra'uff, at first only a name on a computer hard drive acquired in Afghanistan, as a young British convert to Islam, Richard Reid, who tried and failed last in December 2001 to ignite plastic explosives packed into the soles of his shoes during an American Airlines flight over the Atlantic.

Other investigations traced the al-Qaeda assassins of an Afghan warlord fighting the Taliban back to London, and determined that over a three-year period Osama bin Laden himself, using just one of possibly many satellite phones available to him, had placed 238

---

12. Thunder's Mouth Press/Nation Books, 2002.

calls—of a total of 1,100, more than to any other country—to numbers in Britain. In late 1998 bin Laden discovered that the CIA had been picking up his calls on this phone, and he turned to other means.

Few things irritate intelligence professionals more than loose charges that they were snoozing at their desks on September 11. If one of them were to sit down to explain to skeptical journalists "on background" just what the CIA was doing to track the terrorist problem, the evidence cited would include hundreds of intelligence officers with support from numerous contract personnel using sophisticated equipment costing zillions of dollars and aided by friendly intelligence services throughout the globe and much else. Gathering information on a big scale is what the CIA has learned to do over the last half-century. The effort to keep track of the Russians began in the 1940s with a handful of agents of doubtful allegiance trying to count tanks on flatbed railcars, but by the end of the cold war the overhead reconnaissance program alone employed battalions of photo interpreters (PIS), each responsible for a small piece of the land grid of the Soviet Union.

All day five days a week and on weekends at the least blip of something interesting these PIs checked a never-ending river of images with a resolution in yards, then feet, and finally inches for signs of a new bump on tank turrets, different antennae on the roof of the local KGB office, too many fresh graves in a gulag cemetery, a new highway turnoff, or, God forbid, the characteristic outbuildings, concrete pourings, and cone-shaped hole of an intercontinental ballistic missile silo with antennae pointing to an azimuth on a beeline for the American missile fields in North Dakota. No expense and no human effort was spared in this effort and the result was very good coverage of the military capacities of the Soviet Union. Terrorism gets the same sort of budget and manpower now.

But sometimes more is not better, and sometimes information is not intelligence. What's missing from the story of September 11 so far is a sense of why the United States got sucked into the vortex of violence in the Middle East, and how we ought to proceed now that al-Qaeda and other terrorist organizations have decided we are Enemy Number One. Neither of these questions was addressed in the only official inquiry yet released, a study made public on July 17 by the Subcommittee on Terrorism and Homeland Security of the House Intelligence Committee. After several days of testimony by officials of the CIA, the FBI, and the National Security Agency (NSA), the committee issued a brief list of practical recommendations for tightening up. At the top of the to-do list were recruiting spies, especially those with access to terrorist groups, and hiring people, now in short supply, who can speak and translate the relevant languages. To speed up the spy effort, the committee urged the CIA to abandon forthwith rules adopted in 1995 that increased the number of hoops that officers in the field had to jump through in order to recruit spies with a history of torture or murder. (The CIA's director, George Tenet, complied within the week.)

The FBI, the committee said, should strive above all to prevent terrorist acts, and place second the effort to gather evidence to make prosecutable cases. The NSA should "change from a passive gatherer to a proactive hunter" of ways to eavesdrop on terrorists talking to each other. Most of the issues addressed by the committee had already been raised by journalists and frustrated intelligence officers like Robert Baer, but some were new. For example, the committee cited a report circulated by the CIA's Counter-Terrorism Center only a month or two before September 11 under the title "Threat of Impending al-Qaida Attack to Continue Indefinitely." The agency's "no threshold" policy of reporting every threat, no matter how trivial or vague, was more hindrance than help, the committee suggested.

But only half-disguised in the report's sober language was the committee's frustration with the agency's "excessive caution" in the field where intelligence wars can be won or lost. Needed now, the committee said, was a commitment to "going on the offensive against terrorism." Marching orders for the CIA have changed radically over the years: agency coup-plotters were praised in the 1950s for ridding President Eisenhower of inconvenient regimes in Guatemala and Iran, then pilloried in 1961 for trying the same in Cuba. Under President Reagan the CIA allegedly trained Nicaraguan guerrillas in how to assassinate Sandinista government officials; under President Clinton in 1995, embarrassed by a revelation that it had been routinely paying a Guatemalan colonel who had killed and tortured Americans, the agency embarked on an "asset scrub" to get criminals off the payroll. CIA officials insist that in the years since no potential spies have been rejected because they were beyond the pale, but the House committee vigorously demanded rescinding the 1995 rules anyway. But more significant than any single white-gloves-only rule has been the slow growth of a careerist caution in the agency and the FBI alike which some intelligence officers—by no means all—describe as a "risk-averse culture." What this means in practice is summed up by a sign which long hung over the desk of a CIA officer stationed in Rome:

> Big ops, big problems.
> Small ops, small problems.
> No ops, no problems.

The no ops–no problems mindset before September 11 is well described in *The Cell*,[13] a useful narrative by three journalists, part personal account and part old-fashioned street reporting, which gives flesh to the dry and condensed recommendations of the House intelligence report. At the heart of the book is the story of FBI agent John O'Neill, at first a source and later the friend of ABC television reporter John

---

13. John Miller, Michael Stone, and Chris Mitchell, *The Cell: Inside the 9/11 Plot, and Why the FBI and CIA Failed to Stop It* (Hyperion, 2002).

Miller, chief among the three authors of *The Cell*. As a bureau specialist in terrorism, O'Neill investigated the first World Trade Center bombing and later worked the ground in Saudi Arabia and Yemen, where his protests against the stonewalling of local police during the investigation of the bombing of the uss *Cole* in October 2000 led the American ambassador, Barbara Bodine, to urge the Yemeni government to bar him from the country. This among other frustrations persuaded O'Neill to resign from the bureau in disgust at the age of fifty-one. He was promptly hired as director of security for the World Trade Center and he died there, not a week into the job, on September 11.

The Cell is one of the first of what are sure to be many books about September 11 but it is distinguished by Miller's involvement in the story before the attacks occurred, and especially by his account of a trip to Afghanistan in May 1998 when he "interviewed" Osama bin Laden in northern Afghanistan. After hard traveling and much waiting by Miller and his crew, bin Laden arrived amid a crescendo of welcoming gunfire, surrounded by seven bodyguards, and with al-Zawahiri and Mohammed Atef at his side—the latter killed in Kabul last November by American bombs. At six feet three inches bin Laden was the tallest in the group; he wore a green army field jacket; he greeted Miller with a firm handshake; his voice was "soft and slightly high, with a raspy quality that gave it the texture and sound of an old uncle giving good advice." The "interview" was limited to bin Laden's answers to questions Miller had earlier submitted in writing while Miller nodded helpfully on camera. Nothing was translated at the time and there were no follow-up questions. Only later did Miller learn what he had been told.

It was simultaneously little and much—little in the sense that it rambled, added few details to what was known of bin Laden or al-Qaeda, offered no door to dialogue; and much because bin Laden answered a question rarely addressed or even raised since September 11: Why was he angry at America?

The American imposes himself on everyone. Americans accuse our children in Palestine of being terrorists—those children, who have no weapons and have not even reached maturity. At the same time, Americans defend a country, the state of the Jews, that has a policy to destroy the future of these children....

Your situation with Muslims in Palestine is shameful—if there is any shame left in America. Houses were demolished over the heads of children. Also, by the testimony of relief workers in Iraq, the American-led sanctions resulted in the death of more than one million Iraqi children. All of this is done in the name of American interests. We believe that the biggest thieves in the world and the terrorists are the Americans. The only way for us to fend off these assaults is to use similar means. We do not worry about American opinion or the fact that they place prices on our heads. We as Muslims believe our fate is set.

Nothing that bin Laden told Miller in his soft voice, or that he has said or written elsewhere, suggests that al-Qaeda's war on America can be settled at the negotiating table. But that, according to Rohan Gunaratna, an academic expert on terrorism who teaches at the University of St. Andrew's in Scotland, should not prevent Americans from seeing that the war has a political context, and will be won or lost at least in part by political means. Gunaratna is one of those academics, common in America and Britain, who speaks as often to assembled generals and colonels as he does to college students. He has traveled frequently to Afghanistan and other battlegrounds, has interviewed many terrorists and intelligence officials, and has read widely in the literature of Islamic fundamentalism. His *Inside Al Qaeda: Global Network of Terror*[14] is a careful and methodical account of bin Laden's emergence as a leader, and of al-Qaeda cells active around the

14. Columbia University Press, 2002.

world. As a handbook, *Inside Al Qaeda* does the work of many tomes, but its chief strength is to be found in Gunaratna's final chapter, where he argues that the political war will be ignored at America's peril.

Islamic fundamentalism and hostility toward the West did not begin with bin Laden, Gunaratna stresses, but it was his leadership which built the first broadly based Islamic terrorist organization with a global reach and ambition to match. Al-Qaeda, not some vague anti-American feeling among Muslims, destroyed the World Trade Center and aspires to do worse, and Western security cannot be assured until it is crushed. Gunaratna is blunt in saying that bin Laden is the problem and killing him the solution. "Just as Nazism effectively died with Hitler," he writes, "Islamism of the Al Qaeda brand is likely to die with Osama. His death will break the momentum of the campaign."

But America and its allies, Gunaratna argues, must not ignore the issues that arouse and anger the Muslim world, beginning with the fate of the West Bank Palestinians. He quotes a leading Islamic cleric, Sheikh Abdel Rahman al-Sudeis, who attacked "the state terrorism of international Zionism" in Mecca on the final Friday of Ramadan in December of 2001. "Are we incapable of finding just solutions to stop the flow of Muslim blood?" the Sheikh asked. It is the invitation to seek "just solutions" which America ought to heed and pursue, Gunaratna argues. "As long as Al Qaeda . . . can appeal to Muslims worldwide" on the unresolved disputes over Kashmir and Palestine, he argues, there will be a steady flow of new recruits for bin Laden's jihad. "The key to strategically weakening [al-Qaeda] is to erode its fledgling support base—to wean away its supporters and potential supporters," he writes. "The widespread support it enjoys today is driven by the strong belief among Muslims that the West has persistently wronged them. . . ."

Gunaratna's judgment on the war so far is mixed. Most of the physical assets of the Taliban and al-Qaeda in Afghanistan—weapons stockpiles, training camps, offices, and laboratories—have been destroyed, he says, but the Americans erred badly in not giving Pakistan time to pressure Mullah Mohammad Omar and his government to cut free from bin Laden. The resulting alliance of necessity between Taliban and al-Qaeda forces has survived the first months of the war in Afghanistan, and their capacity to go on fighting should not be underestimated. The worldwide roundup of al-Qaeda activists has been broadly effective but Western intelligence services have had little luck in penetrating activist groups.

The biggest American success, in Gunaratna's view, was "in creating a fragile international coalition...by painstakingly building an international consensus against a common threat." But now, in his view, America risks shattering the alliance by a unilateral attack on Iraq—doubly foolish because, in his view, Iran is the real state sponsor of Islamic terrorism. Attacking Iraq would "create the conditions for a fresh wave of support for Islamists" and in the end "the victor will be Al Qaeda." Americans have received and ignored this sort of advice before. The French, for example, warned the Americans not to plunge into Vietnam. But some people you can't tell anything.

War to the knife with Iraq seems to be firmly placed on the White House agenda. At West Point in June President Bush said the United States was ready to launch preemptive strikes against hostile states developing weapons of mass destruction, and in July, speaking to units of the 10th Mountain Division freshly returned from Afghanistan, he said it again: "America must act against these terrible threats before they're fully formed.... Some parts of the world, there will be no substitute for direct action by the United States. That is when we will send you, our military, to win the battles only you can win."

Backing up these often repeated threats are plans on the drawing board in the Pentagon. Americans got their first look at what the US Army's Central Command has in mind from a June 23, 2002, *Los Angeles Times* article by the military analyst and air-war expert

William Arkin, who described "Polo Step," a plan to invade Iraq with up to 250,000 troops on three fronts. When Eric Schmitt of *The New York Times*, using Arkin as a principal source, followed with a second, more detailed story on July 5, Secretary of Defense Donald Rumsfeld denounced leakers of the plan and asked the Air Force Office of Special Investigations to track down the guilty party. "It is wrong," he wrote in a memo. "It costs the lives of Americans. It diminishes our country's chance for success."

But the reason Arkin was given the story in the first place, and the reason he passed it on to Schmitt, was the widespread skepticism among high-ranking military officers that the plan took advantage of American strengths or was likely to work at an acceptable cost. It called for a large-scale war in the classic American style—a huge air campaign to destroy hundreds of targets in Iraq, army divisions crossing the border on three sides, and a march on Baghdad. "The Pentagon doesn't go anywhere with light luggage," Arkin told me recently. Munitions for the war have yet to be moved to the theater of operations, or even received from manufacturers, and no American ally in Europe or the Middle East has expressed support for an invasion of Iraq before giving him at least one chance to readmit UN weapons inspectors. In his speech before the United Nations on September 12 President Bush recited the ten-year history of Iraqi intransigence but also left the door about half-open for a renewed Security Council effort to compel Saddam Hussein to abandon once and for all his efforts to acquire weapons of mass destruction. Bush set no deadline for success or else, but the tone of his speech made it clear that he did not intend to wait long, and that "regime change" in Iraq remains central to his administration's grand strategy for the war on terror.

Is this a good idea? That's a question which requires intelligence in the classic sense, not just information. American leaders have been convinced before that the nation's safety required them to go to war —against Cuba in 1961, when a not-so-secret rebel army trained and equipped by the CIA got no further than the beach at the Bay of Pigs; and against North Vietnam in 1965, when the prospect of an imminent Vietcong defeat in the South prompted President Lyndon Johnson to launch an air campaign to force Hanoi to the negotiating table. The CIA was full of doubt the second time around, but there is no stopping a president and his advisers once they have talked themselves into certainty. At that point the agency begins to shorten its reporting focus until nothing is visible but the details.

How this works was explained to me more than twenty years ago by a former high CIA official who attended many White House and Pentagon briefings on the "progress" of Operation Rolling Thunder to punish Vietnam from the air. The President, the secretary of defense, the secretary of state, the national security adviser, and the Joint Chiefs of Staff beginning in February 1965 were for several years convinced that steadily intensifying American bombing raids on North Vietnam and on the supply routes south through Laos called the Ho Chi Minh Trail would eventually convince Hanoi that the war could not be won. At that point the North would come to the bargaining table and the United States in some meaningful sense would "win" the war in Vietnam.

High American officials didn't simply believe this; they had staked their careers, their reputations, and their place in history on it, and the ante on the table was the blood of American boys. Briefing the principals on the "progress" of the bombing presented an awkward challenge for the CIA because the agency never collected any information from any source that said or suggested the strategy might be working—no reports from highly placed agents in Hanoi, no whispers from Soviet or Chinese officials that General Vo Nguyen Giap was losing heart, no overhead reconnaissance suggesting that the North Vietnamese truck fleet was tending toward zero, or the bridges weren't being fixed, or less was going in at the top end of the Ho Chi Minh Trail and days were stretching to weeks and months when nothing came out the bottom end. That was the reality of the matter, I was told, but you can't tell them if they won't listen.

So, lacking good news, the CIA narrowed its focus. It painted no rosy pictures and disseminated no false figures. It simply said that the capacity of North Vietnam to ship supplies south was X, that American bombings raids at level Y would on average interrupt Q percentage of the truck traffic; that a P level of warfare in the South required T tons of supplies from the North, and so on for as long as high American officials were willing to sit while CIA briefers flipped through visuals droning numbers. The closest the CIA ever came to saying that the emperor had no clothes was to say that the level of bombing we have achieved has not ended the capacity of the North to wage war, if they choose to go on. The numbers in the CIA studies were information; the intelligence—the judgments that mattered—had to be read between the lines.

The invasion of Iraq is not imminent. Centcom's plan is still on the drawing board. There is plenty of time for wise heads to have second thoughts about widening the war on terror in order to win it. In mid-August 2002 senior figures from the Republican establishment, including the first President Bush's national security adviser, Brent Scowcroft, and retiring House minority leader Dick Armey, all counseled caution. President Bush has since promised to seek authority for military action from Congress, and a full-scale debate has been joined. Somewhere along about now would be a good moment for American intelligence organizations to contribute their thoughts on the wisdom of an Iraqi campaign, but that is not what presidents traditionally want from the secret arm of government.

More than a decade ago Robert Gates, the only CIA intelligence analyst ever promoted to run the agency, remarked in an article that directors of central intelligence rarely showed up on center stage when presidents were hammering out big foreign policy decisions. When it comes to war with Iraq, what the White House will want from the CIA is detail—target coordinates for Scud missiles, where Saddam Hussein is sleeping nights, the agency's best estimate of the L level of bombing required to knock out P percentage of Iraqi tanks before Hussein can make use of his weapons of mass destruction, designated U for Unknown. Nothing the CIA is likely to say will cast doubt on the American ability to win such a war. But will a bloody, humiliating defeat of Iraq make us safer in the long run, or instead only fan the flames of hatred for America on which terror feeds? For the answer to big questions of that sort presidents and their advisers often feel they have done enough when they have consulted each other.

—*The New York Review of Books*, September 26
and October 10, 2002

INDEX

Aaron, David, 329
ABC News, 210
Abel, Col. Rudolf, 140
academia, blacklists in, 91
Acheson, Dean, 87, 148, 197
Adams, James, 307n, 316
Adams, Sam, 281–282
Adler, Solomon, 86
Aegis defense system, 244
Aeschylus, 202
Afghanistan: al-Qaeda in, 390, 405,
    415–416; bin Laden in, 362,
    366–367, 376, 413; and cold
    war, 129; and Iran, 286, 381;
    language in, 375–376; the Muj
    in, 285–288, 324, 335, 366;
    proxy wars in, 324; Soviet inva-
    sion of, 152, 284–288, 303, 323,
    335, 339n; Soviet withdrawal
    from, 284–285, 332; Taliban in,
    xx, 409, 415–416; US military
    in, 376, 416
Africa: attacks on US embassies in,
    361; Cuban armies in, 281, 284,
    323; proxy wars in, 324;
    revolutionary movements in, 51
Agency, the, see Central Intelligence
    Agency

agents, see spies
Ahearn, Jim, 402
Air Force, US: analysts in, 222–224;
    arms escalation by, 384; and
    Cuba, 167, 197; intelligence
    efforts of, 233, 243, 417; recon-
    naissance satellites of, 236, 305;
    and Russian bombers, 222–223
Akhmerov, Itzhak, 90
Albania, planned invasion of, 20
al-Fatah, 407–408
Algiers, OSS in, 9
*Alleged Assassination Plots
    Involving Foreign Leaders*
    (Church Committee), xvii
Allende, Salvador, xiv, 352
al-Qaeda, xix–xx, xxii, 366–368,
    369–370, 382, 388, 390, 404,
    405, 409, 411, 413–416
*Al-Qaeda: The Terror Network that
    Threatens the World* (Corbin),
    409–410
al-Zawahiri, 413
American Communist Party: black-
    lists of, 91; and civil rights, 196;
    and FBI, 87–88, 399; founding
    of, 81–82; and left-wing causes,
    87, 91, 105, 107–108; and

Castro, Fidel: and Bay of Pigs, x,
53, 344–345, 379; and
Communist Party, 160, 196;
industry nationalized by, 356;
plots against, x–xiii, xvii, 53–55,
133, 189, 190, 197–200, 212,
214, 215, 351, 357–358, 359,
386, 387; revolution of, 159,
160, 303
Cave Brown, Anthony, 7, 12–13,
14, 16, 17
CBRN weapons, 364
Cell, The (Miller et al.), 412–413
Central America, *see* Latin America
Central Asia, the Great Game in, 45
Central Intelligence Agency (CIA),
45–57, 261–268, 361–380;
annual surveys of, 383; in anti-
Castro plots, x–xi, 54, 55, 133,
199–200, 214, 215, 357, 359,
387; antiterrorist activities of,
405–412, 419–420; arms-
control bias of, 226; "bad
secrets" released by, 262,
264–265; and Bay of Pigs, 153,
197, 214, 330, 343–346, 357,
379, 387, 418; and Berlin, 127,
130, 131, 134, 139, 141, 144;
Board of National Estimates
(BNE), 222; congressional investigations into, 264, 279, 386, 411;
counterintelligence (CI) branch
of, 113–114, 125, 311, 313, 314;
Counter-Terrorism Center (CTC)
of, 361, 363, 371, 406, 411;
covert actions of, 55, 56, 103,
132, 152, 154, 215, 350, 371;
see also specific nations; cut-
backs in, 374–377, 409; declassified documents of, 130, 262,
300, 332, 343, 360; difficulty of
writing about, xiv–xv, 317; dirty
tricks by, xiii; drug experiments

of, 387, 401; and ELINT,
243–245; "excessive caution"
exercised by, 411–412; failures
of, xviii–xix, 303, 319, 321,
353–354, 361–380, 387–390,
408, 410, 418–419; FBI cooperation with, 316, 388, 392; "fizz
kids" of, 103; glory days of,
200, 270; history of, xviii,
301–304, 371, 387; and
HUMINT, 230; internal investigations of, 295, 346, 373–374,
397–398; and Kennedy family,
189, 195, 199, 200; and labor
unions, 102–103; Langley HQ of,
230, 264, 284, 329; loophole in
charter of, 4; mail-intercept program of, xiii, 262; misreading of
evidence by, 226, 311; moles in,
115, 116, 119, 130n, 136–137,
307–318, 391–393; morale in,
121, 374; Office of Policy
Coordination in, 19, 302; Office
of Security in, 113; OSS as pre-
cursor to, 12, 18, 32, 112;
Pentagon vs., 52, 162, 371; plausible deniability of, 55; president
as overseer of, x, xiv, xvi, 55, 56,
279–280, 336, 369, 387,
418–420; protection of its secrets
by, x, 398; reorganization of,
121–122, 125, 267, 311,
371–375, 379, 386–387; self-
criticism in, 373–376; and
September 11 attacks, xviii–xix,
361–364, 367–372, 374–377,
379–380, 381–382, 387,
388–390, 405–406, 408–412;
single outcome forecasting in,
387–388; Soviet/East European
(SE) Division of, 309, 311; successes of, 19–20, 304, 354; Task
Force W in, 215, 359; uniform

29, 33–34, 49, 63; Soviet agents
in, 289, 307; surrender of, 15,
43, 49, 127; Third Reich in, 22,
30; and ULTRA, 13, 14, 104; war
criminals of, 21, 36; Weimar
Republic in, 36; in World War II,
see World War II
Germany Underground (Dulles), 49
Giancana, Sam, 212
Gibbon, Edward, 211
Gisevius, Hans Berndt, 23, 27, 31,
35, 40, 44
Goerdeler, Carl, 24
Goering, Hermann, 37, 39, 192
Gold, Harry, 63, 64, 67n, 75, 86
Goldberg, Stanley, 73n
Goleniewsky, Michal, 114,
115–116, 120
Golitsyn, Anatoli, 116–121, 123,
124, 130n, 294, 295, 313
Golos, Jacob, 99
Gomulka, Wladyslaw, 53
Goodman, Mel, 331–332
Goodwin, Richard, 206
Gorbachev, Mikhail, 110–111, 123,
308; and Afghanistan, 287–288;
and end of Soviet Union, 141,
341; glasnost of, 110, 325, 339;
and Star Wars, 333, 334; system
inherited by, 269, 319, 324; tin-
kering with the system, 96, 322,
325, 326–327, 333, 339
Gordievsky, Oleg, 93, 339
Gouzenko, Igor, 92, 293–294, 295
Government Communications
Headquarters (GCH), 240
Great Britain: and Afghanistan,
286; appeasement policy of,
25–26, 28, 42, 192, 194; Arab
terrorists in, 408–410; and atomic bombs, 63, 94–95; and Baltic
republics, 290–292; Cambridge
Five of, 97, 99, 101, 298; and

Central Asia, 45; code-breakers
in, 13, 14, 49, 104, 231–232,
240–241, 245; as cold-war target, 143; events leading to war
in, 25–31; and German
Resistance, 25, 30–31, 40–43;
and the Great Game, 45; and
Iran, 145–148, 150–152; and
Irish Republican Army, xxii;
Kennedy as ambassador to, 8,
192–194; Official Secrets Act in,
95, 146, 350; OSS X-2 branch in,
111–112; SIS of, see Secret
Intelligence Service; Soviet agents
in, 289–290; war declared by,
29; war intelligence conducted
by, 11, 13, 14, 49, 104, 231–232,
240–241, 245, 271; XX (Double-
Cross) Committee of, 112, 114
Great Mole Hunt (1960s), 130n,
137n
Greek Way, The (Hamilton), 201
Greenglass, David, 65, 67n, 82, 84,
86, 97
Greenglass, Ruth, 82, 84, 97
Gromov, Anatoly, 116
Gromyko, Andrei, 16, 160, 162
Grose, Peter, 45, 46, 49, 50, 52–54,
56
Grossmann, Werner, 141–142
Groves, Gen. Leslie, 66, 70, 71, 73
GRU (Soviet military intelligence),
88, 92, 133, 134, 136N, 161,
162, 289, 308
Guantánamo, Cuba, 161
Guatemala, CIA activities in, 52,
103, 147, 153, 387, 412
Guevara, Che, 281
Guillaume, Gunter, 140, 143
Gulf States, governments of, 368
Gulf War, xx–xxi, 257, 326, 366,
387
Gunaratna, Rohan, 414–416